A
PRACTICAL
APPROACH
TO
SECONDARY
SOCIAL
STUDIES

A PRACTICAL APPROACH TO SECONDARY SOCIAL STUDIES

Walter E. Sistrunk
Mississippi State University

Robert C. Maxson
Auburn University at Montgomery

WM. C. BROWN COMPANY PUBLISHERS
Dubuque, Iowa

*This
book
is
dedicated
to
our
wives,*
Marian
and
Sylvia*.*

CONTENTS

Foreword   **xiii**

Preface   **xv**

Acknowledgments   **xvii**

Chapter I   **The Purpose of Social Studies in American Secondary Schools**   **1**

Needs of Youth, 1
Goals of Social Studies, 5
Specific Purposes of Teaching Social Studies, 10
Assumptions, 11
References, 16

Chapter II   **Philosophical and Psychological Foundations of Teaching**   **17**

Influence of Philosophical Beliefs, 17
Principles of Learning, 23
Psychology and Learning, 27
References, 31

Chapter III   **Secondary Social Studies Curriculum Patterns**   **33**

What Should Be Taught, 36
Typical Social Studies Curriculum Patterns, 38
    Junior High School, 39
    Senior High School, 40
Other Social Studies Curriculum Patterns, 41
    Non-graded Schools, 42
    The Middle School, 43
A Possible Future Curriculum, 43
References, 45

**Chapter IV   The Social Disciplines as a Basis for the Social
Studies Curriculum**   **47**

History, 50
Government (Political Science), 53
    Political Science as Science, 54
    Political Science as Philosophy, 55
    Fields of Study, 55
        Public Law, 55
        Political Parties and Public Opinion, 56
        Comparative Government, 56
        Public Administration, 56
        International Relations, 57
        Political Theory, 57
    Relation to Other Social Sciences, 57
Sociology, 58
Geography, 62
Economics, 63
Teaching Social Studies by the Inquiry or
        Discovery Method, 65
References, 69

Chapter V   Methods of Teaching Social Studies   **73**

Student Learning Activities, 74
Criteria for Selecting Method, 76
Skills to Be Learned, 76
The Lecture, 80
Non-Expository Methods of Teaching Social
        Studies, 81
Socialized Recitiation, 81
The Project Methods, 82
Problem Solving, 84
The Fine Art of Questioning, 86
Contract Grading and Assignments, 88
    Examples of High School Contracts, 90
Use of Teaching Games in Social Studies, 91
    Types of Games, 91
    Teacher's Role, 92
    Advantages of Games, 93
    Disadvantages of Teaching Games, 93
    Examples of Teaching Games for Social
        Studies, 95
References, 98

Chapter VI   **Planning for Teaching**   **101**

Long Range Planning, 103
Courses of Study and Units, 103
Origins of Unit Planning, 104
Steps in Writing a Unit or Course of Study, 104
The Purpose of Behavioral Objectives in Teaching, 107
Sample Daily Lesson Plans, 113
References, 121

Chapter VII   **Evaluating and Reporting Pupil Progress**   **123**

The Meaning of Evaluation, 123
Purposes of Evaluation, 123
Purposes of Testing, 126
Teacher-Made Tests, 126
Instructions to Students, 129
Standardized Tests, 129
Scoring Tests, 130
Other Means of Evaluation, 131
Effects of Testing on Students, 132
Marking and Reporting Pupil Progress, 132
Commercial Tests and Where They Can Be
        Purchased, 135
References, 143

Chapter VIII   **Trends in Social Studies Teaching**   **147**

Team Teaching, 147
Small Group Instruction, 150
Large Group Instruction, 151
Independent Study, 151
Seminars, 153
Advanced Placement, 155
Teaching the Slow Learner, 156
    Teaching Methods, 156
    Evaluation of Teaching Methods, 157
Remedial Reading in Secondary Schools, 157
Teaching the Educationally Disadvantaged, 159
    Problems in Teaching the Disadvantaged, 160
References, 164

Chapter IX   **Current Events, Controversial Issues, and Student
Attitudes**   **167**

Selection of Current Affairs Topics, 168
    Teaching Techniques, 168

Handling Controversial Issues, 169
Changing Students' Attitudes, 170
The Community as a Social Studies Laboratory, 172
References, 174

Chapter X   The Selection and Use of Social Studies Materials   177

Types of Media Available in Social Studies, 178
    Textbooks, 178
    Standards for Evaluating and Selecting Textbooks, 180
    Library Books, 183
    The Textbook as a Basis for Method, 183
    Workbook and Teacher's Manuals, 186
    Audio Visual Materials, 186
    General Selection and Use of Audio Visuals, 188
    Opaque Projector, 190
    Overhead Projector, 190
    Filmstrips, 191
    The Slide Projector, 192
    Use of Globes, Maps, Graphs, and Charts, 193
    Globes, 193
    Maps, 193
    Graphs, 194
    Charts, 195
    Use of Time Lines, 196
Programmed Instruction and Other Related Media, 199
    Programming as a Remedial Method, 202
    Use of Programmed Materials in Social Studies, 202
    Computer Assisted Instruction in Social
            Studies, 203
Information Sources for Selection of Media, 206
References, 209

Chapter XI   Duties of Teachers Not Directly Related to Classroom
               Instruction   213

Classroom Management, 213
Teachers Role in Guidance and Counseling, 220
Relationship with Principal and Superintendent, 230
Directing Co-curricular Activities, 224
    Purposes, 225
    The Sponsor, 226

Sponsoring Student Council or Student
Government, 228
The Advisor's Role, 228
Types of Student Councils, 230
Problems of Student Councils, 232
Other Tasks of Teachers, 233
References, 236

Chapter XII **The Making of a Professional** **239**

Typical Social Studies Degree Program, 239
Initial Certification, 240
Adequate Preparation for Teaching Social Studies, 241
Professionalism and the Teacher, 241
Faculty Morale and Welfare, 244
Measuring Teacher Competency, 246
Professional Growth, 249
References, 251

Appendix A Course of Study—Fifth Grade Social Studies **259**

Course of Study—Sixth Grade Social Studies **275**

Appendix B Teaching Unit—Seventh Grade Geography **297**

Teaching Unit—Eighth Grade United States History **331**

Teaching Unit—Ninth Grade Civics **357**

Teaching Unit—Tenth Grade World History **381**

Teaching Unit—Eleventh Grade American History **393**

Teaching Unit—Eleventh or Twelfth Grade
Social Studies **435**

Teaching Unit—Eleventh and Twelfth Grade Economics **455**

Teaching Unit—Twelfth Grade American Government **463**

Index **483**

FOREWORD

The body of knowledge available to teachers is constantly increasing at an accelerated rate. One of the major tasks of teachers of social studies is that of simply keeping up with new information in the academic disciplines within the social sciences. In addition, the theoretical base undergirding the process of teaching is constantly being further developed.

In the face of the above demands on social studies teachers, the need for sound social studies teaching techniques becomes increasingly critical. In 1958, with the launching of Sputnik, there was a shifting of emphasis in the schools to the fields of science and mathematics. Some of the best brain-power, as well as resources, available to education was directed toward the technical aspects of the curriculum. During the latter half of the sixties it became evident that the most pressing problems facing America—its people, its cities, its land, its government and the environment—were social in nature. These have to do with racial integration, poverty, pollution, population, loss of individual identity, and living in a complex industrial society in the latter third of the twentieth century. In short, the social sciences are back at the forefront in the school curriculum.

The creation of new knowledge in the social sciences coupled with the increasing body of theory and research in teaching has created new needs for textbooks in teacher training programs and reference books for teachers of social studies. The authors of this book have attempted to bridge the chasm between theoretical bases, research findings, and practice in the secondary classroom. Both Dr. Walter Sistrunk and Dr. Robert C. Maxson were qualified to undertake just such an awesome task. The resulting product should benefit both the teacher trainee and the practicing teacher of the social sciences. The authors have both taught in high schools and both are currently faculty members in universities where they are involved in training school personnel. Both authors are knowledgeable in psychological and philosophical foundations of teaching and both are capable of building sane and solid educational techniques on those foundations.

A major strength of the book is its practical approach to the teaching of social studies. The student is lead through the development of a rationale for teaching into the step-by-step preparation of teaching materials and the planning of the structure within which learning takes place.

The authors emphasize the importance of the teacher in the student-centered social studies classroom. There is a delicate balance between the use of tried and proven techniques and encouragement of an open atmosphere which enhances the opportunity for creative thought so desperately needed in the world today. The approach suggested by the authors of this publication is simply for teachers to work hard at the planning process in order that exciting things can go on in the classroom. Many exciting activities are planned, while other exciting things take place in classrooms as a result of spontaneous events and thoughts. It is suggested here that the teacher begin each class with a plan for teaching but to deviate from that plan to whatever degree it seems appropriate to do so. The authors view the student as being capable of a certain amount of self-direction.

Of special significance are the numerous illustrations, examples and practical suggestions for teaching behavior. The prospective or practicing teacher should find the cookbook approach helpful in preparing for teaching social studies. The book is practical enough for the classroom teacher who desperately needs advice in meeting the day-to-day demands of the modern high school yet scholarly enough for use in a sophisticated teacher training program. The proper blend of theory, research and practical application results in an excellent publication.

James O. Williams, Chairman
Division of Education
Auburn University at Montgomery

PREFACE

This book was written to help prospective and in-service secondary social studies teachers teach more effectively. It is designed as a college textbook for a social studies methods course; but it might well serve as a reference on methods, planning, and materials for student teachers and experienced teachers who wish to improve their instructional practices.

Chapter One describes the general purposes of secondary education, and the particular purposes of the social studies in the secondary and middle schools of the United States. Chapter Two is a brief treatment of the philosophical, psychological, and learning foundations of classroom teaching. Long technical explanations of complex philosophical and psychological positions were not attempted; but, a short practical explication of the implications of several broad positions for teaching were given. In a similar vein, no lengthy, complicated exposition of the many and often difficult learning theories was included; instead, a few practical ideas about learning in classroom situations were stated and some brief statements about how to apply these rules were made.

Chapter Three is devoted to a description of typical curriculum patterns in middle and secondary schools. Chapter Four is a simplified statement of the contribution of the social disciplines to the social studies and an explication of the use of the disciplines and their means of inquiry as a basis for the social studies curriculum. Some attention is given to teaching by inquiry and discovery methods.

Chapter Five is a practical and tried approach to methods of teaching social studies. Most of the major methods are described and some attention is given to how to use each in the most effective way. More practical uses of method and of planning for teaching are found in detail in the units and courses of study which make up the appendix. Chapter Six is a step-by-step explanation of long and short range planning for teaching. The material in Chapters Five and Six and in the appendix presents method and planning in enough detail for a teacher to choose almost any means of teaching social studies effectively.

Chapter Seven is a description of good marking, grading, and reporting practices with a brief description of evaluation. It is not a chapter on testing and measurement, and was not so intended. Chapter Eight deals with some trends and newer methods in teaching social studies, and some problems social studies teachers face. Chapter Nine is an important and practical approach to teaching current events and controversial issues, and some means of effecting changes in student attitudes.

Chapter Ten is a description of how to choose social studies materials wisely and how to use them in the most effective manner to help the teacher achieve student growth objectives. Chapter Eleven is devoted to classroom management, discipline, cocurricular activities and other non-instructional duties of teachers. Chapter Twelve is the making of a professional teacher.

The authors thought it important that a practical book such as this one should reflect the work of social studies teachers who have developed methods, units, objectives, courses of study, and daily lessons and used them in their classes. Therefore, at least some kind of teacher-made plans for each grade—five through twelve—is included in the appendix. These materials were put in the appendix to preserve their teacher-made characteristics, and to prevent them from interrupting the reader's thought in the text itself. The appendix is long because of the inclusion of these units, which are complete with objectives, methods, tests, outline of content, and bibliographies and daily lesson plans in many cases. Very few changes were made in any of the material in the appendix, since the authors wished these plans to reflect the work and thought of the practitioners, rather than theirs.

Every effort has been made to make the book simple, understandable, practical, and yet thorough enough for a reliable reference work. It is hoped that it will serve the needs of social studies teachers in their planning and teaching.

Walter E. Sistrunk

Robert C. Maxson

ACKNOWLEDGEMENTS

This book grew out of the authors' experience in teaching student teachers methods of teaching social studies, and more recently out of their work with experienced teachers in a consultative capacity. The book is our response to the needs of the teachers and students with whom we have worked. We are grateful for their help and suggestions, and in many cases for the courses of study, units, and other teaching plans which they generously shared with us.

Our personal notes and lesson plans were used extensively in the development of this book. Every effort was made to give credit to the source of the materials' used. We sincerely hope there have been no oversights in this respect. We are thankful for the scholarly work of the many authors referenced herein, and the work of hundreds of others which we read but did not reference. We owe a particular debt of gratitude to those school districts with whom we worked in developing the courses of study and units outlined in the book. We are thankful for the work of our secretaries: Lynn Carroll, Janet Sexton, Kathy Hawthorne, and Connie Rodgers, and to our respective universities, which made the work possible. A special debt is owed to Mary Kathryn and David Sistrunk, both of whom are social studies teachers, for selecting the units and courses of study and preparing them for inclusion in the appendix.

W. E. S.
R. C. M.

The need of youth are many and diverse.

Photo furnished courtesy of Elmore County Public School, Wetumpka, Alabama.

Chapter I

THE
PURPOSE
OF
SOCIAL
STUDIES
IN
AMERICAN
SECONDARY
SCHOOLS

The social studies are concerned with man and his interaction with his social and physical environment. The social studies delve into processes of human relationships, interactions and governance. Never in history has it seemed more important that students be helped to understand that the varied ways of living in the world are not odd, but reasonable, when seen in terms of the natural environment in which people live. Understanding why people live as they do in other countries encourages an attitude of respect for and realistic understanding of other people.

The social studies must assume a major share of the responsibility of preparing students to live effective, productive, useful lives as citizens of the United States and the world.

The time appears to be crucial for fostering the attitude that good government requires an intelligent citizen who obeys laws, participates actively in government and community, and works constructively to preserve and improve the American way of life.

Needs of Youth

The educational system of a democratic society must be prepared to satisfy the needs of students for growth in mental and physical health and growth in moral and ethical values. Students need to learn recreational, social, educational, moral and vocational skills and concepts. To be effective, the needs of the gifted and well-adjusted as well as the less apt must be met. Therefore, each person must be helped individually and as a member of society to make the best possible adjustment to everyday life and to his role as a citizen of the United States. The secondary social studies curriculum includes many of the

1

activities and experiences that have been planned to help facilitate pupil growth as a person and citizen. Thus we must rely on the teaching of social studies as an instrument through which our youth can be helped to meet their needs and through which the culture is passed on to each generation.

Bernard cited the needs of adolescents as stated by the National Association of Secondary School Principals under the heading "The Ten Imperative Needs of Youth"[1]

1. All youth need to develop salable skills and those understandings and attitudes that make the worker an intelligent and productive participant in economic life. To this end, most youth need supervised work experience as well as education in the skills and knowledge of their occupation.

2. All youth need to develop and maintain good health, physical fitness, and mental health.

3. All youth need to understand the rights and duties of the citizens of a democratic society, and to be diligent and competent in the performance of their obligations as members of the community and citizens of the state and nation, and to have an understanding of the nations and people of the world.

4. All youth need to understand the significance of the family for the individual and society and the conditions conducive to successful family life.

5. All youth need to know how to purchase and use goods and services intelligently, understanding both the values received by the consumer and the economic consequence of their acts.

6. All youth need to understand the methods of science, the influence of science on human life, and the main scientific facts concerning the nature of the world and of man.

7. All youth need opportunities to develop their capacities to appreciate beauty, in literature, art, music, and nature.

8. All youth need to be able to use their leisure time well and to budget it wisely, balancing activities that yield satisfactions to the individual with those that are socially useful.

9. All youth need to develop respect for other persons, to grow in their

---

1. Harold W. Bernard, *Psychology of Learning and Teaching* (New York: McGraw-Hill Book Company, Inc., 1954), p. 265.

insight into ethical values and principles, to be able to live and work cooperatively with others, and to grow in the moral and spiritual values of life.

10. All youth need to grow in their ability to think rationally, to express their thoughts clearly, and to read and listen with understanding.

Meeting these ten needs of youth are certainly as imperative charges to social studies teachers today as they were when first articulated. The need to help students meet each of these needs is a proper purpose of social studies in secondary schools. Each of the ten imperative needs of youth can serve as a guideline for the development of a number of teaching objectives in any social studies course at any grade level.

The American Association of School Administrators in a publication called *Imperatives in Education,* 1966, pointed out twelve significant problems and challenges which face all young people of the seventies. Each of these twelve problems point to the purposes of teaching social studies in secondary schools as a means to help students acquire abilities to deal successfully with these challenges.[2]

1. Technological advance has created new relationships between people, education, and work, with technical skills and knowledge taking priority over the capacity to endure hard physical labor.

2. The specter of unemployment is worrying families, frustrating neighborhoods, and haunting political leaders at a time when there are more people employed than ever before.

3. More young people are entering the labor force during a period when job opportunities in the unskilled and simpler occupational fields are markedly decreasing.

4. Science and mathematics are becoming increasingly important in almost every facet of the total culture and are affecting the lives of people in every family and neighborhood in a vital way.

5. The security of the nation as a whole is dependent upon the expansion of economic enterprise and upon scientific advancement.

6. Ideological conflict is gripping the world, with much of the public budget, much public policy, much effort in military defense, and much of the thoughts of people devoted to meeting this challenge.

2. American Association of School Administrators, *Imperatives In Education* (Washington, D. C.: 1966), pp. 2-4. Used by permission of the publisher.

7. Common problems and issues submitted to the people for decision at the ballot box are becoming increasingly complex and frustrating

8. Rapid change in communication and travel is bringing nations all over the world into closer touch with one another and increasing the need for better understanding of the cultures, institutions, mores, languages, and goals of all peoples.

9. Mass migration of people from the country and smaller towns and villages to large centers of population and from the centers of cities to the suburbs, is producing inevitable cultural clashes that shake institutions, disturb long-established customs, set values in new perspectives, color political actions, disrupt systems of school support, and leave indelible marks on the behavior patterns and characters of children.

10. Different ethnic, racial, and cultural groups of people are vigorously struggling for recognition, full rights, fair employment practices, non-discrimination in housing, and higher levels of living.

11. Pressure tactics, emotional displays, and florid propaganda are displacing reason and the exercise of sober judgment in approaches to the solution of common problems.

12. Demands for education beyond the high school are exceeding the capacities of institutions of higher learning. Rising standards for admission and escalating tuition charges are compounding the problem.

It is important to examine statistics on pupil enrollment when studying student needs. Enrollment in all types of institutions reached a record 57,200,000 in 1967. High school enrollments in grades nine through twelve increased 3% from 13,300,000 to 13,700,000. Nearly 2,700,000 students or about 75% of the age group graduated from high school in 1967, and 40% of these high school graduates continued on to college. There were over 200 million Americans in 1970 with a projected population of about 300 million by 2000. When one stops to realize that about 30% of the population of this nation are students at one level or another at any given time, and when one thinks of the crisis in population density and environmental control, he is forced to consider the importance that social studies in our educational system must play in helping students to live with their problems.

One of the reasons for the existence of school systems is recognition of the need and the acceptance of the responsibility for planning a program to satisfy the needs of these millions of students. Government, parents, and community share in deciding the purposes of social studies; but the decision about what to teach and how to teach it rests mainly in the hands of teachers, administrators, specialists, and other school personnel. This is true because about all anyone external to a classroom situation can do is plan, hope, and provide facilities. This is called the *curriculum planned*. When a teacher closes the door and starts to teach, the students receive what is offered. We call this the *curriculum had*.

Goals of Social Studies

There is a need in a complex society such as the United States to provide youth with a wide range of skills which will be of value to them as adults in assuming the many responsibilities of citizenship. The social studies portion of the curriculum is responsible for the development of many of these needed skills. A better understanding of the goals of the social studies program may be obtained by examining some of the goals listed in the chapter that have been deemed important by various writers and groups.

Fraser and West listed objectives for high school social studies proposed by a group of social studies teachers as follows:[3]

The social studies program should help each student achieve at the level of his individual capacities and become an effective citizen in our democracy. The effective citizen exhibits competence in the areas of human relationships, personal-economic affairs, socio-economic affairs, political affairs, and international affairs. To be competent in these areas, the citizen must;

1. Understand and apply important generalizations in each area.
2. Attack problems in these areas in a rational manner.
3. Locate and gather information in these areas.
4. Evaluate information in these areas.
5. Organize information and draw logical conclusions.
6. Work effectively with others.
7. Communicate effectively with others.
8. Consider events in historical perspective.
9. Consider events in terms of spatial relationships.
10. Maintain an active interest in current affairs and social science materials.
11. Exhibit attitudes consistent with democracy.

Goals for the social studies as seen by the teachers of Prince George's County Public Schools, Upper Marlboro, Maryland are:[4]

I. Behavior Patterns

The major function of the social studies, it is generally agreed, is to make of each young person an intelligent, functioning citizen of a free democratic

3. Dorothy McClure Fraser and Edith West, *Social Studies In Secondary Schools* (New York: The Ronald Press, 1961), pp. 39-40.
4. Board of Education, Prince George's County, *A Curriculum Guide in Social Studies I* (Upper Marlboro, Maryland: 1965), pp. 3-4. Used by permission of the publisher.

society. The objectives of the social studies program should look to the appropriate patterns of behavior. A good citizen engages in activities which will:

1.   give him a respect for and appreciation of other individuals and groups.
2.   give him a concern for the welfare of others.
3.   give him a feeling of belonging.
4.   lead him to accept his duties and obligations.
5.   stimulate intellectual curiosity.
6.   give him an ability to reach tentative decisions based upon sound thinking.
7.   provide him with the opportunities to act consistently on the decisions he has reached.
8.   give him self-direction and an understanding of his own abilities, interests and needs.
9.   encourage him to seek better ways of doing things.
10. help him to recognize and appreciate our cultural heritage.
11. enable him to acquire the necessary skills for living in a democratic society.

II.   Content

Since an understanding and mastery of pertinent content is necessary to development of good civic behavior, certain criteria for the choice of this content are essential. The goals of a free, democratic society as reported in *A Guide to Content in the Social Studies* are the bases used for the development of the curriculum guide for the social studies program in the secondary schools of Prince George's County. These fourteen themes are:

1.   the intelligent uses of the forces of nature.
2.   recognition and understanding of world interdependence.
3.   recognition of the dignity and worth of the individual.
4.   the use of intelligence to improve human living.
5.   the vitalization of our democracy through an intelligent use of public educational facilities.
6.   the intelligent acceptance, by individuals and groups, of responsibility for achieving democratic social action.
7.   increasing the effectiveness of the family as a basic social institution.
8.   the effective development of moral and spiritual values.
9.   the intelligent and responsible sharing of power in order to attain justice.
10. the intelligent utilization of scarce resources to attain the widest general well-being.
11. achievement of adequate horizons of loyalty.
12. cooperation in the interest of peace and welfare.
13. achieving a balance between social stability and social change.

14. widening and deepening the ability to live more richly.

The Muncie Community Schools, Muncie, Indiana list these as general objectives in the teaching of social studies in the senior high school:[5]

A. Improvement of the individual's ability for self-realization

1. to develop alert, sensitive and inquiring minds.
2. to develop skills in getting information, thinking critically, and expressing objective evaluations.
3. to foster in the individual, moral and spiritual values necessary for the realization of human worth.
4. to help the individual to realize his own potential and to assume the responsibilities of daily living.
5. to promote self-discipline.
6. to help the students learn to participate as leaders and followers in democratic group action.
7. to encourage students to live a life enriched by continuous and broad social studies learning.

B. Improvement of civic and social relationships

1. to help students learn to live in harmony with people of different abilities and cultures.
2. to develop intelligent pride and faith in our political and social heritage.
3. to develop interest, understanding, and appreciation for the cultures of all people so our local and world differences and problems will yield to some solution.
4. to develop a basic background of facts upon which wise civic and social decisions may be based.
5. to instill in the individual a desire for improvement of the world in which he lives.

C. Improvement of economic relationships

1. to develop an awareness of man's economic relationships to his environment.
2. to develop an appreciation for the services of all occupations.
3. to help the individual gain the knowledge that will encourage him to become a productive worker and an intelligent consumer.
4. to develop an awareness of the inter-dependence of all people.
5. to develop a better understanding of our own economic heritage so that we can retain the worthwhile aspects of this heritage and build on it for future improvement.

---

5. Muncie Community Schools, "Social Studies Volume III: Senior High School (10-12)," Muncie, Indiana, 1965. Used by permission of the publisher.

Four major purposes of the social studies, according to Quillen and Hanna are:[6]

1. To give to pupils the truest and most realistic knowledge that is possible of the community.
2. Preparation of pupils for promoting a wiser and more effective cooperation among regions, areas, individuals, groups, communities, states, and nations.
3. To develop character: to give the pupils a love of truth, an appreciation of the beautiful, a bent toward the good, and a desire and will to use knowledge for beneficient social ends.
4. To give pupils a purpose and a prerequisite to the attainment of other purposes; it is training in the intellectual processes indispensable to the functioning of society.

Moffatt wrote that the objectives of the social studies program are usually stated in terms of knowledge, understanding, skills, habits, and attitudes.[7]

The basic purpose of the social studies program is to provide the motivation, understanding, knowledge, and skills necessary for informed and active citizenship in the United States of America. Ideally, each pupil who completes the program should understand the basic principles upon which his nation functions and should be motivated to support these principles actively as a patriotic, participating citizen. The selection of social science materials for inclusion in the school curriculum is made with this purpose in mind. The social studies program is intended to offer opportunities for each pupil to develop:

1. Knowledge of how such physical factors as climate and topography affect the lives of people in various regions.
2. Knowledge and understanding of how various groups of people have developed social institutions suited to their needs.
3. Knowledge and understanding of the historical backgrounds of the government and institutions developed by the people of the United States and of the social, economic, and political problems faced by this country and its people during the past two centuries.
4. Understanding of and a loyalty to the principles upon which the government of the United States is based.
5. Understanding of the problems faced by the United States in its role as a leading world power, both at home and abroad.
6. Those skills, habits, and attitudes essential to good citizenship in a democratic republic. These include the personal skills needed by each individual to make use of the various sources of information commonly available in the social science fields. Skills and attitudes are included

---

6. James I. Quillen and Lavone A. Hanna, *Education for Social Competence* (Chicago: Scott, Foresman and Company, 1961), p. 61.

7. Maurice P. Moffatt, *Social Studies Instruction* From Prentice-Hall, 1963, pp. 17-18.

which are requisite to life in a society where a citizen is expected to work cooperatively with others and to assume the proper obligations of citizenship.

The goals of social studies concern themselves with citizenship and individual needs as seen by McCreary.[8]

Civic responsibility is the paramount goal of social studies instruction. Social studies are not a mere reduction of the social science disciplines of history, geography, political science, economics, sociology or psychology to high-school stature, but are intended to be an adaptation of such parts of those disciplines as are most appropriate to high school youngsters and the goals of secondary education conceived in terms of the needs of individuals and society.

It seems appropriate at this point to assert some goals for citizenship education. Daniel Roselle reported twelve goals from a 1965 Civic Education Project sponsored by the National Council for Social Studies and funded by the Danforth Foundation.[9] The goals of citizenship education as set forth by Roselle are paraphrased as follows:

1. Citizens should be committed to both individual freedom and equality for all as provided for in the United States Constitution.

2. Citizens need to recognize that we live in a rapidly changing world and need to be receptive to new ideas, and ways of living.

3. Citizens must make constructive value judgments which enable them to function in a rapidly changing society.

4. Citizens must accept responsibility for participation in public decision making through their appropriate representatives.

5. Citizens need skills in solving current social, economic, political, and cultural problems.

6. Citizens should take pride in American accomplishments; but should also understand and appreciate the contributions of other to countries civilization.

7. Citizens should appreciate and understand science and its impact on mankind.

8. Eugene McCreary, "The Crisis Threatening American Education," *Social Education,* 27 (April, 1962), p. 177. Reprinted with permission of the National Council for the Social Studies and Eugene McCreary.
9. Daniel Roselle, "Citizenship Goals For A New Age," *Social Education,* (October 1966).

8. Citizens need to have economic opportunity and security for them-
    selves and they should value both for others.

9. Citizens need to be sensitive to the uses of the creative arts as means
    of human expression and personality development.

10. Citizens should be compassionate, sensitive, just, and aspiring.

11. Citizens need to understand that survival of the human race is depend-
    ent upon reduction of international tensions.

12. Citizens must develop principles consistent with democracy and they
    must apply them daily.

Specific Purposes of Teaching Social Studies

Students need to learn democratic participation. Participation can be emphasized through the teaching and promotion of good citizenship practices in
the social studies classes. Some challenges of social studies are: teaching students an understanding of international relations and world problems; helping
students develop skills in human relationships, such as participation in affairs
of the community, state, and nation; and providing instruction in how to share
the responsibilities of good citizenship.

The main obligation of teaching good citizenship lies with the teachers. The
teacher may illustrate democracy by giving pupils a choice of several alternative assignments which they may elect to do. The teacher should provide
opportunities for majority opinion to prevail about some decisions so that
students will learn respect for the position of the majority. Teachers should
also encourage classroom discussions, so that students will experience disagreement and compromise. Discussion encourages inquiry and thinking, and
teaches respect for the opinions of others. Teachers should encourage class
elections so pupils can learn responsibility by being elected to do a task for the
class. In elections pupils learn to appreciate their voice in the final decision.
Students need to learn how to disagree without being disagreeable.

Dedication to freedom can be achieved more fully from a study of other
lands and people. The teacher can emphasize how some people are still being
persecuted and enslaved, and in this way may heighten the students' appreciation of the Americans experience.

Teachers can encourage students to make critical appraisals of the basic
institutions of society and to analyze causes and conflicts in various situations.
Politics is the means and process of democratic government. Today the teacher

can honestly and openly teach politics in the classroom. While this may not have always been the case, students now can become acquainted with the nature of the political process in community, state, and nation. Democracy can survive only through an educated citizenry. Some of this education must be acquired by means other than direct teaching of government, history, and citizenry. Democratic participation can be best fostered in the schools by encouraging students to participate in collective decision making.

Teachers should strive to build healthy, open attitudes. Teachers will need purposeful planning and direction of learning activities to achieve maximum growth in positive attitudes. Balance must be maintained between freedom and control. Both the teacher and the school must be careful not to be too domineering or too permissive. The teacher must help students to develop an appreciation of law as the protector of all citizens. Discipline is a necessary ingredient of life and only those able to discipline themselves can enjoy life fully in a free society.

The classroom teacher is the most important single factor in providing a democratic atmosphere. The success of any program of democratic participation will depend upon his ability to recognize opportunities for using democratic principles in classroom situations. The teacher needs to know how to foster a democratic classroom atmosphere and to know when and how to ask questions which guide and stimulate the student's thinking. Such teachers will allow opinions to be given without showing disapproval, and they will accept a reasonable solution which may not be their own.

A democracy requires citizens who can think their way through to a satisfactory conclusion according to the available data and established standards. It is imperative that teachers help students learn to think reflectively. Freedom to speak and to think one's thoughts can be fully learned only when teachers let pupils know from experience that what they say will not meet with ridicule, punishment, or sarcasm. Teachers who try to promote democracy need to be mature enough to accept criticism, to value difference, and to grant the right to dissent. Teachers must believe that children are people and have rights no one may deny or abuse if they are to achieve growth in good citizenship.

Assumptions

There are several basic assumptions about teaching and learning which serve as a basis for this book. These assumptions are stated below:[10]

---

10. Walter E. Sistrunk, *A Theoretical Framework for Instructional Practice,* Bureau of Educational Research, Mississippi State University, 1971.

1. It is assumed that growth is always the aim or goal of teachers as they plan and as they instruct.

2. It is assumed that the kinds of pupil growth for which teachers of social studies are nearly always striving, are in both the affective and the cognitive domains. Social studies teachers do want their students to grow in:

   a. the acquisition of information (facts)
   b. the ability to inquire (learning how to learn)
   c. the ability to think (creatively, reflectively)
   d. mental health
   e. emotional control (mature independence)
   f. self-adequacy and self-trust
   g. moral commitment (values)
   h. democratic participation
   i. appreciation of beauty
   j. concern for others
   k. leadership.

3. Learning of social studies, attitudes, and principles of human relations is affected by teacher-pupil interaction, which influences pupil-pupil interaction patterns.

4. Teacher behavior affects what students learn, no matter what the teacher wishes or plans. Since the teacher represents authority and society, what he does in classroom situations as he plans and teaches determines to a great extent the opportunities a student has to learn facts, acquire attitudes, and develop predispositions to inquire.

5. Knowledge exists on a continuum from least verifiable to most verifiable and is undergoing constant and rapid change and growth. All divisions of knowledge into subjects are arbitrary and man-made and exist only for convenience in inquiry and teaching.

6. Effective instruction must provide effective working groups which are skilled in developing and achieving individual and common goals.

7. Leadership in classroom situations is a transactional role and is dependent upon the needs of individuals within a group, group needs, and the qualities of the teacher in given situations.

8. The United States is a pluralistic society with cultural, social, political, and ethnic roots in many lands throughout the world. Individuals, institutions, and groups with divergent views and values exist within our society as the result of some felt human need or problem. The existence of each divergent and conflicting concept, feeling, or group implies the need. These conflicting needs, feelings, concepts, and groups can serve as a medium for the exploration and trial of ideas and views in a manner

essential to maintaining the vitality and strength of a dynamic and democratic citizen and a viable free American society.

9. The fundamental moral principle upon which free societies rest is the dignity and worth of each human being. Honest and effective instruction must support and encourage free and unrestricted exercise and exchange of human intelligence and effort as the most positive force we can use in building a better society. Any society functions within a framework of laws and rules, yet there must be adequate provision for peaceful social change in keeping within the exercise of reason and free discussion. In a free society the government belongs to the living people, and since the schools are a function of government they too, belong to the people now living. All children of all the people must have optimum opportunities to develop themselves through education to their fullest extent and capacity without undue and arbitrary restrictions or barriers. Effective instruction must recognize that each person has something worthy to contribute and it must provide ways of encouraging the unique growth of each child toward his potentials. *The slogan of many American educators "to take each child where he is and take him from there as far as he can go" ought to be the central purpose of all schooling in any free society,* since the strength of the republic does not lie in some folk spirit of the people but it rests upon the broad and competent shoulders of free, thinking, whole individuals who are doers and planners of their individual and collective destinies.

10. Free societies are based upon two noble but seemingly contradictory principles. These are the notions of being free and equal at the same time. Indeed, if one accepts a negative definition of freedom as the absence of restraint and the common definition of equality as sameness then one could not be both free and equal. However, if one defines the two ideas positively then an individual must be free to be equal. Let us state the two ideas positively so that they make sense. Freedom is the power to make effective choices; equality is the individual's right to develop his personal uniqueness to the fullest possible extent. Therefore, *effective instruction in a free society demands that students be taught how to make their own effective choices* and that they be encouraged to become increasingly more unique rather than more like everyone else. At the same time, each student must be taught that his power to make effective choices and exercise his equality is dependent upon restraint and responsibility, not the absence of them. No free society can long survive unless people exercise restraint and respect for others.

The foregoing ten assumptions together with several in Chapter Two serve as a conceptual framework for the authors' beliefs about the purposes of social studies. The last three assumptions are peculiar to teaching social studies in free societies. *A main purpose of all education in a free society is to teach pupils how to govern themselves; hence, effective instruction in such societies must give some attention to teaching pupils by precept, example, and exposition how to live a productive and contributing life in a free society.*

The goals for the teaching of social studies as enumerated in this book show a thorough commitment to providing each pupil the opportunity to realize his potentialities to the fullest; and belief that teachers must continue their commitment to society and to students in their efforts to prepare all youngsters to be socially competent in this modern world. The social studies—anthropology, geography, history, sociology, civics, economics, government, and related disciplines—are vehicles through which our schools and its teachers strive to see that appropriate social studies goals become a reality of growth for each individual pupil. Emphasis on habits, attitudes, understanding, knowledge, and skills are essential in the efforts of our citizenry to function in an increasingly complex and bewildering world. *The purpose of social studies is therefore to teach people how to be better people and how to live effective, fruitful, contributing, happy lives while preserving a free society.*

Teaching is influenced by one's personal belief about the nature of man, the nature of learning, and the nature of knowledge. The influence of a teacher's philosophy on his teaching will be briefly discussed in the next chapter.

PROBLEMS AND QUESTIONS FOR STUDY OR DISCUSSION

1. If the social studies are concerned with man and his interaction with his environment and with other men, what are some of the implications for the changing purposes of the social studies from the changing social scene?

2. How does the philosophy of government in a nation influence the purposes of teaching social studies in secondary schools? For example how does the purpose of teaching social studies in Castro's Cuba differ to that of the regime of Battista?

3. Do the fundamental needs of youth change as the social, economic, and political conditions change in a nation?

4. The secondary schools were established initially to prepare people for the liberal arts college and ultimately for life as a professional person or governmental leader. Later, the secondary schools came to exist mainly to acculturate immigrants. What do you think the appropriate purposes of the secondary schools and of the social studies as part of them should be now?

5. One of the ten imperative needs of youth is the need to understand the significance of the family. Some social scientists are writing that the family and the church have lost much of their significance for many young people. Discuss the implication of these changes for teaching social studies.

6. It has been said that the *curriculum had* is always the implementation of the philosophy and beliefs of the teacher. What does such a statement mean in terms of your teaching?

7. List several ways technological change has affected the social studies in the last twenty years.

8. Discuss the implications of the emphasis on teacher accountability for the purposes of social studies.

9. Justify teaching the battle of Manila Bay or Lake Erie in the light of what you think the purpose of social studies should be.

10. What are the implications from the turbulent domestic scene for teaching citizenship?

11. Develop both a set of purposes for any social studies course at any grade level of your choice, and a brief statement of the philosophy upon which you base these purposes.

12. Write a statement of purpose for teaching social studies to an ethnically different class, or to a class of disadvantaged students.

13. Discuss the meaning of the statement: *the classroom teacher is the most important single factor in providing for a learning atmosphere that is conducive to growth in the ability to participate in democratic self government.*

14. The authors have stated the basic assumptions about teaching and learning which they think of as the essential foundation of a good social studies program. Discuss each of these assumptions and try to list four or five teaching implications of each assumption. Make an effort to add at least one essential assumption of your own.

15. Choose assumption number five or number eight and write a defense or criticism of it and its implications for teaching secondary social studies.

16. Add to the list asserted in assumption two other appropriate types of growth which the social studies should promote.

17. What are the implications for writing behavioral objective, choosing content, and use of learning activities from assumptions nine and ten?

18. Make a list of the various purposes of social studies asserted in this chapter and try to think of at least one specific way to teach to achieve each.

19. How does the purpose of instruction differ from the behavioral or educational objectives?

20. Do you agree with the assertion that social studies teachers must cease to strive for coverage of content and emphasize teaching students how to learn and how to make decisions? Why do you feel the purpose of social studies should be learning how to inquire on the one hand, or learning subject matter on the other hand? What are the implications for choice of content which can be drawn from your position?

REFERENCES

American Association of School Administrators. *Imperatives in Education.* Washington, D. C.: 1966.

Board of Education, Prince George's County. *A Curriculum Guide in Social Studies I.* Upper Marlboro, Maryland: 1965.

Fraser, Dorothy McClure and West, Edith. *Social Studies in Secondary Schools.* New York: The Ronald Press Company, 1961.

Hillway, Tyrus. *Education In American Society.* Boston: Houghton Mifflin Company, 1961.

McCreary, Eugene, "The Crisis Threatening American Education." *Social Education.* Vol. XXVI, No. 4 (April 1962).

Mayer, Martin. *Social Studies in American Schools.* New York: Harper Colophon Books, Harper and Row Publishers, 1963.

Michaelis, John U. *Social Studies for Children in a Democracy: Recent Trends and Developments.* Englewood Cliffs, N. J.: Prentice-Hall, Inc., 1963.

Moffatt, Maurice P. *Social Studies Instruction.* Englewood Cliffs, N. J.: Prentice-Hall, Inc., 1963.

Muncie Community Schools. *Social Studies Volume III: Senior High School (10-12).* Muncie, Indiana: 1965.

National Council For The Social Studies. *What Is A Good Citizen.* (A Civic Education Project, 1965).

Quillen, I. James and Hanna, Lavone A. *Education for Social Competence.* Chicago: Scott, Foresman and Company, 1961.

Roselle, Daniel. "Citizenship Goals for a New Age," *Social Education.* (October 1966).

Sistrunk, Walter E. *A Theoretical Framework For Instructional Practice.* Bureau of Educational Research, Mississippi State University, 1971.

Chapter II

PHILOSOPHICAL AND PSYCHOLOGICAL FOUNDATIONS OF TEACHING

Teacher practice is influenced by what the teacher believes about human nature, the nature of knowledge, the nature of learning, motivation, truth, values, and personality development. Teachers make decisions about objectives, methods, and choice of content based on these assumptions. Since this is the case, a teacher's personal philosophy may, in effect, influence his students' opportunities to learn.

Complicated philosophical and psychological positions are not explicated in this book. Instead the authors explored the influence of teachers' deepest held beliefs about students and subject matter. In doing this some propositions which seemed reasonable are asserted.

The field of social studies is as wide as the universe and as long in the past as the history of man, plus all that went before man learned to write history or keep archives. The social studies as taught in secondary schools draws from anthropology, archaeology, economics, geography, history, political science, psychology, philosophy, sociology, social psychology, education, religion, literature, languages, the natural sciences, the physical sciences, art, agriculture, music, and mathematics together with some concepts drawn from all the applied sciences and vocations. The social studies are the teachable versions of knowledge drawn from all these disciplines in an effort to help students understand and manage themselves and their environment.

Influence of Philosophical Beliefs

Because the field of social studies is so vast, and because what teachers do and believe influences what students become, teachers should strive to develop a consistent set of values to guide their practices. Every teacher of social studies makes countless decisions each day based upon his values, and based upon the priority which he places on each of these values. Teachers may not be con-

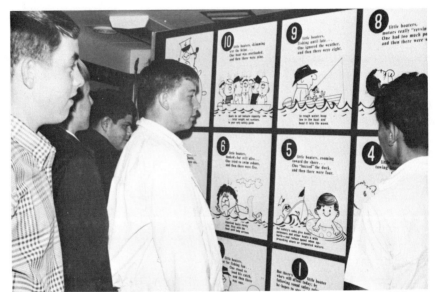

Photo furnished courtesy of Elmore County Public School, Wetumpka, Alabama.

Pupils use their own initiative, interests, and skills in developing projects.

Photo furnished courtesy of Elmore County Public School, Wetumpka, Alabama.

scious of these underlying assumptions which govern their behavior; nevertheless, their teaching is largely determined by these deeply held convictions.

All men learn who they are and what they are from the actions and words of those who surround them. A teacher who believes that all men are evil must always be on guard against student misbehavior. Such a teacher will need quiet classrooms so that his exposition can be heard. Each student will be required to complete identical assignments and take identical tests. Teachers who believe that "idle hands are the devils workshop" will give homework just to keep students busy, not to promote appropriate student growth. These are only a few examples of the influence of controlling assumptions on teacher behavior. There are limitless possible examples of such influences on teacher actions.

There are several major philosophical positions held by most social studies teachers in the United States today. The oldest of these is idealism. Idealists believe the main purpose of education is to discover eternal truth and to teach facts. Realism is the next most ancient belief, it differs in important respects from idealism principally in the manner of investigating truth. The Thomist position and its modern versions such as neo-classicism is a kind of combination of idealism and realism. All these philosophies tend toward belief in schools as a means of passing on the cultural heritage. They believe the function of all learning is discovery of eternal truth. Such teachers are committed to the classical curriculum with emphasis on learning for its own sake and high academic standards. Memorization and drill as a means of teaching are the main methods used by teachers adhering to these philosophical positions. All of these positions hold to the belief in mental faculties, mental discipline, and transfer of training which can be developed through exercise.

Teachers who subscribe to classical philosophies generally emphasize subject matter for its own sake. Coverage of material often becomes the major thrust because of commitment to eternal verities. Teaching people how to be democratic or how to be free becomes largely a matter of talking to them about government and responsibility. Social studies becomes the memorization of dates, biographical data, names, events, and other content without encouragement to explore meaning. Since there are eternal verities, teaching is mainly a matter of telling students what the verities are and having them memorize them. The emphasis in social studies is on learning about the past as a means to understanding the present and preparing to accept the future.

Most teachers who subscribe to classical philosophies are suspicious of change, wary about man's attempts to govern himself, and to control what happens to him. There is a tendency to look backward, to be nostalgic, to be traditional, to be overly insistent upon stability, and to preserve what is. The great strength of teachers who subscribe to classical ideas about knowing, learning, and human nature is in their commitment to well established values

	I Theory of Learning	II Psychological System or Outlook	III Assumption Concerning the Basic Moral and Psychological Nature of Man
Mind Substance Family	1. Theistic mental discipline	faculty psychology	bad-active mind substance continues active until curbed
	2. Humanistic mental discipline	classicism	neutral-active mind substance to be developed through exercise
	3. Natural unfoldment	romantic naturalism	good-active natural personality to unfold
	4. Apperception or Herbartionism	structuralism	neutral-passive mind composed of active mental states or ideas
Conditioning Theories of Stimulus- Response (S-R) Associationistic Family	5. S-R bond	connectionism	neutral-passive or reactive organism with many potential S-R connections
	6. Conditioning (with no reinforcement)	behaviorism	neutral-passive or reactive organism with innate reflexive drives and emotions
	7. Reinforcement and conditioning	reinforcement	neutral-passive organism with innate reflexes and needs with their drive stimuli
Cognitive Theories of Gestalt-Field Family	8. Insight	Gestalt psychology	naturally-active being whose activity follows psychological laws of organization
	9. Goal insight	configurationalism	neutral-interactive purposive individual in sequential relationships with environment
	10. Cognitive-field	field psychology or relativism	neutral-interactive purposive person in simultanious mutual interaction with environment, including other persons

1
and Their Implications for Education[1]

IV	V	VI	VII
Basis for Transfer of Learning	Main Emphasis in Teaching	Key Persons	Contemporary Exponents
exercised faculties, automatic transfer	exercise of faculties—the "muscles" of the mind	St. Augustine, John Calvin, J. Edwards	many Hebraic-Christian fundamentalists
cultivated mind or intellect	training of intrinsic mintal power	Plato, Aristotle	M.J. Adler, St. John's College
recapitulation of racial history, no transfer needed	negative or permissive education	J.J. Rousseau, F Froebel	extreme progressivists
growing apperceptive mass	addition of new mental states or ideas to a store of old ones in subconscious mind	J.F. Herbart, E.B. Titchener	many teachers and administrators
identical elements	promotion of acquisition of desired S-R connections	E.L. Thorndike	J.M. Stephens, A.I. Gates
conditioned responses or reflexes	promotion of adhesion of desired responses to appropriate stimuli	J.B. Watson	E.R. Guthrie
reinforced or conditioned responses	successive, systematic changes in organisms' environment to increase the probability of desired responses (operants)	C.L. Hull	B.F. Skinner, K.W. Spence
transposition of insights	promotion of insightful learning	M. Wertheimer, K. Koffka	W. Köhler
tested insights	aid students in trial-and-error, goal-directed learning	B.H. Bode, R.H. Wheeler	E.E. Bayles
continuity of life spaces, experience, or insights	help students restructure their life spaces—gain new insights into their contemporanious situations	Kurt Lewin, E.C. Tolman, J.S. Bruner	R.G. Barker, A.W. Combs, H.F. Wright, M.L. Bigge

Educational Publishing Inc. Reprinted by permission of Van Nostrand Reinhold Company.

and principles. They are usually stable people and as a result they are usually stable teachers. Their greatest problem is a reluctance to face reality which in this country is often change.

Many social studies teachers claim to adhere to some form of pragmatism, or one of the other more modern philosophies. Some, in fact, are pragmatists, reconstructionists, logical positivists, or existentialists, but most of those teachers who say they are pragmatists may really only be practical minded idealists. *A pragmatist looks to the consequences of his acts as a guide to his practices. Do social studies teachers really consider consequences when they teach or plan?* Many of today's students may be existentialists in their value systems. Thus their views of truth, morality and ethics can and often do, frustrate social studies teachers, especially those who are somewhat idealistic. Both those who tend to be pragmatic and those who tend to be classicists may be annoyed and dismayed by the values held by many students in the secondary schools today.

The reconstructionist teacher thinks of the school as an instrument to reconstruct or remake society. The existentialist's viewpoint is that each student should hold his own values. Most teachers are somewhat eclectic in their view of man, knowledge, learning, and values. Most believe there are some eternal verities, some need for drill and mental discipline, and a great deal of need for practical and democratic participation. Most teachers know that people really do arrive at their own values whether we wish them to or not. Teachers should examine those beliefs that underlie their actions and assumptions as teachers. They should examine the consequences of these assumptions in terms of influence upon students.

Sherman Frey and Earl Haugen have a good description of the relationship of learning theories, psychological systems, and who favors each in Table 1 on the preceeding pages.

Principles of Learning

Some rules of learning are presented in the section which follows. Many educators have found these principles to be experimentally correct with most students and in most classrooms. These statements do not pay homage to any particular theory of learning, and the authors are not pretending that they are stated in exact, scientific, or exhaustive terms. The statements are intended to be usable and practical. They constitute a mass of highly individualized information, and are not oriented to a particular classroom method or philosophy. We have found reference to them to be useful to us in our teaching; however, each teacher should integrate them into some kind of functionally operating process of instruction by the development of his own ideas about learning and teaching.[2]

Complex classroom learning proceeds best from wholes to parts and then back to wholes.

Most learning occurs in patterned ways, a student gains insight as he sees relationships and derives meaning from the context. Some students do learn mainly from a step by step *splitting* process, but many do not and most of the more creative students learn mainly by *grabbing*.

Learning in a piecemeal fashion is inefficient.

People learn facts and skills better when they are presented in a meaningful pattern, not piecemeal as isolated items to memorize. Facts and skills are easier learned when part of a job, game, or project. Then we learn them as we use them, not in isolation.

There are no average pupils.

The notion of averageness is largely a myth. Such things as grades, which are an average of numerical scores, or an average of letters assigned as marks are wrong even for the pupil they are computed about. These means are doubly damaging when they become a standard to measure everyone by. Any standard we have will be unattainable for some and too easy for others.

People differ in countless ways.

People are not created equal in any way and they become more unequal each day they live. Every classroom has students who can do any task assigned better than others, and easier. We need all kinds of people in our society. Why should we try to make people who are different do exactly the same things? Equal treatment does not mean identical treatment. Fairness does not mean that everyone does identical homework assignments.

Teach the skills and concepts you want directly.

Pupils are not born with the skills and knowledge they need, and they do not have either when they come to class, that is why they are there. We can not always depend upon other or previous teachers to teach students the skills and concepts prerequisite to adequate growth in our grade or subject. Therefore, when we get students who can not do the things they must do to succeed, such as read, the only sensible thing we can do is teach them the skill they need.

There are no muscles of the mind that can be strengthened by exercise in wrestling with difficult problems.

The mind is not a muscle which thickens or grows stronger by lifting mental

2. Mimeographed. College of Education, University of Florida, 1965.

weights. The intellect is not like a knife that can be sharpened by honing on a grindstone. If there were muscles of the mind then failure would be good for people, and so would busy work. Don't isolate concepts from the context in which they belong; don't contrive difficult work for students just because its good for them to fail sometimes.

A person can not learn only one thing at a time.
It is impossible to turn the world off while one concentrates on learning some one concept or skill. The student responds to his total surroundings. Learning will proceed better from projects, tasks, participation, and inquiry, so why not use this fact to facilitate teaching?

Participation makes learning easier.
Personal participation by the student is essential to efficient learning of complex social concepts and skills.

Learning is facilitated by realistic and abundant practice.
Students need practice in the many creative, intellectual, political, and social behaviors we want them to master as part of their social studies courses.

People learn through their individual efforts to satisfy their own needs.
People need to do what they do, whether or not they realize this consciously. Actions taken in the effort to satisfy personal needs cause learning.

Motivation is the key to learning.
People learn more and better those things they want to learn. The urge to learn may stem from need, fear, inborn drive, curiosity, puzzlement, challenge, the need for dominance, mastery, or from love. Whatever the source, the drive to learn must be present for the person to be an effective learner. The more the urge to know comes out of the inner drives of the learner the easier it is for him to learn.

Personal interest in what is to be learned is the key force in unlocking the power to learn.
People are interested in those things they feel a part of, and those things they feel have meaning for them. Teacher's who do not capitalize on student interests are not using their best teaching tools very effectively.

Acceptance of class objectives and purposes as his own greatly enhances the student's interest, which helps him find meaning in what is being taught.
We do not teach to get interest, but if interest and acceptance of purpose is not present, then learning will not prosper.

Well established purposes precede effective learning.
Students must have well established purpose which has been internalized before effective learning can occur. Therefore, class objectives should be carefully established, and each student should know exactly what he is to learn and do.

Readiness is another key to learning.
People will not, and indeed can not, learn much when they are unready, have not been prepared, or do not have prerequisite skills and concepts. Thus preparation for learning is very important to effective learning situations.

Discovery of personal meaning helps people learn quickly and lastingly.
The teacher often perceives meaning in learning situations that the pupils do not perceive. It is only as the pupils begin to see personal meaning in what they are doing or learning that effective mastery of a skill or concept will occur.

Students need to be challenged, but not threatened.
The art of teaching is how to challenge without threatening the self-concept, or values of the pupils. What is a challenge to one student may well pose a threat to another. Thus teachers must be alert to detect which way the pupil feels, challenged or threatened. Too much emotional tension reduces efficiency of any behavior.

People usually learn more and better from success than from failure.
No organism thrives on failure. Just as plants need sunshine, water and good soil to flourish, so does the learner need a learning climate that is supportive.

Personal activity helps a student gain insight.
People learn what they do more effectively than they learn from being exhorted. The more extensive and intensive a student's personal activity the greater growth he will have, within some limits of common sense.

Students learn the parts they play.
The roles pupils are to play in life will not be new to them if these roles have been played in school. For example, democracy is something people do, not something people talk about or are talked to about.

A person's surroundings directly influence what he learns.
Make something you want students to learn part of their lives and they will find learning it much easier and more meaningful.

Classroom conditions and organizations which simulate lifelike situations en-

hance learning and retention of what is learned.
Methods and materials should be as lifelike as is practicable.

Use of several of the senses simultaneously enhances learning and reinforces retention.
When a pupil only reads or only listens or only looks or only touches he is forced to rely on one cylinder learning, use of several senses at once helps him master the concept or skill.

Learning is made more effective by firsthand experience.
The kind of knowledge and learning that results from firsthand experience differs greatly in kind and quality from learning because we have read or heard about something. Yet, in schools we can not provide large amounts of firsthand experience because of the limits of space and time. School is intended to be shorthand for experience.

People grow and learn in individual ways continuously throughout life.
It is not possible for any group of students to move through any course or grade in a smooth and even way. Some will outgrow others. There is no reason why every student should have exactly the same assignments, nor do exactly the same things, because they certainly will not know exactly the same things after having a course.

Some authorities say that children learn more in the first three or four years of life than in any other comparable period.
The home influences and the peer group influences what a student will learn or can learn at school. Thus effective schooling is dependent upon improving the environmental influences to which pupils are exposed.

School is only one of many institutions which affect what students learn.
The church, home, community, family, peer group, and numerous other groups and agencies all operate on each student; he learns from all these sources and from the mass media. Much of what we try to teach him in school is in conflict with his most cherished values learned at home, in church, or on the street. This conflict reduces the efficiency of his learning.

Effective learning is often lowered by ill health, malnutrition, or poor mental health.
Because of this and other factors we need to know our students and their background if we are to help them learn more effectively. Confusion in the behavior of a student often results from teacher demands that are beyond his physical or mental capacity.

Learning proceeds from where the student is; asking him to do things he can't do frustrates him.

If students have not mastered prerequisite skills or concepts, they can not learn what is now demanded. Class objectives may be constant, and perhaps they should be, but if objectives are either too easy or too difficult for very long, students will lose interest, become bored, or frustrated, or all three.

Clear communication of goals, assignments, and concepts are essential for students to behave effectively as a result of classroom instruction.

Teachers who are learners and scholars themselves are usually more effective in producing learning and scholarship in their students.

At least some of the things students are expected to learn should be above the lowest cognitive level.

One of the main goals of social studies is to produce a citizenry that can make its own personal and collective decisions in a wise and effective way.

Because this is a free society, students must learn the processes of participative decision making by doing them, not just be being told about them.

Psychology and Learning

Teachers need to study principles of psychology, learning theory and human growth so that they can use these principles intelligently in planning and guiding their instruction. No pretense is made that these enormous and complicated fields have been completely covered in this book. What has been done is to develop and expand a few ideas from these areas which may prove useful to the social studies teacher.

This book is based on several basic assumptions about knowledge and learning in classroom situations. These assumptions follow:

1. Teacher beliefs, assumptions and behavior influence what is learned no matter what the teacher's intentions may be.

2. Teaching is dependent upon effective communication. Most classroom communication is verbal in nature. Civilization, and indeed life itself, is dependent in complex, modern societies such as ours upon man's ability to codify knowledge and recover it through the use of symbols. Survival of civilization is dependent on man's increasing ability to use symbols to convey knowledge and to use stored symbolic material to create new knowledge.

3. Knowledge exists on a continuum from least verifiable to most verifiable and is constantly changing. Therefore, teachers should stress learning to learn rather than acquisition of facts, only.

4. Teaching is goal-oriented human behavior; the goals are student achievement or learning of predetermined concepts, facts, attitudes, and means of inquiry. Since teaching is human behavior, it can be learned and improved by study and design. Most people can teach better than they do.

5. It is important to understand that human growth and development takes place in a social milieu, and is thus directly affected by social, cultural, peer group, and family forces which operate to help create a student's character, personality, and self-image. The school is a part of this cultural context and exists within the broader culture to serve the purposes of the society in helping shape the individual to its way of life while not destroying his own urge to be unique and creative. It is recognized that biological factors have important effects upon human growth and development and it is recognized that heredity does to some extent determine the capacity for growth which any individual has. Certainly there are wide variations from person to person in any given intellectual, physical, or personality characteristics and clearly there is no clear line which separates hereditary biological influences from environmental influences in the shaping of any given individual.

6. It is also a singular fact that man is the only self-conscious organism of which we have any knowledge. Man is an organism that learns who he is and what he is by how others react to him and to what he does. He learns his selfness by what he sees reflected in the eyes and actions of those with whom he interacts in face-to-face groups for the most part. It is one of the most remarkable phenomenon of which we have cognizance that man is a thinking, planning, problem-solving, political animal; but he is also a rationalizing, excuse making, self conscious, remorseful being. It is an equally remarkable fact that men find it necessary to teach what they have learned to their young usually in artificial cultural environments called schools. Because of these individual and societal needs, the school program and the plans of instruction devised by individual teachers must provide for a maximum of positive experiences which bring growth in confidence and increased optimism and hope for each child as his individual needs are met and as he is acculturated. Teachers should remember at all times that not only is man a being; but that he is also a being who is in a constant and continuing state of becoming throughout life from birth to death. Thus each person's growth is unique, yet there are many ways in which each person's growth is similar to that of every other person.

7. Motivation is closely associated with the view of the individual as an integrated and organized whole being. Individual motivation is unique to the particular person and it is constant throughout life, even though

it involves a multiplicity of changing and shifting desires and needs. The position taken in this book is that any given person is always motivated to protect and enhance the self-image which he holds; therefore, he acts and reacts as he does in any given situation because of the way he perceives the elements of the particular situation. Thus given his particular self concept he can act or react in no other way at any given moment of time. The argument often advanced about intrinsic versus extrinsic stimuli and their influence on an individual's motivation is thus irrelevant to this postulate since the self of a given person arranges and selects elements from any given situation that are congruent with its needs and rearranges these elements as it integrates them into its phenomenal field. Even the arguments between the several schools of psychology seem to have little relevance to the uses of motivation in a classroom situation since all of them are concerned with optimum challenge and minimum threat to the learner. The learner is always motivated to protect and enhance his self-image; thus, to be eclective, instructional activities must be structured to respond to individual needs and to provide opportunities for success in terms of individual standards as well as absolute standards.

8. Learning involves the selection of various elements from the environment by the individual, the organization of these elements into a personally meaningful experience. and the integration of this experience into the self-system of the individual. It follows that learning is an individual experience which is continuous as the organism lives and functions. Thus the effective program of instruction must be and always is aimed at individuals rather than the mean of the group. This is true whether or not the teacher wishes to teach individuals.

9. One of the unexplained paradoxes of educational and psychological measurement is that most data are reported in terms of central tendencies rather than as divergencies from the average. Teachers know that people are individuals with unique powers and widely divergent creativity drives, yet we are too often unwilling or unable to provide the kind of instruction which permits and encourages each learner to become increasingly more himself and more unique. Students do learn in unique ways, in spite of teacher's frequent refusal or inability to provide for individual learning and individual ways of coping with a problem. Therefore, it is imperative that effective instruction be aimed at individuals not average of groups.

10. Aggregations of students become a group as they interact with each other in the establishment of common objectives, norms and beliefs, a system of communications, and an organization for the implementation of their joint aims and desires. The behavior of individuals is influenced most by interaction with and within groups which meet their needs through support for the attainment of their individual purposes. It seems reasonable, therefore, to assert that constructive change in behavior of an individual is greatest when he is a participant

in making group decisions.[3]

PROBLEMS AND QUESTIONS FOR STUDY OR DISCUSSION

1. What is your educational philosophy:
   a) in terms of what you believe about the deity?
   b) in terms of your belief about the essential nature of mankind, and thus of student behavior?
   c) in terms of your belief about the nature of knowledge?
   d) in terms of what you think about how people learn and why they learn?
   e) in terms of the nature of communications in classroom situtations? Just what do you think the use of symbols (words and numbers and other symbols) should be in conveying knowledge to students?

2. What do you think the teacher should do while in the classroom? Do you think teachers should do most of the talking and students most of the listening? Or do you prefer to rely upon an activity type curriculum and teaching method, based mainly on students learning by discovering as they do? Do you think teachers should take charge of a classroom and give it a sense of direction, or should the objectives be determined by the students? Perhaps you favor some position other than any of these; if so state it and defend it.

3. Why should social studies teachers strive to develop a consistent set of values and a philosophy that is not too eclectic? Perhaps social studies teachers should be more eclectic in their values than most teachers. What do you think about this, and why?

4. Can talking to students about good government do much about promoting their growth in the ability to govern themselves? Why, or why not?

5. What should the role of subject matter be in a social studies classroom?

6. How would a teacher who is thoroughly pragmatic act if his students are not showing adequate growth toward the stated behavioral objectives?

7. How would a teacher who is thoroughly committed to the classical philosophies or to their newer offspring, neo-essentialism, react to the discovery that his students were not learning as much subject matter as he deemed desirable?

8. Some teachers and many students really subscribe to some form of existentialism. What would such a person's reaction likely be to a poor set of test scores?

3. Sistrunk, op. cit.

9. Write an essay discussing the implication of your answers to questions six, seven, and eight.

10. Which philosophical position and which psychological school of thought largely underlies the *structure of the disciplines approach* to social studies curriculum and teaching?

11. What does a reconstructionist think the purpose of teaching social studies should be?

12. Which philosophy and which psychology adheres to the mental discipline theory of education? Is there any value in the notion of mental discipline?

13. Examine Frey and Haugen's chart on learning theory, philosophy, and psychology and pick out your position. Then show how the position you have picked controls what you choose as content, and how it is presented.

14. Study the principles of learning and try to show how you can apply each of them to the teaching of at least one social studies concept. Perhaps these principles of learning can help guide you as you develop a teaching unit, as outlined in chapters five and six.

15. Study one of the sets of behavioral objectives and the matched methods and content in one of the units in the appendix and make a list of the principles of learning used and the ones ignored or violated. Write down what you think the consequences of these uses or violations could be in terms of change in student behavior.

16. Write out a practical statement of philosophy and of learning principles of your own. Strive for a consistent viewpoint as you do this.

17. Study the authors' assumptions in chapter two and try to discern their implications for teaching. Perhaps you might find it rewarding to examine these assumptions in the light of the units in the appendix or the material on methodology and behavioral objectives in chapters five and six. Are there implications from these assumptions and the ones asserted in chapter one that seem to form a consistent view of human nature, human behavior and teaching?

18. Which one of these assumptions has tremendous implications for the organization of classrooms for teaching and learning? One of these has implication for the choice of content, another one for evaluating student progress. Can you identify these underlying assumptions and explain their meaning satisfactorily?

REFERENCES

Bernard, Harold W. *Psychology of Learning and Teaching.* New York, Toronto, London: McGraw-Hill Book Company, Inc., 1954.

Carter, William L., Hansen, Carl W., and McKim, Margaret g. *Learning to Teach in the Secondary School.* New York: The Macmillan Company, 1962.

Douglas, Leonard M. *The Secondary Teacher at Work.* Boston: D. C. Heath and Company, 1967.

Frey, Sherman H. and Haugen, Earl S. *Readings in Classroom Learning.* New York: American Book Company, 1969.

Gross, Richard E. and Zeleny, Leslie D. *Educating Citizens for Democracy.* New York: Oxford University Press, 1958.

Hilgard, Ernest R. *Introduction to Psychology.* New York: Harcourt, Brace and World, 1962.

Lambert, William, and Lambert, Wallace. *Social Psychology.* Englewood Cliffs, N. J.: Prentice-Hall, Inc., 1964.

Morse, William C., and Wingo, G. Max. *Psychology and Teaching.* Chicago: Scott, Foresman and Company, 1962.

Principles of Learning. College of Education, University of Florida, 1965. Mimeographed.

Sistrunk, Walter E. *A Theoretical Framework for Instructional Practice.* Bureau of Educational Research, Mississippi State College, 1971.

Chapter III

SECONDARY SOCIAL STUDIES CURRICULUM PATTERNS

Some writers maintain that the world has not had a normal day since the outbreak of World War I; some others think that World War III began when Frederick invaded Silesia in 1636; still others view the industrial revolution and its consequences as the main causative agent of the problems of our times. A few people are claiming that we are now living in a post industrial age in such nations as the United States, Great Britain, West Germany, and Japan. Whatever the cause, most social scientists are in agreement that ours is a troubled time. These troubles are compounded by: the revolution of rising expectations, the emergence of new nations and the increase of nationalistic feelings in many world regions, the speed of transportation and instant communications, and world wide mass media that not only report events instantly, but in many cases make events.

During this century the United States has been involved in two world struggles for its very life, two other far away lengthy and agonizing foreign wars on the mainland of Asia. We have experienced the great depression of the thirties; we have seen the dreary predictions of Malthus begin to come true; our technology threatens to overwhelm the planet with refuse and pollution; we have created the power to destroy all life as we know it; and we have witnessed enormous changes in the customs and mores of our people.

People have come to live with all kinds of unspeakable fears and undreamed of potentials for both good and evil as an everyday and continuous thing. No one knows any real security, even though we are more prosperous than ever before, and even though we are better educated and have more people employed than ever before. In only thirty years we have proceeded from the air age through the atomic age, jet age, the hydrogen

Teachers should encourage classroom discussions.

Photo furnished courtesy of AUM Learning Resource Center and Montgomery County Public Schools, Montgomery, Alabama.

The middle school concept implies new and unique methods of instruction.

Photo furnished courtesy of E.K. Wood, Director, Banks Model School Project, Pike County Public Schools, Troy, Alabama.

age, Sputnik, and the exhilaration of putting men on the moon. The cold war has caused us to keep a peace time draft for the first time in our history. World leadership has been thrust upon us, whether we wanted it or were able to handle it or not. Citizens of the United States have grown used to being called ugly Americans around the world and we have even accepted communism in our next door neighbor. Change and uneasiness are the hallmarks of our times; and it is not just the rapidity of change that causes us to be fearful, it is the nature of the changes taking place all around us. These are changes in our most fundamental and cherished values and customs, and no suitable alternative value systems seem readily available to us.

Urbanization has been a trend throughout this century with the added movement of many middle class people to the suburbs in the last decade. Our largest cities are becoming rundown islands of minority peoples in a sea of white people. Unrest seems to be the order of the day in many major cities, most are in a state of perpetual crisis. Constant technological change and planned obsolescence produce a daily deluge of new and different products, and a variety of schemes to tell us that we can not do without a product that replaced last week's indispensable product!

These and other changes going on here and abroad influence economic, political, and social events; thus the social studies must do something about teaching our young people how to cope with change as a phenomenon, as well as the changes themselves. Our school systems are and will continue to be charged with the responsibility for developing individuals competent to function in a democratic society, which includes the phenomenon of changing values, no matter what the situation may be at a given time.

When Sputnik was launched, the groups most interested in technology, science, and mathematics had a field day with the hysterical reaction and shock of the average American. It was incomprehensible to most ordinary men that the Russians could be ahead of us in science, so the reasoning went. It is in the nature of free societies to expect much of their schools, and to quickly find fault with them when things seem awry. Thus, money was poured into the building of new curricula in the sciences, in mathematics, in technological subjects, and to some extent in communications. It did not seem to occur to anyone that the sciences were already several hundred years ahead of our knowledge of how to live with what their handmaiden-technology-could produce. Social studies and humanities were given short shift. However, that is beginning to change and people are now coming to advocate social research and development of a more meaningful and relevant social studies curricula for the secondary schools. Progress has been and continues to be slow in improvement of the social studies.

Many colleges and universities, private and governmental agencies are showing an awareness of the need and are beginning to try to devise newer social studies curricula. These efforts are bound to bring change in what is taught and how it is taught, and hopefully some of the changes will represent improved curricula. Efforts now in progress should provide us with the data needed as a base for improved courses of study for the secondary social studies, revived interest in them, and revived interest in the humanities.

There has been a feeling among teachers and scholars that changes in the social studies curricula are necessary. Many changes have been made in the social studies on a piecemeal basis; but a major overhaul is needed. There are those who suggest that the overhaul be undertaken with the same enthusiasm and extensiveness as that experienced in the sciences and mathematics.

The problems as seen by Carr are: (1) choosing material from the mass of information; (2) a general lack of interest on the part of the public, and many who would like to see things remain as they are; (3) because the social studies field deals with human relationships, it is inextricably bound up with values, beliefs, traditions, local customs, prejudices, and a host of other intangibles; (4) a curricular offering which is not understood, which seems to threaten cherished values and beliefs, or which appears to be based on opinion and imprecision, is viewed with skepticism; (5) hundreds of millions of dollars have gone into research, sponsored by the national government, in the physical and biological sciences, but only a tiny amount has been given to support research in the social sciences and even less to support the improvement of the social studies programs in schools; (6) scholars in the social science disciplines have in the past done very little to help; (7) state legislatures have commonly engaged in the curriculum-building process through the introduction of courses which have taken valuable time away from that needed for a well-balanced social studies program; and (8) inadequate communication which precludes objective study of controversial problems.[1]

What Should Be Taught

Recently there has been a trend to reexamine the entire structure of the social studies curriculum from kindergarten through grade twelve. Current suggestions for consideration are.[2]

1. From the book *The Social Studies* by Edwin R. Carr. © 1965 by the center for Applied Research in Education.
2. Association of Teachers of Social Studies of the City of New York, *Handbook for Social Studies Teaching* (New York: Holt, Rinehart, and Winston, Inc., 1967).

Type of Content: Teach subject matter.
Proposed by: Charles R. Keller, Director, John Hay Fellows. Highlights and Reasons for Program: We should rid ourselves of the idea that history and social studies have the job of making good citizens. Attitudes cannot and should not be taught in formal classroom situations; we weaken education when we try to do so. Students should study subjects and learn facts and ideas—how to think, how to understand.

Type of Content: Educate for citizenship.
Proposed by: 32d Yearbook American Association of School Administrators, NEA.
Highlights and Reasons for Program: In the United States the need for people educated in citizenship and the need for free public schools cannot be separated; programs must be so broadly and soundly concerned that all our children, youth, and adults become more competent to carry responsibility; pupils should know the events of history, conditions of geography, principles of government, sociology and so on.

Type of Content: International approach.
Proposed by: Everett Clinchy (President, Council on World Tension): Frank Graham, UN Conciliator; Willis Griffin, International Development Administrative Coordinator.
Highlights and Reasons for Program: Social studies suffer from imbalances too much weight on the United States and particularly geared to the United States outlook today. Schools should adopt a comparative method for teaching—look at other cultures as normal patterns for these peoples.

Type of Content: Psychological or "know the child".
Proposed by: Frank Riessman, College of Physicians and Surgeons, Author *The Culturally Deprived Child.*
Highlights and Reasons for Program: Effective education of the "one in three" who is deprived requires a positive understanding of his traditions and attitudes and a pragmatic view of education. The deprived child is an anti-intellectual, physically oriented learner.

The preceding ideas have served to stimulate thought and debate on what should be taught. Exploration by scholars and teachers will continue in a concerted effort to come up with a program that meets the objectives of social studies and is palatable to those in the field.

It has been suggested that changes which began in the 1940's have continued and can be summarized as:

1. World history has largely supplanted ancient, medieval, and modern European history.

2. Government is being more widely offered and required in senior high schools.
3. Economics is being more widely offered and required in high schools.
4. Geography is moving fairly rapidly into the senior high schools.
5. The offerings, particularly of electives, are becoming more diverse.

Distinguishing characteristics of the emerging social studies curriculum include emphasis on a unified social studies program with emphasis on concept formation and renewed commitment to the learning process. Behavioral objectives will be the key from which the entire instructional program will derive its sense of direction.

It is likely that the social studies will show some of the following trends: (1) inclusion of more content from economics, anthropology, sociology and geography; (2) various cross-disciplinary approaches in an attempt to teach social concepts in context; (3) more emphasis on the structure of the disciplines; (4) more field tested teaching materials.

There is a concerted effort by private as well as governmental agencies to improve the social studies program as evidenced by the number of projects that have been undertaken. While some people in the field believe that progress is being made, others feel that progress is too slow or is yet to begin.

Most writers on social studies content still appear to be committed to the concept of citizenship and preparation for it, with expansion of social studies coverage to provide more meaningful and up-to-date knowledge, attitudes and skills. While there are efforts to standardize the curriculum, this still appears to be in the future despite the mobility of the population and its impact on our educational system.

It appears that we are currently in a period of experimentation in the use of methods. There can be no criticism of this process as long as some progress is being made, and we do not lose sight of the objectives of the program, and try our best to secure more effective methods.

There is a trend in the social studies toward massive curricular developments at a national level, cooperation among social scientists and social studies educators, utilization of curriculum engineers and behavioral scholars and emphasis on the structure of knowledge.

Typical Social Studies Curriculum Patterns

The usual organizational structure of the American secondary school is grades seven through twelve. Grades seven, eight, and nine are generally referred to as the junior high school and grades ten, eleven, and twelve as the high school or senior high school. The middle school concept, which will be discussed later in this chapter, is becoming more common as a substitute for the junior high school.

The junior high school and high school may or may not be housed in the same complex. The trend has been to combine them in the same building in rural and small town areas. The small student population can be better served by the teaching faculty when organized as one unit. There is often better building utilization when all six secondary grades are combined in sparsely populated areas.

The trend in the larger, more urban, school districts has been to house the junior and senior high school separately. Those grades designated as junior high are often on a self-contained campus. Many junior high schools are housed in structures formerly occupied by senior high schools, but more progressive school districts are designing buildings specifically adapted to the unique needs of junior high students.

The writers of this text support the concept of buildings specifically designed for the junior high school or middle school based on needs of that age student. The concept of grades ten, eleven, and twelve composing a comprehensive senior high school seems logical. It also appears desirable to have a separate campus for the junior high school or middle school because of the obvious physical and social gap that exists between the younger students and the older high school students.

Although the social studies curriculum appears to be somewhat similar nationwide, there are some variations in the social studies courses offered in the middle, junior, and senior high schools. The courses offered, required and elective, are usually dependent upon the school enrollment and the characteristics of the community.

Junior high school

Over 70% of the nation's high schools require social studies of all students in grades seven, eight, and nine. There is a virtually uniform social studies requirement for all pupils in these grades, regardless of the size or type of school. Although social studies electives are uncommon in grades seven and eight, there are some electives offered in grade nine. Approximately 30% of the schools do not require a particular social studies in grade nine, thus providing opportunities for electives at this level.

The usual required courses in junior high school are geography in grade seven, United States history in grade eight, and civics in grade nine. Civics may or may not include at least one semester of state government. When an elective is offered in the junior high years it usually means making civics an elective instead of a required course. Many ninth grade students take driver education or a vocational course which precludes a social studies course.

It appears the following social studies curriculum would be appropriate and typical for a junior high school.

	Required	Electives
Grade 7	Geography	None
Grade 8	U.S. History to 1877	Economic Geography
Grade 9	Civics	State Government
		Economic History

Figure 3-1. Typical Junior High School Social Studies Curriculum.

Senior high school

The high school curriculum, like that of the junior high school, tends to be reasonably uniform all over the country and has experienced few changes during the last fifty years. The greatest departure from the traditional pattern has occurred in the elective area. The specific courses which have found popularity include sociology, social or family living, economics, and consumer education.

The characteristics of the community and the enrollment of the school are having a greater impact on the number and type of electives being offered than on what courses are required. The number of electives is somewhat a function of the size of the high school. The type and depth of the elective offerings often reflects the economic and cultural level of the community.

The average senior high school might adopt the following social studies curriculum pattern.

As indicated earlier, the social studies curriculum has experienced some recent changes, but generally there has been criticism of the social studies curriculum because of slowness of change. Some of this criticism may be entirely justified. However, in the absence of any substantial research that other curricula in the social studies courses would be better, it appears that the suggested social studies curricula will meet the needs of most American high schools, if properly taught.

	Required	Electives
Grade 10	None	World History
		European History to 1700
Grade 11	U.S. History since 1877	Economics
		Sociology
		European History since 1700
Grade 12	Problems of Amer. Democracy	Family Living
		Consumer Education
		Economics
		Sociology

Figure 3-2. Typical Senior High School Social Studies Curriculum.

Other Social Studies Curriculum Patterns

There have been attempts by various school systems to break the lockstep syndrome of the traditional ladder or graded school organization. Most of these innovations have met with limited success. This indictment is based mainly on the fact that many of the changes have received verbal support, but little actual support when it came to application. No doubt most of the refusal to adopt curricula that depart from the traditional is a function of the lack of finances. Voters have a tendency not to support any change which cannot be clearly justified in terms of measurable and visable results to be obtained from the expenditure. Two meritorious approaches that have been receiving a great deal of attention in recent years are the nongraded school and the middle school.

Nongraded schools

The unique contribution of the nongraded school is its apparent ability to provide for individual differences and eliminate learning gaps. Schoolmen have carried on endless dialogue about teaching individuals rather than averages, but historically they have done little in the way of implementing it.

The philosophical principles behind the nongraded idea are:

(1)   Learning should be continuous.
(2)   Children grow at different rates.
(3)   School programs should be flexible.
(4)   Greater achievement results out of success.[3]

The social studies curriculum, in both the required and the elective areas, may be similar to that of the graded school. The difference is that the student can pursue a subject or area of social studies until he has mastered it. Rigid time standards are removed and each student progresses at his own rate in each subject. The student works at his own level and does not compete with other students in the same way as he does in graded curricula.

Nongraded organization often means more work for the teacher, but it does appear to contain potential benefit for the student. The method of instruction will vary from school to school. A program that is specifically adapted for one school may not be as effective in another school.

Melbourne High School in Melbourne, Florida has become one of the most widely known nongraded schools in the country during the last ten years. The Melbourne plan is based on phases, ranging from phase one which is remedial to phase six which is reserved for the academically talented. An eleventh grade student, who is not doing well in school, may have the following schedule at Melbourne High School.

English – Phase I – Remedial
Math – Phase 2 – Intermediate
Art – Phase 4 – Depth Study
Biology – Phase 2 – Basic Study
History – Phase 2 – Basic Study

It is apparent from the schedule that the nongraded school helps eliminate grade mindedness both on the part of the teacher and the student.

3. Hugh Perkins, "Nongraded Programs: What Progress," *Educational Leadership,* 19 (December, 1961), pp. 166-169, 1940. Reprinted with permission of the Association for Supervision and Curriculum Development and Hugh Perkins. Copyright © 1961 by the Association for Supervision and Curriculum Development.

The middle school

The middle school is essentially just what the name suggests, an intermediate school, a school between two other schools. To try to make a comprehensive definition of a middle school, we must assume it to have a unique philosophy and an organizing principle to implement its purposes. The organizational pattern should cover those age levels where the greatest number of pupils enter and complete the period of pubescence. It appears, based on these criteria, that grades five through eight would be the most appropriate for the middle school.

The social studies offered in the middle school varies from school to school, depending upon the philosophy of those charged with administering the program. The nature of the curriculum will also be somewhat dependent upon the extent of departmentalization. In general, a typical middle school social studies program would not differ dramatically from the offerings found in upper elementary and lower junior high school grades.

An area where the middle school faces a problem is that of training its teachers. It has taken the junior high school many years to attain enough status, stability, and experience in the eyes of colleges of education to warrant special courses being established in junior high school teaching and administration. If an education student is interested in teaching in the five-eight middle school, what area will he specialize in, elementary, junior high, or secondary education? State departments of education will have to find ways to certify teachers and administrators. Standards for accreditation will need to be developed as will new curricula and new media. This is not an insurmountable problem and it does appear the middle school concept will continue to expand.

A Possible Future Curriculum

No curriculum should be organized on subject matter only or on child needs and experience only. Rather any curriculum should be based on those *concepts* and *skills, knowledges, understandings, attitudes,* and *habits* which a person will need to live and function in his world. These learnings, together with the structure of subject matter, serve as the basis for selecting student growth objectives and content. Together they serve as the main determiner of the best instructional organization and the most desirable method for teaching this particular content to this particular learner at this particular moment in time.

The curriculum should draw concepts, skills, and knowledge from all the disciplines into which man has divided the world's storehouse of knowledge in an ordered sequence fitted to the student's needs and capacities in such a way as to help him reach *his* unique potentials most effectively.

Such a curriculum and instructional arrangement requires a total rearrangement of subject matter and instruction. This approach might be called *S* imultaneous *I* ndividualized *M* ultiple *P* rogress *L* earning *E* xperiences. *SIMPLE* is a good name for the *S* equentially *O* rganized *C* oncept *C* urriculum, *SOCC*. *SIMPLE* would be achieved by using *SOCC* as a means of examining what people need to know and be able to do after school, and then organizing these concepts and skills in such an individualized tailor-made way as to help them most in growing toward these goals. *SOCC* was probably what educators had in mind when the curriculum was first organized many years ago, but much has been added to it, the nature of knowledge has changed, man's needs are more complex, and schools *cannot* produce the *universal man* anymore. It appears that many recent innovations in school practices such as flexible scheduling, inquiry methods, the curriculum projects, programmed materials, use of electronic media, and the growing use of media centers all tend toward *SOCC* and all will help achieve *SIMPLE;* but none really vary enough elements of instruction and curriculum to do very much about individualizing learning or teaching. More talking is done about individualizing instruction than action. Too much classroom teaching is still aimed at averages, testing for convergent learning, and rigid conformances to others values upon the urging of authority.[4]

PROBLEMS AND QUESTIONS FOR STUDY OR DISCUSSION

1. What are the curriculum implications of the assertion that the world has not known a normal day since World War I?

2. How should American involvement in Vietnam, Korea and other regions of Asia affect what you teach in social studies?

3. How should the changes going on in our larger cities affect the social studies curriculum?

4. Is there any logic to the sequence of social studies courses usually offered in secondary schools? If not, what sequence do you think they should be in? Why?

5. Design a social studies scope and sequence for grades five through twelve that is based on some different rationale than the traditional history and geography offerings.

6. Read some of the recommended curricula for American secondary schools that are organized on a different basis than the typical pattern described in this chapter, such as the ones described by James B. Conant; Hilda Taba; Kimball Wiles, Broudy, Smith and Burnett; or J. Lloyd Trump.

4. Sistrunk, op. cit.

7. Study some of the literature about the middle school and about the junior high school and decide which organization you think is more educationally sound.

8. Study the periodical literature about curriculum reform in the social studies and write a short paper stating the reasons why there has been so little of it in comparison to science or mathematics education.

9. Read the latest reports on two or three of the current curriculum projects in the social studies and report on them to the class.

10. How does a teacher or a school provide balance in the social studies curricula?

11. How can you tell if one social studies course is well articulated with the rest of the program of social studies courses at your school? How can you determine the relative articulation of social studies with science, mathematics, and language arts?

12. When you write a teaching unit or course of study, how can you check its scope, sequence, articulation, fit, pacing, reward, and degree of relevance to the purposes of social studies? How can you determine if the curriculum fulfills the needs of the students and the community?

13. How do the social studies differ from the social sciences?

14. What are the appropriate determinants of the content of the social studies?

15. What should be the main purpose of the social studies in junior high school or the middle grades?

16. Devise a non-graded, fused, social studies curriculum for the senior high school.

17. The authors have recommended a future curriculum that is dramatically different from most present day social studies curricula, and equally different from most reformer's dreams of what the social studies curricula should be. This recommended curriculum is subject centered, yet learning centered in that it rests on the notion of breaking each subject down into its component parts and restructuring both sequence and scope. Study *S I M P L E* and its practical application *S O C C* and try to write a three or four week unit that incorporates its basic design.

18. Apply the concept above to restructuring the entire secondary social studies program in terms of what concepts should be taught, *which* ones should be first, and *what* behaviors students should learn as a result of social studies courses.

REFERENCES

Alexander, William M., Williams, Emmett I., et. al. *The Emergent Middle School.* New York: Holt, Rinehart and Winston, Inc., 1969.

Carr, Edwin R. *The Social Studies.* New York: The Center for Applied Research in Education, Inc., 1965.

Conant, James B. *The American High School Today.* New York, Toronto, London: McGraw-Hill Book Company, Inc., 1959.

Fenton, Edwin. *Teaching the New Social Studies in Secondary Schools: An Inductive Approach.* New York: Holt, Rinehart and Winston, Inc., 1966.

Gulley, Halbert E. *Discussion, Conference, and Group Process.* New York: Rinehart and Winston, 1966.

Perkins, Hugh. "Nongraded Programs: What Progress." *Educational Leadership.* (December, 1961).

Sistrunk, Walter E. *A Theoretical Framework For Instructional Practice.* Bureau of Educational Research, Mississippi State University, 1971.

The Association of Teachers of Social Studies of the City of New York. *Handbook for Social Studies Teaching.* New York, Chicago, San Francisco, Toronto, London: Holt, Rinehart and Winston, Inc., 1967.

Veatch, Jeannette. "Improving Independent Study." *Childhood Education.* Vol. XLIII (January, 1967).

Weber, Del and Haggerson, Nelson L. "Broad Trends and Developments in the Social Studies Today." *The Social Studies.* Vol. LVIII, No. 1 (January, 1967).

Chapter IV

THE
SOCIAL
DISCIPLINES
AS
BASIS
FOR THE
SOCIAL
STUDIES
CURRICULUM

We have discussed in the preceding chapter the typical curriculum found in most secondary schools in the United States, and some of the other ways social studies curricula are organized. It is necessary that some attention be given to the rationale for choosing the content of the social studies curriculum, and to whether the content chosen will accomplish the stated purposes of the social studies in the secondary schools.

One of the rationales most often advocated for improvement of existing social studies programs is the structure of the disciplines. This concept is rooted in Spencer's question, "What knowledge is of most worth." Most of the national curriculum projects in science and mathematics are based on the structure of the disciplines approach to choosing content and method. Phillip Phenix published a paper in 1956 in which he advocated the thesis that because of the proliferation of knowledge, all curriculum content should be composed of key concepts drawn from the disciplines as such.[1] Phenix viewed both content and method as derivative from the peculiar means of inquiry in each discipline. Many educators found merit in his proposal and proceeded to build whole new curricula for secondary mathematics and science around the structure of the disciplines. More recently some social studies curricula have been built on the means of inquiry or discovery of the several social sciences.

There are several strengths to inquiry method. One of the more obvious advantages to inquiry method and the structure of the disciplines is that it teaches students how to inquire, how to learn what they will need to know at

1. Philip H. Phenix, "The Use of the Disciplines as Curriculum Content" in, *"The Subjects in the Curriculum: Selected Readings."* (Frank L. Steeves, Editor. New York: The Odyssey Press, Inc. 1968).

History composes the greatest portion of the social studies curriculum.

Photo furnished courtesy of AUM Learning Resource Center and Montgomery County Public Schools, Montgomery, Alabama.

Students find geography one of the most exciting courses in the curriculum.

Photo furnished courtesy of AUM Learning Resource Center and Montgomery County Public Schools, Montgomery, Alabama.

some future time, rather than memorizing a large storehouse of facts. Transfer of learning is facilitated because method and material are one. Simplification of complex concepts and procedures is made easier and generalization is easier since it is a prime objective of inquiry. The object of schooling is to substitute a shortened, simulated experience for the longer and more difficult experience of life. In order to do much at school learning, students must learn how to use symbols in an abstract way. The goal of teaching is to promote understanding and proponents of the structure of the disciplines approach believe that their method facilitates student learning of abstract, symbolic reasoning. It is believed that the act of discovering or rediscovering knowledge intrigues students and leads them on to inquire more, and to inquire more deeply. School people have long claimed that one of their main goals is teaching students how to think; generally we have not been very successful in helping most people learn to think in a very scientific fashion. The process of inquiry, indigeneous to the several disciplines, requires rigorous thinking, thus it was reasoned that the disciplines approach would teach students how to think. Indeed, there is some evidence that the new science and mathematics courses have helped teach some students how to think more carefully. This is especially true for the gifted student, and is true for thinking about math and science problems. The social sciences are only now beginning to develop inquiry based secondary curricula. The method of discovery or inquiry seems admirably adapted to teaching most secondary social studies courses, so perhaps the results will be gratifying.

One must wonder, however, if Spencer's question about knowledge is the appropriate criterion for selection of either content or method in the social studies. Certainly, there is much knowledge in the social sciences that students need to know; certainly we want young people to know how to learn in the social disciplines; certainly we want students to know how to participate in group discussions and decisions; and certainly we want students to learn how to think about social questions. There can be no quibble with students' need to develop their ability to inquire. Yet, thoughtful social studies teachers or thoughtful parents, must ask themselves if the question of the phenomenological psychologists, *"What can man become?"* isn't a more important criterion of the worth of both social studies content and method than the question, *"What knowledge is of most worth?"* Perhaps this is not an *either/or question,* but, rather, *a both/and question.*

It does seem that an examination of the contribution of some of the social sciences and their respective means of inquiry should follow. The authors have used the inquiry approach and the discovery method in teaching social studies to students in several social studies courses and at various age levels with success. The disciplines approach to social studies teaching has merit, especially in teaching students how to gather information and form generalizations. A discussion of the social disciplines most common to secondary schools follows.

History

History composes the greatest portion of the social studies taught in the secondary and middle schools of the United States; therefore, it seems appropriate to consider it first among the disciplines in this discussion. History is a vast, ancient, and complicated discipline which draws on most other disciplines, including the humanities in an effort to describe the record of human existence. History is unique among the social disciplines because it is so broad and because it is a three dimensional discipline, the third dimension being time. The dimension of time gives history its perspective and may account for its continued popularity as a part of the secondary curriculum, at the expense of some of its younger, and seemingly more useful, sister social disciplines. Many definitions have been offered for history, none completely adequate; but history has been described as the record of everything man has said, done, or thought, and that it is our best reconstruction of what men have done and how they did it.

Herodotus is reputed to be the father of western history. Thucydides is generally credited with originating historical method. The histories of the ancients, and indeed those of the nineteenth century before about 1870, were very literary and were very unscholarly by modern standards. Some say that is precisely why we enjoy reading Herodotus, Josephus, or Plutarch–their works are literary.

St. Augustine gave history its first careful and recognized philosophy. His writing was meant to be theologically persuasive, and was. Leopold Von Ranke ushered in the modern era of history in the last part of the nineteenth century. It was Von Ranke who established careful and scientific methods for verifying authenticity. He stressed the need for the historian to consider his philosophy, and the equally important need for the reader to be aware of the philosophy of the writer. Von Ranke developed the tool by which modern history has grown into a deeply respected discipline, *the historical seminar.*[2] The seminar as a means of investigating truth, together with the canons of verifiability developed by Von Ranke and his followers are the elements from the structure of history as a discipline, along with a sense of time and causation that we should stress in secondary social studies. The methods of empirical investigation developed by the graduate schools of history have had a profound influence on the other social sciences.

The historian is trying to reconstruct the past, thus all records of what men have done, thought, and planned are grist for his mill. The historian must gather information from many sources; he must exhaust primary sources and evaluate existing secondary sources so that he can obtain a clear picture of an

2. Donald V. Gawronski, *History: Meaning and Method* (Illinois: Scott, Foresman & Co., 1967).

event or a personality before he is even ready to write a rough draft. All sources must be checked for competency, accuracy, completeness, truth, verifiability, corroboration, and the personal intent of the witnesses before a historian can feel competent to generalize about his subject. If we could teach this careful scientific, cool-headed, detached attitude to students, history would have made a mighty contribution. The hallmark of the historian is careful research, reluctance to judge, and skepticism about those who make sweeping generalizations claiming too much knowledge of a person long dead, or an event long past. History is an effort to reclaim the past, but the past can rarely, if ever, be totally reconstructed. Most history, as most current news stories, is a narrative that ties together the public statements, letters, assertions, and acts of men of prominence. Obviously much of the real story is never available to the public, since men's public personalities and pronouncements bear scant resemblance to their private thoughts and actions in many cases.

There are four basic types of sources upon which the historian relies for his information: *primary, secondary, remains,* and *traditions.* Primary sources constitute such things as verifiable documents, letters, manuscripts, diaries, and eye-witness accounts. Any primary source is dependent upon the witness' firsthand knowledge of the topic, his competence to understand the issue, and his relative lack of bias. Thus, those primary sources which the witness had reason to believe would not be made public are usually reckoned of great importance in shedding light on a topic. Secondary sources are the works of other writers on the same subject, or the expert opinion of someone, or the judgment of someone not present. Secondary sources, no matter how carefully documented, or how well written always suffer from the handicap of being hearsay historical evidence. Remains are such things as clothing, buildings, artifacts, works of art, food, pottery, armor, weapons, etc. There are scientific methods of verifying the age of most types of remains. Traditions are similar to secondary sources in being hearsay, but they are usually not carefully researched or documented and they are usually oral rather than written, having been handed from one person to another until generally believed.

A research historian, as any other scientist doing research, is supposed to enter upon his study without preconceived opinions of truth. It has been said that if one's mind is made up about a conclusion, then he can do no bona fide research about that particular issue or topic. Research is supposed to be an honest search for data which can lead the researcher to *any conceivable* conclusion. It is not uncommon, however, for the historian to embark upon a study with a number of preconceived conclusions. Indeed, sometimes he is simply trying to prove his point.

There are many special types of history such as: economic history, political history, history of agriculture, history of education, history of science, church history, regional history, and many others. There are several basic schools of historical philosophy or thought which determine the interpretation put on reconstructed events or people by the historian. Some of the main schools of history are: providential, cyclical, scientific, dialectical, economic, progressive, and Social Darwinist.

The beliefs of a textbook writer about these or other schools of historical thought inevitably influence the slant of his presentation; the beliefs of a social studies teacher about the nature of history inevitably influence the way he teaches history. A teacher who believes in the cyclical theories typified by the writing of Oswald Spengler and Arnold Toynbee isn't likely to teach history as dialectic in the Hegelian tradition. Someone who believes that an economic interpretation of history is the best one, such as the view of Charles Beard, will not be comfortable with providentialism. Many Americans have an inner conflict that revolves around the progressive viewpoint that man can actively plan his future effectively. Most of us believe this to some degree, but are drawn away from its full implications by our most deeply held beliefs which stem from the Judaeo-Christian ethic. The nature of history and its means of inquiry have much to offer to the young person in secondary school, if taught in a thorough and interesting way.

History is a subject that can influence the future citizen as few others can because knowledge of where we have been as a people contributes to understanding of the present situation and some insight into what the future may bring. One of the highest priorities of the schools today is to provide students with knowledge of people in other countries, knowledge of our government and way of life, and knowledge of what the future may be like. History is the best story we can reconstruct of man's story, so it is vitally important that students understand world conditions and their causes. Therefore, history should be one of the best taught and most loved subjects in the secondary school curriculum. However, it is not. Most surveys indicate that history is the most disliked course which the students must take. Such a situation desperately needs to be corrected. The cause is too often lack of knowledge of history and its means of inquiry.

Many secondary history courses are taught as shallow survey courses, and often entirely by the teacher reading from his notes or the text. The problem is in part the result of inadequate undergraduate preparation; but more often than not competent history teachers are available and seeking positions but are not hired. In some cases competent social studies teachers are on a faculty, assigned out of their field or to some trivial duty while the administration assigns a less competent person to teach history. Traditionally, social studies has been what was taught by the assistant coaches, whether prepared or not. There is nothing wrong with coaches teaching history or any other social studies class; but, if a coach is going to teach anything in the classroom, he should make certain that he knows what he is doing and that he does it well.

Many history teachers are not professionals, and have little knowledge of the real purpose of the discipline. Too often school libraries are inadequate for students to learn anything about the means of historical inquiry. Often, this is the fault of teachers who do not ask for materials. Frequently, history is taught in the driest, most uninteresting manner possible. Since all of these conditions can exist in the same school, small wonder that students scorn history as the most unpopular subject of all!

Improvement of the teaching of history is dependent upon better trained teachers who know what the structures of the disciplines are and who are capable of scholarly inquiry themselves. History can contribute much to student growth in the ability to inquire, the ability to think, and growth of value systems if presented in a more thorough and interesting fashion. History is the most inclusive of the social disciplines and it is the area that gives the student some perception of time. It is too valuable a discipline to be taught as it sometimes is. History was once the social studies, and it still is the largest part of them in most schools. The history teacher needs to learn how to be a director of learning, rather than someone who engages daily in oratory efforts aimed at his class.

Government (Political Science)

A simple and workable definition of political science is needed as a basis for understanding its nature and the means of inquiry peculiar to it. There is disagreement even among political scientists about what the discipline is.[3] We can avoid the problem of abstract definitions by simply saying that, from the practical viewpoint, political science is the study of governments and how they function, or ought to function. Everyone comes into contact with agents of the government such as judges, teachers, policemen, firemen, mail carriers, and many others. Everyone's life is affected by the things done by our elected officials, such as congressmen, president, governor, legislators, school board members or aldermen. These offices are not separated but are interwoven into a complex network which comprise the levels of government which serve our needs and regulate our conduct. Political science is the study of government, therefore it is the study of governmental institutions, constitutions, laws, and the people who make them and who conduct the business of governing. Understanding the behavior of the people in government means understanding people's political behavior. A workable definition of political science then, means the study of the art, science, and philosophy of government and those who participate in governance.[4]

3. Dell G. Hitchner and William H. Harbold, *Modern Government: A Survey of Political Science* (New York: Dodd, Mead, and Company, 1962).

4. Ibid, p. 7.

An understanding of political science as a discipline is made simpler by dividing it into several sub-divisions: (1) the nature of the discipline, its definition, objectives, and its criteria for truth; (2) the several sub-fields within political science, public law, public administration, political theory, political parties, comparative government, international relations, public opinion, local and municipal government, state government, the federal administration, and legislation; (3) the relationship of political science to other social sciences; (4) the tools used to help collect and interpret data about government.

Government is more art than science; but the study of government is the study of political activity which requires the use of rigorous scientific method. Thus the study of political science requires both art and science. Judgment by humans of other humans and of situations is the natural order of things in government, especially in free societies. Democracy is somewhat inefficient by its nature; some political scientists would despair of a society ruled in an orderly, scientific manner on the ground that it would of necessity be dehumanized. There is evidence that government as we know and like it is a practical art acquired largely from long experience, and dependent upon the gift of getting along with people. The successful statesman or politician is a master craftsman, his success depends upon skill, talent, and experience, and more perhaps than any other work, reputation of past performance. Bold men of genius have made possible many of our governmental advances. However, even if those who say that government is art are correct, we need not depend upon art to study and analyze it. It will help us to understand the behavior of people in politics and government if we look at government from the point of view of science and philosophy as well as art.

Political science lies between the humanistic studies and the physical sciences, and always has elements of both. Therefore, political science will probably never become simply a system of collecting facts, but will retain its humanistic elements.

Political science as science

Scientific knowledge is defined as organized and verifiable knowledge, based upon observation and experience. The process of government is, according to this definition, a science. Scientifically based knowledge is available to people involved in the governmental process, and a scientific method may be applied to political science including the definition of the problem to be solved; the acquisition of relevant data; the construction of hypotheses or tentative theories, to explain the data in terms of the problem; and, finally the verification, or attempted verification, of the hypotheses. This is not to say that political science is a rigid science that can control and predict; there are few, if any, unvarying and universal factors or terms of measurement. The study of political science is concerned with bettering its present methods of obtaining and evaluating data.[5]

Political science as philosophy

Political philosophy furnishes us with insight through which we can evaluate intelligently the institutions and politics of the concrete political world. Philosophy provides the answers to many questions, in particular the objectives which the institutions of government seek. Philosophy is systematic thinking; therefore, it is necessary for the proper operation of politics. To achieve any success, political observers must bring their social life into proper view, and gain an understanding of the goals of political action. Then we can understand the processes and actions of government. This is politics as philosophy.

The objective of political science is not the cultivation of patriotism, but the furthering of knowledge. Political science is concerned with mankind as political units. It traces political life from its earliest beginning. It also considers the development of the state from simple to complex.

Fields of study

The separate fields of political science have a variety of approaches and materials they employ, yet they overlap. They are simply rough groupings of materials pointing out areas of specialization, and they permit some division of labor for scholars and students.[6]

Public law

Public law deals with governmental authority. It concerns individual relations with their government, following a set of fixed rules. It includes constitutional law, or laws dealing with governmental powers; administrative law, dealing with rules of governmental agencies; and the law of criminal offenses, which are offenses against the public. Public law differs from private law in that private law regulates the relations of individuals with each other, whereas public law regulates the individuals relations with the government and society at large. The role of the political scientist is to determine the rules, the way they are established, changed, and function. Political scientists study how power is obtained and how it is used in running a government.

5. Ibid. pp. 9-10.
6. Ibid. p. 13.

Political parties and public opinion

Parties and opinion deal with public policy, and are concerned with political power. This field includes the practices of politics; the organization and function of political parties, the foundation and operations of interest groups in politics, and examples of leadership.[7] A political party is a group of organized citizens acting as a political unit, who use their voting power to try to be in control of the government and thus carry out their policies. Competing political parties are the force that is necessary to keep the state's political machinery in operation. They exist in democracies, and *only* in democracies. In fact, it is political parties that make democracy workable in large areas, because they are the unifying agency. Political parties give the citizens a voice and make the public opinion known.

Comparative government

This field is a study of the political experience, institutions, behavior, and processes in the major systems of modern government.[8] This field of study emphasizes the similarities of major modern governments, determines what are variables and invariables in political systems, and points out those that are unique and those that are common. The political systems usually studied in a course of this type are those of Western Europe, Great Britain and the Commonwealth, and the United States, and occasionally those of the Far East and Latin America. Also, the Soviet Union and other Communist countries are being studied more closely.[9] Other systems may be of particular interest because of various reasons: common origins, similar structures, geographical or cultural association, or relation to a great power. Subjects of recent attention in comparative government include post-war constitution-making, the sources and character of leadership in dictatorial states, variations in the assumption by governments of increased economic responsibilities, the adaptation of western political institutions by the newer African and Asian states, patterns of federalism, the role of legislative second chambers, and devices for promoting ministerial responsibility and stability in parliamentary governments.

Public administration

This field is focused on public policy—its application and enforcement. Administration takes place at all levels—local to international—and is shared by all branches and organs of government. Policy execution and policy formation overlap. It deals with such topics as policy-making, organization in ad-

7. Ibid. p. 14.
8. Ibid. p. 14.
9. Ibid. p. 15.

ministrative-operations, ordinance-making power, personnel recruitment and management, public funds, natural resources, and interest groups.

Courses in this field are varied. They may deal with phases of public administration such as personnel administration, public finance, public planning, and administrative management. Or, they may deal with government programs in such areas as national economy, housing, social security, or natural resources.[10]

International relations

International relations is divided into three major areas: international law, international politics, and international organization. International law is concerned with rules and practices of international relations. International politics deals with power and influence between states of the world. International organization deals with the structure and agencies of the governments of the world. The political scientist analyzes interrelationships among states of the world.

Recent areas of interest in international law are rules developed by international organizations, rules concerning criminal law, jurisdiction over water and in the air. International politics currently is concerned with theories for handling international tension situations, propaganda warfare, diplomatic strategies, security systems, foreign policies, and balance-of-power. International organization is presently concerned with such issues as international administration, institutions and personnel; ways to bring about peace; and international enforcement.[11]

Political theory

This field considers politics philosophically and speculatively. The purpose of political theory is to give meaning and a sense of direction to particular subjects of political investigation. This area is the broadest of all fields of political science. Two specific tasks for political scientists lie in this field. One is to provide a basic definition. The second is to reveal the underlying nature, functions, and purposes of the political community.[12] Courses in political theory are devoted to research and political knowledge, to analytical theory, and to political thought.

Relation to other social sciences

The social sciences consider man in society. To more clearly understand why man behaves as he does, we may isolate certain types of behavior into

10. Ibid. pp. 16-17.
11. Ibid. pp. 17-18.
12. Ibid. p. 18.

several sciences. Although political science is a large area of study in itself, it is not detached from the other social sciences.

The relationship of political science with history is immediately obvious. The two are very closely related. Political science draws from history for much of its data. History includes the political activities of man; thus it is of interest to the political scientist. Political science is in a peculiar sense dependent upon history. This is so true that some persons have argued that if history is well taught, there is no need of a separate course in civics. History furnishes information concerning past states, the causes of their successes and failures, and helps answer the questions concerning the best systems of government.

Political science was once studied in conjunction with economics in a study known as political economy. Today, though they are separated, they are still related. A part of economics concerns the wealth of the state. Certain subjects are of concern to both sciences—taxation, currency, governmental industries. Economics is concerned with them because they deal with wealth; political science is concerned with them because they deal with governmental administration. No hard and fast line divides politics and economics. The study of sociology deals with man's social relations whereas political science is concerned with political relations only. Political science, therefore, is a subdivision of sociology, restricting its material to a much narrower area.

The political activities of man are always greatly influenced by his geographical environment. It partially determines the particular needs for his political system, and automatically groups man. Also, geography has been important in the determination of the nature of international relations between states.

The study of political science is important to the people of America as a training for good citizenship. Citizens of this democracy are obligated to inform themselves on public matters in order to make good contribution to the governmental process, and this task, in essence, is the purpose of political science.

Sociology

Sociology originated about one hundred years ago as an offspring of philosophy. However, philosophy had to first be separated from theology before sociology could become distinct. The Socratic Method was responsible for the transition of thought from theology to philosophy, because it searched for a procedure which would establish a criteria of truth within the thought process itself. Socrates had laid the foundation for rational proof, which was developed more fully by Aristotle in his syllogisms. Greek philosophy contributed to social science indirectly, by way of the rational proof. Just as the rational proof was a basic element for science, it was also important for sociology.

Sociology is also based on history. Auguste Comte, the father of sociology, relied directly on history to try to establish laws of the regularities of social events. Perhaps it would be more understandable to show how sociology is different from other disciplines rather than how it is like them. Sociology generalizes about social events, but unlike folk wisdom, it looks for abstract knowledge not limited by time and place. It seeks abstract knowledge, but unlike religious thought, it is not subordinate to sacred institutions or beliefs. It tries to establish knowledge based on inherent standards of validity, but unlike philosophy, it is empirical. Sociology seeks empirical knowledge of social events, but unlike history, it looks for the general instead of the unique.

Sociology owes much to both the humanities and the sciences. The idea of a genuine social science came largely from science itself. It extended the scientific method to the social world of man, so that the economic, political, legal, religious, familial, and other institutions came to be studied empirical-ly.[13]

Sociology in particular is interested in the general study of human social behavior; the structure and functioning of societies, groups, communities, and institutions; and social change.[14]

Sociologists have certain fields that they study in detail, such as the family, the community, and population. They deal with characteristics common to all groups and societies, so they must study social classes, social prestige, rank, discrimination, and power. They investigate human social life as the product of four factors—biological heredity, natural environment, the group, and culture.[15]

Sociologists are interested in how ideas influence people's behavior. For example, one widespread idea is that one race is genetically inferior to another in mentality. The majority group in a society may use this idea to discriminate against a minority group. As the result of discrimination and denial of equal opportunity, the minority group becomes handicapped in its achievements. Their inferior performance is then used by the majority group as proof of the theory of racial inferiority. So one can see how ideas, even though they may be false, can greatly influence people's behavior.

Sociology can be broken down into six areas in general:

13. Don Martindale, *The Nature and Types of Sociological Theory* (Boston: Houghton and Mifflin Co., 1960).
14. Robert L. Sutherland, et al. *Introductory Sociology*, 6th ed. (New York: J. B. Lippincott Co., 1961).
15. William Ogburn and Meyer F. Nimkoff, *Sociology*, 4th ed. (Boston: Houghton Mifflin Co., 1964).

(1)   Social theory is taught as a history of thought. It deals with the social structure, the social order, and social change.

(2)   Social control is concerned with the ways in which members of a society influence each other to maintain a social order. An example is the socialization process; this is the way we learn the expected behavior patterns.

(3)   Social change studies technical innovations, the analysis of cultural diffusion and culture conflict, and the investigation of social movements.

(4)   Social processes are the patterns of social change used to interpret social behavior.

(5)   Social groups include integrated group behavior, collective behavior, mass behavior, and public opinion.

(6)   Social problems are the study of social conditions which cause difficulties for many people and which the society is trying to eliminate. Examples of social problems are juvenile delinquency, crime, alcoholism, suicide, narcotics addiction, mental disorders, racial prejudice, industrial conflicts, slum areas, etc.

In order for sociological concepts to have meaning to students in the social studies, the schools themselves must adapt to the real world in which they exist. Schooling is ineffective when its goals and methods are at odds with competing forces in the students' environment. When one's purpose is to teach civility and tolerance, but outside social patterns teach meanness and narrowness, the school may have little impact in accomplishing these goals.

Most citizens have not grasped the full meaning of the technological age we face or the responsibilities they hold in our intercultural and interdependent civilizations.

Sociology plays an important role in general education in several ways. It liberates the student from the narrow spheres of time, place, and circumstance; students should realize that there are other races, regions, classes, religions, neighborhoods, and nations, and that beneath the cultural differences, all human societies are essentially the same. Sociology introduces students to the nature and function of logic and the scientific method; they learn to deal not only with the concrete, but with the abstract, as culture, norm, folkway, status, role, authority, and institution. It stimulates students to reflect on the relationship between the individual and society. It has a place in the history of human thought; it studies the nature of human groups and the character of human relationships as they have evolved through history.[16]

Most teachers of social studies give some allegiance to the notion of teaching students how to learn (inquire). Indeed use of inquiry as a method of teaching is increasing. Inquiry, using the methods of the social sciences, seems to be a vehicle through which students can be taught how to learn, think, problem solve, and develop solutions to future problems that require both analysis and synthesis. The purpose avowed by many social studies teachers is to help their students reach a deeper and more meaningful understanding of what the human condition is and can be through social inquiry. The teacher tries to help students discover the conditions of mankind in the world, how things got as they are, and what conditions may be like in the near future. This strategy is designed to encourage students to think of the social sciences as tools that a reasoning mind can use to analyze what is happening in the world, and what we may reasonably expect to happen to ourselves.

Various kinds of subjects suggest themselves as appropriate for investigation through the inquiry method in the social disciplines. One type of subject is individual role conflicts. Another is the conflicts that develop between different institutions in a society as these institutions attempt to satisfy the needs of us, the client system. Study of the conflicts between institutions is helpful to the student in gaining insight into his own interpersonal conflicts and the causes of them. An example of a conflict between ideas and institutions in the United States is the need for efficiency in running our schools, which calls for large classes, electronic media, computerized schedules, reliance on lectures, rigid schedules and nationally standardized performance criteria for teachers and students. Our national commitment to individualization of instruction, to developing each teacher and each student's potentials to their fullest is in conflict with efficiency. There is at least some evidence that efficiency in schooling is a very inefficient way to educate people who are expected to reason, think, and be free.

Simple resolution of the interpersonal tensions this causes will not ameliorate the problem, since it is a societal problem, not a personal one. Inquiry training using the tools of sociology, can help students understand these institutional conflicts and how they get internalized into the personality structure of individuals. Efforts to teach students how to do social research should be carefully fitted into a total program of schooling. Administrators and teachers should consider the nature of the inquiry, seek the help and cooperation of the community, and choose and define the goals carefully. An imaginative, resourceful, intelligent teacher can utilize any of the social disciplines and their several means of inquiry to help students gain understanding and insight into the essential human condition. Concepts and means of inquiry from sociology and political science are useful in any social studies class, and are used by most

16. Charles H. Page, Ed., *Sociology and Comtemporary Education* (New York: Random House, 1964).

teachers. Students need not wait until they can take a course in sociology, as such, to learn how sociologists seek answers to social problems.[17]

Geography

There are many schools of thought in geography such as: human geography, physical geography, cultural geography, political geography, economic geography, cartography, and oceanography. The study of geography includes: physical features, such as mountains, plains, plateaus, rivers, oceans; animal and plant life indigeneous to a geographical region; climate, rainfall, temperature; agricultural products, soil types, pests; products of industry; demography, density of human population, trends in population, relative urbanization, the quality of human existence; and the interaction of all these elements in making up the total human political, social, and ecological condition in a nation, or region.

Man has had geographical (political) boundaries between peoples since before the dawn of time. Geography has exerted an immeasurable influence on the culture of man, his style of life, the wars he has fought, the religions he has believed in, his political persuasions, his history, and his relations with his neighbors. Consider for a moment the influence of the Pyrenees and the Rhine on the language, culture, and economic conditions of the people who live on either side of them! Consider what the Pyrenees may have meant to the preservation of Christianity in Europe. Think for a moment about the meaning of Britain being an island. Imagine what Europe would be like without the Gulfstream, or what the United States would be like without the oceans on either side and the mighty Mississippi flowing down the middle. These are only a very few of the illustrations of the influence of geography on the lives of men in various places. It has been said that *all* wars, in one way or another, have been fought over territory, geography! It is this sense of territory (land) that lies at the heart of economic thought and planning, and that is the basis for Marxian thought about private property. Think of the world events that have been influenced by geography, such as the direction rivers flow along the eastern slopes of the Appalachian mountains in the southern and northern United States and the influence this had on agriculture and later on the course of the Civil War. It is difficult to see how anyone can teach any other social discipline without relying heavily on concepts drawn from geography.

Early geographers studied geography for various reasons such as religion, making war, map making, commercial ventures, outlining routes for pilgrimages, tracing the course of streams, or the crest of mountain chains, and most often of all to establish boundaries between states. Most early geographers'

17. P. Schlechty, "Teaching Strategies in Social Inquiry," *The High School Journal,* LIII (December, 1969).

methods were imprecise, consequently their maps and their narratives were rather casual in nature. Most of them did not try to show the relationship of climate and terrain to culture or to history. They described what they thought existed. Geography as a means of describing something is a very old field of study; but it was not until the nineteenth century that modern means of inquiry were developed by geographers. Humboldt and Ritter are usually credited with laying the foundation for modern scientific geography. Today there are numerous highly specialized fields within the broad area of geography. Geography in the hands of professional geographers is an exact science. We do not wish to teach secondary students how to be oceanographers, demographers, or cartographers, but we do want to teach them a sense of place, and its influence on the lives of men. Every event had to happen someplace, and most happened as they did partly because of the peculiarities of that particular place.

People establish nations, enact legislation, develop customs and mores, have rulers, communicate, make war, grow crops, fly, create art, worship, conduct scientific investigations, and sometimes try to improve their lot while on this planet. All these efforts are influenced by climate, terrain, natural resources, rainfall, temperature, soil type, and many other geographic phenomena. The forces of nature make soil, collect deposits of minerals, and fossil fuels, move these things through the operation of erosion, provide an environment for flora and fauna all without too much influence by the efforts of man, at least in the past. These forces make possible life itself and influence the quality of it in any locality, in countless ways.

The teacher who uses geography as a means of enriching his history teaching will have more interested and more enlightened students. He should teach students where things are or were, how climate, terrain, and resources contributed to what men did, and he should teach students a sense of direction. Geography and its means of inquiry can contribute greatly to the growth of secondary social studies students.[18] [19] [20]

Economics

Economics is often called the dismal science. It is in some respects the most exacting of the social disciplines, therefore many, if not most, people who are preparing to be social studies teachers avoid it. A great many social studies teachers have had only one college course in economics, few have had more

18. J. O. Broek, *Geography: Its Scope and Spirit* (Columbus, Ohio: Charles E. Merrill Books, Inc., 1965).

19. R. J. Chorley and P. Haggett, *Frontiers in Geographical Teaching* (London: Methuen & Co. Ltd., 1965).

20. Richard Hartshorne, *Perspective on the Nature of Geography* (Chicago: Rand McNally and Co., 1960).

than the minimum required for a degree in general social studies. Consequently, many teachers are very poorly prepared to teach economics. This is also true to a degree with sociology and geography. One wonders if anyone can be prepared to teach five or six different disciplines.

The need for personal and national economic competence is increasing rapidly. The complexity of governmental, business, and private economic affairs is growing with the size and nature of our institutions. Jefferson once said, *he who expects to be both ignorant and free expects what never was and never can be.* We can restate his assertion about economic literacy as, *he who expects to be ignorant of economics can be neither free or economically solvent as a person or as a nation.* Free societies are dependent for their very life upon an enlightened citizenry, and a free economy is absolutely dependent upon the economic competency of its participants. This is even more true of a modified free economy such as ours now is. Economic education provides the tools of analysis and reasoning which our citizens must have to make intelligent personal and private decisions about the government, the economy, the ecology, and foreign affairs throughout their adult lives. Citizens need not be economists but they must be competent to consume economic data and make value judgments based on these data.

Our living standard—the hope, envy, and despair of the whole world—is dependent on economic literacy. Human freedom in a nation such as ours can not be had if people are in economic shackles brought about by their own ignorance. The ability to meet the needs of our people at home, defend ourselves from attack, and meet our obligations abroad are all dependent on an economically enlightened people. Our economic system is challenged on every front today. Every newspaper carries stories almost daily about industrial pollution, inflation, the national debt, voters repudiating bond issues because taxes are too high, the balance of payments, the welfare state, the decline in the price of stocks, huge conglomerate corporations on the verge of bankruptcy, the wage-price spiral, the plight of the cities, rising interest rates, rising costs of college education, and unemployment of young people. These are only some of the daily economic problems which we face as private persons and as citizens.

People have studied economics since civilization began. However, most people attribute modern scientific study of economics to Adam Smith who published his most famous work in 1776. The thinking of the bankers and political philosphers of the Renaissance and Reformation periods had laid the groundwork for Smith's monumental contribution to economics. He was followed shortly by contributions of Malthus, Ricardo, Mill and others of the classical economists. The thinking of these men seemed inadequate to some people such as Karl Marx, who wrote his monumental *Das Kapital* in the latter half of the nineteenth century. Economic thinking has been further modified in this century by the contirubtions of such men as Keynes and Galbraith.

There are other social disciplines which contribute to the social studies in important ways, these disciplines have not been discussed here since they are seldom taught as such in secondary schools. All the social sciences described in this chapter—except history—share certain common characteristics. The means of inquiry in history has been described in sufficient detail earlier in the chapter, but the means of inquiry of the other disciplines might need restating. Sociology and political science both rely on surveys, opinion polls and the use of statistics. Economics relies on primary documents as does history and geography, but it uses statistics more than any other social discipline.[21]

Anthropology and history share the concept of studying a culture or a people over a period of time. They also share many of the scientific means of dating artifacts, documents, and other phenomena. Many of these tools used to verify social data were developed by the sciences such as archeology and paleontology. Many of the means of finding information used by all social scientists were first developed by historians. Geography is closely related to several of the biological and physical sciences in its methods of inquiry, but is also reliant on statistics and historical proofs. In short, while the social sciences differ from each other, differ from the behavioral sciences, differ from the biological sciences and the physical sciences all share a common search for truth, a common skepticism and a common devotion to rigorously applied research methodology. Each of the social disciplines has something to offer the teacher and the student of social studies.

Teaching Social Studies By The Inquiry or Discovery Method

Teaching students by the inquiry method requires them to use their powers of inductive reasoning. Induction is the reasoning process used to reason from a particular and personal experience to a generalization. Inductive thinking requires the student to proceed from the concrete perception or experience to the abstract generalization. He must move in his thinking from the particular to the general. Induction is not taking a position and then seeking evidence to support it; rather induction is asking what is or why and seeking information that may provide answers. Inquiry learning does not begin with an axiom or proposition and then proceed deductively to logical conclusion. Inquiry leads, at most, to probabilities, rarely to certainties. Induction is the method of scientific inquiry; but it is also the most often used method called common sense, on which we base our daily behavior.[22]

21. Edward C. Prehn, *Teaching High School Economics* (New York: Pitman Publishing Corporation, 1968).

22. Edwin Fenton, *Teaching the New Social Studies in Secondary Schools: An Inductive Approach* (New York: Holt, Rinehart, and Winston, Inc., 1966).

There is considerable emphasis on teaching the structure of the social disciplines in the newer approaches to teaching social studies. The non-expository methods described in later chapters of this book are mainly based on teaching students how to inquire, or discover, or, more explicitly, to learn. The inquiry approach is one of the more promising concepts in teaching, and is even more crucial to learning, especially transfer of learning. We have described some of the contributions which the social sciences can make to the secondary social studies curriculum earlier in this chapter. Perhaps the most important contribution of the disciplines is their means of investigation. We want students to learn how to acquire information, how to generalize, how to arrive at valid value judgments, and how to transfer school learning to lifelike situations. But it is doubtful if we want to make research historians or sociologists or any other kind of social scientist of secondary school students.

Many teachers teach by the inquiry method without consciously trying to do it. They require students in problems of democracy courses to investigate problems, collect evidence, draw conclusions, and generalize. Occasional and incidental exposure to the structure of a discipline and use of the means of inquiry peculiar to it are not enough to assure that the students will master the technique of discovery or inquiry. Students need to learn the method of each of the social sciences explicitly. This requires the teacher to teach them the steps of the mode of inquiry in each discipline. Teachers must help students master the cognitive learnings essential to careful investigation and thinking in the social sciences. Each skill and each concept must be taught explicitly until students have mastered it. Accurate work in the social sciences requires a thorough knowledge of the cognitive skills of each of them, and these skills must be related to the cognitive objective of the lesson if students are to learn the means of inquiry effectively. Mastery of cognitive skills requires practice, practice of the equivalent skill, not of some other behavior. The social studies should place more emphasis on understanding and upon critical thinking, and upon learning how to approach learning rather than avoid it.[23] Facts are important, but they are not important as goals for students to memorize so that they can replicate them on test day. Unless teachers know the importance of the means of learning and the necessity to teach it directly, it will not be mastered by most students. One of the more common complaints voiced by experienced secondary social studies teachers to the authors is that their students do not know how to study. What they mean is that their students do not know how to inquire or learn; the real cause of this is the students' inability to see any purpose in the implicit objectives of the lessons. A great many students find school to be an unpleasant place, a nice place to escape from either in day dreams, by failing, by misbehavior, or by actually absenting themselves from classroom situations. It is reasonably certain that students

23. Ibid.

who are busily engaged in inquiring into something interesting will be motivated, will not be bored, and will not seek to escape.

Most social scientists believe in the significance of the philosophical, normative, cognitive, and aesthetic character of the thought in their respective fields and related fields. Many of them disagree, however, on how much attention should be given to teaching the structure of the respective disciplines. More social studies teachers err on the side of too little emphasis than on the side of too much emphasis on scientific approaches to knowledge.

Expository techniques of teaching are almost the only methods in common use in the secondary schools before the curriculum projects in science and mathematics of the past decade. Expository teaching is still the most common method in use in most secondary social studies classes. Teachers, like others, learn what they see their teachers do, not what they are told to do. Most college instruction is expository; thus it should be expected that secondary teachers will teach mainly by exposition since that is the way they were taught. Exposition has its place in the methods which teachers use and should use, and it is an important place; however exposition should not be the only way a teacher ever presents a lesson, to do so is to presume that talking is teaching and that teaching is synomous with learning. Such assumptions are fallacious and reliance upon them has caused the nation untold woe. Surely, there must be a place for some guided discovery, some free inquiry, some consistently scientific method of arriving at truth, which we teachers can and will use.

Teachers should use the structure of the disciplines, as they use all other concepts and methods, when most appropriate, and when best fitted to a particular student or a particular purpose for a class. Students need to learn how to listen, how to take notes, how to read a lesson, how to use a map, how to determine chronology, how to make reports, how to answer specific questions; but they also need to know how to know, how to find out, how to learn, how to generalize, how to apply their knowledge to unfamiliar situations, and most of all how to create new knowledge as the need arises. Discovery of the structure and regularity of a discipline is a wonderful and fulfilling experience for young people. In a world that is as restive as ours is, and that is accumulating knowledge at such an astounding rate, and changing with such enormous rapidity, perhaps the central question for the social studies should be, *What knowledge will be of most worth to students as a basis for creating new knowledge, which will help them reach their potential?*

The method of discovery has a highly motivating effect on students. Almost without exception, the students, directly or indirectly, demonstrate a great deal of personal involvement with the material under discussion. There is wide classroom participation and intensive utilization of library resources. The motivating effect of discovery is due, in large part, to the game-like situation which reinforces the element of perplexity and incentive to explore.

The teacher indirectly encourages student exploration by stubbornly refusing to provide ready-made answers.

PROBLEMS AND QUESTIONS FOR STUDY OR DISCUSSION

1. What is meant by *the structure of the disciplines?*

2. What contribution can this concept make to the practical everyday teaching of social studies?

3. Why did the concept of the structure of the disciplines arise as a means of choosing content, objectives, and method?

4. Can you devise a means of teaching history using the structure of history as the controlling factor in choosing content and method?

5. What is the nature of history as a discipline?

6. What contributions have the means of inquiry of the sciences and of anthropology made to the study and teaching of history?

7. What are the features of history as a discipline which sets it apart from the other social sciences?

8. State the canons of historical proof and investigation and show how secondary school students might use them as a means of finding meaning from subject matter.

9. What are some of the tools of investigation of sociology, economics, and political science?

10. What is the *inquiry* method of teaching the social studies? Write a lesson plan showing how your students will learn through inquiry.

11. What do proponents claim the advantages of learning by inquiry to be? What happens to the traditional lecture, exposition, or discipline of the teacher when students are taught by inquiry method?

12. Does *inquiry differ from discovery method?* If it does differ, what are the main differences?

13. How does one measure student growth in classes taught by inquiry or discovery?

14. What is the reason for so many people becoming excited about the use of the structure of disciplines as a basis for deciding what and how to teach?

15. Locate as many different secondary teaching programs for the social studies as you can that are based on the disciplines, inquiry, or discovery. Compare these designs for teaching to the unit plan method described in chapter six and to the units in the appendix. Can inquiry be used in unit plan teaching?

REFERENCES

Bach, George Leland. *Economics and Introduction to Analysis and Policy.* Englewood Cliffs, New Jersey: Prentice-Hall, Inc., 1968.

Barnes, Harry Elmer. *A History of Historical Writing.* Norman: University of Oklahoma Press, 1937.

Baxter, Maurice, Lorrell, Robert H., Wiltz, John E. *The Teaching of American History.* Bloomingfield: University of Illinois Press, 1964.

Bourne, Henry E. *The Teaching of History and Civics in Elementary and the Secondary Schools.* New York: Longmans, Green, and Company, 1902.

Broek, Jan O. M. *Geography: Its Scope and Spirit.* Columbus, Ohio: Charles E. Merrill Books, Inc., 1965.

Chorley, Richard J., and Haggett, Peter. *Frontiers in Geographical Teaching.* London: Methuen & Co. LTD., 1965.

Cole, Donald B., and Pressly, Thomas. *Preparation of Secondary School History Teachers.* Washington D. C.: The American Historical Association, 1968.

Committee for Economic Development. *Economic Literacy for Americans.* (February, 1962).

Dahl, Robert A. *Modern Political Analysis.* Englewood Cliffs, New Jersey: Prentice-Hall, Inc., 1963.

Fairgrieve, James. *Geography and World Power.* New York: E. P. Dutton & Co. Inc., 1941.

Fenton, Edwin. *Teaching the New Social Studies in Secondary Schools: An Inductive Approach.* New York: Holt, Rinehart & Winston, Inc. 1966.

Fischer, Eric, Campbell, Robert D., and Miller, Eldon S. *A Question of Place.* Arlington, Virginia: Beatty, 1967.

Fling, Fred Morrow. *The Writing of History.* New Haven: Yale University Press, 1926.

Foster, Michael B. *Masters of Political Thought.* Vol. I: *Plato to Machiavelli.* Boston: Houghton Mifflin Company, 1941.

Frankel, M. L. *Economic Education.* New York: The Center for Applied Research in Education, Inc., 1965.

Gawronski, Donald V. *History: Meaning and Method.* Illinois: Scott, Foresman and Company, 1967.

Gettell, Raymond Garfield. *Introduction to Political Science*. 2nd ed. revised. Boston: Ginn and Company, 1922.

Gross, Richard E., Frainkel, Jack R., McPhie, Walter E., eds. *Teaching the Social Studies*. Scranton: International Textbook Company, 1969.

Hartshorne, Richard. *Perspective On The Nature of Geography*. Chicago: Rand McNally & Co., 1960.

Hitchner, Dell G., and Harbold, William H. *Modern Government: A Survey of Political Science*. New York: Dodd, Mead, and Company, 1962.

Jaspers, Karl. *The Origin and Goals of History*. New Haven: Yale University Press, 1953.

Jones, Roy E. *The Functional Analysis of Politics*. London: Routledge Kegan Paul, 1967.

Kohn, Hans. *Reflection On Modern History* Princeton: D. Van Nostrand Company, Inc., 1963.

Mayer, Martin. *Social Studies in American Schools*. New York: Harper Colophon Books, 1962.

Martindale, Don. *The Nature and Types of Sociological Theory*. Boston: Houghton Mifflin Co., 1960.

Moffatt, Maurice P. *Social Studies Instruction*. New York: Prentice-Hall, Inc., 1950.

Ogburn, William, and Nimkoff, Meyer F. *Sociology*. 4th ed. Boston: Houghton Mifflin Co., 1964.

Page, Charles H., ed. *Sociology and Contemporary Education*. New York: Random House, 1964.

Prehn, Edward C. *Teaching High School Economics*. New York: Pitman Publishing Corporation, 1968.

Roseman, Cyril, Mayo, Charles G., and Collinge, F. B. *Dimensions of Political Analysis*. Englewood Cliffs, New Jersey: Prentice-Hall, Inc., 1966.

Rubinstein, Alvin Z., and Thumm, Garold W. *The Challenge of Politics: Ideas and Issues*. Englewood Cliffs, New Jersey: Prentice-Hall, Inc., 1970.

Schlechty, P. "Teaching Strategies in Social Inquiry," *The High School Journal*. Vol. LIII (December, 1969).

Steeves, Frank L. *The Subjects in the Curriculum*. New York: The Odyssey Press, Inc., 1968.

Stern, Fritz R. *The Varieties of History.* New York: Meridian Books, 1956.

Stewart, Kathryn B. *Studies in How We Live.* Haverford, Pennsylvania: Haverford House, 1963.

Sutherland, Robert L. *et al. Introductory Sociology.* 6th ed. Chicago, Philadelphia, New York: J. B. Lippincott Co., 1961.

Valkenburg, Samuel Van. *Elements of Political Geography.* New York: Prentice-Hall, Inc., 1940.

Walch, J. Weston. *Colorful Economics Teaching.* Portland, Maine: J. Weston Walch, Publisher, 1954.

Whitbeck, Ray H.; Thomas, Olive J. *The Geographic Factor.* New York: The Century Co, 1932.

Woolridge, S. W. *The Spirit and Purpose of Geography.* London: Hutchinson & Co., 1958.

Group projects play a major role in the teaching of social studies.

Photo furnished courtesy of Elmore County Public School, Wetumpka, Alabama.

Much of what students learn comes from other students.

Photo furnished courtesy of Elmore County Public School, Wetumpka, Alabama.

Chapter V

METHODS
OF
TEACHING
SOCIAL
STUDIES

Every teacher is concerned with the question of what method or methods to employ to help students learn the desired concepts, achieve the desired objectives, and learn the process of democracy. Achievement of the lesson objectives is a mutual enterprise between the teacher and the student. There is no one best method or "magic solution" to teaching. Instead, there are many methods which have been employed successfully by teachers which lend themselves to use under different sets of circumstances which include consideration of the teacher, the learner, the material to be covered, the objectives, and the resources available.

Any exhaustive list of specific methods would be very lengthy. Generally, however, there are three fairly distinct categories of teaching technique, with infinite variations, and each associated with a philosophy. (1) The most traditional organization of material and method assumes essential passivity of the students, arranged in fixed positions and responding only to the authority of the teacher. (2) A contrasting view of learning and human nature has produced a reaction to the idea of the student as an "empty vessel" to be poured full of authoritative wisdom. Whole systems of education have come to be based on a thoroughgoing permissiveness, where in students were allowed and encouraged to pursue their own way through whole courses of study. This led in most instances to less than desirable outcomes. (3) Both passivity and permissiveness have been combined to produce a better balance of practice. Neither rigid control nor complete classroom and curricular anarchy is permitted to override good judgment and balance in the use of teaching methods.

Each of these general methodologies is identifiable in direct proportion to the teacher's understanding and acceptance of a theory of learning. The behaviorist, for example, would be inclined to feel sympathy for some sort of activity program, and even though he only lectured to his class he would probably want them to exhibit some kind of activity to reinforce their learning. There are many different theories of learning, few of which are based on completely scientific findings. There is still much to learn concerning the actual process and nature of learning since no general rule can yet be stated as the best theory of learning or the best teaching method. If it is remembered that all of the learning theories and all of the methods have been shown to be useful in various situations, there will be less difficulty in choosing a particular tool for a particular task.[1]

Student Learning Activities

Kenworthy has prepared a comprehensive list of student activities or learning experiences which teachers can use to help students achieve the goals of social studies.[2]

A.   Talking activities

    1.   Asking questions of teacher, other pupils, visitors
    2.   Answering questions of teacher, other pupils, visitors
    3.   Telling about a trip or other experience
    4.   Taking part in a panel or round-table discussions
    5.   Taking part in a debate
    6.   Serving on a committee
    7.   Sharing in a buzz group (a small group talking over a problem or topic for a short time without changing seats, reporting to the class on its findings or opinions
    8.   Interviewing people in the community or school.

B.   Written activities, assignments, and work

    1.   Taking notes on books, talks, panels, encyclopedias, etc.
    2.   Writing original materials—plays, poems, essays, diaries, etc.
    3.   Writing "reactions" to a book, play, movie, trip, or TV program
    4.   Taking tests of various kinds
    5.   Preparing an article or editorial for the school newspaper
    6.   Writing a letter to a newspaper or a Congressman or some other person.

C.   Listening activities

    1.   Listening to radio or television programs
    2.   Listening to class discussion, panel, debate, etc.
    3.   Listening to local forum, city council, or other meetings

1. James High, *Teaching Secondary School Social Studies* (New York: John Wiley and Sons, Inc., 1962), pp. 140-141.
2. Leonard S. Kenworthy, *Guide to Social Studies Teaching in Secondary Schools* (Belmont, California: Wadsworth Publishing Company, Inc., 1966), pp. 82-83.

      4.   Listening to comments and instructions of teacher.

D.   Visual activities

      1.   Looking at and studying pictures, maps, cartoons, charts, or graphs
      2.   Observing a film, filmstrip, slide, or other visual aid, such as a movie or television program
      3.   Looking at bulletin boards or other displays.

E.   Service or action activities

      1.   Collecting money, clothes, books, or other materials
      2.   Earning money for service projects, such as Red Cross, United Community Fund
      3.   Serving on school patrol, student council, or other groups
      4.   Conducting a local poll or survey in the school or community
      5.   Preparing a list of inexpensive community recreational resources
      6.   Taking part in a clean-up campaign.

F.   Arts and crafts activities

      1.   Taking photographs for use by the class
      2.   Preparing various kinds of maps for use by class or school
      3.   Collecting and mounting pictures, maps, charts, etc.
      4.   Preparing a bulletin board
      5.   Preparing models or mock-ups.

It should be noted that while all of these methods can be used to teach, none of them are things teachers do. Teacher centered activities are discussed later in this chapter.

> We should not expect that our students will learn to think critically as a by-product of the study of the usual social studies content. Instead, each teacher should determine what concepts are essential—e.g., that have relevance— if his students are to perform the intellectual operations deemed necessary to critical thinking—such as, for example, the formulation and evaluation of hypotheses. How to do each of these should be taught explicitly to the students. Situations as similar as possible to those in which the students are to use their competencies should be set up in the classroom, and the students should be guided in application of the concepts learned to other situations.[3]

3. James P. Shaver, "Educational Research and Instruction of Critical Thinking," *Social Education*, XXVI (January, 1962), p. 16. Reprinted with permission of the National Council For The Social Studies and James P. Shaver.

Criteria for Selecting Method

Some criteria are needed to help in deciding which method is best for teaching a given concept or achieving a given objective. The following are some assumptions which may help the teacher in the decision making process.[4]

1. The nature of the topic determines method to some degree.

2. The needs of students and the class are the major factor in identifying the proper methodology.

3. Variety is a factor in selecting methods. Learning takes place best when there is interest.

4. Individual, small-group, and large-group experience should be provided.

Edgar Dale of the Ohio State University has depicted the variety of methods possible in a dramatic visualization which has been called a "Cone of Experience." Each method has its place but slower students learn best in most instances when the methods at the bottom of the cone are used.

Skills to be Learned

The social studies teacher is concerned not only with developing understandings and attitudes but also with developing social studies skills which are equally important. Carr identifies these skills as (1) critical thinking, (2) communication skills, (3) the use of maps and globes, (4) the use of graphic materials, and (5) the use of skills of time and chronology. He further stated that these skills are all essential to learning, understanding, and using the social studies and that none can be taken for granted, assumed to come naturally, or adequately learned through incidental instruction.[5]

The categories of skills to be developed includes:

1. creative thinking

2. critical thinking

3. work habits and study skills

4. Kenworthy, op. cit., pp. 78-88.
5. From the book *The Social Studies* by Edwin R. Carr. © 1965 by the Center for Applied Research in Education.

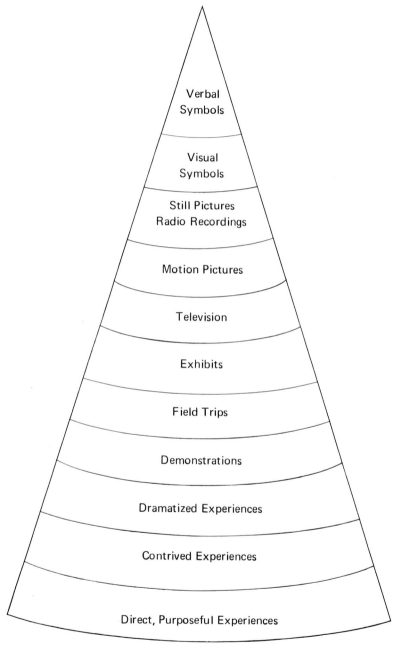

Figure 5-1. Dale's Cone of Experience.[6]

6. Edgar Dale, *Audio-Visual Methods in Teaching,* Hinsdale, Illinois: The Dryden Press, Inc., 1954).

4. map skills
5. research skills
6. using libraries materials
7. outlining
8. note-taking
9. keeping a notebook
10. written reports and term papers
11. summarizing
12. discussion
13. committee work
14. interviewing
15. reading the newspaper
16. speaking effectively
17. effective listening
18. problem solving
19. evaluation
20. gaining information from books
21. the making of bibliographies
22. preliminary steps in examining a subject
23. map interpretation
24. graphic interpretation
25. reading, writing, and speaking.[7]

The following are skills which are usually designated as primarily intellectual.

1. Skill in methods of obtaining access to information
   a. Use of libraries and institutions
   b. Use of encyclopedias, handbooks, documents, sources, authorities and statistic collections

2. Skill in the sifting of materials and the discovery and determination of authentic evidence—in the use of primary sources

3. Skill in the observation and description of contemporary occurrences in the school and community

4. Skill in methods of handling information
   a. In analysis—breaking down large themes or masses of data into manageable units and penetrating to irreducible elements
   b. In synthesis—combining elements, drawing inferences and conclusions, and comparing with previous conclusions and inferences— logical and systematic organization
   c. In map and chart making and graphic presentation

5. Skill in memorizing results of study—with consciousness of application to new situation by exact reference and analogy

7. Maurice P. Moffatt, *Social Studies Instruction* From Prentice-Hall, Inc., 1963, pp. 131-148.

6. Skill in scientific method—inquiring spirit, patience, exactness, weighing evidence, tentative and precise conclusions.[8]

The 1965 edition of the "Space Curriculum Guidelines" published by the Brevard County Board of Public Instruction, Florida, tied together techniques and resulting skills they facilitate.[9]

TECHNIQUES

1.	Lecture – discussion	—listening, note-taking, analyzing, interpreting
2.	Use of Library	—card catalog, guides, references, selection
3.	Original work (art, writing, cartoons)	—imagination, organization, inquiry, problem solving
4.	Guest speaker	—listening, note-taking analysis, interpreting
5.	Field trip	—observation, evaluation, synthesizing
6.	Review of literature	—interpreting, synthesizing analysis, reporting, evaluating
7.	Make newspaper of period	—organizing, writing, summarizing, interpreting, analogizing
8.	Debate	—data gathering, classifying, speaking
9.	Role-playing, sociodrama	—imagining, interpreting, projecting
10.	Research	—note-taking, classifying, using files
11.	Question and answer	—inquiring, speaking, theorizing
12.	Groups (committees)	—interacting, social behavior, speaking
13.	Bulletin board, graphs, models, etc.	—observing, interpreting, visualizing, symbolizing, analyzing
14.	Map reading	—interpreting, visualizing, symbolizing, analyzing
15.	Seminar	—evaluating, speaking, group process, reporting
16.	Forum	—analyzing, group process, speaking
17.	Reports	—writing, research, evaluating, speaking
18.	Hypothetical problem-solving	—imagining, inferring, experimenting
19.	Model situations	—analyzing, interpreting, evaluating

The teaching of skills is an integral part of the social studies program and makes an important contribution to the individual growth and behavior of the student. Skills have value to the learner since they serve as tools and machinery which assist him in the learning process. The learner becomes a more competent person as he masters these skills and becomes more able to use them as resources that assist him in solving the problems of his every day life as a citizen of our democracy.

8. Helen McCracken Carpenter, *Skills In Social Studies* (Washington, D.C.: National Council for the Social, Twenty-fourth Yearbook, 1953).
9. Brevard County Board of Public Instruction, *Space Curriculum Guidelines,* 1965 Edition, (Florida, 1965).

The Lecture

Lecture or any other form of expository teaching should be used sparingly at the secondary level as its use tends to require that students be inactive, passive learners. The lecture as a method is in great contrast to other methods such as problem solving, where the group is active in learning and presenting information. One of the most difficult problems of lecture is getting and holding the attention of the class. Another problem with lecture is that many students have difficulty in following the theme.[10]

College bound young people need training in listening to the lecture method; therefore, its judicious use should not be discouraged. Use of lectures with some variation to permit interruptions for questions and discussion can make it more successful in many situations. Lectures can be and are used successfully in large classes in advanced social studies particularly where resource personnel are used.

The teacher should keep in mind the following cautions when using the lecture method or other means of exposition.[11]

1. Choose the occasion for a lecture with care.
2. Prepare the content carefully.
3. Provide an outline for the class to follow, preferably mimeographed.
4. Anticipate questions.
5. Prepare maps, illustrations, drawing, charts, and source materials to brighten the talk and sustain interest.
6. Follow-up the lecture in subsequent meetings of class. Question the class on content of the lecture; assign homework questions based on the lecture material, include test questions in examinations.

Most expository methods of teaching tend toward the top end of Dale's Cone of Experience. Formal lectures, unsupported by audio-visual aids, are at the very top of the cone as far removed from real experience as possible. Students who have low retention levels may actually gain very little from the formal lectures. Preparation for fruitful participation as a citizen of a free society makes it imperative that students learn how to participate effectively in group discussion and problem solving processes. Because of these student needs, social studies teachers need to vary their expository techniques through guided classroom discussions, seminars, problem solving, projects, and other teaching techniques.

10. Moffatt, op. cit., p. 111.
11. The Association of Teachers of Social Studies of the City of New York, *Handbook for Social Studies Teaching* (New York: Holt, Rinehart and Winston, Inc., 1967), p. 85.

Non-Expository Methods of Teaching Social Studies

Most surveys of secondary school students reveal greater distaste for social studies than for any other subject in the curriculum. One cause of these feelings of dislike for social studies may be the insistence of many social studies teachers upon talking at their students as they explicate content and as their students take notes. Such social studies teachers have come to rely on the old adage, "tell them what you are going to say; say it; then remind 'em of what you said." Their teaching has become telling. They rely mainly on textbooks as a guide to exposition of facts, names, dates, places, events, and generalizations. The emphasis is upon passive listening as teachers tell students about yesterday's politics and wars and require automatic replication of these assorted data upon cue. These teaching procedures are hardly calculated to produce thinking, growth in ability to inquire, or learning how to live in a democratic society.

Many teachers seem to have forgotten how teaching began, which was the Socratic dialogue as a means of assisting students with the birth of ideas. Discussion as a variation of straight exposition helps students discover meaning for themselves; through Socratic intellectualization of data; through reflective thinking as a means of removing perplexity; and through discovery of meaning or truth, often by having an "aha" experience. Furthermore, discussion facilitates growth of the ability to inquire (learn). Important as all these teaching methods are in facilitating student intellectual growth, they are of far less significance for the learner than the opportunities which discussion provides for him to interact with his teacher and peers.

Maintenance of our freedom demands citizens who know how to engage in dialogue, how to think, how to participate, how to elect, and how to disagree with tolerance for the disagreements of others. Teachers who use a variety of other methods, as well as lecture, are likely to have students who are more interested in social studies. Nonexpository teaching techniques are more likely to produce mature, effective citizens than simple lecture, and they are at least as effective in teaching factual data. Some more specific examples of nonexpository teaching techniques will be discussed.

Socialized Recitation

The socialized recitation affords a greater opportunity for pupil participation than most other methods. The teacher functions more as a guide and consultant than as an authority figure. Pupils function in a cooperative manner by making contributions, asking questions, and attempting to solve problems. This method may be used for formal presentations as well as informal, although most formal lessons require more structure and organization. Each student may be assigned to, volunteer for, or be selected for specific tasks of responsibility in the more formal application of socialized recitation whereas in informal uses the leadership may shift from one student to another in the course of the discussion.

The teacher acts as a supervisor and resource person who retains control of the learning situation. The teacher lends encouragement and endeavors to see that every pupil has an individual contribution to make to the class. The alert teacher may engage in preplanning, motivating, and evaluating the individual student or the class.

The Project Method

The project method is sometimes the outgrowth of the study of a problem or topic and is considered an activities approach to learning. It provides activity for the learner as he experiences growth through his efforts to obtain his own objectives. Pupils use their own initiative, interests, skills, and experience in their efforts to identify problems, collect data, and complete projects of their own. The teacher should study his class, and know their interests and abilities before deciding whether the project is appropriate to achieve the goals of the teaching unit.[12]

The project method of teaching is a form of coordinated activity that is directed toward the learning of a significant skill or process. The project may also involve the acquisition of much useful information, and inevitably affects growth of attitudes and interest.

When teaching social studies by the project method the teacher will need some guiding principles to help him determine what constitutes a suitable student project. Having pupils do projects because they like to do them is not a sufficient guarantee that the activity is worthwhile, but the worthwhile project usually does originate with the pupil. The project should have value as subject matter and the pupils need to accept the project purpose as their own. Too many projects fail to achieve the objectives because they are little more than busy work. The time and energy spent on such projects must be justified by the results. The teacher must help students choose projects so that the required subject-matter will be covered and the project should have social as well as individual value. Students are not always resourceful in thinking up problems and projects so the teacher should be alert to help them find projects of interest and if the pupils are not resourceful in thinking up projects it will

---

12. Edgar Wesley and Stanley Wronski, *Teaching Social Studies in High Schools* (Boston: D.C. Heath and Company, 1958), p. 423.

become necessary for the teacher to introduce them. This can be a drawback to the method. Mistakes will be made in student approaches to projects, but, if the teacher is too anxious to eliminate all student errors, he will take most of the responsibility away from the pupil and the undertaking will lose its appeal to the student and will, in short, cease to be his project. Some teachers will be tempted to step in and do the work themselves rather than see students waste so much time and produce such crude results. The student may appear to be learning more and better than he actually is. The surest test of mastery is the ability *to do*. Execution of projects tests the pupil's ability *to do*. The project method places the responsibility for evaluation where it should be, directly on the pupil himself. He, and not the teacher, is the judge of his work.

The teacher's role in project teaching is a varied one. The teacher may be a leader, chairman, authority, judge, advisor, guide, or friend as the occasion may require. The teaching of social studies by the project method requires more of the teacher than merely keeping pupils at work at some interesting task. Since teaching by projects will make it impossible to follow the textbook, logical presentation of subject-matter is more difficult. This can be an advantage for the pupil; but it places a heavy burden on the teacher. Nevertheless, this handicap can be overcome by resourceful teachers. The project method arouses and maintains the interest of the pupil. It does this by the fact that the purpose, which creates the desire to carry through the activity, is the pupil's own. It appeals to strong natural tendencies within pupils. The strongest of these is the desire for self-expression. It develops student responsibility and initiative. The burden of planning and executing the project is placed on the pupil. He is given plenty of opportunity to plan and to carry out his plans. It provides for rational, as well as for practical learning. Pupils see a reason for learning facts, rules, and principles. They see a relation between classroom learning and reality.

Since the project is not a method implying daily assignments, the question may be asked how it will affect the existing curriculum? It is difficult to teach by means of projects when exact curriculum requirements are set. Project teaching assumes latitude and a certain degree of freedom in the handling of subject-matter. It assumes teaching by units rather than pages. There have been a few attempts to reorganize the entire curriculum in terms of projects.

In most social studies classrooms there is too little time to do any work with individual students. The use of projects is one of the better ways to accomplish some form of individualized instruction of each student. Projects are also one of the better ways to help students of varying ability levels. The project utilizes the most effective level of Dale's Cone of Experience more fully than most means of teaching social studies.

Problem-Solving

Problem-solving as a method of teaching initially gained impetus from John Dewey's description of reflective thinking which is sometimes described as the complete act of thought, or the scientific method of inquiry. The general application of problem solving includes the following steps: (1) defining the problem; (2) analyzing the problem and setting up tentative hypotheses; (3) collecting, evaluating, organizing, and interpreting data; (4) forming conclusions; and (5) testing conclusions. Proponents of problem solving as a method of teaching claim a number of advantages for it as outlined below.

(1) It is believed to be more consistent with our knowledge of the learning process and to promote greater understanding and longer retention than traditional methods do. (2) It lends itself to the study of personal problems and to problems of the society in ways which are difficult with other methods. (3) It is possible through the proper use of problem-solving to develop in students a quality of open-mindedness and a willingness to withhold judgment until all the facts are in. (4) It provides students with a means of evaluating problems which can be generalized for use in solving problems with which they may be faced in the future. (5) It is more democratic with student participation throughout the process. (6) It relies on student's interests and thus has a powerful motivating function. (7) It requires the use of a variety of materials and sources and thus makes dependence on a single textbook impossible. Some might view the last statement as a disadvantage of its use.[13]

For problem-solving to be successful certain conditions must exist. These are:

(1)   Students must recognize the problem as being important to them.

(2)   The problems studied must be suited to the maturity of the students—neither too easy nor too hard.

(3)   The classroom atmosphere must encourage free inquiry.

(4)   Materials suitable both to the students and to the problems must be at hand or readily available.

(5)   The teacher must know enough about the problems studied so that he can provide required guidance and direction.

13. Carr, op. cit., pp. 54-55.

A number of different techniques have been suggested as means of stimulating the problem solving approach to teaching. The case study, in which students are given basic information on a certain problem or issue and are asked to draw conclusions, stimulates thought and discussion. Through the case study, value conflicts are exposed when students study the problems that simulate real situations. This is a way of bringing vitality into the study of the social studies and can aid in developing skills in formulating and testing alternative solutions to problems. The use of simulation is a valuable technique. The approach provides students with a situation which has the characteristics of an actual problem or issue and in which opportunities are provided to make decisions on problems which seem realistic in nature.

The use of source material from history or other social science may provide the raw data by which students can develop an understanding of a particular historical period or significant social issue. Problem-solving is one of the most useful techniques in individualizing instruction. Teacher differentiation of assignments is necessary for effective problem-solving. There are a number of factors to consider in making assignments in problem solving. The teacher must decide whether or not using the problem solving approach would allow him to cover the course material he wishes to cover in the time alloted. The teacher must decide if he will present the problem to the class as a whole to be worked on collectively or to allow each student to work individually.

Group problem solving does not always incorporate the best ideas of its individual members. The teacher must consider the age and past experience of the students in relation to the difficulty of the problem.

Many educators feel that the problem solving method is a good idea in theory, but they are fearful of its actual application to the classroom situation. The adoption of the problem solving method presents many problems for the teacher. This method requires more preparation on the part of the teacher. The teacher can not predetermine the content of the course, therefore he must be flexible enough in his planning to permit the students to engage in a study of problem situations. Some issues and problems are controversial and the teacher must be prepared to deal with them. Students will need to be evaluated on the basis of how well they are able to work with the process of learning rather than upon their ability to assimilate information. Problem solving enhances the student's ability to criticize ideas in an unbiased manner. It develops the ability to assume a tentative attitude about concepts. Pupils learn to plan because they assume the responsibility of planning. They learn to know how to reach a relevant conclusion. These abilities collectively comprise the ability to think independently.

The adaptation of the problem solving method has implications for both the organization of the classroom and the selection of content for the social studies. Teachers need to become stimulators and directors of the learning process and attempt to establish a classroom climate in which creative problem solving can take place. Students discover for themselves the causal relΩtionships which exist in society and examine crucial issues which have current national significance.

Our survival and our livelihood depend upon problem solving. Today, people in our society are not required to make individual decisions about many of the problems related to daily living. Instead, they speak and act through groups in all areas of their lives. If the decisions made are to be ones which are best for all citizens we must have individuals in leadership roles who can implement problem solving techniques in reaching these decisions. There must be a total social group which has these same abilities so the problems and the solutions to them are understood by all.

The Fine Art of Questioning

Discussion and informal lecture techniques depend upon questioning as a main means of concept development and promotion of growth. Some teachers are very supportive of students with their questions; others are threatening. Some simple guidelines ought to be used by teachers as they question and guide discussion. A few of these are listed below.

1. Questions should be pertinent to the subject, appropriate to the time and place, and should be understandable.

2. The teacher should guide all questioning except when students are teaching.

3. Students should know the ground rules for asking questions and for answering them.

4. Teacher questions should serve educational purposes.

5. Teachers should not ask nor permit others to ask personal or embarassing questions.

6. Questions should be tailored to student abilities. This is one of the better ways to individualize instruction and every student can contribute something worthwhile if the teacher will work at it.

7. Teachers should make certain that each student has opportunities

to answer questions. To do this teachers can require that no student volunteer information or raise his hand until a designated time.

8. Always ask the questions before naming the student who is to respond because this requires all students to listen to the question.

9. Make certain that the question is clear. One way is to have the student repeat what he understood the question to be.

10. Ordinarily questions asked of students in open textbook situations are worthless as devices for teaching concepts. Such questions reward the quick and the good reader, they do not require thought or even memory.

11. *Avoid* telling a student he is either *right* or *wrong* when he answers. Instead ask other students to agree or disagree, to add information, or to change answers. Telling a student that he is wrong makes him fear the next question and may stop him from thinking.

12. Be fair, give everyone a chance.

13. Ask questions of those who seem inattentive. When students know they may get a question at any time, it helps keep their attention.

14. *Why* questions and *how do you know* questions are usually better than *what, when,* or *who* questions as means of teaching concepts or affecting attitudes.

15. Play Pass the Question Game with students by letting them choose a consultant or permitting them to pass the question to another student. These games cut down on guessing, wild or "smarty" answers. They increase the number of participants, and the quality of answers. There are no techniques that will inform the teacher so quickly of student abilities as these questioning games.

16. Sometimes, it is a good idea to work out a daily grading scheme for your questioning games such as: baseball; pass the question; can you add anything; who did it or said it; or the 'consultant' game. Each acceptable or contributing answer receives a given number of points, each wild guess loses a like number and in pass the question all who have passed it to the wild guesser lose something. Those

who pass to contributors receive some points but the contributor gets more.

17. Socratic questioning is a fine technique for forcing more able students to examine their knowledge, attitudes, and beliefs.

Contract Grading and Assignments

A major concern of educators today is meeting the needs of students with all kinds of abilities in the same classroom. Social studies teachers are faced with an even greater challenge in individualizing instruction than are most other secondary teachers since most social studies classes are heterogeneously grouped. The use of discussion, problem solving, projects, individualized assignments, and group work have been developed.

All these methods will help individualize the learning experience provided for each child. However, the contract assignment and grading method will permit the social studies teacher to use many means of tailoring learning for each student without using all of the available classroom time. The authors have used contract assignments and grading successfully for several years in secondary schools and on the college level. Examples of typical high school social studies contract assignments will be shown.

There are several principles which should be followed in using the contract method. Following these simple precepts will do much to insure acceptance of the method by principal, parents, and students.

1. Get permission to use the contract method from the appropriate administrator, principal, or department head.

2. Make certain that students understand the contracted assignments and mark they can receive.

3. Give parents time and opportunity to understand the method, its purpose, and its possible consequences.

4. Allow students some choice of materials to be learned within any given contract.

5. Get parental understanding of each contract, preferably in writing.

6. Devise some ground rules for contracting such as:

a) Contracts must be completed on time or grades will be lowered.

b) Percentage of contract based on test grades, classroom performance, and classroom behavior.

c) No contract may be raised during its life; but any "A" or "B" contract may be lowered.

d) Let it be known that you will stick to the contract and that you expect each student to do no less.

e) Provide for periodical review of and renewal of contracts.

f) No contracts below "C".

g) Must meet an objective of the Course of Study.

7. Explain how much class time can be devoted to the contracted assignments.

8. Make sure all students understand that while the grade is contracted, still minimum mastery as indicated by test scores is expected.

9. Let students know you will still teach and will still give tests, evaluate, and otherwise be in charge of guiding the learning experiences.

10. Provide some conference time to help students with their contracted assignments.

11. Provide for adequate group work.

12. Prepare a list of possible individual and group projects.

The contract plan will help students learn, and it will remove some of their anxieties if you are as careful in planning for contract learning as you would be for any other method of instruction. No gimmick can take the place of a good teacher who plans carefully, is knowledgeable, and is creative and caring. All efforts to teach by student centered rather than teacher centered activities require more thought and more careful teacher preparation. Most such methods are also more effective in helping students attain behavioral and educational objectives than is simple teacher exposition of content. Students do learn by experience, as do all others including teachers. Experience is not the only way students learn, but it may be the most effective way to change behavior permanently. The contract plan is also very good at teaching students the consequences of responsibility, which is certainly a major goal of the social studies teachers.

Examples of high school contracts
"A" Contract

1. A biographical report

2. A report on selected research topics (both written, one oral)

3. Read all of basic materials, fifty additional pages from selected material.

4. Exhibit competence in understanding concepts and definitions used. Display initiative and inspiration in search for new topics and information.

5. Work on at least two committees or panels, chair one of them.

6. Average of 90 on tests.

7. Exhibit superior citizenship qualities throughout (democratic participation).

"B" Contract

1. One report, biography or research topic, must be written and oral.

2. Read all basic materials and twenty-five extra pages from selected bibliography.

3. Understand most concepts, definition, etc. Display initiative in search for new knowledge.

4. Serve on at least two panels or committees and really work on one of them.

5. Average 80 on tests.

6. Exhibit good citizenship qualities throughout. (Use and practice of democratic processes).

"C" Contract

1. One report either written or oral.

2. Read all basic material.

3. Understand a majority of concepts, definitions, etc. Really try to find new information.

4. Average 70 on tests.

5. Show adequate citizenship qualities throughout. (Knowledge of and use of democratic processes).

Grades of D or F will be given to those who fail to meet the "A", "B", or "C" contracts. Contracts of "A" or "B" may be reduced by mutual consent but may not be raised. Grades will be lowered on "A" or "B" contracts if work is not up to standard or is late without permission.

Use of Teaching Games In Social Studies

The idea of using games as a teaching method is rapidly becoming popular in the field of education. Many people think this idea is new; although, educational games have actually long been in existence. Long ago Prussian generals used to study modern military tactics by moving objects to different positions on a board. This game became known as chess. During World War II the general trend was to play war games in history classes. As this idea caught on, games came into common usage in business and management.[14]

The term *educational game* has many implications, but it is basically a representation of a physical or social phenomenon.[15] The term may be further defined by adding that the game is a simplification of the real world or a representation of some actual period or sequence of events.[16] Educational games and simulation games are much the same in that real life situations are portrayed and emphasis is not based completely on competition. Emphasis is placed on methods used to achieve victory rather than victory itself.[17] Educational games may be played through the use of computers or props such as cards and paper money.

Types of games

Games are basically divided into two groups: board games and role-play games.

14. Roger Kasperson, "Games as Educational Media" *Journal of Geography,* Vol. 67 (October 1968) pp. 409-22.
15. M. Kysilka and V. Rogers, "Simulation Games. . .What and Why," *Instructor* (March, 1970), pp. 94-95
16. Kasperson, op. cit.
17. From *Games For Growth* by Alice Kaplan Gordon. © 1970, Science Research Associates, Inc. Reprinted by permission of publisher.

Board games are those games in which the action involves movement around a gameboard. Monopoly is an example of the board game.[18]

Role-play games are those which involve human relations. This type of game is one of the best to use in the classroom. The only necessary materials are the scenario, which sets the scene, and the profiles, which supply needed information. These two materials, plus a set of rules, are all that are needed to play the game.[19]

Included with these two broad types of games are the book-review games. Students can create serpentine games by using their imagination after reading the book.[20]

Newest in the game field is the computer game. The computer and the student interact. The computer asks a question and the student responds. The computer in turn responds to the answer given and the cycle is then repeated.[21]

Games are an effective educational media when used as a supplement to other materials. Students are encouraged to use their imagination and enthusiasm when participating in games. Games motivate learning in that students absorb knowledge in the process of competing to win.[22]

Teacher's role

With the use of games the role of the teacher changes from that of leader and judge to that of coach or referee. The teacher uses her knowledge to help the student reach *his* objectives. Special materials are prepared for the teacher. The day before the game is to be played the teacher should give to the students a copy of the rules of the game, brief the class on the rules, and give the students a general knowledge of the game. The teacher should play the game beforehand and rework the game, if necessary, to meet the needs of the students. During the game the teacher can move around the room offering suggestions.[23]

Before the actual playing of the game the teacher should ask herself these questions about the value of the game:

1.   Is the game fun?

2.   Are the elements of the game related to the subject?

18. Gordon, ibid.
19. Fred Rasmussen, "Science Teaching And Academic Gaming," *The American Biology Teacher,* (December, 1969).
20. Jean Phillips "Book-Review Games" *Instructor,* (November, 1967).
21. Gordon, op. cit.
22. Larry Nelson, "Games Motivate Learning," *Clearing House,* (March, 1962), pp. 400-02.
23. Gordon, op. cit.

3. Is the game behavior specific?

4. Can a child teach the game to his peers?

5. Does the loser benefit in some way?[24]

Advantages of games

There are advantages for the student and the teacher in the use of games in the classroom. In playing games the student assumes a role, interacts with others, and learns to make decisions based on the actions of others. Through these activities he is able to build his confidence. The student is given the chance to develop new strategies and new games through the debriefing session.[25] The game keeps the student's attention much longer than other methods of teaching. Games also contribute to the socialization of the student by bringing the past or the future to the present.[26]

The game relieves the burden of grading from the teacher. The student determines his own grades through the outcome of the game. The teacher can, however, evaluate concept development and social-emotional development without the use of traditional methods of evaluation.[27]

Disadvantages of teaching games

The disadvantages of using games as a method of teaching are fewer than the advantages. The greatest disadvantage is that the amount of knowledge absorbed is hard to measure. Also, the student often places much more emphasis on winning than on learning.[28] Other complaints are that games are sometimes too costly and, as compared to other methods, too time-consuming.[29]

As mentioned earlier, students often find social studies the most boring of subjects offered in the high school curriculum. This is due to the fact that the material is frequently presented in dry text. Social studies should, however, be of prime interest since it deals with life and living. The creative teacher can find the use of games very effective in the classroom. The text can be used in the teacher's summary after the students have participated in the games. The use of games in a history course is particularly effective. The students are forced to make decisions involving timeless problems faced by the world.

24. "Games Children Play To Learn," *Grade Teacher,* (October, 1969).
25. Kysilka, op. cit.
26. Kasperson, op. cit.
27. Kysilka, op. cit.
28. Kasperson, op. cit.
29. Kysilka, op. cit.

Crucial decisions in the game make the issue relevant to the lives of individual students.[30] The student is permitted to take any action to solve problems and then immediately knows the outcome. This method of instruction allows the student to experiment with problems and solutions, while the classroom becomes a laboratory. The students are having a direct impact on the writing or making of history in the classroom.[31]

The slow learner may benefit from the uses of games more so than the average or the gifted child. Games allow the slow learner to take on new personalities and enter into competition with others.[32] Those students who are not drawn out by games tend to ask questions of their peers and are thereby not embarassed by being asked questions they cannot answer.[33] Slow learners understand games and can participate; whereas, with older methods they could seldom do either. Games give these students a chance at success, since they are qualified in problem-solving and decision-making.[34]

The gifted student also derives benefits from the use of games. The game can be played so that the student will not be able to memorize materials, but must analyze, comprehend, and evaluate problems. The teacher may make the games harder for these gifted students.[35]

The student should do research work, memorize important facts and dates, take notes and discuss the material before the game. After the game a test may be given to be sure the student understands important facts that were discovered during the game.[36]

The use of games in the social studies curriculum is an ideal method of individualized study. Each student determines his own grade by participation in class activities; thus, much of the burden of grading is lifted from the teacher. The slow thinker is motivated into action, while the gifted student may be challenged by finding solutions to problems. The needs of all students may be met in that they are being trained in problem-solving and decision making, both of which are necessary to survive in the world today. Games are indeed most helpful. Some research, however, has shown that games are no more effective than other methods in the teaching of knowledge. The greater value of the use of games lies in the fact that games often raise the student's levels of interest and motivation.

30. Gordon, op. cit.
31. Kysilka, op. cit.
32. Bernice Ignatoff, "Games Add Fun To Learning," *Forecast For Home Economics,* (March, 1966).
33. Nelson, op. cit.
34. Gordon, op. cit.
35. Ibid.
36. Nelson, op. cit.

Some examples of teaching games for social studies

Countdown

A rocket ship with a "launching" button is drawn on the board. The numbers 1-10 are placed on both sides of the ship. The class is divided into two groups and asked questions alternately. When a correct answer is given the numbers are erased beginning with number ten. The countdown has begun! With a missed question there is a mechanical malfunction, countdown has to be stopped and is started again at ten. The first team to blast off wins the game.[37]

Beat the experts

Five of the best students in the class are chosen to serve as a panel of experts. The experts are quizzed by the class on the day chosen for the game. The class scores when the panel misses a question. The panel scores when they answer a question. Panel members may not consult with each other except on a bonus question which is more difficult than individual questions. Bonus questions should come at regular intervals. A time limit placed on the questions helps keep the game moving.[38]

Inter-nation

This game deals with a five country struggle for power. The students also deal with the outbreak of World War I. They draw maps to indicate changing conceptions of relationships among the nations.[39]

Democracy

The students assume the role of legislators and take part in activities carried on in the state or national legislatures such as caucuses and committee meetings.[40]

Steam

This game is a senior high school game for economics. The student deals with economic applications of steam engines to coal mining in the eighteenth century England. The students must decide on technological innovations under competitive market conditions.[41]

37. Ibid.
38. Ibid.
39. Roger Kasperson, op. cit., pp. 409-22.
40. Clarice S. Stoll and Sarane S. Boocook, "Simulation Games For Social Studies," *Audiovisual Instruction,* (October, 1968) pp. 64-6.
41. Kasperson, op. cit.

Market

Players assume the role of wholesalers, retailers and consumers. The consumers buy essential goods and other items. The wholesalers and retailers sell as much as possible at the highest rate of profit. The wholesalers and retailers set their own prices which may be raised or lowered depending on how many people want to buy their goods and how badly the goods are wanted.[42] Several teaching games have been described which can be used to help students of different interests and abilities learn more in social studies classes. The games described are helpful but they consume a great deal of classroom time. Alice Kaplan Gordon has written a book, *Games For Growth,* published by SRA, College Division, 165 University Avenue, Palo Alto, California 94301, 1970. Gordon's book has an excellent description of many useful social studies teaching games available commercially.[43]

There are many methods and techniques of teaching available. However, preceding the use of any method or process must come the proper planning for instruction. Planning ahead with full expectation of realizing the advantages and limitations of each method and with due consideration for individual student differences, as well as individual teacher difference, puts us in a much better position to evaluate the appropriateness of a given method or presentation as a means to the best possible goal achievement. The teacher should have the courage to experiment with methods as he attempts to find those best fitted for attaining given objectives. Without experimentation to meet individual teacher needs and student objectives we may end up with a classroom of students who are bored, disinterested, and gaining little from the course solely because of the method of presentation.

Of all the methods, the ones that appear to be the most useful for teaching social studies are the ones that permit group discussion in one form or another. Students who participate in preparation and presentation of material themselves learn it better than students who merely listen. Because each student must find personal meaning, and must reflect this in the course of the discussion, the class and work related to it are likely to be more interesting to him. Knowing that he may be called on at any moment, and will be expected to make a contribution of some substance, keeps each student more alert to what is going on in the classroom. The teacher, in turn, hearing the part-conscious, part unconscious results of instruction come pouring out of his charges, learns something of what is being learned by the students from what they have read and heard.

42. Gordon, op. cit.
43. Ibid.

PROBLEMS AND QUESTIONS FOR STUDY OR DISCUSSION

1. What is the role of method in teaching?
    a)   what role should teacher activities play in the teaching learning situation?
    b)   what role should learning activities play in the classroom situation?
    c)   what is meant by learning from action, or doing?

2. What is the "empty vessel" theory of learning and teaching?
    a)   which philosophical and psychological positions outlined in Chapter Two, support the contentions of those who pour information into the "empty vessel"?
    b)   what is the principal teaching method of this viewpoint? Has it any place in teaching social studies?

3. What problems have arisen from some methods and curricula which have been developed as a reaction to the "empty vessel" idea?

4. Is there any one best method of teaching social studies for all teachers in all situations?

5. It is often said that students learn more and in more depth when taught by a variety of methods, if this is true what psychological principles might help us understand it?

6. What should determine a teacher's choice of method?

7. Examine the list of different kinds of methods listed in this chapter and develop at least one specific way of using each in a classroom situation.

8. Devise a method that utilizes each of Dale's cone of experience levels to teach the same concept or skill to the same class.

9. Devise three methods of teaching seventh grade students to think critically about geography.

10. Show how you might use the problem solving method to teach an economics class about the balance of payments, or the types of taxes.

11. Choose a lesson that you think lecture is the best method for and support your choice by citing reputable authority.

12. State three methods for increasing students ability to listen effectively.

13. How should students learn to read maps or charts?

14. What is homework good for as a teaching method?

15. How does a bona fide discussion differ from: conversation, a bull session, question and answer, a catechism, student reports, problem solving, or brainstorming?

What should the role of the teacher or discussion leader be in a discussion type lesson? What is the place of the statement, *That's wrong,* in discussion taught lessons?

16. Devise a method to teach chronology.
    Show how to give individualized assignments in social studies and how to measure pupil growth when this is done.

17. How can you use tests as method for teaching?

18. How do introductory, developmental, and culminating methods differ in purpose?

19. What is the purpose of audio-visuals in teaching?

20. Devise a method of teaching that capitalizes on each of the principles of learning enumerated in Chapter Two.

21. Make a one week problem solving lesson utilizing the appropriate means of investigation in a given discipline.
    Make a list of thirty appropriate project lessons for any social studies course and grade.

22. Why do some writers put so much emphasis on non-expository techniques of teaching social studies, especially problem solving, programmed learning, inquiry, discovery, projects, and above all discussion?

23. Write a one week lesson plan using problem solving as a means of structuring the content, and the Socratic questioning technique as an in the classroom means of exploring meaning.

24. Work out a means of using the *pass the question* method.

25. Work out a set of social studies contract assignments for United States History.

26. Devise as many means of enriching your teaching with audio-visual aids as is practical, especially the use of video tape. There are many suggested uses of audio visuals in the units which are in the appendix.

27. Decide on a means of keying each method to each objective and to a means of choosing content and evaluating progress so that any given method used will be likely to help students learn the desired behavior.

REFERENCES

Arnoff, Melvin. "A Comparative Problems Curriculum." *Social Education.* Vol. XXX (February, 1966).

Brevard, County Board of Public Instruction. *Space Curriculum Guidelines, 1965 Edition.* Florida, 1965.

Carpenter, Helen McCracken, *Skills in Social Studies.* Washington, D. C.: National

Council for the Social Studies, A Department of the National Education Association, Twenty-Fourth Yearbook, 1953.

Carr, Edwin R. *The Social Studies.* New York: The Center for Applied Research in Education, Inc., 1965.

Dale, Edgar. *Audio-Visual Methods in Teaching.* Hinsdale, Illinois: The Dryden Press, Inc., 1954.

de Bono, Edward. *New Think.* New York: Basic Books, Inc., 1967.

Dunfee, Maxine, and Sagl, Helen. *Social Studies Through Problem Solving.* New York: Holt, Rinehart and Winston, Inc., 1966.

Ediger, Marlow. "Middle East: Problem-solving Unit on a Tension Area." *The Instructor.* Vol. LXXVIII (January, 1969).

"Games Children Play To Learn." *Grade Teacher.* (October, 1969).

Gordon, Alice Kaplan. *Games For Growth.* Palo Alto, Calif.: Science Research Associates, Inc., 1970.

High, James. *Teaching Secondary School Social Studies.* New York, London: John Wiley and Sons, Inc., 1962.

Ignatoff, Bernice. "Games Add Fun To Learning." *Forecast For Home Economics.* (March, 1966).

Kaltsounis, Theodore. "Problem Solving in the Social Studies." *Education.* Vol. LXXXVI (February, 1966).

Kasperson, Roger. "Games As Educational Media." *Journal of Geography.* Vol. LXVII, (October, 1968).

Kenworthy, Leonard S. *Guide to Social Studies Teaching in Secondary Schools.* Belmont, California: Wadsworth Publishing Company, Inc., 1966.

Kenworthy, Leonard S. *Social Studies for the Seventies.* Waltham, Mass: Blaisdell Publishing Company, 1969.

Kysilka, Marcella and Rogers, Virginia. "Simulation Games. . .What and Why." *Instructor.* (March, 1970).

Maxson, Robert C. "Diversity, A Key To Their Little Cranial Cavities." *Florida Education.* (Fall, 1970).

Moffatt, Maurice P. *Social Studies Instruction.* Englewood Cliffs, N. J.: Prentice-Hall, Inc., 1963.

Means, Richard. *Methodology in Education.* Foundations of Education. Columbus, Ohio: Charles E. Merrill Publishing Company, 1968.

Nelson, Larry. "Games Motivate Learning." *Clearing House.* (March, 1962).

Phillips, Jean. "Book-Review Games." *Instructor,* (November, 1967).

Rasmussen, Fred. "Science Teaching and Academic Gaming." *The American Biology Teacher.* (December, 1969).

Rimoldi, H. J. A. *Problem Solving in High School and College Students.* Chicago: Loyola University, 1964.

Shaver, James P. "Educational Research and Instruction of Critical Thinking." *Social Education.* Vol XXVI, No. 1 (January, 1962).

Snellenberg, Eleanor. "Try Them On the Category Game." *Grade Teacher.* (October, 1969).

Stoll, Clarice S., and Boocork, Sarane S. "Simulation Games For Social Studies." *Audiovisual Instruction.* (October, 1968).

The Association of Teachers of Social Studies of the City of New York. *Handbook for Social Studies Teaching.* New York: Holt, Rinehart and Winston, Inc., 1967.

Vanderleeden, Ann Flaherty. "Children Love Games." *Instructor.* (April, 1970).

Wellington, C. Burleigh, and Wellington, Jean. *Teaching for Critical Thinking: With Emphasis on Secondary Education.* New York: McGraw-Hill Book Company, Inc., 1960.

Wesley, Edgar B., and Wronski, Stanley P. *Teaching Social Studies in High Schools.* Boston, Mass.: D. C. Heath and Company, 1958 and 1964.

Chapter VI

PLANNING
FOR
TEACHING

Teachers sometimes get so involved in thinking about purposes, philosophy, methods, and content as factors which influence the teaching of social studies that they forget these things are all an integral part of the planning process of instruction. Tying all of these considerations together is the purpose of proper planning. There are differences of opinion as to whether lesson plans should be written and, if so, in how much detail. Generally it is advisable for most teachers to develop detailed written lesson plans for maximum effectiveness.

Written course outlines, units and lesson plans serve several purposes. The teacher who puts down on paper a list of his major teaching objectives and how he expects to achieve them has a useful tool for checking on his own teaching. He can examine his overall plan of organization for teaching and determine how well the different parts fit together. He is in a better position to see the continuity of his plan. This will enable him to fill in any gaps and remedy any inconsistencies in his own thinking or planning. He can usually teach much better if his plans are on paper than if he only developed the plans in his mind.[1] Some indication of the extensiveness and usefulness of the preparation of courses of study is given later in this chapter. These course guides or plans have been taken from those prepared by different schools or school systems. A study of these course guides will aid teachers in understanding the importance and usefulness of their own planning.

The teacher can usually expect the student to get about as much out of instruction as the teacher has put into his preparation. Therefore, successful teaching and planning complement each other. All teachers need to plan their work and the work of their students. Both students and teachers in classrooms where there has been no instructional planning are at the mercy of the textbook writer, helpless in facing the current issues of the day, and are bound to cower before the tyranny of domineering students or immature ones. Such unplanned classroom situations, far from facilitating creativity in teaching and learning as some educators believe, prevent spontaneity and creativity, for both teachers

1. American Association of School Administrators, *Imperatives in Education,* (Washington, D.C.: 1966). Used by permission of the publisher.

Lesson plans should encompass participation activities as well as lectures and exams.

Photo furnished courtesy of AUM Learning Resource Center and Montgomery County Public Schools, Montgomery, Alabama.

Courses of study should include opportunities for the students to voice their opinions and observations.

Photo furnished courtesy of AUM Learning Resource Center and Montgomery County Public Schools, Montgomery, Alabama.

and students. There must be organization and planning for spontaneity and creativity, as there must be for any other learning or teaching behavior. No teacher should use plans as a strait jacket for their classroom teaching activities; but all teachers should plan and should write their plans out in enough detail to guide their practices.

Long Range Planning

Teachers will find a number of types of long range planning in most secondary schools. Social studies programs will usually include one or more of the following kinds of long range planning: curriculum guides, courses of study, resource units, teacher's guides or manuals, student workbooks, textbooks, units of study, and lesson plans. Some schools will have most or all of these general kinds of long range plans for teaching, some will have nothing but textbooks. Most teachers will find it desirable to read and use the plans available to guide teaching, but most will also find it necessary to do considerable planning of their own instructional practice.

One area of planning that is relatively neglected in many schools and by many teachers is that of scope, sequence, articulation, and pacing of learning and teaching in all subject areas. Social studies teachers may be a little worse about failure to plan a totally articulated educative experience for students than some other subject areas, since so many different disciplines are represented in secondary social studies curricula. Teachers should be careful in evaluating the breadth, depth, and ordering of their courses so that they fit logically with other courses being taught.

Courses of Study and Units

The *course of study* or *unit* is an organized body of information and experiences designed to effect significant change of behavior or learning by the student. Some writers make a great distinction between courses of study, resource units, and teaching units. It seems that except for differences in scope, span of time, and detail these differences are mainly one of terminology. The steps involved in preparing all three are identical and the content of each is similar except for the amount of detail in objectives, method, and content. Any unit or course of study should reflect sound scholarship, thought, and careful planning for desirable pupil growth. There can not be any such thing as a good unit or course of study that has low student appeal, or is difficult for teachers to use.

Good units and courses of study require careful identification and statement of behavioral and educational objectives, selection of subject matter on the basis of its expected contribution to student growth, choice of learning and teaching activities designed to assure maximum student growth toward stated objectives, and student evaluations which carefully assess the student growth toward the stated objectives. Content is focused, sampled, and organized rather than included and covered. It is utilized as a means to student goal attainment not something to be memorized as an end in itself.

Origins of Unit Planning

Units and courses of study are instructional devices with attention focused upon utility in teaching for significant educational growth and behavioral change. The modern concept of the unit as a teaching device owes its origin to the writings of Herbart, who formulated five steps in teaching: (1) preparation, (2) presentation, (3) comparison, (4) generalization, and (5) application. More recently Morrison gave five steps: (1) exploration, (2) presentation, (3) assimilation, (4) organization and (5) recitation. Dewey stressed a similar step-by-step procedure in problem solving or thinking: (1) define the problem, (2) collect information, (3) evaluate the data, (4) form a tentative hypothesis or conclusion, (5) act to test the hypothesis.

Steps in Writing a Unit or Course of Study

There are several steps necessary in planning and writing a course or unit of study. These are:

1. decide upon the purpose of including this course or unit of study in the curriculum,
2. decide upon and write the behavioral or educational objectives of the unit (growth of students because of this unit or course of study),
3. choice of methods of presentation (teaching activities and student learning activities),
4. selection and outline of content,
5. evaluation of student progress toward the stated objectives,
6. list of materials, books, and other information sources,
7. preparation of a brief summary or overview of the unit or course of study to be included immediately after the title. This overview serves to orient a reader quickly to the contents of the unit.

An outline of the procedures and format for units and courses of study is included as a guide for teachers' preparation of their own units and courses of study. Units vary in length, from a day or two to a school year. Long range planning varies in a similar way; but should incorporate planning for the whole year as well as daily lesson plans and short unit plans. A sample format for a daily lesson plan is also included for teachers' convenience.

Courses of study and units can not be made by combining daily lesson plans. However, daily lesson plans can and should be made from courses of study and/or from unit plans.

Procedures for Developing
a Unit or Course of Study

1. Title

2. Introduction and Overview

3. Purpose

4. Statement of the specific behavioral or educational objectives (what you are hoping students will learn or be able to do because these concepts were taught in terms of changes in the behavior of students). Some logical arrangements of objectives should be used, such as:

A.	Psychomotor (to do with the body)	A.	Skills
		B.	Knowledge
B.	Affective (to value-personality and morals)	C.	Understandings
		D.	Attitudes
C.	Cognitive (to know-mind)	E.	Habits
		F.	Appreciations

    State all objectives in simple, complete, declarative sentences.

5. Statement of methods used or to be used in this unit or course of study. Methods must be designed to help students attain objectives and to teach the selected concepts in the content chosen.

    A. Teaching methods

        (1) Introductory activities (methods used to introduce new materials, and concepts, and used to capture the attention and imagination of students.) (Use of films, speakers, etc.)

        (2) Development activities (activities used to teach the mate-

rial). Should also include a pretest to determine what students already know.

- (a)   Those things *teachers do* such as: lecture, show films, or ask questions.
- (b)   Those things *students do* as individuals such as: homework, make reports, projects, etc.
- (c)   Those things *students do collectively* or with the teachers such as: a panel, take a test, or engage in real discussions.
- (d)   Provision for optional activities and for teacher-pupil planning, and for individual study.
- (e)   List of ways to encourage students to develop their own methods of learning.

B.   Culminating activities (used to close a unit of course of study)

   (1)   Summary and review.

   (2)   Relation to preceding courses and units and to those that are to follow must be made clear.

   (3)   Show how student growth will be measured and what your students have learned. Relate their learning to your objectives. Tests and other measures of student growth toward objectives.

   (4)   Describe marking and grading practices and procedures to the students.

6.   Outline of Content

A brief outline of the more important facts and concepts to be taught in this unit or course of study. The shorter the unit the more detailed this should be. The outline should always be topical.

7.   Evaluation

A.   Of students by: tests, observation, anecdotal records, reconsideration of objectives. Include examples of each.

B. Of materials by student reactions, by use of checklists, by observations, by personal teacher evaluation.

C. Of questions and activities: of student reactions, of checklists, and of observations.

D. Teacher self-evaluation of the unit or course of study, of method, or self. Revaluation of unit or course of study for future use or needed change.

8. Bibliography and/or list of materials

A. The bibliography must contain books of sufficient variety of interest and difficulty to appeal to the interest and meet the need of every student of the class.

B. Maps, globes, films, slides, filmstrips, specimens, models, pictures, places to be visited, and any other materials of instruction that are to be used or available for use.

9. Units or courses of study should be changed as a teacher goes along. Therefore it is a good practice for a teacher to make daily lesson plans from the course of study or unit and to make written comments on the daily lesson plan after each days work. File these plans and then use them as a helpful guide to reworking the unit or course of study before using it again. These procedures will insure the preparation of better and more realistic planning each year.

The Purpose of Behavioral Objectives in Teaching

The purpose of this section is to answer for the beginning teacher the following questions concerned with behavioral objectives: (1) What is a behavioral objective? (2) Why use behavioral objectives? (3) How are behavioral objectives written? (4) What is an appropriate classification of objectives? (5) How behavioral objectives are selected. (6) How behavioral objectives are used in evaluating a student's progress.

Behavioral objectives are a means of telling the teacher and the student where they are going because "...if you're not sure where you're going, you're liable to end up someplace else."[2] Behavioral objectives are based upon

2. Mager, Robert F. *Preparing Instructional Objectives.* Palo Alto: Fearon Publishers, Inc., 1962, p. vii.

some observed need that existed prior to the statement of the goals, in other words, from needs we state goals, and from goals we state behavioral objectives.[3] A meaningfully stated behavioral objective is one that points out the direction in which to go and then tells one how to know when he has arrived. A behavioral objective describes the desired state of behavior the learner performs when he has successfully achieved and completed a learning experience. An objective is not reached unless the student is influenced to become different in some way other than he was before the instruction was undertaken, because any act of learning should change the behavior of the learner.[4] A behavioral objective is stated in terms of learning outcomes and defined in terms of observable student behavior based on the assumption that efficient teaching and testing require a clear conception of the desired learning outcome.[5] The use of behavioral objectives always presume that someone knows what the student should be able to do.

Why use behavioral objectives?

Behavioral objectives define the behavior the student will demonstrate after he has learned the material or skill. Some of the ways behavioral objectives can help the teacher are listed below:

1. Behavioral objectives provide a means of analyzing the teaching-learning situation and they help the teacher be consistent.

2. They serve as guidelines in attaining general objectives and purposes of the course and of education.

3. They help the teacher select and organize subject matter.

4. They provide and define the prerequisites to mastery of a subject or unit.

5. Behavioral objectives provide direction for the student.

6. They are an appropriate guide for evaluating pupil progress.

7. Carefully defined objectives force teachers to consider the importance of the skills and concepts they are emphasizing and the relevance of what is being taught.

8. They assure the administration that the teacher's objectives are related to those of the school.

9. They provide a means of assuring scope, sequence, and continuity from year to year and unit to unit.

10. They provide a means of informing visitors and substitute teachers of what is going on.

11. They prevent disorder, chaos, and conceptually empty courses.

3. McAshan, H. H. *Writing Behavioral Objectives a New Approach.* New York: Harper & Row, Publishers, 1970, p. 90.
4. McAshan, Ibid, p. 8.
5. Gronlund, Norman E. *Stating Behavioral Objectives for Classroom Instruction.* London: The Macmillan Company Collier-Macmillan Limited, 1970, p. 15.

How does one write behavioral objectives?

One of the major reasons teachers experience difficulty in writing behavioral objectives is that few know how to proceed. The difference between a goal and an objective is specificity. The most important criterion is that the objectives specify the intended behavioral outcomes and how these outcomes will be measured. Behavioral outcomes, if they are met, should always develop the student's ability to think or do. Objectives should thus be written to include all levels of learning. These levels include the following: (1) knowledge of facts, simple recall, the ability to recognize, and to memorize; (2) concept formation such as the ability to cluster and to classify; (3) comprehension such as the ability to translate and to summarize the materials, and (4) the ability to analyze, to synthesize, and to think convergently or divergently.[6] Teachers find other difficulties in writing behavioral objectives other than trying to develop the student's ability to think. Four basic "don'ts" in writing behavioral objectives should help the teacher to avoid some of these problems:

1.   *Do not* describe teacher behavior; do describe student behavior. Describing what the teacher will do is *method* or technique and not student behavioral objectives.

2.   *Do not* state the behavioral objectives in terms of the learning *PROCESS,* but in terms of the learning *PRODUCT. The purpose of behavioral objectives is to change student behavior* after learning and *not* to describe his behavior during learning. *Behavior objectives always describe what the student is to do after teaching.*

3.   *Do not* describe outcomes in terms of topical content, but rather in terms of student behavior. Listing the subject matter to be covered is outlining the content.

4.   *Do not* include more than one type of learning outcome in each behavioral objective.[7]

A guideline for the development of good objectives can be developed from the following questions:

1.   Is the behavioral objective real, important, and practical?

2.   Is it clear what is expected of the student when he has successfully achieved the behavioral objective?

3.   Does the behavioral objective truly represent the original problem, concept, skill or need that was observed or prescribed?

4.   Can the performance that has been specified be accepted as clear evidence that the student has either failed or achieved the objective?

5.   Does the objective tell *what the student is to do, how he is to do it, the conditions under which it is to be performed, the best way the student*

6. Armstrong, Robert J. *The Development and Evaluation of Behavioral Objectives.* Ohio: Charles A. Jones Publishing Co., 1970, p. 19.
7. Gronlund, Norman E. op. cit., p. 35.

is to do it, and *how many in the class should be able to perform the objective?*

6. Is the behavioral objective stated in a simple complete sentence?
7. Is the behavioral objective illusive, or is it explicit, and specific?
8. If you were absent from school, could someone unfamiliar with your class, course content, and teaching techniques evaluate your students with only your behavioral objectives for guidelines?[8]

Writing the actual objective

All teachers should understand and be able to apply the steps in writing all objectives, the classification of objectives and the writing of objectives for specific domains.

All behavioral objectives should include the following in order to be clear, concise, and meaningful:

1. Terminal behavioral variable
2. Instructional variable
3. Institutional variable
4. Method of measurement[9]

An objective stated as follows only achieves variables one and three and is therefore, not a good objective.

$$3 \qquad\qquad\qquad 1$$
Students will learn algebra.

The above statement can be improved by using all four variables in the objective. An example of the improved behavioral objective is as follows:

$$3 \quad 2 \quad\quad 2 \quad\quad 1$$

$$4$$

The *students* will increase their *problem solving skill* in *algebra* as demonstrated by their scores on the *SCAT test.*

1. Behavioral Variables
2. Instructional Variables
3. Institutional Variables
4. Measurement Variables

Avoiding misinterpretation

The behavioral objective that communicates best excludes the greatest number of possible alternatives to the goal. It describes the terminal behavior of the learner so as not to have misinterpretation.

8. McAshan, H. H., op. cit., p. 79.
9. Armstrong, Robert S., op. cit., p. 20.

There are unfortunately many words which can be misinterpreted in many ways. If these words are used then the behavioral objective is open to wide interpretation. Listed below are both ambigous and precise terms.[10]

Words open to many Ambiguous Interpretations	Words Open to Fewer Interpretations
to know	to write
to understand	to recite
to really understand	to identify
to appreciate	to differentiate
to fully appreciate	to solve
to grasp the significance of	to construct
to enjoy	to list
to believe	to compare
to have faith in	to contrast

An example of making an ambiguous behavioral objective meaningful through the use of words open to fewer interpretations is shown below:

1. Poor objective: The students will understand the trade winds.

2. Improved objective: The students will list the causes of trade winds.

This improved objective demonstrates how the student will show his understanding in behavioral terms.

It is all right to include such words as understand and appreciate in a statement of an objective, the objective is not specific enough to be useful until it indicates how the student will demonstrate his understanding and appreciation. A good objective must describe what the learner will be DOING when demonstrating that he *understands* or *appreciates.* Thus, the objective that communicates best is one that prescribes the terminal behavior of the learner well enough to preclude misinterpretation.[11]

The selection of objectives

Properly stated behavioral objectives specify desired changes in the learner. Most teachers find that trivial pupil behaviors are easily stated in behavioral terms, and that although insights are more important, they are too illusive to make good behavioral objectives. Behavioral objectives do not specify only trivial forms of behavior as many teachers seem to think. The example given below clearly illustrates that higher forms of learning can be stated in behavioral terms.

The student will demonstrate his understanding of the causes of the Civil War by writing an essay on a given cause.

10. Mager, Robert F., op. cit., p. 11.
11. Armstrong, Robert S. op. cit., p. 24.

Objectives cannot just be written in behavioral terms but the behavior must be estimated according to the worth of its learning value. A taxonomic analysis of the objective's behavior can be used to rate each objective's purpose. A classification scheme devised by Benjamin S. Bloom is divided into the three major areas that follow:

1. The *cognitive domain* which deals with intellectual behavior and which is divided into five basic levels.

2. The *affective domain* which deals with interests, attitudes, values, appreciations and adjustments of the individual and which is divided into four basic elements.

3. The *psychomotor domain* which deals with skills and which is divided into five basic elements.[12]

The affective domain is not as easily measured because it is highly subjective. How does a teacher measure, for instance, whether or not a student is sixty percent more tolerant of other students' views? Can students pass or fail attitudes at all? A teacher can improve on his judgment of attitudinal changes by recognizing approach and avoidance responses in the behavior of students. A few indicators for both are listed below:[13]

Approach Indicators	*Avoidance Indicators*
1. talk about it	1. speak unfavorably
2. encourage others	2. discourage others
3. read about it	3. approach something other
4. buy books about it	than the subject in question
5. attend lectures or other	4. state "I don't want to learn."
outside activities	5. state "I can't learn."
6. do extra projects	
7. ask frequent questions	

Teachers should try to master the skill of writing objectives in the affective domain as well as the other two domains in order to improve the quality of their behavioral objectives.

The use of Bloom's Taxonomy has two main points: (1) It prevents one kind of learning from excluding all others and (2) It permits different levels of objectives within each domain. Most teachers will be careful to include objectives from the lower levels; but they should also be certain to include objectives from the higher levels of the three domains.

Although Bloom's Taxonomy is helpful, teachers should not become a slave to any classification system. Some objectives include behavior

12. Bloom, Benjamin S. *Taxonomy of Educational Objectives.* New York: David McKay Company, Inc., 1956.
13. Mager, Robert F. *Developing Attitude Toward Learning.* Palo Alto: Fearson Publishers, 1968, p. 21-23.

changes in all three domains and should not be discarded because of difficulty in classifying them. If revising these objectives in order to place them into one of the three domains causes ambiguity and distortion, the original behavioral objective should be used.[14] Any classification scheme should be used as a guide line to help teachers write behavioral objectives and not as a set of rules.

Evaluation based on objectives

Evaluation is a means to an end with no intrinsic value of its own. It is an attempt to determine how successful the students have been in performing the behavioral objectives. All evaluation should be specific, relevant to what has been learned and representative of what has been learned. Students who fail to achieve desired behavioral objectives can be evaluated in two ways: (1) The student is to blame for the failure or (2) The teacher's methods and objectives are in need of revision. In either case evaluation based on whether or not the students have achieved the objectives helps the teacher to improve his own teaching and thus improve the learning atmosphere of the students.

Generalizations

The purpose of teaching is to change the perceptual field of the student and cause growth in his ability to think thus changing the person he is. All teachers should strive to teach the student something of importance. Good behavioral objectives will tell what is important, how much must be specific, and they should also reach the level of most of the students. Students should be encouraged through the use of behavioral objectives to learn to approach their studies and not to avoid them. In the end, teachers hope that students will learn more, behave better, appreciate someone or something, make judgments of their own, become a person of worth and always be moving toward their own objectives.

Objectives are teaching destinations. In any class all students are moving toward objectives. There is always movement, but the teacher should try to make this movement good.

Sample Daily Lesson Plans

All of the following daily lesson plans except the last one were taken from Callahan.[15]

14. Gronlund, op. cit., p. 52.
15. From *Successful Teaching in Secondary Schools* by Sterling G. Callahan. Copyright © 1966 by Scott, Foresman and Company. Reprinted by the permission of the publisher.

Daily Lesson Plan

Specific Objectives:

What to Teach	How to Teach	What Is Needed	Time

Assignment:

Evaluation:

Daily Lesson Plan

Daily Lesson Plan for _____ Date _____

Objectives Stated as Concepts to be Learned:

Other Objectives:

Preliminaries:

Assignments:

What to Teach	How to Teach	Time Used	Materials

Evaluation Procedures:

Daily Lesson Plan

(Title)

Class _____ Unit (No.) _____

Method:

  Discussion _____Illustration _____ Demonstration _____Conference _____Lecture _____

Type of Learning:

  Concept _____ Skill _____Memorization_____Tastes and Preferences _____

Lesson Objectives: _____

_____

_____

What to Teach	How to Teach	Materials

Assignment:

_____

Evaluation:

Daily Lesson Plan

Subject: Time:

Reminders:

Lesson Objectives:

Supporting Objectives	Time	Procedures

Assignments:

Unfinished Business:

Daily Lesson Plan

Class and Grade _____ Unit Title _____

Teaching Method: Discussion ____ Illustration ____ Demonstration ____
                    Conference ____ Lecture ____ Project ____

Type of Objective:
1. Behavioral Objective —

    A. Psychomotor _____ B. Affective _____ C. Cognitive _____
       1. Skills _____   1. Perceiving _____   1. Memorize facts_____
       2. Combination of   2. Responding_____   2. Association _____
          skills & mental   3. Valuing _____   3. Application _____
          set _____   4. Organizing _____   4. Inquiring _____
       3. Habit _____   5. Attitude _____   5. Discovery _____
                                           6. Thinking _____

2. Educational Objective — Knowledge _____   Understanding _____

                            Appreciations _____   Values _____

Lesson Objective: _____
_____

Student Assignment: _____
_____
_____

Concepts to be Taught	Teaching Method or Activity	Time	Materials for Students

Relation to Previous and Future Lessons:

Evaluation:

PROBLEMS AND QUESTIONS FOR STUDY OR DISCUSSION

1. Why is it not logical to try to make a course of study by putting teaching units together?

2. Why doesn't it make sense to make teaching units by just combining your daily lesson plans?

3. What is the reason for long range planning?

4. Is it possible that experienced or very creative teachers do not need to plan?

5. What function does the formulation of carefully developed, behaviorally stated objectives serve in the teaching-learning process.

6. How do you propose to provide continuity in your teaching, how will you articulate your teaching units, how will you provide articulation within the social studies from grade to grade and course to course?

7. How can the social studies be fitted to the sciences, to math, to English and to the various applied subjects so that the student perceives what he is learning as a continuous piece, as is life?

8. Why should all behavioral objectives be written in simple, complete, declarative sentences?

9. If a teacher knows what he wants to teach, why should he bother to write out his objectives?

10. Outline the steps in making a course of study, and the steps in making a teaching unit.

11. How does a teaching unit differ from a resource unit, or an activity unit?

12. State five or six criteria which should be used to decide upon the worth of any objective.

13. Examine the steps in teaching proposed by Herbart, the steps in the complete act of thought (problem solving) asserted by John Dewey, and the steps in lesson planning, write out the similarities between the three and the differences, if any.

14. Write a set of behavioral objectives for teaching one or two concepts, of your choice, from any social studies course. Apply the criteria asserted in this chapter to these objectives to make them behavioral, measurable, important, teachable, and capable of classification; then fit teaching and learning activities to these behavioral goals; then choose the content to be taught, make or select needed audio visual materials; devise a means of evaluating student progress.

15. Write a mini-unit (about ten minutes) to teach before the camera in your micro teaching experience. Teach it, view your performance, critique it, examine the critiques of your fellow teachers; then rewrite the mini-unit and reteach it on video-tape.

16. Develop a list of as many suitable verbs for use in writing behavioral objectives as you can.

17. Do you think either your college professors, who taught you your methods courses or your subject matter courses had any long range plans with behavioral objectives? As you try to recall your high school experiences, do you think very many of your high school teachers had carefully developed long range, behaviorally oriented plans? If your answer to these questions is no, why do you think they had no such plans; and how do you think long range behaviorally oriented plans can help you teach better?

18. Write a complete four to six weeks social studies unit similar in design to some of those in the latter part of this text.

19. Develop a complete set of daily lesson plans from your unit, making sure you have kept in mind the purposes of the social studies, and some of the rules of learning as you planned; also that methods, evaluation, and materials all serve instructional and learning purposes.

20. One of the authors was taught when he was a social studies student teacher a few years ago that too much and too careful planning might inhibit his and his students creativity, so don't do it! Discuss the matter of careful planning and behavioral objectives and try to decide if creativity will be inhibited or enhanced by it.

21. There are other ways to teach than through use of behavioral objectives and unit planning. Write a short problem solving lesson which might last for several days. Show how to use the community to teach socal studies. Develop a discussion oriented lesson plan, or a sociodrama, or a lesson using brainstorming as a means of getting students to participate. Develop a teaching plan which relies on small group work and individual study.

22. Develop a lesson plan that relies on the use of simulation and games, or one that uses the Socratic questioning technique to cause learning by induction.

23. Work out a means of teaching social studies by inquiry or discovery method, putting the burden on students for their own growth.

24. Design a social studies teaching plan for slower students.

REFERENCES

American Association of School Administrators. *Imperatives in Education.* Washington, D.C.: 1966.

Armstrong, Robert S. *The Development and Evaluation of Behavioral Objectives.* Ohio: Charles A. Jones Publishing Company, 1970.

Bloom, Benjamin, *Taxonomy of Educational Objectives.* New York: David McKay Company, 1956.

Burner, Jermone. *On Knowing.* Cambridge, Mass.: The Belknap Press of Harvard University Press, 1961.

Burton, William H. *The Guidance of Learning Activities,* 3rd Edition. New York: Appleton-Century-Crofts, Inc., 1962.

Callahan, Sterling G. *Successful Teaching in Secondary Schools.* Chicago: Scott, Foresman and Company, 1966.

Dewey, John. *John Dewey on Education.* New York: The Modern Library, 1964.

Fenton, Edwin. *Teaching the New Social Studies in Secondary Schools.* New York: Holt, Rinehart, and Winston, Inc., 1967.

Fritz, Dorothy. *Ways of Teaching.* Philadelphia: Westminster Press, 1965.

Furth, Hans. *Piaget for Teachers.* New York: Prentice-Hall, Inc., 1970.

Gronlund, Norman. *Stating Behavioral Objectives for Classroom Instruction.* London: The Macmillan Company, 1970.

Hoover, Kenneth H. *Learning and Teaching in the Secondary Schools.* Boston: Allyn and Bacon, Inc., 1964.

Mager, Robert. *Developing Attitudes Toward Learning.* Palo Alto: Fearson Publishers, 1968.

McLendon, Jonathan C. *Social Studies in Secondary Education.* New York: The McMillan Company, 1965.

Chapter VII

EVALUATING
AND
REPORTING
PUPIL
PROGRESS

The Meaning of Evaluation

The aim of the school is to produce changes in the behavior of the pupil through the acquisition of information, skills, habits, attitudes, appreciations, and interests.[1] Careful evaluation of student growth is necessary to improved instruction.

Evaluation is the process of appraising pupil behavior to determine if and how much of a change toward the instructional objectives has been made. This concept of evaluation requires that the teacher have a clear idea of what his objectives are. Each objective should describe what the learner will do, the circumstances under which he will do it, and how much he will do after instruction has taken place.[2]

In order that an accurate evaluation of pupil progress toward the instructional objectives is made, the teacher will need to know the present level of student attainment. This can be determined by pretesting. Evaluation is a continuous process made necessary because student growth is continuous. Evaluation, therefore, needs to be made continuously.

Purposes of Evaluation

Evaluation serves many purposes. The central purpose, however, is to enhance pupil progress. Evaluation reveals student strengths and weaknesses, and thus enables him to work to overcome his weaknesses.

Evaluation of students' progress tells the teacher if the means he chose to achieve his instructional objectives has been successful. With this evidence the teacher can, if necessary, make changes in subject matter, teaching techniques, and learning activities that are appropriate for his particular group of students.

---

1. Jacob S. Orleans, *Measurement in Education* (New York: Thomas Nelson and Sons, 1938), p. 13.
2. Morris R. Lewenstein, *Teaching Social Studies in Junior and Senior High School* (Chicago: Rand McNally and Company, 1962), p. 457.

Observation is one method of evaluation.

Photo furnished courtesy of AUM Learning Resource Center and Montgomery County Public Schools, Montgomery, Alabama.

Tests, whether teacher-made or standardized, require careful scoring and evaluation.

Photo furnished courtesy of AUM Learning Resource Center and Montgomery County Public Schools, Montgomery, Alabama.

Evaluation provides a means of re-defining objectives. Evaluation of students can reveal whether or not the objectives are realistic.[3]

Another purpose of evaluation is to provide a basis for assigning grades to students. Grades become a part of the student's permanent record, and are used for reporting to parents, computation of credit for graduation, qualifications for college entrance and job opportunities, and awarding of scholarships.

From the evaluation of students, a teacher can determine if the pupils are experiencing any difficulty. This will enable the teacher to decide whether a review is necessary or if he can proceed with new material. Motivation is another purpose served by evaluation. Some students work for grades, if a student knows he is making progress, he will be more highly motivated. Students develop skills in judging their own progress through self evaluation and knowledge of the evaluation of their progress by others. Evaluation supplies the data needed to section and group students in school.

Many people think evaluation and testing are synonymous. Evaluation is more inclusive than merely testing; but testing is the most common means of appraising pupil progress. Tests are the instruments used to collect information about pupil performance.[4]

The primary purposes of classroom tests are to evaluate the student's knowledge and understanding of the material and to evaluate his ability to select, organize, criticize, and present material in a coherent manner. The type of test used depends upon the nature of the material being tested. In general, multiple-choice test items are the most reliable and impartial type of test questions. In scoring test papers, teachers should devise some method for keeping the student as anonymous as possible. Also, each teacher should have other teachers criticize his tests and check his grading of papers periodically. Tests can be of great value to both the teacher and the student when they are used properly.

In planning his tests, a teacher needs to make decisions about the number of tests to be given, and the nature of the tests. He will need to decide whether the tests will be written or oral, long or short, open or closed book, preparation or surprise, paper and pencil, or performance, objective or essay. His decisions should be based on what he wants to measure, the size of the class, and the resources available at the school. With respect to frequency of tests, studies suggest that many tests be given in order that a representative sampling of the pupil's work be obtained.[5]

3. Peter F. Oliva, *The Secondary School Today* (Cleveland: The World Publishing Company, 1967), pp. 386-87.

4. Peter F. Oliva and Ralph A. Scrafford, *Teaching in a Modern Secondary School* (Columbus: Charles E. Merrill Books, Inc., 1965), p. 142.

5. Herbert F. A. Smith, *Secondary School Teaching: Modes for Reflective Thinking* (Dubuque: William C. Brown Company Publishers, 1964), pp. 196-198.

The type of items that fall into the category of the essay type test include: (1) discussion questions, (2) comparison of items, (3) explanation of problems, (4) description, (5) outlining, (6) criticism, (7) analysis, (8) decisions or opinions, (9) showing relationships, and (10) illustration or application. Objective type items include: (1) recall, (2) completion, (3) alternate response, (4) multiple choice, (5) true-false, (6) rearrangement, and (7) matching.

Essay tests have been criticized because they measure a limited amount of content, and must be scored subjectively. The objective type of test is often criticized because it encourages memorization rather than mastery with meaning, and permits guessing. Most experienced educators like to use both essay and objective types of testing in their classrooms. Which type test the teacher chooses should be determined by the kind of growth he is trying to measure.

Purposes of Testing

Behavioral objectives give a teacher a sense of direction when teaching and content and method provide the teaching and learning vehicles. Thus, evaluation becomes necessary to tell us whether we have arrived at the planned destination safely and on time or not. Thus, we test in order to evaluate pupil progress toward the stated objectives and his general educational growth. Testing has become an integral and regular part of the educational scene in most classrooms. All human behavior must be evaluated as a basis for decisions on how to improve our practices. Learning and teaching are no exceptions. Testing is one way of measuring the effectiveness of the curriculum, the learning activities, the teaching method, and the wisdom of the choice of content. Testing, at its best, is also an important teaching and learning experience.

Teacher-made Tests

A well-constructed teacher-made test is the best indicator of a student's achievement in relation to local objectives. While items on a standardized test are objective in nature, items on the teacher-made test may be either objective or subjective. Essay and short-answer questions are examples of the subjective type. Objective items may be true-false, multiple-choice, matching, or fill-in-the-blank.

The main argument of teachers who use essay tests exclusively is that it is the only way to test the student's ability to organize material and to express himself in writing.[6] The good essay question will require students to search out relationships, put concepts into their own words, discerningly select facts for memorization, and organize their thinking to present the material coherently.[7]

However, whether the response is mere recall or reasoning depends on the expected or unexpected nature of parts of the test requirement. Thus, in order for the essay or short-answer questions to be most effective, a part of each item must be new in the sense that it has not been discussed or studied previously.[8] In measuring familiarity of the material or recall, however, the essay question may require the student to generalize, evaluate, or apply material that he is able to reproduce. The essay test may, in addition, point out subject mastery or misconceptions and may reveal creativity not evident in objective tests.

The essay test does have great merit, but there are two main criticisms against it. The first of which is that clever students may sometimes "bluff" their way through questions for which they do not know the correct or expected answer. The other criticism and the more severe of the two is that grading depends too much on the opinions and preferences and, in some instances, the ignorance and dogmatism of the teacher.[9] Such factors as spelling, neatness, promptness, and handwriting may also influence the teacher's evaluation of the student's mastery of the material. The previous criticism of the manner in which essay tests are sometimes graded may be remedied somewhat by having the students identify their papers by number or in some other way to make the student as anonymous as possible for grading purposes. In addition, other teachers can also read the papers, or if this is not possible, the teacher should re-read it after an appropriate lapse of time.

The most common type of test item is the multiple-choice item. This is a widely-used test item and is considered by many experts in the field of testing to be the best measure because a well-constructed multiple-choice item can measure most, if not all, of the things measured by the essay test and can measure them more reliably and more validly.[10] The multiple-choice test can be adapted to any field or material and can be used on almost all levels of learning. It is easy to score, and there is less writing for the student to do. Multiple choice items are sometimes criticized because of the effect of guess-

6. Frances R. Link, "Teacher Made Tests," *NEA Journal,* 52 (October, 1963).

7. Jean Keelan, "Pandora's Box-The Essay Test," *The English Journal,* 53 (February, 1964), pp. 269-71.

8. A. Davis, "Short Answer and Essay Examinations," *Peabody Journal of Education,* 44 (March, 1967), pp. 269-71.

9. P. B. Diederich, "Cooperative Preparation and Rating of Essay Tests," *The English Journal,* 56 (April, 1967), pp. 573-84.

10. Frances R. Link, op. cit.

ing. To cope with this problem, one author has devised a ratio scale.[11] Hoffman pointed out that multiple-choice tests may penalize students with deep, subtle critical minds who see subtle points that others, including the examiners, do not notice.[12] In spite of these shortcomings, multiple-choice test items are probably the most uniform, reliable, consistent, and impartial method of testing that we have at present.

The true-false item is another type of objective test. This type item permits extensive sampling and can be scored very objectively. There are many valid criticisms of true-false tests. For one thing, guessing may be a very serious problem. This problem can be corrected to a great extent by having the students tell why a statement is false or having them make a false statement true. Also, true-false items do not measure understanding or organization as well as other types may. The tendency to "read in things" or to misinterpret the true-false statement is another problem. Several precautions may be used to improve true-false items: (1) be sure that the true-false statement is absolutely true or absolutely false, (2) avoid determiners such as all or always, or indefinite terms of degree or amount such as some or a few, (3) avoid items with more than one statement, (4) avoid an item whose answer depends on one insignificant word, phrase, or letter, and (5) avoid double negatives. The true-false item is difficult to construct and is apt to be the type most disliked by students.

The matching item is excellent for certain types of material such as matching inventors with their inventions or scientists with their achievements. The primary purpose of matching items is to test recognition rather than understanding and other higher levels of learning. The matching item provides for maximum coverage with minimum space and preparation of time. In making matching items, the teacher should cover only one field or idea. The entire matching item should be on one page and should contain no more than ten to fifteen questions. The number of choices for answers should be greater than the number of questions to help prevent students from determining the correct answer by the process of elimination.

Fill in the blank test items greatly reduce guessing and encourage intensive study of the material. This type of item tends to test for isolated facts, however, and encourages "splitting." The scoring of this test is sometimes slow and is somewhat subjective. In writing this type of test, omit only key words or phrases and do not use many blanks. The great weakness of fill in the blanks is that such items test absolute recall, which should not be an objective most of the time.

---

11. Palmer De Pue, "Multiple Choice and The Either-Or Fallacy," *School and Society,* 93 (March, 1965), pp. 154-56.

12. Banesh Hoffman, "Toward Less Emphasis on Multiple-Choice Texts," *Teachers College Record,* 64 (December, 1962), pp. 183-89.

Instructions to Students

Teachers often advise students not to change their answers on a test, but studies of changing answers have shown that the sampled groups, as a whole, definitely improved their scores by changing responses. In one experiment on a group of graduate students, the test papers of the lower-scoring group showed that the probability of improvement by changing their answers was two to one. The probability for the upper group was four to one. Other investigations have backed up these findings, and other authorities agree.[13]

Standardized Tests

The most widely used standardized tests are those made by testing bureaus. These agencies have a staff of experts trained in item writing and construction techniques, technically trained assistants, access to large and representative samples, and laboratory and scoring equipment.[14] These experts are, thereby, able to determine to some extent the reliability, validity, and practibility of the test items they create. Because of these very carefully constructed items, one may more accurately determine a student's standing within a group and may determine variations in performance within the student. However, too much reliance is often placed on standardized tests. A standardized test of achievement may not test closely enough a school's or an individual teacher's instructional objectives. There is a need for improved standardized tests, such as tests of mental abilities that provide a better estimate of potential when school performance is not a valid indicator, and proficiency tests that indicate mastery of particular skills and concepts. Common errors made in the use of standardized aptitude tests are (1) treating the score as a measure of capacity rather than as an estimate of present ability, (2) over-generalizing the meaning of the score, (3) playing down the significance of general ability, (4) accepting the scores as the main indicator of scholastic aptitude even when academic achievement is greatly different, (5) using the test as the main basis for ability grouping, (6) leading students of below-average tested ability out of verbal and abstract courses and activities into more concrete, vocational-type activities, (7) allowing greater precision and constancy to the test score than is merited, and (8) reporting exact scores to students and parents rather than interpreting them.[15]

13. Sidney Archer and Ralph Pippert, "Don't Change the Answer," *Clearing House,* 37 (September, 1962) pp.39-41.

14. Henry E. Garrett, *Testing for Teachers* (New York: American Book Company, 1965).

15. Edward J. Furst, "The Question of Abuses in the Use of Aptitude and Achievement Tests," *Theory Into Practice,* 2 (October, 1963) pp. 199-204.

Scoring Tests

Teachers are influenced by a number of factors when they score a student on classwork or through testing. Most of the time they are unaware of the influences of personal preconceptions, since teachers usually want to be fair and try to do the right thing.

The teacher does not merely check a student's paper for right or wrong answers. When he looks at a particular paper his personal attitude toward that student intervenes. Such factors as student personality, position of the student's parents within the community, the student's popularity among his teachers and his classmates, the student's intelligence or special talents which he exhibits, whether or not the student excels in a sport or school organization, his appearance, and many other things influence the mark any given student receives.[16]

These factors, of course, are unfair to the quiet, shy student, the student from an underprivileged home, and the student who has a behavior problem stemming from an unhappy family life. Some teachers exhibit a marked tendency to mark and grade a test paper on the basis of how well the student's answers agree with their own ideas on the subject matter tested. This is particularly true when essay questions are given.[17] To combat this problem, the teacher could grade each question separately, going through all the test papers before going to the next question. It is also helpful to assign each student a number and have him give his number in place of his name. This eliminates teacher preference toward some students by having them all remain anonymous. Teachers are people, and people like some people better than they do others, and it is doubted if teachers are different.

Besides unit tests, students are also graded on classroom participation, student-teacher rapport, and class conduct. This class participation may take place as a group, panel, or as an individual.

Many teachers place undue emphasis on test papers. These teachers use test scores as a measure of the child's overall ability. This policy is most unfair to the student, for he or she may make lower or higher on one test than on another. The material tested is also limited and cannot possibly be a fair measure of how much the student knows. Perhaps, the student studied the wrong material or did not know the most effective way to study for the course. Many times, a teacher will fail to give the students a proper outline for study.

The student's emotional and physical health also affect his test score.[18] If the student has a cold, fever, or physical pain he will be unable to give his full attention to the test before him. If he has quarreled with his family the night

16. Sterling G. Gallahan, *Successful Teaching in Secondary Schools* (Glenview, Illinois: Scott, Foresman and Co., 1966).

17. Henry E. Garrett, op. cit.

18. Ronald K. Penney, "Reactive Curiosity and Manifest Anxiety In Children," *Child Development* 36 (1965), pp. 697-702.

before, broken up with his girlfriend, or been embarassed or ridiculed by his peers or a teacher earlier in the day, he will likely be affected by these influences on the test. Often sheer nervousness over the prospect of the test will block the student mentally. When this occurs, he should take several deep breaths and sit quietly relaxed for a few minutes before beginning the test.

After giving a test, the teacher should return the papers to the students as soon as possible. At this time he should go over the test with the class and answer any questions that prove difficult. It is also good practice to let the students help in scoring their papers after a test. This helps them understand the grading system and cuts down on complaints about counting off too much for a particular question. Most important of all, the teacher should always explain his grading system to the students before giving a test.

Teachers may find it advantageous to plan a test with the students occasionally as a form of review or to encourage them to study. In such cases, students may be asked to prepare several essay or multiple-choice questions, which may serve as a basis for review and study, and some of the items may later be selected for the test. Cooperative planning of this type may help the students gain some insight into what the teacher expects and is trying to measure, and it will help them understand the difficulties involved in making effective test items. Students are always concerned that the teacher be fair in his evaluation of their progress, helping make the test assures them of its fairness.

Grades and marks sometimes have consequences in the lives of students that are very far reaching; they may become branded as dumbbell, average, a daydreamer, or a superior person because of the marks or scores they made. These categorizations follow him, sometimes into adult life. One reason why some students who appeared to be very poor secondary students become honor students in college is that the college instructor has not seen their permanent record, with its damning scores and grades and the cute little notes about how they behaved in Mrs. Lollypop's 7C social studies class, or the fact that their work was often late and sloppy in Mr. Xanadu's world history class. More often than not, of course, such students are just late bloomers. Grades have considerable social acceptance value, so there is pressure to make good ones.

While grading papers, it may prove helpful to have a note pad handy to record some information. Papers should be marked and returned promptly and discussed in class. A copy of every test given, with an item analysis, should always be filed.

Other Means of Evaluation

Tests provide one means of measurement. Pupil progress not measurable by tests can be measured in a number of other ways. Some of these means follow.[19] Observation of students' behavior in the normal sequence of classroom activities can be made. Anecdotal records can be kept to record classroom activities of the students such as the ease with which a student speaks before groups, cooperation and sharing in group work, and the respect shown for the views of others. Student participation in class discussions, the number and quality of questions asked, the number of times he volunteers, and participation in role-playing can be evaluated.

The teacher evaluates pupil progress by means of written assignments. Opinionaires can be used to survey what the students report to be their values and attitudes. The technique of observation will be needed to determine if the student puts into practice these attitudes and values.[20] Many teachers are not well trained observers, training in techniques of observation and inter-classroom visitation would improve this type of evaluation.

Conferences between the student and teacher serve as a means of evaluation. A teacher can learn about previously undetected facets of the student's feelings, attitudes and interests by informal talks with him. Unfortunately time and space often limit the use of this evaluation technique.

Effects of Testing on Students

Many students, and teachers, are markedly affected by testing and the situations test taking cause. Some students fear tests very little, if at all; in fact, knowledge that a test or examination is to be given only challenges them to study more and better. They become mildly tense which causes them to perform more effectively than they might otherwise be able to. Some students suffer from an all pervading fear of being evaluated by anyone on any criteria, such students tend to freeze in test situations, and thus perform far below their expected capacity. These students are called test-shy.

Marking and Reporting Pupil Progress

Judgment about pupil progress is always relative. A "C" may mean that a child is doing all that he is capable of doing, or it may mean that he is doing average work, depending on the definition of the symbol. Judgment is often relative to the pupil population in the school system.[21] Evaluating a pupil's

19. Gene R. Hawes, *Education Testing for the Millions* (New York: McGraw-Hill Book Company, 1964), pp. 53-55.
20. Oliva and Scrafford, op. cit., p. 146.
21. Charles Walters Odell, *Traditional Examinations and New Type Tests* (New York and London: The Century Company, 1958), p. 166.

ability requires careful study of many aspects of his personality and abilities. In social studies much more is evaluated than basic knowledge of subject matter. The teacher is concerned with a student's personal adjustment, the way he represents his school, and the quality of his answers to the learning situations he experiences. Teachers agree that giving and reporting marks is one of their most uncomfortable responsibilities. Some lack confidence in the marks they assign and others believe marks are fair but find them difficult to defend. The basis for assigning a mark is often unclear; questions occur such as, "Should the intelligent person who loafs be given a low mark?" Should the pupil who adjusts well to his peers but receives failing marks be promoted? Should the pupil who works hard but whose mental abilities are inadequate be promoted in spite of his below average performance on tests and assignments?[22]

Among the more specific purposes of marking systems are to provide a basis for: (1) giving information to parents about pupils, (2) promotion and graduation, (3) motivation of school work, (4) guidance of learning, (5) guidance of vocational and educational planning, (6) guidance of personal development, (7) honors, (8) participation in many school activities, (9) reports and recommendations to future employers, (10) data for curriculum studies, and (11) reports to a school which the student may attend later. Each school system must decide the basic functions or purposes it wants its marks to serve, and the system must provide the ways and means by which these functions can be accomplished. Most schools want a marking system that will provide data for the faculty to better help the pupil to grow toward acceptable goals.[23]

Variations in marking and reporting pupil progress are evident among social studies teachers and school systems and support the idea that there is no common reference point for grades. Some school personnel believe in predetermining the distribution of grades. Probably the system most commonly used is the five point scale of A, B, C, D, and F. One of the earliest methods of marking was the percentage system. In this method marks were assigned on a one hundred point scale with acceptable marks between 70 and 100 and failure marks below 70. This system implied an exact judgment of performance thus it could not be justified by available instruments of measurement.[24] It depended as do all marks on the teacher's estimation of the progress of each pupil.

Some educators have suggested just two categories such as pass or fail, or satisfactory or unsatisfactory for marking systems. This system has not re-

22. R. Kindsvatter, "Guidelines for Better Grading," *Clearing House,* (Fall, 1969), p. 331.
23. J. M. Haskell, "Pass-Fail, A System Worth Trying," *Clearing House* (November, 1967), p. 172.
24. J. L. Philbrick, "Precision in Grading Practices, Panacea or Problem," *Journal of Education Research,* LXII (December, 1968), p. 198. Used by permission of the publisher.

ceived widespread pupil or parent approval. One recent system that has received wide acceptance is the dual marking system. The concept of this system is that a student should be graded both in comparison to his own growth and in relation to others. Its proponents claim motivation for the better and the poorer students. The better students are able to see their progress in terms of national norms in comparison with their ability and it is possible for the slower learner to obtain a mark which is acceptable to him, his parents, and to society.[25]

It is of great importance to social studies educators of today that parents be brought in as partners in the educative process. In addition to the philosophy that education should be a cooperative effort there are other reasons why teachers should share grades with parents. Parents are curious about modern testing programs and are interested in having any information the school has about their child. A large percentage of parents have the ability to understand the test performance of their children and to become more effective in cooperating with schools. Another reason is that if evaluation programs are to be of real value the data collected must be used rather than filed, and discussed with parents rather than simply recorded on the cumulative record.[26]

The conference method of reporting has potential for providing more information and better understanding between home and school. Conferences should not be called only when special situations arise. They should be planned periodically to serve as a regular understanding of the child's progress.[27] Sufficient time must be allowed for the conference, a minimum of thirty minutes appears to be necessary. The teacher should be given ample time to prepare for and hold conferences during his working schedule.[28] Conferences are time consuming and it is true that many parents will not attend, also some students do not want their parents to attend. But schools are now beginning to instruct their teachers on effective conference techniques through in-service education, and it appears these programs will make parent-teacher conferences more effective.

Certainly the teacher's evaluation should be reported to the pupils. Such reports provide some form of motivation for future school work. They also give the pupil information which may help him achieve both immediate and long-term goals, and plan future educational and vocational experiences. The student needs to know his specific learning problems rather than to know in general that he is doing poorly in geography.

25. John Lewis, "Throw the Letter Away," *Balance Sheet,* XLIX (January, 1968), p. 198.
26. Ralph E. Smith and Ralph Tyler, *Appraising and Recording Student Progress* (New York: Harper Bros., 1942), p. 168.
27. Ernest W. Tiegs, *Tests and Measurement in the Improvement of Learning* (Boston: Houghton and Mifflin, 1939), p. 44.
28. M. A. White, "View From the Pupil's Desk," *Educational Digest,* (November, 1968), pp. 32-35.

Report cards used to record the assigned marks can take many forms. Commonly they provide for the recording of marks for all marking periods during the school year. Parents or guardians are usually requested to sign the card before it is returned to the school. Reports of academic achievement are sometimes accompanied by a check list of personality traits and attitudes. The teacher generally checks in any one of several categories of attitude and personality, as unsatisfactory, satisfactory, or improving. If these check lists are carefully worded, they can save the teacher time and effort.

Determining and reporting pupil growth is one of the greatest concerns of teachers, parents, and pupils. Although teachers dislike it, probably no activity has greater potential for interpreting the school program, for securing cooperation between home and school, and for promoting pupil development.[30]

In summary, evaluation in the social studies is the process through which the teacher determines how well his students have learned the understanding, skills, and attitudes which he has tried to teach them. In the process of evaluation the teacher uses both formal and informal measuring devices, and these may be either objective or subjective or both. Usually both informal and formal and both objective and subjective devices are used to make the evaluation process reasonably complete. Teachers use the results of evaluation for marking and grading and as a basis of motivation, reteaching, making changes in method, rewriting objectives and as a guide to selection of content. The young teacher will do well to understand the importance of the evaluation process and the role it can play in assisting him to accomplish his goals. Without an effective evaluation process there will always be mediocre instruction. All evaluation should be based on measurement of pupil progress toward the stated objectives. Teachers must also evaluate their planning, objectives, methods, choice of content, pacing and rewards, and student assignments. Student progress, in most cases, is a fairly good measure of teacher effectiveness.

Commercial Tests And Where They Can Be Purchased

I.   Standardized Tests for Elementary Grades
    A.   Social Studies

American School Achievement Tests: Social Studies and Science. This test requires 50-60 minutes to administer. More information can be obtained by writing Bobbs-Merrill Co., Inc., 4300 E. 62nd St., Indianapolis, Indiana 46202.

30. G. I. Jones, "Time to Evaluate," *Agricultural Education Magazine,* (June, 1967), p. 220. Used by permission of the publisher.

Metropolitan Achievement Tests. Recommended for grades 5-6. This test requires 74-88 minutes to administer. It costs $6.00 per 35 tests and is computer-graded. The Metropolitan social studies tests are the workmanlike products of professional testmakers. The teacher who carefully examines the tests and the materials accompanying them will have no difficulty in making intelligent and effective use of them. More information can be obtained by writing to Harcourt, Brace & World, Inc., 757 3rd Ave., New York, N. Y. 10017.

Stanford Achievement Test. Grades 4-9. The required time for the test is 30-35 minutes. The cost is $4.10 per 35 tests and is IBM-graded. The 70 items of each of the two forms of this test represent a sampling of a great amount of information. Most of the items are factual-seeking rather than problem-solving or thought-provoking. For further information contact Harcourt, Brace, & World, Inc., 757 3rd Avenue, New York, New York, 10017.

B.   Current Events

Nationwide Current Events Examination. Grades 4-8. The time required to administer the test is 40-45 minutes. A new form is issued each April. It can be ordered from Educational Stimuli, 201·2 Hammond Avenue, Superior, Wisconsin 54881.

C.   Geography

Emporia Geography Test. Grades 4-7. Administering time is 30-35 minutes. If one wishes to know whether the pupils in his class are memorizing a large number of place locations and miscellaneous geographical information, this test is useful. For further information, contact Bureau of Educational Measurements, Kansas State Teachers College, Emporia, Kansas 66801.

Modern Geography and Allied Social Studies. Grades 6-10. This test takes 30-35 minutes to administer. It costs 4¢ per test and is teacher graded. This test places major emphasis on trade routes and their products, casual geography (U.S.), casual geography (world), miscellaneous geographical vocabulary, world products (sources and uses), economic and human relations, place geography (Europe and Eastern hemisphere). The test contains good material which individual teachers or principals may wish to evaluate in terms of local courses of study. The test is well worth using and should be an evaluative instrument which will prove helpful to teachers and supervisors in improving instructional techniques. For further information contact Bureau of Educational Measurements, Kansas State Teachers College, Emporia, Kansas 66801.

D. History

History: Every Pupil Scholarship Tests. Grades 5-6. This test requires 40-45 minutes to administer. The cost of the test is 4¢ per test and is teacher-graded. No information on norms or reliability. New forms are issued each January and April. For more information write Bureau of Educational Measurement, Kansas State Teachers College, Emporia, Kansas 66801.

II. Standardized Social Studies Tests for Grades 9-12

A. Social Studies

Citizenship: Every Pupil Scholarship Test. This test takes 30-45 minutes to administer. It costs 4¢ per test plus 4¢ per answer sheet. It is teacher-graded. No data on norms or reliability. It can be ordered through the Bureau of Educational Measurement, Kansas State Teachers College, Emporia, Kansas 66801.

College Entrance Examination Board Achievement Test: American History and Social Studies. This test takes 60-80 minutes to administer. No information on cost, it is IBM-graded. This test places major emphasis on application of what has been learned, rather than recall or facts. Questions deal with government, economics, sociology, geography, and history. Has a reliability of .91. More information can be obtained by writing the Educational Testing Service, Princeton, New Jersey 08540.

College Entrance Examination Board Achievement Test: European History and World Cultures. This test takes 60-80 minutes to administer. No information on cost. It is IBM-graded. This test seems to be well edited and to cover material well. No information on reliability. More information can be obtained by writing the Educational Testing Service, Princeton, New Jersey 08540.

Metropolitan Achievement Test: Social Studies. This test takes 74-88 minutes to administer. It costs $6.00 per 35 tests and is computer-graded. This test measures study skills, vocabulary, and general information. No other data available. More information can be obtained by writing Harcourt, Brace & World, Inc., 757 Third Avenue, New York, New York 10017.

Sequential Test of Educational Progress: Social studies. This test takes 90-100 minutes to administer. The test costs $4.00 per 20 tests and is computer-graded. This test measures indicated abilities and previous knowledge concerning the subject matter. It has a reliability of .84 to .93. This is the leading standardized series of skill test in social studies. More information can be obtained by contacting Cooperative Test Division, Educational Testing Service, Princeton, N. J. 08540

Social Studies 12 (American Problems): Minnesota High School Achievement Examinations. Grade 12 only. This test requires 60-65 minutes to administer. It costs $2.50 per 100 and is graded by teachers. No data available on reliability or normative population. More information can be obtained by writing the American Guidance Service, Inc., 720 Washington Ave., S. E., Minneapolis, Minn. 55414.

B.   Contemporary Affairs

Contemporary Affairs: Every Pupil Test. This test requires 40-45 minutes to administer. It costs 5¢ per test and is teacher-graded. This test is revised each year, so there is no information on reliability. For more information concerning this test contact: Ohio Scholarship Test, State Dept. of Education, 751 Northwest Blvd., Columbus, Ohio 43212.

Current Affairs: Every Pupil Scholarship Test. This test requires 40-45 minutes to administer. It costs 4¢ per test and is teacher-graded. A new form of this test is issued each year. No other information available on reliability or norms. For more information write the Bureau of Educational Measurements, Kansas State Teachers College, Emporia, Kansas 66801.

Nationwide Current Events Examination: This test requires 40-45 minutes to administer. It costs 10¢ per test and is teacher-graded.

New test issued each year. No data on reliability or norms. For more information contact Educational Stimuli, 2012 Hammond Ave., Superior, Wis. 54881.

New York Times Current Affairs Test: Issued monthly through the New York Times School Service program. This test requires 35-40 minutes to administer. It is a teacher-graded test and costs 40¢ per student per week. No other data available. For more information contact New York Times, School and College Service, Times Square, New York, N. Y. 10036.

Newsweek Current News Test: This test requires 35-40 minutes to administer. Its distribution is restricted to schools subscribing to one of the publishers quantity subscription plans. The cost is $1.75 for 17 weeks. Newsweek Educational Division, 444 Madison Avenue, New York, New York 10022.

C.   Geography

Brandywine Achievement Test in Geography for Secondary Schools: Grades 7-12. This test requires 50-55 minutes to administer. It costs $7.00 per 35 tests and is teacher-scored. No manual and no data available on reliability or norm groups. More information can be obtained through Brandywine Achievement Test, Box 526, Coatesville, Pa. 19320.

Physical Geography: Every Pupil Scholarship Test. This test takes 30-45 minutes to administer. It costs 4¢ per test plus 4¢ per answer sheet. It is teacher-scored. No data on norms or reliability. It can be ordered through the Bureau of Educational Measurement, Kansas State Teachers College, Emporia, Kansas 66801.

World Geography: Every Pupil Scholarship Test. This test takes 30-45 minutes to administer. It is teacher-scored and costs 4¢ per test plus 4¢ per answer sheet. No data on norms or reliability. It can be ordered through the Bureau of Educational Measurements, Kansas State Teachers College, Emporia, Kansas 66801.

D.   Economics

A Standard Achievement Test in Economic Understanding for Secondary Schools, Sixth Revision: This test requires 50 minutes to administer. It costs 25¢ per copy and is teacher-scored. No other data available. For more information contact Joint Council on Economic Education, 2nd West 46th St., New York, New York 10036.

Test of Economic Understanding: For High School, College and Industry. This requires 60-70 minutes to administer. Costs $3.00 per 20 test. No other data available. For more information contact the Science Research Associates, Inc., 259 East Erie St., Chicago, Ill. 60611.

E.   History

Ancient History: Every Pupil Scholarship Test. This test requires 30-45 minutes to administer. It costs 4¢ per test plus 4¢ per answer sheet, it is teacher-scored. No data on norms or reliability. It can be ordered through the Bureau of Educational Measurements, Kansas State Teachers College, Emporia, Kansas 66801.

American History: Every Pupil Test: Grades 10-12. It costs 5¢ per test plus 4¢ per answer sheet. This test requires 40-45 minutes to administer and is teacher-scored. No data on norms or reliability. For more information contact Ohio Scholarship Test, State Dept. of Education, 751 Northwest Blvd., Columbus, Ohio 43212.

American History: Every Pupil Scholarship Test. This test takes 30-45 minutes to administer. It costs 4¢ per test plus 4¢ per answer sheet. It is teacher-scored. No data on norms or reliability. It can be ordered through the Bureau of Educational Measurements, Kansas State Teachers College, Emporia, Kansas 66801.

Cooperative Topical Test in American History. This requires 40-45 minutes to administer. This is a series of eight tests covering the period from 1450-1950. The cost is 50¢ for the set of eight tests. It is teacher-graded. No information on norms or reliability. It can be ordered and more information obtained by writing Cooperative Testing Service, Princeton, New Jersey 08540.

Objective Test in American History: Consists of ten unit tests, two semester tests, and one final exam. This test requires 60 minutes to administer. It costs 10¢ per test and is teacher-graded. No data on norms and reliability and no manual. For more information contact Perfection Form Co., 214 West Eighth St., Logan, Iowa 51546.

Objective Test in World History: Consists of ten unit tests, two semester tests, and one final exam. This test requires 60 minutes to administer. It costs 10¢ per test and is teacher-graded. No manual or data on norms and reliability. For more information contact Perfection Form Co., 214 West Eighth St., Logan, Iowa 51546.

World History: Every Pupil Scholarship Test. This test requires 30-45 minutes to administer. It costs 4¢ per test plus 4¢ per answer sheet. It is teacher-graded. No data on norms or reliability. It can be ordered through the Bureau of Educational Measurements, Kansas State Teachers College, Emporia, Kansas 66801.

World History: Every Pupil Test: Grades 10-12. This test requires 40-45 minutes to administer and is teacher-graded. It costs 5¢ per test plus 4¢ per answer sheet. No data on norms or reliability. For more information contact Ohio Scholarship Test, State Dept. of Education, 751 Northwest Blvd., Columbus, Ohio 43212.

F.   Political Science

American Government and Citizenship: Every Pupil Scholarship Test. This test requires 30-45 minutes to administer and is teacher-scored. It costs 4¢ per test plus 4¢ per answer sheet. No data on norms or reliability. It can be ordered through the Bureau of Educational Measurements, Kansas State Teachers College, Emporia, Kansas 66801.

Peltier–Durost Civics and Citizenship Test: Evaluation and Adjustment Series. This test requires 55-65 minutes to administer. It costs $4.10 per 35 tests and is IBM-graded. This test has a reliability of .88. Teachers who wish to receive an estimate of how well their pupils have mastered traditional information contact Harcourt, Brace & World, Inc., 757 Third Avenue, New York, New York 10017.

Principles of Democracy Test: This test requires 40-45 minutes to administer and is IBM-graded. It costs $4.00 per 100 tests. This test has a reliability of .89. With adequate revision, it could become a fine instrument for measuring the results of instruction in American Government classes. For more information write Harcourt, Brace & World, Inc., 757 Third Ave., New York, New York 10017.[31]

PROBLEMS AND QUESTIONS FOR STUDY OR DISCUSSION

1. What is meant by the idea that evaluation is an instructional process?

2. What are the appropriate purposes of evaluation in social studies classrooms?

3. Devise an instrument to evaluate the students' growth from the teaching unit you wrote for the preceding chapter.

4. Write a one or two page recommendation for marking and reporting pupil progress that makes sense to you and that has some support in the literature.

5. How does testing differ from evaluation?

6. What are the relative strengths of each of the types of teacher made test items such as: essay, homework, classroom oral reports, debates, multiple choice items, true-false, fill in the blanks, matching, anecdotal records, and observations? What are the relative weaknesses of each? How should a teacher decide which type to use?

7. List the steps in preparing a test.

8. What is meant by the following terms used frequently in testing: *mean, mode, median, validity, reliability, culture free, intelligence quotient, achievement, non-verbal, standard deviation, standard error of measurement, norms, sample, population, instrument, standardized test, diagnostic test, predictive validity, correlation, standard scores such as stanines?*

9. Can a teacher, or any other evaluator, ever avoid making value judgments about the work of those being evaluated?

10. How can you be sure that your evaluation is fair and accurate? Or can You?

11. Can anyone evaluate the work or progress or growth of anyone else without also evaluating the person?

12. How accurate are teacher made tests in evaluating pupil knowledge?

13. Can the careful statement of behavioral objectives, equally careful fitting of me-

---

31. Oscar K. Buros, Ed. *Mental Measurement Yearbook* (Highland, New Jersey: Gryphon Press). Used by permission of the publisher.

thods, and choice of subject matter make evaluation easier, more effective and more meaningful? Explain your answer.

14. What are the purposes of classroom testing?

15. How do you intend to evaluate your unit or lesson planning, your use of teaching and learning activities, and your choice of material? In short how do you propose to know whether your teaching is effective or not?

REFERENCES

Ahmann, Standley, and Glock, Marvin. *Evaluating Pupil Growth.* 2nd Edition. Boston: Allyn And Heath, 1963.

Archer, Sidney N., and Pippert, Ralph. "Don't Change The Answer!" *Clearing House.* Vol. 37 (Sept., 1962).

Armstrong, Robert J., Cornell, Terry D., Draner, Robert E., and Roberson, E. Wayne. *Developing and Writing Behavioral Objectives.* Tucson, Arizona: Educational Innovators Press, Inc., 1968.

Baker, Eva L., "Effects On Student Achievement of Behavioral And Nonbehavioral Objectives." *The Journal of Experimental Education.* Vol. XXXVII, No. 4 (Summer, 1969).

Bernard, Harold W. *Psychology of Learning and Teaching.* New York: McGraw-Hill Book Company, 1965.

Blatt, Sidney J. *Effects of Test Anxiety and Instructional Context on Problem Solving.* New Haven: Yale University, 1963.

Bloom, Benjamin S., Engelhart, Max D., Furst, Edward J., Hill, Walker H., and Krathwohl, David R. *Taxonomy of Educational Objectives Handbook I: Cognitive Domain.* New York: David McKay Company, Inc., 1956.

Boiarsky, Carolyn. "How to Set, and Meet, Learning Goals." *American School Board Journal.* (December, 1969).

Buros, Oscar Krisen, ed. *The Sixth Mental Measurements Yearbook.* Highland Park, N. J.: Gryphon Press, 1965.

Callahan, Sterling G. *Successful Teaching In Secondary Schools,* Glenview, Illinois: Scott, Foresman, and Co., 1966.

Chansky, Norman M. "Report Cards And Teacher Personality." *The Journal Of Educational Research.* Vol. 57 (1964).

Consalvo, Robert W. "Evaluation and Behavioral Objectives." *The American Biology Teacher.* (April, 1969).

Davis, R. A. "Short Answer And Essay Examinations." *Peabody Journal Of Education.* Vol. 44 (March, 1967).

Deitz, Patricia. "An Oral Performance Rating Sheet." *The French Review.* Vol. 35 (October, 1961)

De Pue, Palmer. "Multiple-Choice And The Either-Or Fallacy." *School And Society.* Vol. 93 (March, 1965).

De Pue, Palmer. "Great Fault In School Marks." *Journal Of Secondary Education.* Vol. 42 (May, 1967).

Diederich, P. B. "Cooperative Preparation And Rating Of Essay Tests." *The English Journal.* Vol. 56 (April, 1967).

Dyer, H. S. "Needed Changes To Sweeten The Impact Of Testing." *Personnel And Guidance Journal.* Vol. 45 (April, 1967).

Engman, Bill. "Behavioral Objectives: Key to Planning." *The Science Teacher.* (October, 1968).

Furst, Edward J. "The Question Of Abuses In The Use Of Aptitude And Achievement Tests." *Theory Into Practice.* Vol 2 (October, 1963).

Garrett, Henry E. *Testing For Teachers.* New York: American Book Co., 1965.

Haberman, Martin. "Behavioral Objectives: Bandwagon or Breakthrough." *The Journal of Teacher Education.* Vol. XIX, No. 1 (Spring, 1968).

Haner, Wendall W. "Test Your Tests." *The Instructor.* Vol. 73 (October, 1963).

Hawes, Gene R. *Educational Testing for the Millions.* New York: McGraw-Hill Book Company, 1964.

Hoffman, Banesh. *The Tyranny Of Testing.* Englewood Cliffs, New Jersey: Prentice Hall, 1966.

Hoffman, Banesh. "Towards Less Emphasis On Multiple-Choice Tests." *Teachers College Record.* Vol. 64 (December, 1962).

Jansen, Udo H. "Grading Practices in Nebraska." *Clearing House.* Vol. 43 (February 1969).

Keelan, Jean. "Pandora's Box—The Essay Test." *The English Journal.* Vol. 53 (February, 1964).

Lange, Phil C. "Taking The Stress Off ·Grades." *P.T.A. Magazine.* Vol. 62 (October, 1967).

Leles, Sam, and Bernabei, Raymond. *Writing and Using Behavioral Objectives.* Tusca-loosa, Alabama: W. B. Drake & Son Printers, Inc., 1969.

Lewenstein, Morris R. *Teaching Social Studies in Junior and Senior High School.* Chicago: Rand McNally & Company, 1963.

Lindvall, C. *Testing and Evaluation.* New York: Harcourt, Brace, & World, 1961.

Link, Frances R. "Teacher Made Tests—Models To Serve Specific Needs." *Clearing House.* Vol. 39 (February, 1965).

Link, Frances R. "Teacher Made Tests." *National Education Association Journal.* Vol. 52 (October, 1963).

Link, Frances R. "To Grade or Not to Grade." *PTA Magazine.* Vol. 62 (November 1967).

Loree, M. Ray. *Psychology of Education.* New York: The Ronald Press Company, 1965.

McCall, William Anderson. *Measurement.* New York: MacMillan Company, 1939).

McLane, Mary, Finkbiner Ron, and Evans Don. "Team Teaching and Objective Evalu-ation." *Clearing House.* Vol. 44 (November 1969).

Mager, Robert F. *Preparing Objectives for Programmed Instruction.* San Francisco: Fearon Publishers, 1961.

Montague, Earl J., and Butts, David P., "Behavioral Objectives." *The Science Teacher.* (March, 1968).

Murray, Thomas R: *Judging Student Progress.* New York: David McKay Co., Inc., 1960.

Ojemann, Ralph H. "Should Educational Objectives Be Stated in Behavioral Terms?" *The Elementary School Journal.* (February, 1968).

Oliva, Peter F. and Scrafford, Ralph A. *Teaching in a Modern Secondary School.* Columbus: Charles E. Merrill Books, Inc., 1965.

Oliva, Peter F. *The Secondary School Today.* Cleveland: The World Publishing Compa-ny, 1967.

Orleans, Jacob S. *Measurement in Education.* New York: Thomas Nelson & Sons, 1938.

Penney, Ronald K. "Reactive Curiosity And Manifest Anxiety In Children." *Child Development.* Vol. 36 (1965).

Robertann, Sister M. "Report Cards Belong To The Stone Age." *The Instructor.* (October, 1967).

Schwartz, Alfred. *Evaluating Student Progress In The Secondary Schools.* New York: Longmans, Green, 1957.

Smith, Herbert F. A. *Secondary School Teaching: Modes for Reflective Thinking.* Dubuque: Wm. Brown Company, 1964.

Wesley, Edgar B. and Wronski, Stanley P. *Teaching Social Studies in High School.* Boston: D. C. Heath & Company, 1958.

Whitaker, J. Russell. "A Fair Test." *Peabody Journal Of Education.* Vol. 45 (September, 1967).

Chapter VIII

TRENDS
IN
SOCIAL
STUDIES
TEACHING

There have been many innovative teaching techniques employed in secondary schools. Some have been found to be "fads" and have fallen by the educational wayside, while others have proven to be meritorious. Regardless of the technique, effective instruction is a function of the teacher. The emerging patterns offered in this chapter are designed to make good teachers more effective. They are not a panacea and will not serve as a substitute for a well-trained teacher with a desire to teach.

Team Teaching

Literature containing clear-cut evidence as to when the team approach was introduced into educational practice is practically nonexistent. In fact, a common definition of team teaching is somewhat difficult to find. Since its inception into educational practice and its entrance into school structural patterns, team teaching, like many other educational innovations, has become a term referred to by several titles, not always synonymous in their meaning. "Cooperative teaching," "collaborative teaching," the "team method," and "the team approach," are the most commonly used terms when reference to team teaching is made.

Team teaching may be defined as an arrangement where by two or more teachers cooperatively plan, teach, and evaluate a single group of students, regardless of the group size. There may, or may not be, larger instructional spaces and longer blocks of time provided specifically for the team teaching.

There are two basic approaches the team effort may take. One approach is the departmental approach. The team is organized to teach a subject or subjects within the social studies department. A team of three may teach only American history to a group of seventy-five students in grade eleven, or a team of three may team teach both American history and economics to a group of seventy-five eleventh graders. In either case, all team members would have social studies backgrounds. But the American history and economics approach

Students find social studies seminars interesting and meaningful.

Photo furnished courtesy of AUM Learning Resource Center and Montgomery County Public Schools, Montgomery, Alabama.

Independent study gives the teacher an opportunity to help the slow learner.

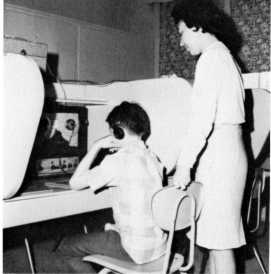

Photo furnished courtesy of Elmore County Public School, Wetumpka, Alabama.

would team social studies teachers with expertise in American history with teachers who are strong in economics. There are advantages to team teaching the same subject. Teachers can more easily coordinate their work since they have similar backgrounds, academic interests, and training. Since they are not combining two disciplines they do not have the problem of putting too much emphasis on one subject and not enough on another.

The other common type of team teaching is the interdepartmental or interdisciplinary pattern. This is an approach in which the team is composed of teachers of different disciplines. A common interdepartmental pattern teams social studies with language arts. The team will have at least one teacher from the social studies area and one from language arts. An interdisciplinary team will usually employ more than a one period block of time. Once the block of time has been assigned, the team assumes the responsibility for scheduling the activities within the block.

The major advantage of the interdepartmental approach is that it prevents the fragmentation of subject matter. It enables the student to more clearly see the relationship that does exist between the various academic areas. Another benefit is the exposure of teachers to subjects other than their own.

The utilization of the block of time assigned to the team is important. If the teaching techniques and methods do not differ from those practiced in the conventional one teacher classroom the maximum benefit is not being derived from the team. An effective way to schedule a period for team teaching is to include time for large group instruction, small group instruction, and individual study activities.

The large group activity is centered around an organized teacher presentation. This may, or may not, be the same team member each time. But the speaker must be dynamic if the method is to be effective. Large group instruction may serve the following purposes:

1. To introduce a new unit or new work.
2. To summarize or conclude a unit.
3. To deliver general information that will be beneficial to the entire group.
4. To perform demonstrations that should be observed by the whole class.

The small group process may find students grouped according to ability, interests, or talents. The individual teacher will lead the small group activity in some instances and will not in others. The small group process serves the following purposes:

1. To enable student to work cooperatively in specific areas of interest.

2.   To provide small group discussion under the supervision of a teacher.
3.   To establish question and answer sessions with a teacher.
4.   To stimulate an open exchange of ideas between students.

The individual study activity provides time for the students to delve into a specific area of interest. The teachers serve only in an advisory capacity and the responsibility for learning is placed squarely on the shoulders of the student. The individual study time may serve the following purposes:

1.   To develop habits of inquiry in the students.
2.   To provide realistic treatment of individual differences in students.
3.   To help create a sense of pride and responsibility within the student regarding his own efforts.
4.   To allow the student to reach his own potential and motivational level and not be limited by the abilities of the other class members.

There appear to be many advantages to team teaching. Any school system would be wise to investigate the vast potential offered by this approach. But it should again be emphasized that teacher attitudes, enthusiasm, skills, and initiative are basically the determinants of the superiority or inferiority of any teaching approach as compared with another.

Small Group Instruction

Students in a small group learn to reinforce and use knowledge gained in a large group or from independent study. It is in small groups that the teacher asks students to form opinions and make decisions.

Small group instruction strengthens the basic skills of speaking, reading, and writing. The teacher can test the skills of the pupil by the student's ability to interpret a document by writing or speaking his ideas.

One of the main functions of a small group is to analyze the content of a large group lecture. The teacher judges how well the student has progressed by his discussion in class. This brings about group activity which allows each student a chance to share his opinions with the class. The students can better understand others, enjoy being with others, develop concern for others, and work together to reach a common goal.

The teacher in a small group serves as an advisor and a resource person. The role of the teacher is to set guidelines for discussion and help students to arrange their thoughts. The teacher should choose a student leader or a chairman and a recorder. The teacher can observe the group better while the student leader sets the pace for the group and gets all group members involved in the lessons. The recorder is charged with the responsibility to record the ideas discussed and the means of research.

The strongest point in small group instruction is that it facilitates individual instruction. When a teacher notices a student's weakness, he can help the student compensate for his weakness.

Large Group Instruction

Large group instruction works best when it is combined with small group instruction and individual study. The teacher in large group classes presents stimulating lectures to hold the student's interest. A teacher is able to prepare a better lecture because he has more time to prepare it and does not bave to worry about presenting the lecture over and over. A film, a television program, or a radio program can be used as a means of covering a topic. These types of activities can bring out points the lecturer would not be able to do. Teachers in large group instruction become specialists because some teachers are able to keep students interested and motivate them better than other teachers.

The large group is to be used either for the presentation of content or for enrichment experiences. Schools must decide whether to base the composition of the group on ability, or place all students in the group. Many schools choose the best teacher to present a lecture while other schools rotate the instructional responsibility among the members of the teaching team. Administrators must decide the length a large group period will last and the number of weekly sessions.

Regardless of whether you have low or high ability students, the basic challenge to each teacher remains the same. That responsibility is to see to it that each learner is challenged according to his abilities and that every effort is made to teach skills that will benefit him at his level of performance.

Independent Study

Independent study is receiving increased attention in many schools. Like many other innovations, this program means different things to different people. One form of independent study is to schedule a specific course or area (such as Latin American culture) and pursue this area in depth, on an individual basis, outside the confines of a classroom. The student has a faculty advisor to offer assistance and also to evaluate the students progress periodically. To get a better insight into how independent study programs operate, two programs that are in practice are described briefly.

One of these programs is at the Abington (Pennsylvania) High School.[1] For about one-fourth of their school time the students are not scheduled for classes. During this unscheduled time—called independent study time—the student may work any place in the building either completely on his own, with a student assistant, with a teacher, or with a teacher aide. No passes are used, there is no attendance check, and the student has almost complete freedom of choice as to where he studies, what he works on, and what kind of assistance he secures. The following are the kinds of independent learning activities that take place during independent study time.

1.   Practicing a skill.

2.   Doing advanced work on a class project, such as a map project in geography.

3.   Getting remedial help from a student tutor or a teacher.

4.   Doing independent research.

5.   Viewing films and filmstrips.

The other independent study program, at Pimlico, Md., Jr. High School, offers an opportunity to selected ninth-grade students to pursue a program on an independent basis.[2] The objectives in organizing their independent study program were (1) to provide an opportunity during the school day for boys and girls to study in depth a topic of their individual interest, and (2) to stimulate a desire for creatively tackling a learning problem on their own. No term papers or examinations are required; additional homework for students pursuing an enriched program in all regular subjects is not expected. Each student is responsible to a faculty advisor selected from the subject field in which the student chooses to work. Typically each teacher has four or five students with whom he will meet at least once a week, usually as a group. The advisor is responsible for screening the student's proposed study plans and for seeing that the student continues to pursue them profitably. During the periods scheduled for independent study, most students usually report to the school library where they read or pursue research as planned.

Independent study does seem to be particularly adaptable to the social

1. Glatthorn and Ferderbar, "Independent Study for All Students," *Phi Delta Kappan,* (March, 1966), pp. 379-382. Used by permission of the publisher.
2. Edward Goldsmith, "Independent Study: Pimlico's Enrichment Program," *Baltimore Bulletin of Education,* (1963-64) pp. 1-7.

studies. The teacher in the traditional school organization might use designated portions of classroom time to allow students to engage in an independent study of those areas of the subject they find especially exciting.

Seminars

A seminar, by definition, is a group of advanced students studying under a teacher with each doing original research and all exchanging results through reports and discussions. The seminar technique can be adapted to any type of classroom organization and any academic discipline, but the concept appears to be particularly applicable to the high school social studies program.

The social studies seminar is ordinarily open to junior and senior students on an elective basis. The course carries a semester or year's credit depending upon the organizational pattern employed by the school. It seems advisable to screen students registering for the seminar, with emphasis being placed more on interest than on ability. The optimum class enrollment is probably about fifteen.

The seminar should not be a survey approach. The seminar is based on the rationale that the student will profit from the opportunity to pursue a specific area of the social studies in depth. The teaching technique would include some teacher presentations to the seminar, but the major thrust should be small group interaction and individual presentations. The student is responsible to the teacher for his work, but he also has the responsibility of sharing his findings with the other class members.

There are two alternative plans that may be followed in developing the seminars. One approach in developing the seminar is to identify one specific area of study, let the course title reflect this area, and expect all the students enrolled in the class to pursue the designated topic. The course title may be, for example, *Seminar on Selected Religions of the World.* The students would work cooperatively and individually in the single investigation. There are several ways the seminar can be organized internally. The most practical method is to sub-divide areas of responsibility among the students with the culmination being the bringing together of the assigned parts to make up the final analysis and report. It appears that this type of seminar is more applicable for the large high school where a number of the seminars covering a variety of subjects can be offered. This plan also appears to have more merit for those schools which offer courses on a semester basis. The teacher may feel that a year is too long to study a somewhat limited topic.

The second alternative is to offer a general social studies seminar for a semester or for a year. After registering for the class the students select a topic to research. This approach is open-ended and provides for much flexibility in individualizing instruction. Prior to the first class meeting the teacher judiciously selects topics for investigation. The topics selected are somewhat dependent upon factors such as the availability of library materials, the cultural status of the community, and geographic location. For example, students living in the southern region of Florida may find a study of the culture of the Latin American countries of great interest. The general social studies seminar approach also permits the student to choose his own topic for research. If the student does request a topic that was not previously recommended he is then expected to justify his request. This includes showing the availability of resources to adequately investigate the topic. This type of seminar has the flexibility that would allow a student to pursue more than one area of interest. It seems advisable for the student to spend at least six weeks on a research topic. This amount of time is probably necessary for the student to complete his investigation and finish his preparation for presenting the results. This second concept for offering a social studies seminar is particularly functional in the small high school where it is not feasible to offer more than one seminar in a given term.

There are numerous methods by which the student could be evaluated in a seminar. A simple pass-fail mark may be assigned, but if this is unacceptable then letter grades can be given without doing violence to the seminar concept. Regardless of the grading technique used, the student should be evaluated on the difficulty of the topic chosen, the amount of research done in investigating the topic, and the analysis and presentation of the results of the study.

Not only is it imperative that materials be available about the topics being researched, but it is also necessary that materials be readily accessible to the students. This means being accessible after school, on weekends, and during the scheduled class period. In many schools the most difficult time to get a student or students into the school library is during their class period. The teacher must establish procedures so that students may go freely from their assigned classroom to the library. The teacher obviously cannot be at both places at the same time, but often there will be members of the class working in both areas simultaneously. It seems desirable to establish a few simple and direct ground rules for conduct in halls and during unsupervised study. These rules need to be made perfectly clear to the students and then enforced.

The seminar is not an unstructured, disorganized class. It is a well planned and often highly organized method of teaching a class. The students benefit from the built-in flexibility and the freedom, but at all times they operate within the superstructure established for the seminar. Learning is not purely incidental, but is preplanned and supervised by the teacher. Each student assumes the responsibility for presenting his findings and conclusions to the total class, which may be in the form of reports and discussions.

The seminar concept has merit in the social studies. It frees the student and teacher from the traditional textbook oriented course and provides the freedom and the flexibility necessary to really individualize instruction.

Advanced Placement

Smart students have often avoided taking classes designed for smart students! Honors programs, or classes for superior students have often meant nothing more than giving additional homework to the student and then grading him harder.

Advanced Placement courses, which are still relatively new in many secondary schools, offer students an opportunity to complete some of their college work while still in high school. This program is a way that high schools may meet the needs of academically superior students by offering them college-level courses. Essentially, it is another means for providing for individual differences, in this case by allowing bright students to take courses which challenge their intellectual abilities.[3]

The Advanced Placement Program is worthwhile because it embodies the basic principle of reward for effort. The student receives more than a letter grade and a pat-on-the-back for the additional effort he puts into his educational program.

Teaching of the academically talented student is receiving more attention. The rapid learner has fundamental needs just as the slower learner and it is the responsibility of our educational system to endeavor to help meet those needs.

The United States application of American democracy has hampered the development of the potential of many students. American democracy has failed to recognize that some persons are less able to do some things than others. The result of this interpretation of democracy has been a concerted effort directed at those of lesser abilities, while often neglecting those students who are gifted. Many of those who possess the greatest potential for becoming tomorrow's leaders have been neglected in the name of economic progress and the process of equalization.[4] "Equality for all" could very well have been the seed which caused a great nation to perish by providing identical opportunities for all, rather than providing educational opportunities according to each one's abilities and needs.

The recent past has seen a new recognition of the phrase "equality for all." The recognition has caused a trend toward the realization that there are intellectual differences in students ranging from those who need special education classes to those who are gifted. Each type of student should be provided

3. E. M. Gerrity, "Advanced Placement," *NEA Journal,* (January, 1965), pp. 22-24.
4. C. Klinger, "We're Wasting The Gifted," *Today's Education,* 58:(Spring, 1969), p. 86.

educational opportunities according to their interest and abilities.[5]

There is increasing concern in educational circles about the student as an individual and providing a program where he has an opportunity to experience some success at his particular level of ability. One of the approaches has been to ability group students into classes based primarily on IQ and communication skills. The argumunts pro and con for ability grouping in some form are many; however, regardless of the position one takes about the effectiveness of grouping there has resulted an even greater awareness that all youngsters do not have the same basic abilities in all academic areas. For a while the major emphasis was on the slow learner and the rapid learner was left to take care of himself. The current trend seems to be toward more recognition of the needs of both groups.

Teaching the Slow Learner

Some special approaches, emphases, materials, and procedures have been developed to assist the slow learner in his everyday learning situation. A discussion about the slow learner and suggestions for the teacher follow.

The usual methods of control do not work well with slow learners because many conventional punishments are actually fun to the slow learner. An example is sending the slow learner to the principal for not doing the assigned work. The slow learner views this as fun because he has escaped from the classroom situation. The teacher must be flexible in his dealings with the slow learner. The teacher should develop methods of teaching which are especially suited for the slow learner. The presentation of information must develop in the student a desire to understand, a desire which may have been dormant for years.

Teachers who are working with slow learners say that it is very important to eliminate competition. Slow learners should be encouraged to learn only for the sake of knowing, and what knowing can do to help them live better lives. Thus, the concept of individualized instruction is most important in helping the slow learner. Most teachers do not assign homework to students who are slow learners since they tend to view it as punishment. Teachers must break complex ideas down into simpler ones so that the slower student can understand them.

Teaching Methods

It almost seems that audio-visual aids were developed especially for the slow learner. In many schools, films are used in place of textbooks or in connection with the text for the teaching of concepts. Through the use of

5. Mildred Fox "Providing For The Gifted" *National Association of Secondary School Principals Bulletin,* 37 (October-December, 1953) pp. 78-81.

pictures the student can visualize concepts that would be only words without any real meaning from reading or listening only.

Another teaching method which has been found to be very successful with the slow learner is creative problem solving. Through this process the slow learner can develop a process of logical thought. Later, this logical thought can be used in other areas of his studies. Creative problem solving can help the slow learner to gain confidence in his own ability to reason. This increased self-confidence can lead to more self-reliance.

Team teaching has been found to help the slow learner. Under team teaching a student can receive more individualized instruction in a subject that is troubling him, while the rest of the class is busy with other subjects. Cooperative planning is necessary if team teaching is to work, since every day must be carefully planned to make maximum use of class time.

Evaluation of Teaching Methods

A teacher may develop a program which he feels is appropriate for the slow or brighter students; however, an essential part of this development is the final evaluation. A teaching method, no matter how well planned, is only good if it aids the student in the learning process.

An important measure of a teaching method is the length of the pupil's attention span. This is particularly important in working with slow learners since their attention span is usually relatively short. If the attention span is long and at a high level, one can safely assume that the teaching method is aiding the student in his growth toward the objectives. Another measure of teaching method is the amount and quality of class participation. A lack of control problems is often indicative of effective teaching methods.

Educators must never lose sight of the fact that every student, regardless of background or ability, must be given the opportunity to become what he is capable of becoming. Every teacher is responsible for helping each student to continue his preparation for citizenship in our democratic system. Whether students are grouped on a homogeneous or heterogeneous basis is not as significant as recognizing the fact that they are individuals and must be accepted as such in our efforts to provide all students with as many skills as possible which will aid them in their citizenship role.

Remedial Reading in Secondary Schools

In order to help the remedial reader, a teacher must first understand the problems as well as the background of this special student. Typically, he went through early school years weak in the decoding skills of primary reading. In junior high, he experienced increasing difficulties in recognizing words and getting meanings, especially when encountering polysyllabic words. This problem was further compounded by the increasing burden of concept difficulty of reading material. When the student entered high school, he was unprepared for the demands of the curriculum. Therefore, because his verbal recognition is weak and his vocabulary small and because he is not experienced in symbolic meaning, the remedial student is unable to read, write, speak, or think at the level usually demanded of high school students. Thus, with the development and capabilities of the remedial reader in mind, the teacher must decide how he can help this student.

In fact, the key to the success of remedial reading programs is motivation. To read well one must want to read well. Motivation might be enhanced if the teacher stressed what reading can do for the student. For example, a student might be more likely to read if he thought that reading would bring him pleasure in future years. A student might be motivated if he was shown his reading scores. If this score is extremely low, the student needs encouragement and advice designed to help him improve. Each remedial reading student should be placed in competition, not with other students, but with himself. The student should be encouraged by discovering that his reading can be improved by keeping him aware of his progress. Simple tests should be given frequently and the teacher can encourage the students by giving evidence of individual progress and by paying sincere compliments to the class as a whole on its improvement. Still another important factor in achieving motivation is the reading material itself, for if this material is not appropriate, the course will not be effective. Interest, quality, and intrinsic worth must all be considered in the selection of remedial reading materials. Even where a need for intensive remedial work exists, it is important to secure the highest levels of material that the student can read. The student should feel he is in friendly surroundings, which are devoid of tensions and are cheerful, and that he is free to study the material which he and the teacher choose.

If the needlessly poor reader has been properly motivated he will probably have made substantial gains within a semester. Mastery of basic concepts can give the remedial reader confidence to move on to more complicated material.

What is the best method to use in teaching remedial reading? Unfortunately some researchers have tended to make exaggerated claims for the methods they have used successfully. Thus machine users, for instance, being able to demonstrate that students improve when using machines, have urged that reading accelerators be used exclusively. Some persons who favor phonetics would apparently ignore everything else. Some who think that small vocabularies are the poor readers' biggest handicap would spend day after day on vocabulary-building devices. Most of these claims are partly true. However, each of the dozens of recommended methods is likely to lead to a special and limited sort of improvement. The best programs are those which are balanced and that borrow some parts from several of the proven methods.

Not all slow learners have reading problems, and not all those who need remedial reading are slow learners. Yet, it is a safe assumption that most slow learners and most disadvantaged students have reading problems. Some reading problems are caused by physical defects, some are the result of various learning disabilities. There is little that a typical social studies teacher can do to help such students, except refer them to the appropriate expert. Most reading problems of secondary students are caused by one or more of the following things, and can be helped in an ordinary classroom: (1) emotional disturbance, (2) conscious refusal to learn, (3) hostility to teacher and school, (4) fear, or dislike of reading, (5) displaced hostility, (6) parental pressure, (7) discouragement, (8) restlessness, (9) day-dreaming. Any of these problems may make a pupil seem slow.

Teaching The Educationally Disadvantaged

Concern about the teaching of the educationally disadvantaged student is a recent phenomenon on the educational scene. Poverty and educational deprivation are not new problems for the United States nor are these problems unique American concerns, but nationwide interest in such problems is recent and is a relatively unique American problem. This interest is the result of many forces, not the least of which is continuing affluence. The United States is committed to full education for all its young people, thus more lower ability and more disadvantaged students are staying in school each year. The nation is more aware of its cultural pluralism than in former years. National attention has been focused in the last decade on the great differences between the poor or the minority child and the child of the more affluent middle class. Money is available to give minority children and the children of poor parents a better than even break in educational opportunity.

It is not always clear who the educationally disadvantaged and the culturally deprived are since not all poor achievement can be attributed to environment or to low income of parents, or even to being non-middle-class. Cultural deprivation is always a relative thing, and is usually a result of the preconceived norms of those doing the classifying, as much as it is the result of anything else. Most educators use the term educationally deprived to include most children of lower class parents, most ghetto children, many rural children of Appalachia, children of migrants, many children of minority racial groups, and many first generation children of poor immigrant parents. In other words, almost any student who is ethnically, socially, or economically different to the middle class majority is likely to be considered deprived by some of his teachers. Furthermore, many such students are, in point of fact, less able to do typical class work. Thus, they are educationally deprived, or disadvantaged simply because they can not do the expected work, or because they perceive no meaning in it and will not do it. Many students from lower class and minority homes do have some sort of learning problem. One of the major purposes of the social studies is to help every student become a worthy and contributing member of society, thus we must teach disadvantaged students more effectively.

There are a number of myths about people in general, and lower class people in particular, that need to be dispelled as a prerequisite to working with disadvantaged children. The first of these myths is that all people are born free and equal. All people are not born equal, and people become more unequal every day they live. Many inner-city poor and rural poor children are born of undernourished mothers and continue to eat a poor diet all their lives. Many grow up in one parent homes, where even that parent works most of the daylight hours. Many poor parents do not know how to care for children. Aspirations of poor children are appallingly low and even more amazingly unrealistic. Books at home are a rarity, parents who are seen reading are even more rare. Appropriate adult models for children of the poor are few. Models for children of some minority groups are even more uncommon. Noise, disease, crowded conditions, rootlessness, apathy, drugs, crime, and violence are part of daily life to many such young people. Some lower class students view any act of simple courtesy or kindness by any adult as a sign of fear or weakness. Thus when a teacher is nice to him, he thinks the teacher is afraid. Such children begin school disadvantaged and get more disadvantaged as far as school work is concerned each day they live.

Contrary to what many middle class teachers think, the lower class child has values, as does the minority child; but his values are very different to those of the middle class about most things, and are quite likely to shock a teacher who is not accustomed to them.

Problems In Teaching The Disadvantaged

The materials are not relevant to the disadvantaged students who can see no relation between the books they study and themselves. Textbooks are generally written for middle-class white children about middle-class white people and have little meaning for the black ghetto child. Some writers think ghetto teachers are those who can find no other place to teach so they go to the worst schools and become the worst teachers.

Many educationally disadvantaged students are intimidated by middle-class teachers and classmates. They are afraid to ask questions which could help them understand the material; so they memorize the material, never grasping the concepts being taught.

The students establish negative attitudes toward their ability to learn, toward teachers, toward school, and toward life. Apathy, low motivation and hostility toward authority are not lower class values, they are mental health problems developed in the environment of lower class homes. The constant tardiness, bizarre dress and speech habits which are characteristic of many lower class students may be offensive to the middle class teacher, but they are the only status symbols the students have. These customs are intended to help them function in their world.[6]

Besides these characteristics, the lower class youth tends to overgeneralize. This is the same as a defense mechanism. A close look at their surroundings makes them uncomfortable.

One research found five problems common to most economically deprived students. These problems are:[7]

1. Insufficient language skills—most economically deprived students do not speak standard English and do not read on their grade level.

2. Weak perception and concentration—the students have trouble with descriptions and abstractions.

3. Orientation to present fulfillment—lower class students are not interested in delayed gratification. They must be rewarded for completed tasks every day.

4. Disoriented to intelligence tests—the students have reading problems and do not speak or understand standard English. Therefore they do not understand intelligence tests and do poorly on them. Standardized tests do not properly measure their intelligence.

5. Slow learning as a way of learning—the students learn by memorization and know no other way. They have always been labled as slow learners.

Teaching lower class children is very different from teaching middle class children who have had encouragement to be creative, independent, self-disciplined, and good students. Lower class students have had little encouragement to go to school in many cases. They are there because the law says they must be, or because there is no place else to go.

Conventional instruction does not reach disadvantaged students very effectively. They have already decided that they cannot learn and school is not a good place to be; conventional education does not meet their needs and represents drudgery.

Only 15 percent of lower class high school students are equipped for pure

6. Joseph Lahman, "Expose-Don't Impose," *National Education Association Journal* IX (January, 1966) pp. 24-26.
7. J. D. Boney "Some Dynamics of Disadvantaged Students in Learning Situations," *Journal of Negro Education.* XXXV (Spring, 1966) pp. 315-19.

academic study. The students can see no relationship between school, where they study purely academic subjects which are of no use to them and to their lives outside. They do not see how school can affect their chances of getting a job. They do not study anything related to jobs they will work at upon graduation. No one has ever succeeded in showing them the advantages of being a good student. No one has ever told them about the financial aid available to them. They know they cannot pay for a college education. All they know is to get out of school and get a job.

In the classroom the relaxed atmosphere approach will not work; the students do not know how to operate in a situation in which they must decide what to study and when to study. The students need intensive guidance and supervision which requires them to do things. The teacher should always be on hand to explain procedures, no matter how simple and the teacher should set down rules which have structured learning activities.

Because self-concept is so important in learning and because disadvantaged students are oriented to present fulfillment of their goals instead of delayed gratification, they should be given tasks that they may complete each day.

Teachers who have successfully taught disadvantaged students say that the main problem they have is developing student interest in new material. They have found the best way to develop this interest is through pictures, discussions, and study trips.

Since the students do have learning disabilities to overcome, it is necessary to present the material in as many concrete forms as possible. Visual aids are effective and should be used for presenting most content. The pupil can hear the teacher present the lesson and he can see it written down on the visual aid and in his book. If there is a film or filmstrip this will reinforce his learning. Visual aids help develop interest in the material presented.

Some teachers do not use a text in teaching disadvantaged students because they say the students can accomplish much more if they are not confined to the text. Those who do use a text do so because they say the students find security in knowing what to memorize.

Many students from lower class homes are role players. Therefore any type of teaching that puts the students into roles will catch their interest and enthusiasm. This helps them learn the material and encourages them to think creatively.

The students can also learn by observing and discussing what material they cannot learn by reading. Any activity that involves the student is much better than one that does not. Since grades and punishment do not motivate the lower class student, the teacher must find something else. The sheer drama of being involved in a learning activity can serve as motivation.

Teaching disadvantaged students requires good teachers and the best materials. If students are to overcome their disadvantages, they must have all the help they can get. Teachers must be specifically trained to make them better equipped to teach in the ghetto and rural schools. The materials and curriculum must be made more relevant to the students. Everything must be done to keep such students who make up the majority of those in inner city schools more prepared to meet the world in which they must live.

PROBLEMS AND QUESTIONS FOR STUDY OR DISCUSSION

1. Examine the *(Education Index)* for articles that seem to indicate newer and promising approaches to teaching secondary social studies, then make a list of:
    a) newer social studies programs that have been developed by practicing teachers, and write for several that interest you. Some of these programs are referenced in the bibliography at the end of this chapter and the next chapter, some at the end of Chapter Four, many references to specific programs may be found in the units and courses of study in the appendix.
    b) research studies in social studies materials or methods.
    c) programmed social studies courses that show promise.
    d) uses of video tape to improve social studies teaching.
    e) specific examples of nongraded social studies programs, use of team teaching, flexible or modular scheduling, the open school concept, innovative middle schools, or individualized instructional programs that are near enough to your school for you to visit them.

2. Study the literature on the several team teaching approaches to teaching social studies and learn how you could teach effectively in each, and the rationale supporting the establishment of each type of team.

3. Study the Trump plan, and the many practical variations of it such as Nova High School, the Brevard County plan, the Montgomery county, Md. plan. There are many variations of nongraded schools, and many of continuous progress schools.

4. Reexamine the recommendation for *S I M P L E* and *S O C C* made in an earlier chapter of this text and try to assess its implications for teaching social studies.

5. Devise an innovative means of teaching current affairs that will interest the students and still cause the desired behavioral changes.

6. Investigate current practices of grouping students for instruction in social studies, and some of the more innovative means of grouping and try to arrive at some sense of how students should be grouped for effective learning, in the light of your educational philosophy, the assumptions asserted in Chapters One and Two, and the purposes of social studies education in secondary schools of a free society.

7. Devise a means of individualizing study through seminars, differentiated assign-

ments, independent study, projects, programmed study, inquiry method, and any other means you can find evidence of effectiveness.

8. Design a means of encouraging your academically talented students to learn more about social studies, to develop their leadership potentials, and to develop their ability to think as a result of independent investigation.

9. Make a list of innovative social studies programs that use the problem solving method, or projects as a main means of teaching, study two or three of them and modify them for your own use.

10. There is considerable material on how to teach social studies more effectively to slow learners and to the educationally disadvantaged students. Many claims are made for these programs, but the evidence seems to be that most compensatory educational programs are far less effective than their originators and proponents had either hoped or claimed. Why do you think this is so? Perhaps you can find evidence that some compensatory programs are doing what their originators claim.

11. If you could have any kind of social studies program you wanted, what would it be like?

12. What do you think of the promises of technology for teaching social studies more effectively?

REFERENCES

Arnez, Nancy L. "The Effect of Teacher Attitudes upon the Culturally Different." *School and Society.* Vol. XCIV (March, 1966).

Bishop, William E. "Successful Teachers of the Gifted." *Exceptional Children.* Vol. 34, No. 5 (January, 1968).

Boney, J.D. "Some Dynamics of Disadvantaged Students in Learning Situations." *Journal of Negro Education.* Vol. XXXVI (Summer, 1967).

Cheyney, A.B. "Curricular Methods used by Outstanding Teachers of Culturally Disadvantaged Elementary School Children." *Journal of Negro Education.* Vol. XXXV (Spring, 1966).

Clift, V.A. "Further Considerations in the Education of the Disadvantaged." *Education Forum.* Vol. XXXIV (January, 1970).

Crow, Lester D., Murray, Walter I. and Smythe, Hugh H. *Educating the Culturally Disadvantaged Child.* New York: David Mc Kay Co. Inc., 1966.

Dailey, J.T. "Talent Training for Culturally Deprived Adolescents." *School and Society.* Vol. XLV (December, 1967).

Elkins, Deborah, Taba, Hilda. *Teaching Strategies for the Culturally Disadvantaged.* Chicago: Rand McNally and Company, 1968.

Fox, Mildred G. "Providing for the Gifted." *National Association of Secondary School Principles Bulletin.* Vol. 37 (October-December, 1953).

Gerrity, E. M. "Advanced Placement." *NEA Journal.* (January, 1965).

Glasman, Naftaly, S. "Teachers' Low Expectation Levels of Their Culturally Different Students: A View from Administration." *Journal of Secondary Education.* Vol. XLV (Febuary, 1970).

Glatthorn, and Ferderbar. "Independent Study for all Students." *Phi Delta Kappan.* (March, 1966).

Goldsmith, Edward. "Independent Study: Pimlico's Enrichment Program." *Baltimore Bulletin of Education.* (1963-64).

Johnson, H.A. "Educational Needs of Economically Deprived Children." *Education Digest.* Vol. XXXV (March, 1970).

Kliebard, Herbert M. "Curriculum Differentiation for the Disadvantaged." *Education Forum.* Vol. XXXII (November, 1967).

Lohman, Joseph D. "Expose-Don't Impose" *National Education Association Journal.* Vol. XIX (January, 1966).

Maxson, Robert C. and Williams, James O. "Fail-Teach-Pass: A Rational Basis of Instruction for Failing Students." Kappa Delta Pi *Record,* Vol. 7 No. 4. (1971).

Plowman, Paul O. "What Can be Done for Rural Gifted Children and Youth" *The Gifted Child Quarterly.* Vol. XII No. 3 (Autumn, 1968).

Wisniewski, Richard. *New Teachers in Urban Schools: An Inside View.* New York: Random House, 1968.

Students learn outside of the classroom.

Photo furnished courtesy of E.K. Wood, Director, Banks Model School Project, Pike County Public Schools, Troy, Alabama.

Effective teaching techniques involve the presentation of learning materials in an interesting manner.

Photo furnished courtesy of AUM Learning Resource Center and Montgomery County Public Schools, Montgomery, Alabama.

Chapter IX

**CURRENT
EVENTS,
CONTROVERSIAL
ISSUES,
AND
STUDENT
ATTITUDES**

Any statement of the goals of teaching current affairs requires a restatement of the purposes of all social studies teaching. The objectives of teaching contemporary affairs are similar to those of the whole social studies field. Although contemporary affairs constitute only a part of the social studies curriculum; the curriculum without contemporary affairs is inadequate and incomplete. Thus the objectives which are claimed for contemporary affairs very properly reflect those of the whole social studies program. Current events are taught to help students:

1. understand the problems of the United States in the world situation,
2. obtain knowledge for understanding of future events,
3. develop an understanding of other peoples and places,
4. follow changing institutions and trends in our society,
5. learn skills of reading and listening with comprehension, of recognizing propaganda, of reading maps and globes,
6. find social studies more interesting and more timely,
7. select significant issues from the mass of daily events,
8. develop independent thinking and judgment in problem solving.

The teacher of social studies cannot restrict instruction solely to what has gone on in the past. He must be prepared to guide discussions of events as they occur and may happen in the future. Our students live in the world today as it exists and they are interested in most issues of the day. The ever increasing abundance of news sources and the advancements made in the communication media, as a whole, has certainly served to stimulate interest in current affairs.

Selection of Current Affairs Topics

The following criteria are useful guidelines for the selection of current affairs topics. (1) Is the topic related to the course of study? It may sometimes become necessary to rule out some important topics in order to allow time for the inclusion of other current topics that are more closely related to the regular work. (2) Does the topic lend itself to a "then-and-now" treatment? Students should be helped to establish connections and parallels between historical events and current situations. The current topics that are selected should serve to illustrate persistent and significant issues or trends. The teacher must determine which events of the day are merely interesting items and which are likely to be continuing issues that will shape future events.

The relationship of the topic to the broad educational goals of the social studies is of utmost importance. Sports events and disasters crowd the news media, but are inappropriate topics for lengthy development. The development of such items in the classroom does not normally contribute to the attainment of social studies objectives.

The event used should be widely reported, and useful and appropriate materials should be available to the students. In most cases, there are plenty of materials.

The topic should be appropriate for the pupil's age and ability level. The teacher must consider the composition of his class in terms of pupils' intellectual abilities, levels of maturity, scholastic backgrounds, interests, and experiences in selecting current topics. For example, while it might be appropriate to discuss the European Common Market in detailed economic terms and its impact on the balance-of-payments problem in a senior economics class, it would not be purposeful in a seventh grade class in world geography where a more elementary and simplified treatment of the Common Market would be appropriate.

Teaching Techniques

Methods of teaching current affairs should be varied depending upon the class, the nature of the issue, the objectives of the lesson, and the materials and resources available.

If the teacher wishes to incorporate current affairs within the regular lessons he must continually be aware of the daily world scene. He can use a contemporary event to motivate students to study a lesson or an assignment. The teacher should use events that are sufficiently recent and well publicized that are to be important and will be remembered by the students. In a developmental lesson, current events can be used to illustrate the aim of the lesson, to provide the basis for an application of the concept being learned, or they can be used to supply content for a thought-provoking question. Current events can be taught outside the classroom. Opportunities are available to the teacher to involve the entire school with a presentation of current affairs in an assembly program by a social studies class. Bulletin boards and exhibits prepared by members of a social studies class can also be displayed for the entire student body of a school.

Handling Controversial Issues

The term controversial issue is used to designate any topic or problem about which there are actual or potential conflicts of opinions. History is the story of controversy and it is impossible for a teacher of the social studies to avoid dealing with controversial issues in the classroom, and even on occasions raising a few of his own. Controversial issues include not only those which affect students directly, but those which trouble the adult world, those which are present and those which can be foreseen, those which are soluble and those which are insoluble, those which are local and those which are world-wide, those which deal with facts and those which deal with policies.[1]

Growth in abilities to recognize, investigate, and evaluate controversial issues ranks as a major objective of social studies. The issues chosen should be pertinent to the content of the course and the objectives. The issues included in social studies classes should be social in nature and recognizable.

There are some issues so fraught with feeling and emotion that they are avoided entirely in the school curriculum. A nationwide survey conducted several years ago by the NEA revealed that the following subjects are often forbidden in the schools: religion, sex education, local politics, communism, socialism, public ownership, national politics, race relations, labor management, the United Nations, and various aspects of local school policy and administration.[2]

No doubt many of the issues that were considered too controversial a few years ago are being discussed openly and without fear today. Nevertheless, teachers are still faced with the problem of selecting those controversial issues that are worthy of attention and that can be taught effectively.

Some of the techniques used for study of controversial issues are:

1. Students may debate the issue or conduct a panel discussion on the issue.

2. Students may present oral reports giving their own findings and

1. Edgar Wesley and Stanley Wronski, *Teaching Social Studies in High Schools* (Boston: D. C. Heath and Co., 1958), p. 9.
2. Gerald Leinwand and Daniel M. Feins, *Teaching History and the Social Studies in Secondary Schools* (New York: Pitman Publishing Corporation, 1968), p. 129.

reaction to the issue.

3. Students may interview other students and adults to gain a consensus of opinion on the topic.

4. Students may dramatize the issue by means of simulation and role-playing.

In using any of the above techniques it is hoped the student will develop a sense of intellectual curiosity that will stimulate him to gather information outside of class. As students seek, organize, and record pertinent information, they should reach some conclusions of their own.[3]

The teacher's role in dealing with controversial issues is one of stimulator and consultant. He should not influence the students opinion on a topic by telling his views too early in the period of study. He should not persuade, but inform, he should withhold his opinion unless asked. In fact, he may honestly hold no conclusive opinion on any of the topics discussed. While a teacher is not expected to be perfect, he should serve as a model to students by his behavior.[4] The teaching of controversial issues requires the highest type of scholarship.

If the only problems taken up in the classroom were those upon which we all agreed, some of the richest material with which men and women in society must deal would be excluded. The skills that students acquire through the careful study of controversial issues rank among the most valuable learning that they can experience in social studies.

Changing Students' Attitudes

One of the most misleading myths is that you can't change attitudes. Social studies teachers have never accepted the contention that a person possesses permanent and unyielding attitudes that can never be altered. This denies one of man's greatest capacities—that of change as a result of cognitive learning.

There has been considerable disagreement among social studies teachers as to which types of activities are most productive in affecting attitude reorganization. Maxson conducted research in an effort to gain insight into the processes of attitudinal change of high school seniors. As a result of his study he suggested the following hypotheses:

1. The most desirable and lasting attitudinal adjustments will result from an honest presentation of the issue—showing both sides of the question and encouraging a critical evaluation on the part of the students.

3. Maurice Moffatt, op. cit., p. 41.
4. Jonathon McLendon, *Social Studies in Secondary Education* (New York: Prentice-Hall, Inc., 1950), p. 41.

2. Modifiability of attitudes are most likely to occur when students have the opportunity to discuss the issue and have interaction with their peers and teacher.

3. Attitude change is most likely to occur if the teacher is not perceived as trying to impose his values on the group.

4. The more a student is motivated to learn about issues dissonant to his own, the more likely he will be to experience an attitudinal change.[5]

The studying of controversial problems is one technique that might be used in attempting to modify attitudes. Since the study of social studies involves controversial issues, this technique can easily be incorporated into the instruction. Using this approach, various possible courses of action are stated and analyzed in terms of reasons why each might be selected, the behavior involved, and the consequences of each choice.

Social studies teachers are more and more turning to simulation to effect attitudinal shifts. Simulations are more than fun and game. They may range from the very simple, developed by the teacher, to extremely complicated, requiring computers. Simulation is being used with much success in the area of human relations.

Presenting examples is another method that is used to change attitudes. Both children and adults tend to emulate the conduct of those whom they admire. Pointing out the great, famous, or popular individuals who held certain attitudes, made certain decisions, or behaved in given ways, frequently influenced attitudes.[6]

The requiring of selected readings may have an impact on the students attitudes. Our educational system is based on the premise that people are influenced by what they read. There is clear evidence that reading can change the attitudes of students, and there is confirmation of the assumption that reading, reinforced by listening, discussion, and conversation will change attitudes more effectively than reading alone.[7]

Since attitudes are learned it would appear to be a simple matter to modify or replace an undesirable attitude by learning another one. But this is not the case; attitudes are not as easily modified or replaced as they are learned. More research is needed to explain both the persistence and modifiability of attitudes.[8] Even with the obvious difficulties, however, attitudes of students can

5. Robert C. Maxson, "Attitudinal Change as a Function of Communication Effectiveness," *Trends in Social Education*, (Fall, 1969), p. 8.

6. Lowry Harding, "Techniques for Changing Value-Patterns," *Educational Research Bulletin*, (April, 1947), pp. 97-100.

7. Frank Fisher, "Influence of Reading and Discussion on the Attitudes of Fifth Graders Toward American Indians," *Journal of Educational Research*, November, 1968), pp. 133-5. Used by the permission of the publisher.

8. William Lambert and Wallace Lambert, *Social Psychology* (Englewood Cliffs: Prentice-Hall, Inc., 1964).

be changed through classroom instruction. The teacher needs to know what he wants, where he wants to go, and what his objectives are. Then he can look for ways to achieve them.

If attitudes are to be affected by the educational experience, it seems clear that the social studies teacher is destined to play a major role in doing it. The teacher of social studies can provide guidance and deliberate help to students as they search for values upon which to form their attitudes. The quest for positive attitudes should be a prime focus of the social studies program. Facts may change, and skills may vanish, but attitudes can make the crucial difference in the individual lives of youth and the society in which they will become the adult citizens and leaders.

The Community as a Social Studies Laboratory

The student in the modern secondary school has a right to know what is happening in the world around him. A rather intensive study of one's own community will yield much insight into attitudes and events in other parts of the world. It is of great importance that the social studies teacher treat the community realistically and honestly. Realistic and honest treatment of the community includes consideration of conflicts, and tensions as well as trends and achievements.

There are three basic ways the social studies teacher may use the community as a laboratory.

1.   *Observational Approach* — This method consists of activities in which the social studies student learns through passive listening and observing. These activities would include lectures, oral reports, films, filmstrips, slides, tapes, records, and reading. It is somewhat questionable whether the community is being used as a laboratory when this approach is being used exclusively.

2.   *Field Trip Approach* — The field trip is one of the oldest, and most effective, social studies teaching techniques. This approach takes the student into the community and gives him a first hand look at facets that he may not be familiar with. The field trip must be well planned and related to the unit being studied if it is to achieve maximum effectiveness. The field trip is not a panacea and should be used only when the objectives cannot be accomplished as well by the observation method.

3.   *Human Resource Approach* — Teachers have long recognized the value of "outside" resources in supplementing the instructional program. It is becoming increasingly more difficult to transport students to the desired resources, thus the resource must be brought to the school. The human resource file is an organized effort to develop a bank of resource persons who can come to the children.

Teachers are often pleasantly surprised when they discover how many "interesting" people live in their community. A careful survey usually turns up people who have either traveled extensively, held important and unusual jobs, or have had other experiences that have educational value. These become target people for the teacher's resource file.

There are numerous ways the teacher may tackle the development of a resource file. He may do it himself or suggest it as a faculty project. The construction of the file can become a meaningful learning experience for the students. They may help in initiating the search for talent, conducting interviews, and confirming visitation dates.

The first step in developing the file is to identify potential resource people. These should be persons who have had experiences worth sharing. It is hoped that student interactions with the person will produce desired learning outcomes. Once the person has been identified he should be contacted and his willingness to share his experiences ascertained. If the potential resource is willing to donate some of his time to the school then the following information should be attained and typed on a card to be placed in the human resource file.

1. The resource person's name, address, and phone number.
2. Personal history of the resource person that would be relevant to his discussion with the students.
3. The subject area in which the resource person has expertise and is willing to share with the students.
4. The specific day or days the resource person is available to visit the school.
5. The most convenient time during the day for the resource person to visit the class.

It should be pointed out that a human resource file is never complete. It must be continually revised as new potential resource people move into the community and existing resource people move away. But once the teacher has constructed his initial file it then becomes a matter of coordinating the identified resource talent with his teaching unit and lesson plans.[9]

PROBLEMS AND QUESTIONS FOR STUDY OR DISCUSSION

1. Students generally dislike the current events day found in most social studies classes, they tend to view it as drudgery, boring and meaningless. Teachers often express dislike of teaching current events, and some teachers even show open disgust about teaching them. Why, then should we continue to teach

9. Robert C. Maxson, "The Human Resource File," *The Instructor*, (August-September, 1971).

a topic that is admittedly poorly taught, and openly disliked by both teachers and students?

2. What should a social studies teacher do about his feelings when controversial topics arise in class unexpectedly?

3. Design a brief problem oriented unit to teach an issue you deem controversial or design one to change student attitudes.

4. Establish a set of criteria for the selection and teaching of current affairs topics in any social studies class or grade.

5. Devise a means of using newspapers and magazines more effectively in teaching students how to understand current events, and how to evaluate news stories, editorial comment, and bias in the reporting media.

6. Set up a scheme for handling "hot topics" in your classes, it may prove helpful to examine the means other teachers report as being effective.

7. Write a short unit designed to change students attitudes toward some issue or ethnic group or person, remembering that students, like other people, change their value systems slowly and very gradually.

8. Discuss the concept of academic freedom that is likely to arise when social studies teachers attempt to teach concepts or actions to their classes about which the teacher feels strongly, but about which the community may feel strongly in a different way. What should the principal and the community expect from you as a social studies teacher in these areas?

9. What are your feelings about teaching sex education? Americanism versus Communism? Drug abuse? Communal living? Social protest?

10. Would you like to teach a social studies course that was mainly a "rap session"? Why or why not?

REFERENCES

Fisher, Frank. "Influence of Reading and Discussion on the Attitudes of Fifth Graders Toward American Indians." *Journal of Educational Research.* (November, 1968).

Lambert, William and Lambert, Wallace. *Social Psychology.* Englewood Cliffs: Prentice-Hall, Inc., 1964.

Leinwand, Gerald, and Feins, Daniel M. *Teaching History and the Social Studies in Secondary Schools.* New York: Pitman Publishing Corporation, 1968.

McLendon, Jonathon C. *Social Studies in Secondary Education.* New York: The Macmillan Company, 1965.

Massialas, Byron G. and Kazamias, Andreas M. *Crucial Issues in the Teaching of Social Studies.* Englewood Cliffs, N. J.: Prentice-Hall, Inc., 1964.

Maxson, Robert C. "Attitudinal Change as a Function of Communication Effectiveness." *Trends in Social Education.* (Fall, 1969).

Maxson, Robert C. "The Human Resource File." *The Instructor.* (August-September, 1971).

Sistrunk, Walter E. *The Teaching of Americanism versus Communism In Florida Secondary Schools.* University of Florida (Gainesville: 1966) Unpublished Dissertation.

Sistrunk, Walter E. *The Teaching of Americanism versus Communism In Secondary Schools.* (State College, Miss: Bureau of Educational Research, Mississippi State University), 1968.

Wesley, Edgar B., and Wronski, Stanley P. *Teaching Social Studies in High Schools.* Boston, Mass: D. C. Heath and Company, 1964.

The use of audio-visual equipment is becoming commonplace in social studies instruction.

Photo furnished courtesy of E.K. Wood, Director, Banks Model School Project, Pike County Public Schools, Troy, Alabama.

Chapter X

THE SELECTION AND USE OF SOCIAL STUDIES MATERIALS

The purpose of education, generally, and of social studies, specifically, determines *what* is included in the secondary social studies curriculum. Philosophical beliefs of the public, the students, and especially the teachers influence what is taught, why it is taught, and the way it is presented. Principles of learning and psychology are relied upon as guides in choosing student growth objectives, method of teaching, learning activities, and content.

The first step in planning for instruction in any course is to determine the desired educational outcomes; the next step is to state these outcomes in behavioral, measurable, observable terms. Once the student growth objectives have been determined, the destination of the course, unit, or lesson has been decided. The next step in planning for effective teaching is choice of materials which will make up the content of the course, unit, or lesson. The method of instruction, and learning is then chosen which seems best adapted to teaching the students the chosen material. Learning is evidenced by behavioral change. We teach to cause people to act differently than they did before they had the experience offered. Their behavior changes because they have learned something. Thus, while it is true that we want to teach *students rather than subject matter;* still *we must teach students something, otherwise the course or lesson will be conceptually empty.* Such courses may have a sense of destination if the objectives have been carefully defined but they are likely to promote unpredictable arrival times and unexpected behavior because content was not carefully selected to fuel the vehicle of learning. Materials must be carefully selected and presented in order to insure maximum desired student growth. No task of the teacher is more crucial than the selection of teaching and learning materials.

Kimball Wiles wrote in *Teaching For Better Schools,* in 1959 that,

> The key to better schools is better teaching. . .a greater number of special services, a wider range of instructional services will not result in better schools unless teaching is improved. What the individual teacher does as he works with children is the crucial question.[1]

His assertion seems crucial to the issue of selection and use of social studies materials by classroom teachers. Selection and use of materials is always an important part of the duties of the social studies teacher. It is vitally important to have adequate material readily available to cope with the everyday needs of both teachers and students. There are a number of criteria which should be applied to the selection and use of any media.

Types of Media Available in Social Studies

Development of the printing press is usually reckoned as one of the great milestones in the history of mankind. Modern man is bombarded from every side and in every conceivable way, through every sense, often all at once by media. The mass media of television, motion pictures, newspapers, books, radio, billboards, and countless other devices are constantly employed to influence what we know, and therefore what we think, believe and buy. It seems impossible that it was only a little while ago that books were very rare, and were copied by hand, or were not available. Even as late as the American Revolution books were quite rare, few of the founding fathers ever had access to more than a few dozen. Under such conditions selection of materials was not too great a problem, the problem was finding anything at all for people to read. Franklin promoted the first circulating library in an effort to alleviate this condition. However, books and libraries remained meager in America throughout the last century, except in a few large cities or cultural centers near well established universities. Generally the only readily available media were newspapers, almanacs, a few magazines, and the textbook.

Early in this century the types of media began to change with the advent of motion pictures, radio, and later talking pictures, television, video tape recorders, and many other devices. Maps became more common and better prepared; many kinds of graphs, charts, tables and other graphic devices came into common use as a means of conveying information to others in a quick, concise, and accurate fashion.

Textbooks

Books were scarce and the population was mobile in the early days of our country. Teachers were meagerly trained and poor, often working only three

1. Kimball Wiles, *Teaching For Better Schools* (Englewood Cliffs, N. J.: Prentice Hall, Inc., 1959).

or four months of the year; and often they carried all their material with them from town to town and school to school. It was out of the frontier condition that the need for some simple instructional device was born; thus the textbook was developed. The textbook was meant to serve as a course of study, a source of objectives, a ready reference, a sort of lay version of holy writ as applied to secular knowledge. Most authorities agree that the textbook was indeed the course of study, the library, the source of method, and the curriculum.[2] As a result of a long process of historical evolution and development, the textbook of today is a complicated product. This is especially true of texts in the secondary social studies, since the social studies are derivative in terms of content from half a dozen or more disciplines, and are derivative in terms of method from three or four more subject areas. Many social studies texts are accompanied by numerous teaching aids such as manuals, teacher's annotated editions, books of readings, student workbooks, map exercises, and projects.

The textbook has exerted, and continues to exert a powerful influence on the social studies since it often serves as the only, or nearly only, source of material the teacher reads or has students read. More often than not the textbook influences the choice of objectives, the methods used, and the means of evaluation as well as the content taught. The textbook may not be as influential as in past years, but even today in many classrooms *the textbook at least dictates what is not taught!*

Textbooks are still the most used social studies materials in secondary schools. This may not be the best way to facilitate learning; but most teachers rely upon the textbook because it is the most available material and because it is approved by the state or the district or both. Many teachers feel that they can not pick material more wisely from the plethora on the market better than the textbook writer did. Some social studies teachers have so many students and so many daily preparations that they feel impelled to trust the textbook writer to choose their material for them. Textbooks are always available and always have the sanction of authority, and very often the kind of achievement tests given are keyed to the material usually in standard textbooks.

A good textbook is a course of study and is designed to provide a source of audio-visual aids, a series of suggested learning activities, suggestions for measuring learning, suggestions for enrichment, and for teaching. In short, a well constructed and well written book is one of the most useful devices a social studies teacher can rely on. A teacher who is unfamiliar with a subject should read the adopted textbook, or perhaps several different ones as a prelude to attempts to write his own course of study or organize the course into units and lessons of a teachable nature. Many teachers and professors view the text as a humble device which is simple to the point of being laughable. They assume

2. John A. Nietz, *Old Textbooks* (Pittsburgh: University of Pittsburgh Press, 1961).

that all its points, concepts, and teaching devices are self explanatory, and that any normal student can learn all there is in one by a casual perusal. In reality this is far from the case with most texts. Most texts are compact, complex, complicated organizations of both subject matter and method; therefore, effective use of them requires understanding and skillful study. Every author has peculiarities of style and organization. An understanding of these, plus an understanding of his purposes, helps both the teacher and the student to derive maximum benefit from the text.[3]

Better textbooks are arranged so that the student is able to at least glean a workable knowledge of the subject from an orderly reading of them. Many better texts have study helps, or directions spotted throughout. Most have summaries and questions that can be used to stimulate thought.

Standards for evaluating and selecting textbooks

Many states have adopted textbooks for all courses, and most of those which have local option have encouraged local districts to adopt their own. Many teachers of social studies may not ever serve on an adoption committee, but many others will, and still others will serve as members of library advisory committees. It seems, therefore, that a brief set of criteria should be asserted as a beginning screening device for the use of any book, especially a textbook. Any book should be evaluated in the light of the needs it is intended to satisfy, the purpose for which it will be used, the students' age and reading level, the organization of the content, the recency of the material, the relative lack of bias, and the factual nature of its contents.

There are many means of evaluating textbooks and other materials, which may be adopted or widely used in schools. Some states have a state textbook commission that actually adopts texts. Some states have no state adopted texts, but leave the choice of texts entirely to the local schools or school systems. A few of these systems permit the individual teacher to choose any textbook he wants, as most college instructors do. A common arrangement for choosing textbooks, in most of the arrangements described above, is to have an advisory committee of social studies teachers that actually reads the books available for a grade level and subject and then assigns a point rating to each. The adoption commission then chooses a text or several texts based on a composite of the ratings given books by the advisory committee and based on the cost of each proposed book. It is common practice in many states and school systems, now, to adopt several texts thus permitting an individual teacher or school to choose one of them. Whatever the means of screening textbooks for adoption, it seems likely that the teacher will personally be involved at some time with the choice

---

3. Edgar B. Wesley and Stanley P. Wronski, *Teaching Social Studies in High Schools* (Boston: D. C. Heath and Co., 1964).

of a textbook. Social studies teachers in most schools must choose, make, buy, and develop audio-visual materials, and in most schools, at least one social studies teacher serves as a member of the library committee, which makes recommendations for additional library books, atlases, maps, charts etc. Several means of screening books are listed in an effort to show some of the means teachers have found useful in deciding on the usefulness of books.

One widely used means of evaluating books is to teach from them for a semester or a year, or in the case of a library or reference work to have several students read or use them. This method is time consuming, some students do not find this interesting, and there is an element of exploitation of students in it, so some authorities believe. Another means of evaluating prospective books or texts is to ask a group of teachers to read the book and rate it on a predetermined scale. Many schools consult book reviews by professional reviewers before even reading it themselves. Sometimes the prospective book will have been analyzed and compared to other books with which it competes. Some adoption committees ask friends in other schools to recommend texts for possible adoption, some consult with subject matter and curriculum experts before deciding on four or five possible texts from which one or two will be adopted after careful analysis and reading.

There are many scales which have been designed to help the practicing teacher choose texts, books, and audio visuals more adequately. Some of the better known ones are in Edgar Dale's, *Audiovisual Methods in Teaching,* and in some of his earlier works.[4] A good scale for the choice and use of audio-visuals may be found in Brown, Lewis and Harcleroad, *A-V Instruction: Materials and Methods.*[5] There is a good treatment of the selection and use of materials in de Kieffer and Cochran's, *The Manual of Audio-Visual Techniques.*[6] Haas and Packer provide an excellent description of the selection and use of materials in, *Preparation and Use of Audio-Visual Aids.*[7] *How To Use Audio-Visual Materials,* by John Bachman is a very good book on this subject.[8] There are many other fine works available to help the teacher select and use social studies materials effectively.

The American Library Association has a number of publications which list criteria for the selection and use of texts, books for the school library, and audio-visual aids. Louis Shores has a good general work, *Instructional Materials,* which the teacher may find useful in helping choose materials more

4. Edgar Dale, *Audio Visual Methods in Teaching* (New York: The Dryden Press, 1969).

5. James W. Brown, Richard B. Lewis, and Fred F. Harcleroad, *A-V Instruction: Materials and Methods* (New York: McGraw-Hill Book Company, 1964).

6. Robert E. deKieffer and Lee W. Cochran, *The Manual of Audio Visual Techniques* (Englewood Cliffs, N. J.: Prentice-Hall, Inc., 1962).

7. Kenneth B. Haas and Harry Q. Packer, *Preparation and Use of Audio Visual Aids.* (New York: Prentice-Hall, Inc., 1950).

8. John W. Bachman, *How To Use Audio-Visual Materials* (New York: Association Press, 1959).

wisely.[9] Some of the departments of the NEA have published yearbooks devoted to the social studies at various times.

State textbook adoption commissions or local committees evaluate and adopt texts usually, thus individual teachers are forced to depend on their evaluations, at least in a general way. Other evaluations of any materials may be found in the book review sections of various professional journals. There is still a need for some brief general criteria which the teacher can use as a guide to selecting materials which students will use and study. Some very general criteria follow:

1. What is the reading level of the material?
2. Is the scope of the material adequate and suitable for the purpose intended?
3. Is the sequence of the content appropriate and logical?
4. Is the material factual and free of bias?
5. How well is the content articulated with the preceding and the following course?
6. Has the author made provision for adequate variation in assignments and in pacing as the material is taught?
7. Are adequate teaching aids available for it?
8. How recent is the material?
9. Is the material appropriately illustrated?
10. Is the content organized to facilitate the achievement of student behavioral goals?
11. What is the physical makeup of the book, its format, size of print, type of paper, binding, etc.?
12. Is the content realistic for students of this age and experience? Is the style interesting and readable?
13. Does the book have adequate bibliographies and references?
14. Can the material be used to stimulate thought and inquiry?
15. Does the material or audio visual device serve the purpose of this lesson, unit, or course?
16. Has the writer left sufficient room for a flexible approach.

There are many other criteria which may and should be applied to the selection and use of specific materials and devices used in the instructional program such as cost, ease of acquisition, safety of use, and ease of duplication and student use. The manner of use will determine which text or other material is chosen, to some extent. If a text is to be used as a total course of study, it should differ in important ways from one which is chosen as supplementary reading. There are many roles which the textbook may play such as presenter of content, developer of study habits, common denominator for testing, or an

9. Louis Shores, *Instructional Materials* (New York: The Ronald Press, 1960).

aid to learning.[10] Every effort should be made to serve the needs of the teacher and of the students in promoting learning when a text is chosen or used.

When a textbook is evaluated and chosen, or when any other material is chosen for inclusion in the social studies, any one of the general criteria may serve as a rationale for rejecting it, but usually rejection or inclusion is based on an overall evaluation of the worth and usefulness of the book or other material. Judicious use of these or other more specific criteria in the selection of any material should insure that the material will serve the purpose for which it was intended.

Library books

Library books are very important materials in the teaching of social studies. It is just as important to establish careful criteria for the selection of materials which will be housed in the library or media center as it is for selecting textbooks. Actually the only real difference is that library books, reference works, and some audio visual media are not kept in the classroom and are not used as frequently as texts, or in quite the same way; therefore, materials selected for the library or the media center do not have to be as compact, portable, or flexible as those used in the classroom or taken home daily. Many schools have committees that advise the librarian on the acquisition of new materials, usually at least one of the social studies teachers serves on this committee. Each of these school library advisory committees usually have their own rules and procedures. A wise new teacher learns what these are so as to avail himself of the opportunity to recommend acquisitions for the library or the media center. Similar criteria as those established for textbooks should be used for selecting library books, reference works, and audio visual media.

The textbook as a basis for method

Social studies materials must be used to serve educational ends if they are to be of maximum use. Reading may be the most efficient way to acquire information; but learning may be facilitated by other more realistic means, such as field trips, films, exhibits, dioramas, or video tape. Generally social studies textbooks should be used as compact, portable, personal reference works, not as basal readers, and not as a device to lock every student into identical daily assignments. Some students may read a text in depth, others may skim over the material searching for needed information. Others may refer to the bibliography for outside sources of reading. Pupils may be permitted to establish their own purposes and means of using textbooks such as to

10. Brown, Lewis, and Harcleroad, op. cit.

make a point, satisfy curiosity, settle an argument, answer a question, or form an opinion.[11]

Just as there are different kinds and levels of growth in students, there are different types and levels of textbook teaching. One of the more unworthy uses of a textbook is that of providing material which each pupil memorizes and replicates on cue. Perhaps a bit more worthy use of a text occurs when a teacher assigns designated reading from a text and then devotes the class time to questioning the students for understanding on what was read. Another textbook use requires students to read designated pages or materials, then prepare outlines, summaries, or parallel accounts to hand in or be shared with the class. A textbook may be used to cause pupils to learn to read, to analyze, to outline, to summarize, and to learn how to learn and study. Thus the textbook becomes a means to the end of learning, not a basis for evaluation of memorization. Some teachers are more independent of textbooks, they superimpose on them an independent organization of their own, usually in the form of courses of study and units of teaching materials with carefully developed behavioral objectives and methods of teaching, learning, content, and evaluation chosen to fit the best possible facitation of the stated objectives. Students use the text as a basis for further search for meaning, but the teacher and the students fill in the broad outlines of the course and of the lessons as they go. This is not done by the textbook writer. Some teachers take this method to its logical conclusion and do not rely upon the text at all for content, method, objectives, organization, scope, sequence, pacing or anything else. For such teachers the textbook is a resource just like any other material, no more or less useful. Such teachers and students are free to pursue discussions,engage in problem solving, or any other activity or learning they deem desirable. The only possible problem with such teacher independence is that it may be difficult to tell whether the course is serving its avowed educational purpose or not.

Many people are critical of textbook teaching, others favor slavishly following the textbook because they believe it guarantees coverage and uniformity from class to class. De Bernardis listed some apparent defects or problems with too much reliance on the textbook in 1960.[12]

The textbook is deadening to the good student, when no other materials are used.

No single textbook is suited to the interests and abilities of all students in any class.

11. Virginia D. Moore, "Guidelines for the New Social Studies," *The Instructor.* LXXIX (February 1970), pp. 112-13.

12. Amo. De Bernardis, *The Use of Instructional Materials* (New York: Appleton-Century-Crofts, Inc., 1960).

Reliance on the textbook does not encourage development of initiative and self-direction in students.

The textbook determines the scope of the course, thus students are not encouraged to work up to the level of their capacities.

The textbook encourages belief in the infallibility of printed matter, and reliance on a single source for information.

Use of textbook teaching provides little opportunity for students to compare and contrast and evaluate different points of view and thus develop critical abilities.

Reliance on textbooks encourages poor reading habits and rote memorization.

The textbook encourages both teacher and students to routinize the teaching-learning situation.

A good teacher is the key to good textbook utilization.

A teacher's educational beliefs, values, and understandings determine to a great degree his use of textbooks and other learning materials. Just as his value system determines his choice of objectives, his purpose, and his methods, it determines his choice of materials. Teachers who believe that social studies are the study of man's struggle with his environments in cultural settings will recognize a limitless range of possibilities open to their students which can not be learned from textbooks alone. Such teachers will choose a variety of materials and audio visual devices that are calculated to appeal to a variety of individual student interests. A non-textbook approach to teaching implies a willingness to move away from coverage of content toward a program that will encourage students to discover and inquire. Perhaps ceasing to rely on the text as the only, or even main source of material implies the teachers's acceptance of the need for all kinds of learning experiences to satisfy all kinds of student needs as part of a good social studies program. Students can learn from the printed word, but that is not the only media from which they learn, nor is it the most common one outside of schoolroom situations.

Textbooks remain the most commonly relied upon instructional device in most social studies classes, and they will very likely remain the most used instructional tool for a long time to come in spite of the great technological advances that the makers of audio visual media are making. Reliance on the textbook does sometimes encourage teachers to force students to memorize facts and does sometimes lead classroom experiences to become a dreary and dull business for many students. However, use of the textbook as the main source of material does not force poor teaching, or even dull teaching. A reasonably imaginative teacher can put a text in its place anytime and can use it as a base camp for further explorations of the mountain of learning. Beginning teachers who try to teach without reliance on a good textbook may be moving into an intellectual wilderness without a map and/or landmarks that will help them and their students reach their destinations safely.

Workbooks and teacher's manuals

Teacher made lesson plans and courses of study are being replaced in some schools by commercially prepared workbooks and teacher's manuals. These devices are usually designed to cover a semester or a year, are usually keyed to a particular textbook, and usually incorporate suggestions for objectives, methods, assignments, questions, and evaluation. Many of the newer ones are not keyed to a single text but are written for use with five or six different standard textbooks, with cross references to each. Such a manual is very helpful to even the most sophisticated social studies teacher because the drudgery is removed from teaching by a multiple textbook approach.

Some commercial companies now have kits of materials on the market that include, films, filmstrips, tapes, maps, student programs or workbooks, teacher's manuals, and tests all sold in a package to teach a given course. These kits are usually well prepared and useful; most teachers will like them, but they allow even less latitude for the teacher and student to choose goals and content and method than a typical text. Because the teacher's time is limited, and it takes time to prepare a good course of study with appropriately selected materials, methods, evaluation, and behavioral objectives the manual or the complete audio-visual kit is welcomed.

The makers of the science and mathematics curriculum projects discovered that teachers more readily adopt a new method or curriculum, if it is presented as a complete package. Such materials always reflect the viewpoint of the writers, and they are prepared with no knowledge of the particular characteristics of the students in the users' school. In spite of these drawbacks, preplanned and prepackaged materials will grow in popularity and will be widely used. Teachers need to think about the implications of permitting someone who does not know their students to decide on objectives, content, method, and evaluation. A good manual or kit of audio-visual helps is a useful and important tool, but such devices do foreclose many of the teachers' and the students' options.[13]

Audio-visual materials

The practice of using a great variety of audio visual materials and devices is growing in popularity among social studies teachers. Wider usage of such materials does not mean that audio-visuals should not be subjected to the same

13. Wesley and Wronski, op. cit.

careful scrutiny as a basic textbook, nor does it mean that greater use of audio-visuals will guarantee greater growth of students toward the desired objectives. Careful selection of audio visual media along with planning and timing can add much to a classroom learning situation that will provide richer, more rewarding learning for students and more effective instruction for teachers.

Much has been written in this chapter and elsewhere about the relationship of objectives to method, to content, and to evaluation in instructional situations. The model shown below depicts this relationship graphically.

There are many types of audio visual devices and materials that are easily obtained and used in teaching social studies. Audio visuals are not a substitute for reading material, for classroom or home study, discussion, or for problem solving as a means of teaching or learning; nor are audio visuals ever a suitable substitute for a qualified, concerned teacher. Audio-visuals may vary from very complicated and expensive devices such as television, video taping, or 16mm movies to the simplest kind of poster or simply writing on the chalkboard. Some of the types of audio visual devices and materials available are: motion pictures, television (both commercial and educational), radio, video recordings, audio tapes, records, filmstrips, film loops, still pictures, cartoons, drawings, charts, graphs, bulletin boards, flannel boards, chalk board, transparencies, slides, opaque projections, exhibits, posters, maps, globes, mi-

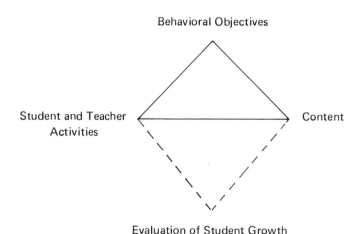

Figure 10-1. Instructional Planning.

meographed materials, time lines, dioramas, magazines, newspapers, books and many more.

General selection and use of audio-visuals

Audio-visuals are most effective as resources for the creative teacher. The traditional term, *audio-visual aids*, was well chosen. They are tools that extend, rather than displace, the capacities of the teacher. The social studies teacher may profit from, but should not limit himself to, the suggestions of the producers of audio-visual materials. He should use audio-visuals to help serve the purposes that he, the teacher, is attempting to achieve. Audio-visuals are most appropriate as aids to teachers when they serve the teacher. Five kinds of instructional situations in the social studies commonly call for the use of audiovisual aids, assuming that appropriate specific aids are available. These five types of situations involve the elements of teaching reality, securing motivation, promoting efficiency, teaching a sense of time, and giving a quick general impression.[14]

Beyond the recognition of a general need for audio-visuals, use in a particular instance should be determined by the characteristics of a given filmstrip, chalkboard illustration, or other audio-visual aid. Appropriate materials are those possessing pertinence to the topic, adequacy of depth and breadth in coverage, accuracy in content, and suitable level for students. Fortunately there is a variety of sources from which audio-visual aids are available listed in various directories, catalogs, and bibliographies, which include price and rental fees. Teachers should secure, or arrange to have sent to their schools, at least one copy of such directories if they are not already available in the school. Because many new commercially prepared audio-visuals appear each year and depositories often expand their collections, it is best to make sure that the latest directories are on hand. Every social studies department should have a card file identifying the films and other commercially produced audio-visuals that are available to the local teachers. Their ratings of the material should be noted, thus providing valuable information for their fellow teachers.

The teacher's next step is to plan the use of the material. The particular way in which an audio-visual should be used depends on both the purpose it is intended to serve and the characteristics of the specific material selected. Planning is simplified when the material is readily at hand and can be analyzed or reviewed in advance by the teacher. Many audio-visuals are borrowed from distant sources; and there may be a delay in planning the use until shortly before the actual time of use. In any event, *the teacher has a professional obligation to preview material that he does not already know well.* It is insuffi-

14. D. Schute, "An AV Try for Better Public Relations," *Educational Screen and Audio-Visual Guide,* (February, 1960), pp. 76-7.

cient to have a salesman's, a catalog's or another teacher's favorable recommendation. Because it is furnished free by the originating source, another
sponsor, the school system, or a friend, is not adequate justification for devot-
ing class time to a film, filmstrip, or recording. Previewing or examining an
audio-visual aid is done for purposes of (1) deciding whether to use the material, and (2) securing a basis for selecting the ways in which the material will
be used.[15]

Fundamental to achieving maximum learning from the use of audio-visual
aids is the teacher's preparation of the students. The routine, unstimulated,
and unguided use of materials has been widely criticized. The desired learning
is more likely to result if the students have some awareness of what kind of
learning they are expected to gain from the material. In his advance examination of audio-visuals the alert teacher will have identified points which will
require clarification. He will want to identify content related to what the
students are studying, terms and features unfamiliar to students, ideas to be
emphasized during classroom use, and other aspects of subject matter presented in or suggested by the audio-visual aid.

The next step is actual presentation of the material in the classroom. It is
important that the teacher know how to operate equipment. Even when there
is a student operator, he sometimes needs help loading or running a projector
or other audio-visual devices. There are also factors such as satisfactory room
darkening, seating arrangements, and the like to be arranged before the use of
projection equipment can be most effective.

Materials that reproduce sound ordinarily preclude the teacher from instructional opportunity during their presentation. Up-to-date equipment, however, increases such opportunity. Some motion picture projectors permit rapid
reverse of film or reshowing a scene without sound, thus facilitating comments
by the teacher and students.

Another step in the use of audio-visuals involves follow-up activity. Because presentation of these aids provides, at most, incomplete learning, teachers should have students engage in one or more appropriate activities designed
to follow up or reinforce learning begun in the presentation. For example, a
class may take notes on a filmstrip, it may discuss information presented in
a film, it may write a collective set of conclusions or individual summaries, and
it may construct aids similar to those presented. Reinforcement activities may
accompany a presentation or they may literally follow it in a sequence of
learning activities. It is best for any follow-up to come as soon as practicable
after the presentation.

Audio-visual aids are becoming more available than ever before. It would
be well for each teacher to visit the material center of his school district for

15. G. A. Brouwer, "Helping Teachers Use Audio-Visual Materials," *The National Elementary School Principal,* 40 (January, 1961), pp. 31-4.

an orientation on what materials may be on hand or that may be procured within available resources. There are private companies and many local, state, and federal agencies that can provide a wealth of information. The quality and proper use of these materials remains the responsibility of the teacher.

Opaque projector use

The opaque projector involves the projecting of flat pictures on a large screen in order for the entire class to see them. The use of opaque projectors with pictures is almost limitless. It is among the easiest of all audio-visual materials to operate. You have only to place the material in it, turn on a light, and focus a lens. It projects pictures ranging in size from a postage stamp to regular size paper and it also projects small objects such as coins, medals, and shallow dishes.

A major advantage of the opaque projector is the endless source of free materials that can be used. Opaque pictures come from everywhere—magazines, newspapers, books, and catalogs. Commercial sets of pictures developed around one subject may also be purchased.[16] Because of the amount of material available, it is necessary to consider carefully what should be used. The material should be interesting enough to catch the students' attention; it should be large enough to be seen clearly; the information should be important to the topic being discussed; the material should be accurate; and it should be well-produced, realistic, and attractive. Students can participate in the choosing of these materials; thus increasing their interest in the unit being covered. The only disadvantages are having to darken the classroom and the size of the machine.

The overhead projector

The overhead projector is similar to the opaque projector in style and inexpensiveness. The overhead projector, however, projects transparencies rather than pictures. The transparencies can be purchased commercially or easily prepared by the instructor. Transparencies dealing with social studies subjects can be purchased from several commercial firms.

The principal advantage of the overhead projector is that the teacher stands in front of the room facing the class, while projecting the transparency above and behind him. The teacher can work on the transparency while projecting it, thus illustrating as he explains. In social studies, overhead projectors are especially useful in presenting maps.

16. E. W. Hodes, "How Audio Visual Aids Make Teaching and Learning Easier," *Educational Screen and Audio-Visual Guide*, 39 (December, 1960), pp. 644-45.

Filmstrips

One of the most popular audio-visual aids in the classroom is the filmstrip. One of the major advantages of filmstrips is that they allow time for the students to think about and to discuss the subject. They may also be used by students on an individual basis for remedial work or enrichment activity. Among the other advantages are the moderate cost for both the filmstrips and the projectors, the variety of films produced, adaptability to the class, and ability to gain and hold the attention of the audience.

Because there is such a variety of filmstrips available, the social studies teacher must set up some criteria for selecting them. He must first decide what his subject matter is and then decide the purpose for showing the strip. Filmstrips can be used in a variety of methods—to introduce the unit, to illustrate some point, or to summarize or review the unit. Other criteria to consider in selecting filmstrips are; the logical organization of the material, good technical quality, accurate information, and adequate treatment of the subject. There are many sources from which filmstrips may be obtained. Companies that produce filmstrips have catalogs with listings. The *Educational Media Index* is a good source for finding filmstrips as are the magazines, *Educational Screen and Audio-Visual Guide.* Descriptions of free filmstrips are found in the *Educator's Guide to Free Filmstrips.*

Filmstrips are very useful in teaching social studies but they should never be just shown and forgotten. A filmstrip should be taught. Begin this by selecting the strip to meet the need; never use a strip just because it is available. The first step in teaching with filmstrips is to preview the filmstrip. This can be done by the teacher alone or with the aid of a few students. In the preview the teacher must make certain the subject is on, or can be adapted to, the unit. The teacher should also determine the main points and decide on questions for class discussion. Before showing the film the class should be prepared for it. There is no particular way to develop class readiness. One of the most common techniques is telling the students they are about to see a filmstrip and briefly describing it. More interest may be aroused by asking questions before showing it or by asking the students to evaluate the filmstrip.

The filmstrip is an effective teaching tool to be used when it is not necessary to portray motion in order to have the subject understood. In social studies it is not always necessary to show motion; in fact, it is often helpful to be able to stop and study individual frames in detail. This is important especially in history because it gives the students the opportunity to study the manner of life in the past—the clothes, architecture, equipment, and other details. Filmstrips are especially useful in geography because the facts and statistics of faraway places are presented in a more acceptable manner; thus, the students learn more because they are interested.   .

The slide projector

The slide projector produces much the same effect as the filmstrip. Slides are more difficult to handle because they are separate and easily disarranged. The chief advantage is that the teacher can make his own while visiting historical places. In teaching with slides you must aid the students in interpreting them because there are no captions describing the scene. Teachers must preview slides carefully to insure that they will be in correct order while showing them. Commercial slides are produced in sets which can be tailored to fit the teacher's needs by simply removing those not applicable. Elsie P. Heyl's booklet, *Where To Buy 2" X 2" Slides: A Subject Index,* is a good reference for purchasing commercial slides.

Free films are available to the schools from commercial concerns and governmental agencies. Many of the free, sponsored films are advertising or promoting something, therefore, the teacher must be certain that the material is pertinent to the class objectives before showing. There are many sources for ordering films. Catalogs put out by various groups, professional educational journals, and advertising literature put out by producers are examples. The *Educational Media Index, Educational Film Guide To Free Films,* and *A Directory of 16mm Film Libraries* are among the leading catalogs listing films.

Some criteria to remember in selecting social studies films are that the films used should be appropriate for the grade level of the students; they should be in logical order; they should have only a few significant objectives so all can be treated clearly; and they should be of good technical quality. History films should demonstrate change and show the development of civilization. Geography films should show relationship between man and his physical environment. Government films should show the duties of citizens, while economic films should explain the economic institutions of the world.

Teachers should preview the films and prepare the students for them. Students should be told what they are expected to learn from the film and should be tested on it. Learning is probably increased when there is no note taking required and by reshowing the film. One of the key points to remember in teaching with films is that learning is increased through discussion. The teacher should choose films that will encourage the students to think and want to learn more after seeing the film. The teacher must know why he is showing the film and should show the film when it will do the most good. It is important not to show several films consecutively. In fact, it is best to show only one film, preferably not over twenty minutes in length, during a class period. The actual projection of the film is one of the most important duties of the teacher. The projector should already be set up before the students arrive for class. Regardless of the quality of the film, it will not be an effective learning experience unless the projection equipment is run smoothly.

Students do learn from audio-visual aids if they are properly presented. Teachers must prepare themselves before using these materials in the classroom. Audio-visual aids have to be taught and not merely shown in order to provide adequate learning experiences for the students.

Use of globes, maps, graphs, and charts

There has never been a time in history when it was so important for a person to know as much as possible about the world in which he lives. He needs to know more about the general size and shape of the world and places in the world, more about relationships involved in getting to these places, and also more about the relations of this part of the world to other parts of the world. Naturally, the devices to which we turn in acquiring this knowledge are globes, maps, graphs, and charts.[17] [18] [19]

Globes

Only a globe can represent the earth's surface correctly with respect to size, shape, area, scale, distance, and direction. The fact that a globe is not capable of showing enough detail is its main limitation.

In geography the use of the globe is obvious. It is a valuable aid in teaching classes about wind systems, ocean currents, and the changing of the seasons. It is also valuable in showing the relation of grid systems, such as latitude and longitude. The globe is a good representation of the comparative size and shapes of continents and nations, of true routes between places, and of true distance and direction.

The use of the globe in the early years of school is basically for familiarization and preparation for application of concepts. It is in the junior and senior high school where the globe is actually used in various subjects. Unlike a map, graph, or chart, the globe is basically used in geography and history classes because it has relatively little application in classes concerned with the other social studies. The history of the area they are studying could have been affected by problems of communication or transportation such as waterways, mountains, deserts, or hostile intervening countries.

Maps

Maps are used to a greater degree than globes in the social studies curriculum. There are many types of maps, such as the physical relief map that is used to show physical characteristics of the earth's surface, the political map

17. R. Machlin, "The Use of Overlay Charts," *Arithmetic Teacher*, 8 (December, 1961) pp. 433-35.
18. "Maps" *The Instructor*, 39 (October 1960). pp. 90-1.
19. R. A. Mangive, "Map Thinking and Map Making," *The Instructor*, 72 (February, 1963), p. 128.

which is used to represent political units on the earth's surface known as countries, and climatic maps which are used to show the climate and temperature of various countries. Most social studies teachers regard the availability of maps as a necessity to effective teaching. Maps and product maps serve their purpose in directing students' attention to what various regions grow. Population, agriculture, minerals, fuels, and transportation routes may all be represent ed on maps for specific courses of study. There are many possible types and uses of maps that may be incorporated into the geography curriculum.

Maps are incorporated very well into the history curriculum. Historical maps have value in that they show change and development. Maps of the United States, for example, show exploration and settlement of different sections of the country. There are maps useful in teaching history that show the growth of new territories and states, westward expansion, and other historical changes. With an exceptionally creative teacher, maps can be one of the most fascinating and most interesting methods of teaching history. Certain eras and important situations can be made to come alive with some realistic thinking on the part of the teacher. The teacher needs to help students feel history to make it become realistic. Specific instances in American history that could be taught this way are boundary disputes, such as Florida, Maine, the Rio Grande, the Gadsden Purchase, and the "Fifty-four Forty or Fight" issues.

Whatever the subject, the map to be used for any particular presentation should be one that is designed to meet specific needs. The student should be able to go to a wall map and find places, measure distances, explain facts represented by symbols on the map, and understand the differences between such maps as the political, physical, and product maps. There should not be just one, but a variety of maps in every classroom in which social studies are taught. Wall maps, atlases for consultation, and maps in textbooks or for individual study should be provided in the classroom and like other aids must be kept updated and in good repair for maximum benefit.

Graphs

A graph is a picture which employs various symbols to represent data that are to be used for analysis or comparison. A graph is a means of breaking down cold statistics into a language that can be understood by the student. The student, when using a graph, needs a background of information to which the graphic information can be related and he must understand the symbols used and why certain ones represent specific things. Also, after developing the ability to read and understand graphs, the student must be able to compare the information and use this knowledge in relation to other course content.

There are several types of graphs used extensively. The first of these is the circle graph, sometimes called the "pie" graph. This is the most easily read of all graphs. The circle graph is useful in all the social studies as it can depict the percentage of each country's contribution of iron ore to the world total in geography courses, the percentage of men in the Civil War from each state in history courses, the percentage of votes each state contributed to the election of a President in government courses, or the population percentage of ethnic groups living in New York slums in sociology courses. Almost any type of information may be represented in a circle graph.

Another type of graph is the bar graph which has two or more single bars arranged for comparative purposes. The bar graph is very versatile and can be used in the same courses as a circle graph, but it is used more to compare totals than to show percentages.

The pictorial graph may be used in many of the ways the bar and line graphs may be used. They are not quite as exact as other graphs because there is a certain amount of estimation on quantity.

The area graph is used to a lesser degree because it is easily misinterpreted by using area or surface to show comparison. However, when used they are employed to show a relationship between two or three related totals.

Graphs are chosen for use because of specific qualifications concerning what is to be presented, but any graph used draws on the student's ability to think, compare, relate, and use the information to achieve desired results.

Charts

There are three basic types of charts: the "flow" chart, the "flip" chart, and the "tree" chart. The "flow" chart is referred to as organizational in that it can be used for showing the organization of almost anything. It is also used in all branches of the government to indicate to employees the relation of their specific office to the overall organization of the department.

The "flip" chart is actually a series of charts, usually mounted on an easel, in which a topic is presented sequentially. Each page of the chart is displayed as the material which it represents is explored, explained, and discussed. This chart is especially useful in any subject that has material that may be presented in a sequential manner, or step by step.

A "tree" chart is shown as a tree with branches and can be used for demonstrating relationship or development. It can be used for tracing the development of a company or an organization such as a political party with the branches showing the new parties. It can also be used to show the development of our government and the growth of its branches into the legislative, executive, and judicial branches. The "tree" chart is useful in almost any social studies course.

It should not be taken for granted that the students have any understanding of how to use these aids. There may not have been any previous experience on which they could have built such knowledge. Many students do not have the ability or capacity to understand using these aids without special explanation. It is the responsibility of the teacher when he uses these aids to insure that his students have an adequate understanding of maps, charts, etc. to benefit from his instruction.

Use of time lines

The purpose of the time line is to develop a concept of time as the students gain a sense of time. They learn to use and understand events in their time context. Here is an example on the use of the time line. In this method you use events in chronological, geographical, social, and political context.

The student, after being introduced to the use of time lines, derives more benefit from those which he himself devises and constructs. Time lines, parallel

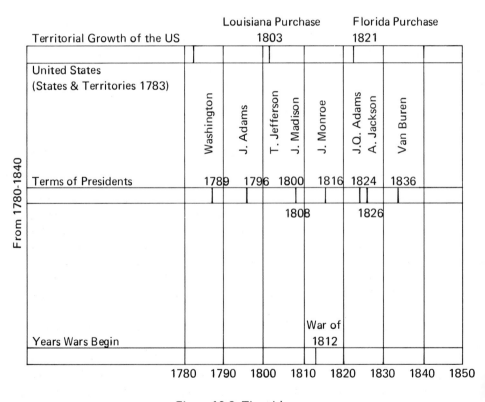

Figure 10-2. Time Line.

columns, biographical charts, and dynastic charts are all designed to promote a clearer appreciation of chronology. Such chronology may be employed as a tool in helping secondary students understand one of the basic ideas behind all history study, the relationship between stability and change. Whether one teaches chronologically or topically, the strands of certain central concepts run through all of history as continuous strands even though conditions may have changed between any two historical periods.

It is doubtful if a teacher should ever require a list of dates to be memorized. Dates to be learned should evolve from the materials rather than the materials from the dates. Yet, history without adequate chronology is meaningless. The teaching of dates should be directed toward the building of an inclusive idea of chronology rather than mere emphasis upon replicating specific dates, but it is well to remember that specific dates assist in the building of this general chronology. The following rules may be of help in teaching dates and chronology:

1. List related events in the order of their occurrence.
2. Ascertain approximate dates by reference to specific dates.
3. Give the length of time between two related or similar events.
4. Relate specific events to periods or general movements.
5. Associate the contemporary events that occur in different countries.
6. Compare the duration of two movements.
7. Place events by centuries, decades, or years.
8. Assign events for each of the years in a list.
9. Associate men and events and apply the dates for either to the other.

The social studies make constant use of the names of cities, countries, states, rivers, and people of note. Every teacher recognizes that it is idle to talk about St. Louis as a center for manufacturing shoes if the pupils have no idea where the city is; that the Battle of Tours can have only a vague meaning if the pupils have no idea where it occurred, or when, or who fought there; and that Iraq has no meaning until it exists somewhere. Consequently, great attention must be given to place as well as time. This involves frequent use of globes and maps, as well as constant inquiry, explanation, and drill.

Time and place are inextricably interwoven. The Indians sometimes referred to a journey as so many "sleeps." The proverbial fisherman refers to a period of time or a distance as so many "pipefuls." The very conception of "miles per hour" is a complex interweaving of time and distance. Each type of concept seems to support the other, and both seem to be fundamental to any clear understanding of the social studies. The teacher should have the

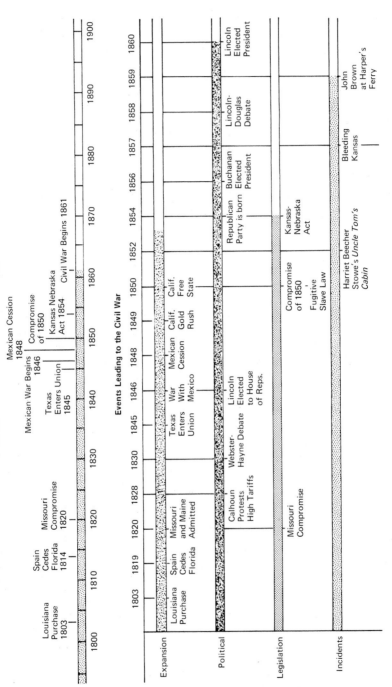

Figure 10.3.

pupils select a few important dates and place them on a time-line. This is a good outside assignment. In class the pupils can compare the dates they selected, which is a good learning experience for them.

Programmed Instruction and Other Related Media

It has often been observed that if education is to keep pace with a rapidly changing and expanding world, there must be major break-throughs in school education. Among the very important new tools being made available to teachers is *programmed instruction*. In programmed instruction, the concepts are presented to the student by means of specific sequentially placed statements called frames. The program, whether presented by a teaching machine or in book form, leads the student through a body of material in steps. The learner sees a frame, responds to it, and receives an indication of whether his response is right or wrong.

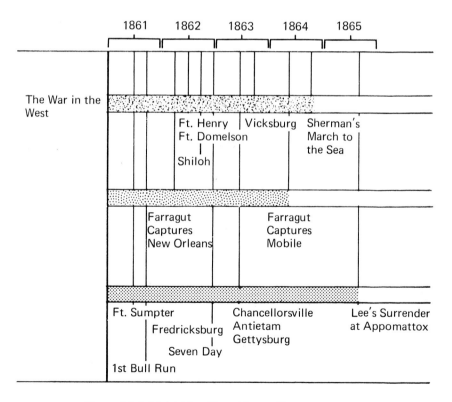

Figure 10.4. Multi-Line Time Line to Teach Relations.

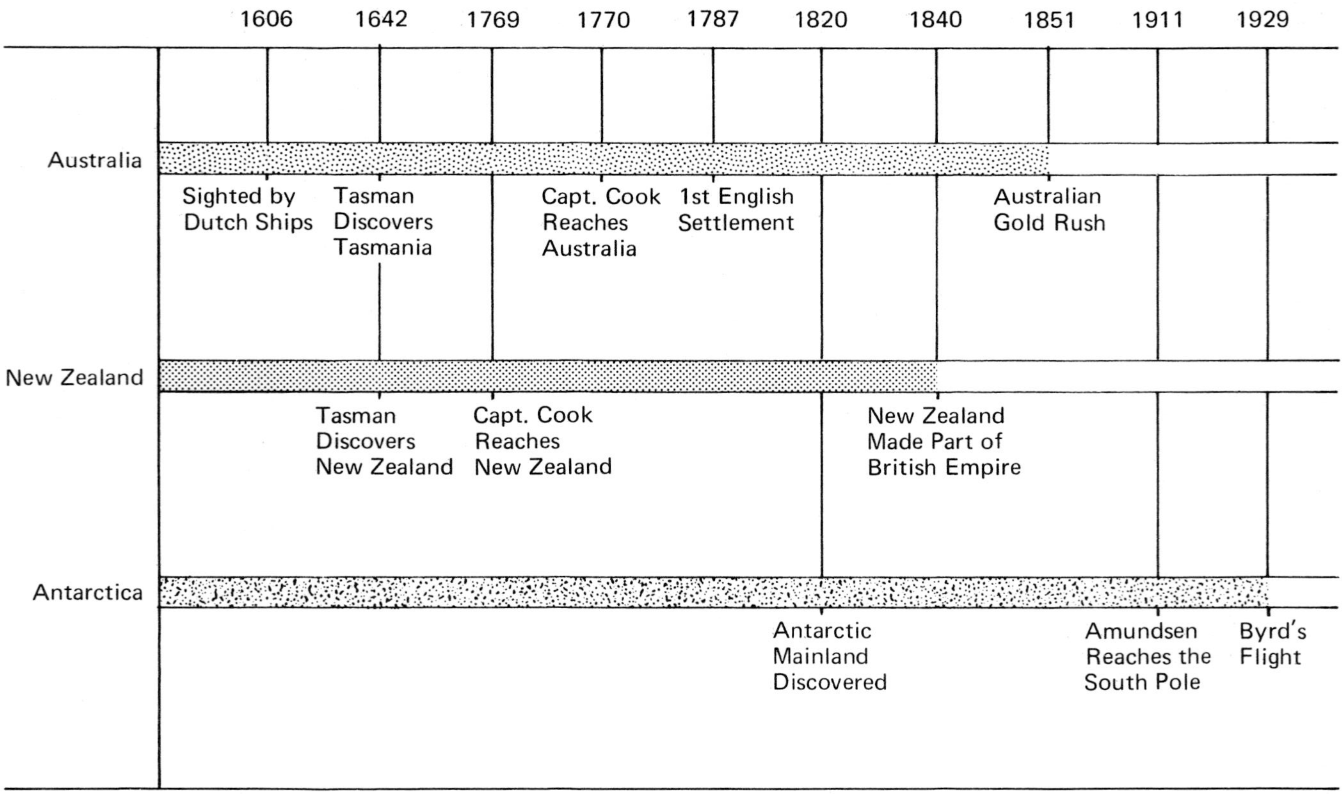

Figure 10.5. **Geography** (all work on the Time Lines should be done by the students).

Although the research shows little advantage of programmed over conventional instructional methods, there is a place for auto-instructional tools in the classroom. They save considerable amounts of teacher time, allowing the instructor more time to assist individual pupils. They are effective tools for remedial teaching. They cause the learner to be actively responding at all times, in contrast to the passive learning that often takes place in conventional situations.

Programmed instruction will never be able to replace enlightened, capable teachers, but it may be used as an effective supplement to teacher instruction. Programmed instruction can make it possible for a teacher to clarify less and stimulate more. More important, it enables teachers to meet the needs of the individual learner in both small group and tutorial situations. Programmed learning may be used to save substantial amounts of teacher time. Programmed learning supplemented by systematic teacher instruction can result in a significantly superior level of achievement.

Programmed instruction may be used effectively when a greater amount of teacher-pupil interaction is desired, such as in tutorial, study hall, or learning laboratory types of classroom situations. On the other hand, when the highest level of achievement is desired, programmed learning may be employed to supplement regular teacher instruction. In such cases, much teacher time may be saved because the programmed materials teach the student the fundamentals, thus allowing the teacher to add to what the pupil has already learned from the program. The teacher will then be able to help the student to enlarge on, relate to and use what he has learned, to help him to seek, to solve, and to state new problems, and to express himself more often in the form of intelligent, well-phrased questions as well as in thoughtful, well-composed answers.

Programmed instruction has implications for the teacher outside the classroom as well as in the classroom. The time saved by use of programmed instruction can be spent by the teacher in the selection of the best possible programs for his subject matter and for his particular students. Programmed instruction requires that the teacher know more than ever before, because one student in the class may be very advanced in the program, while other students may be progressing very slowly. Therefore, in order to answer questions from both types of students, the instructor must know, not only the fundamentals, but the entire scope of his subject matter.

The aspect of pupil growth in which programmed instruction makes its most important contribution is in the intellectual realm. There is some evidence, in the area of cognitive growth, which suggests that programmed instruction may help students to learn to ask questions and to solve problems more effectively. However, most authorities believe that programmed instruction is, by its very nature, limited to material in which there are right and wrong answers. Structured information, concepts, and identification of key elements are all of such a nature, that they can be put into programs calling for a series of "correct" responses. Much school learning is of this kind, but some of it is not. Programmed instruction can teach factual background, but beyond this, where intelligent opinion can differ, it can only help identify the alternatives. It cannot ask any questions to which several original answers are equally correct. Therefore, the teacher may use programmed methods to develop a background of information in his students, but in order to develop their analytical and integrative skills, he must use some other method.

There are a number of questions which have been posed concerning programmed instruction. One such question involves the mode of presentation. A program may be presented by a machine or in book form. Pupils using programmed texts complete work in less time than do those using machines. When time is an important factor, the instructor may use the programmed text approach.

Programming as a remedial method

The research reviewed shows that programmed instruction holds promise as a remedial supplementary teaching technique with some students having a history of repeated failure in academic subjects. Students of limited ability need supervision when using programmed instruction. Low achievers of limited ability generally are not sufficiently motivated to use programmed materials on an independent basis—programmed materials do not in themselves provide sufficient motivation.

This has great implications for the teacher. He may use programmed instruction to correct skill weaknesses in students. If they may go back and learn concepts they failed to learn previously, students will be able to more successfully learn what is being presented presently in the course. The teacher must carefully supervise this remedial work, making sure that the student is doing the program correctly and stimulating the student to want to learn.

Use of programmed materials in social studies

The disciplines of science and mathematics have been involved in the programmed instruction movement for over ten years. The social studies educators have not had much enthusiasm for the movement. In fact, some social studies educators have been among the critics of automating education. There have been only a few programs provided for use in the social studies. The National Council of Social Studies reports a lack of sufficient information about the use of programmed materials in social studies teaching.

Educators have claimed several reasons for the limited use of programs in social studies. Some of the reasons are included in this paragraph. The social studies content and purposes are not adaptable to programming. The processes of problem-solving, critical thinking, controversy, and imagination are not used effectively in present programs. The real reason social studies programs are not used deals with the teachers. The teachers do not have a knowledge of the concepts and principles of psychology used in programming.[20]

There are many ways of teaching history or political science, there are innumerable variations in the meaning of terms, and the programmer has no standard authority to which he can turn. Most of the social sciences are not limited to empirical observation, though they make use of it; in fact, it can be argued that nearly every important assertion in political science is a subjective and normative judgment. The field covered by each of the social sciences is not precisely defined. It is not always possible to state where politics ends and economics or sociology begins. The relationship between propositions in the social sciences, hedged in as they are by normative conclusions, cannot be described logically in all cases. Finally the social sciences are not always open to systematic division into small component units which can then be reassembled like building blocks. This combination of characteristics poses a serious problem for the programmer; he must seek authoritative assistance in defining the area to be covered, the meaning of terms within the respective disciplines, and the best means of approaching the subject matter, and these points are open to violent controversy among social scientists themselves.[21]

A program should be planned according to the student's background and level of preparation. According to the reinforcement learning theory, the most effective learning takes place when the student makes a correct response and this response is immediately reinforced. The object, then, in writing every frame in the program is to lead the student to make a specific response that can be promptly reinforced.

Computer assisted instruction in social studies

Proponents of computer-assisted or programmed instruction in social studies claim four advantages. These advantages are listed below:

1. Possibility of providing completely individualized instruction according to the individual's needs and responses.

2. Useful as a stimulating and gaming model.

20. Albert G. Gleep, "Programmed Instruction in Social Studies," *Education,* LXXVIII (November-December, 1967), p. 119.
21. Edward B. Fry, *Teaching Machines and Programmed Instruction* (New York: McGraw-Hill Book Company, Inc., 1963).

3.   Allows the teacher, if claims are true, to rise to higher levels of intellectual and creative endeavor. The teacher may be relieved of much of the volume of routine work.

4.   Diagnostic in nature, plus student involvement, reinforcement, immediate confirmation of response.[22]

Critics of this technique are alarmed by the programmer's attempt to transform teaching from a subtle art into a precise science. They warn that the technique contains a number of serious defects. These critics say that programmed instruction discourages critical thinking. The critics say that programmed instruction fosters only rote learning and memorizing of facts; and prevents the student from exploring a discipline on his own, thus discovering basic principles. The critics believe that programmed instruction is a joyless and uninspiring way to learn because they believe it is both mechanical and monotonous.[23]

Some opponents of computer-assisted or programmed instruction in social studies claim that there are several limitations to programming. Some of these limitations are listed below:

1.   The functions which the computer is best suited to handle in education are not yet defined.

2.   Few instructional programs at the present time have been "engineered" through a series of empirical trials and revisions.

3.   There are likely to be deleterious social and emotional effects from this type of instruction on students, especially young children.

4.   The present lock-step system of education makes use of CAI or programming difficult.

A multitude of practical problems must be solved if computers or programs are to have widespread use in educational situations. If these problems can be solved, and if the full potentials of high-speed data processing can be realized throughout the educational situations, we may expect some of the greatest, and perhaps most significant, changes seen in education for hundreds of years.

22. William E. Schall, "Automation in Social Studies Education: Highlighting Computer Assisted Instruction," *Peabody Journal of Education,* XLV (November, 1967), pp. 162-68.
23. Alferd de Grazia and David A. Sohn, Eds. *Revolution in Teaching* (New York: Bantam Books, 1964).

Leonard W. Ingraham suggested two areas of computer application that are seen for possible use with social studies. One of these areas would be learning history and the social sciences by discovery or inquiry. In this method, a dialogue system would permit the student to conduct a genuine dialogue with the computer. The second area as seen for computer application uses simulation. Simulation refers to an artificial representation of situations that occur in the real world. In computer simulating, the student is presented with information about some problem situation. Simulation is usually used for the purpose of analysis and learning. The proponents of programmed instruction tell us that permanent learning of factual material is facilitated when the learner wants to acquire, retain, and use the facts. The facts are organized into appropriate learning units; the learner makes correct responses on the first try; correct responses are reinforced and errors are corrected immediately. Distributed practice is carried out until the facts are firmly established, and each individual proceeds at a rate appropriate for him.

The social studies teacher should know the following things about the computer and computer-assisted instruction to use it more effectively. The teacher should first understand that the computer operates only according to detailed instruction (input) written by a human programmer. The teacher should realize the student is located at some kind of a console or station, which is connected to the computer by telephone wire or coaxial cable. The student will have before him a television screen, a light-pen, a typewriter keyboard, or possibly earphones and a microphone, and he is required to respond to messages received through these media. The majority of the teachers do not know enough about computer-assisted programming to use it effectively. Therefore, their lack of knowledge is a limitation of the use of programming, simulation, or CAI.[24]

Many educators are concerned with the effects on students of continuous exposure to programmed materials over a relatively lengthy period of time. Classes using programmed instructional materials to replace the textbook were compared to conventionally taught classes in a one semester American government course. The following conclusions were drawn from the study.[25]

1.   The instructional material used in this study was found to be an effective teaching device.

2.   The programmed material in this study was found to be more efficient than conventional instruction in total time involved.

3.   Enthusiasm for the program, very high in the initial phases, was reduced significantly over a full semester.

24. Schall, op. cit.
25. Kenneth A. Otting, "Programmed Material Versus the Textbook: A Comparison of Effectiveness and Efficiency and Motivational Aspects in a Twelfth Grade American Government Course," *Dissertation Abstracts.* XXV (March, 1965), pp. 5157-5159.

4.   Dissatisfaction with the experiment was strongly related to the limitation
     on group work and discussion.

5.   The more able students show a more favorable attitude toward experience
     with and possible further use of this program in American government.

Information Sources For Selection of Media

Textbooks:
Literary Bulletin
American Educational Catalog
Textbooks in Print
Standard Catalog for High School Libraries

Reference, reading books, and periodicals:
Guide to Reference Books, Winchell
A. L. A. Subscription Book Bulletin
Basic Reference Sources
Standard Catalog for High School Libraries
Recommended Library Books for Schools
Booklist
New York Herald-Tribune
Librarian's Guide to Periodicals   Faxon
Periodical HandBook   Mayfair
Periodicals Directory   Ulrich
Reader's Guide to Periodical Literature
U. S. Government Publications
Manual of Government Publications   U. S. and Foreign
How to Locate Government Publications

Radio:
Listener's Guide   Columbia Broadcasting Co.
Scholastic Teacher
Educator's Guide to Free Tapes, Scripts, Transcriptions

Records and tapes:
Educational Screen
Audio-Visual Instruction
Audio Guide

Library Journal
Educational Record Catalog   RCA
Dealer's Catalogs

Pictures:

Encyclopedias
Textbook Companies
Pageant of American History
Educational Index
Magazines
The Picture File   Norma Olin Irelands
Pamphlet File

Posters:

National Safety Council
National Association of Manufacturers

T.V.

Educational T.V. and Radio Center, Ford Foundation
Stations National and Local
Educational Screen

The reader will find more complete sources of various kinds of social studies materials and some applications of them to teaching situations in the several units and courses of study in the appendix. The authors did not include more exhaustive lists of source materials because such lists are in the units and because the need determines the selection and use of materials and audio visuals.

PROBLEMS AND QUESTIONS FOR STUDY OR DISCUSSION

1. What should determine the selection of social studies materials?

2. Decide upon the criteria you will use to screen each type of social studies material such as: library books, textbooks, maps, charts, graphs, transparencies, bulletin board displays, films, video taped materials, and presentations by resource persons. Write your criteria into a four or five page guideline that can become a part of your regular planning materials.

3. How can you effectively use textbooks in your classroom without slavishly permitting the writer to dictate your every plan and action?

4. Start a cardboard box file collection of magazine articles, pictures, news stories, editorials, and other materials which you may need for resource material at some future time.

5. Make a set of transparencies and outline maps to accompany your unit.

6. Make a time line to go with the teaching unit you prepared for Chapter Six.

7. Video tape several sequences of lessons and critique them so that you can work on correcting problems in presenting material or using it to best advantage.

8. Devise a means of having each of your students develop and make some useful social studies teaching material.

9. Make a list of fifty to one hundred paperback books which you think might make the beginning of a classroom library for social studies.

10. Make a history test using maps as the means of testing.

11. With the help of your librarian, department head, supervising teacher, or media person, make a list of suitable reading material for both fast and slow learners in your classroom. This is especially difficult, since by the eleventh grade the reading level in a heterogeneously grouped social studies class may range from third grade to the third year of college.

12. Work out a proposal to select out of class projects and materials cooperatively with the science and English departments.

13. Why do so many social studies teachers rely upon textbooks as their courses of study, their teaching units, and their only lesson planning?

14. Evaluate the practice of having each student read a paragraph from the textbook to the class in a sort of round robin pooling of oral reading abilities. Do you think such practices are likely to stimulate students to inquire, and to think?

15. Examine the workbooks in use at your school, if any are, and the teacher's manual for the textbook you use and try to think of better means of utilizing them to promote student learning.

16. Use the model for teacher planning shown in this chapter to help you select the material for a unit. Use one of the teaching units in the appendix and see if you can improve on the selection of material to facilitate the stated behavioral objectives.

17. Acquire one of the commercially prepared guides to sources of free and inexpensive teaching materials. Then write several of the sources for some of these materials, evaluate these materials for lack of bias, general format, teachability, and reading level.

18. Work out a plan to have a class of slower to average students make their own social studies book from mail order catalogs, automobile technical manuals, instructions from the government, newspaper want ads, and other common and easy to acquire materials.

19. Select a set of films, filmstrips, transparencies, and maps to accompany a teaching unit.

20. Make certain you can operate all the common audio visual teaching devices such as: film projectors, filmstrip projectors, opaque projectors, tape recorders, video-tapeing devices, cameras, and machines used to reproduce materials.

21. Write the local school supply firms in your area and ask for a copy of their latest catalog.

22. Get the latest film rental catalog from your nearest and most appropriate agency.

23. Acquire a programmed social studies book or other type of material and try it with a few students.

24. Decide what you are going to do about teaching some remedial reading to those students who have reading problems, and acquire some materials to teach them from.

REFERENCES

Bachman, John W. *How to Use Audio-Visual Materials.* New York: Association Press. 1959.

Bragdon, Henry Wilkinson. "Dilemmas of a Textbook Writer." *Social Education.* Vol. XXXIII (March, 1969).

Brouwer, G. A., "Helping Teachers Use Audio-Visual Materials." *The National Elementary School Principal.* Vol. 40 (January, 1961).

Brown, James W., Lewis, Richard B., and Harcleroad, Fred F. *A-V Instruction: Materials and Methods.* New York: McGraw-Hill Book Company, Inc., 1964.

Bulter, Frank A. *The Improvement of Teaching in Secondary Schools.* Chicago: The University of Chicago Press, 1948.

Chabe, Alexander M. "Evaluating Social Studies Textbooks." *Education.* Vol. LXXXVI (January, 1966).

Charters, W. W. *Methods of Teaching.* Chicago: Row, Peterson, and Company, 1912.

Dale, Edgar. *Audiovisual Methods in Teaching.* New York: The Dryden Press, 1969.

de Bernardis, Amo. *The Use of Instructional Materials.* New York: Appleton-Century-Crofts, Inc., 1960.

de Kieffer, R. E., and Cochran, Lee W. *Manual of Audio-Visual Techniques.* Englewood Cliffs, N. J.: Prentice-Hall, Inc., 1962.

Deterline, William A. *An Introduction to Programmed Instruction.* Englewood Cliffs, New Jersey: Prentice-Hall, Inc., 1962.

Edgerton, Ronald B. "Odyssey of a Book." *Social Education.* Vol. XXXIII (March, 1969).

Freedman, Florence B., and Berg, Esther L. *Classroom Teachers Guide to Audio-Visual Material.* Philadelphia: Chilton Books, 1967.

French, Henry Pierson, Jr. "A Study of Difference in Students' Learning of Chinese and Japanese Culture Concepts Using Lecture and Intrinsically Programmed Methods." *Dissertation Abstracts.* Vol. XXIX (December, 1968).

Friedman, Kopple C. *How to Develop Time and Chronological Concepts.* Washington, D. C.: NESS, 1964.

Fry, Edward B. *Teaching Machines and Programmed Instruction.* New York: McGraw-Hill Book Company, Inc., 1963.

Garner, W. Lee. *Programmed Instruction.* New York: The Center for Applied Research in Education, Inc., 1966.

Gleep, Albert G. "Programmed Instruction in Social Studies." *Education.* Vol. LXXVIII (November-December, 1967).

Grazia, Alferd de, and Sohn, David A., eds. *Revolution in Teaching.* New York: Bantam Books, 1964.

Griffin, Paul F. "The Importance of Media in Geography." *Social Education.* (November, 1967).

Haas, Kenneth B., and Packer, Harry Q., *Preparation and Use of Audio Visual Aids.* New York: Prentice-Hall, Inc., 1950.

Hall-Quest, Alfred Lawrence. *The Textbook.* New York: MacMillan Company, 1918.

Hendershot, Carl H. *Programmed Learning: A Bibliography of Programs and Presentations Devices.* Saginaw, Michigan: Scher Printing Co., 1964.

Hodes, E. W., "How Audio-Visual Aids Make Teaching and Learning Easier," *Educational Screen and Audio-Visual Guide.* Vol. 39 (December, 1960).

Hughes, John L. *Programmed Instruction for Schools and Industry.* Chicago: Science Research Associates, Inc., Publishers, 1962.

Kinder, James S. *Audio-Visual Materials and Techniques.* New York: American Book Company, 1959.

Lambert, Philip, ed. *The Teacher and The Machine.* Madison, Wisconsin' Dembar Educational Research Services, Inc., 1962.

Machlin, R. "The Use of Overlay Charts." *Arithmetic Teacher.* Vol. 8 (December, 1961).

Mangine, R. A. "Map Thinking and Map Making." *The Instructor.* Vol. 72 (February, 1963).

"Maps." *The Instructor.* Vol. 70 (October, 1960).

Martorella, Peter H. "Carl L. Becker and Secondary Social Studies." *Social Studies.* Vol. LVIII (October, 1967).

Moore, Jerry R. "An Experiment in Programmed Instruction: Voting in Iowa Ninth Grade Civics." *Dissertation Abstracts.* Vol. XXV (March, 1965).

Moore, Virginia D. "Guidelines for the New Social Studies." *Instructor.* Vol. LXXIX (February, 1970).

Muessig, Raymond H. "Bridging the Gap Between Textbook Teaching and Unit Teaching." *Social Studies.* Vol. LIV (February, 1963).

Nietz, John A. *Old Textbooks.* Pittsburgh: University of Pittsburgh Press, 1961.

Popham, W. James. *Systematic Instruction.* New Jersey: Prentice-Hall, Inc., 1970.

Rogers, Vincent R. "Social Studies Minus Textbooks." *Instructor.* Vol. LXXIX (February, 1970).

Rose, Homer C. *The Instructor and His Job.* U S of A.: American Technical Society, 1961.

Schall, William E. "Automation in Social Studies Education: Highlighting Computer-assisted Instruction." *Peabody Journal of Education.* Vol. 45 (November, 1967).

Schute, D., "An AV Try for Better Public Relations." *Educational Screen and Audio-Visual Guide.* (February, 1960).

Shores, Louis. *Instructional Materials.* New York: The Ronald Press Company, 1960.

Tali, Ronald Harry. "The Use of Programmed Materials for Teaching in the Social Studies." *Dissertation Abstracts.* Vol. XXVIII (November-December, 1967).

Trow, William Clark. *Teacher and Technology.* New York: Appleton-Century-Crofts, 1963.

Wesley, Edgar B., and Wronski, Stanley P. *Teaching Social Studies in High Schools.* Boston: D. C. Heath and Company, 1966.

Wesley, Edgar B. and Wronski, Stanley P. *Teaching Social Studies in High Schools.* Boston: D. C. Heath and Co., 1964.

Wiles, Kimball. *Teaching for Better Schools.* Englewood Cliffs, New Jersey: Prentice-Hall Inc., 1959.

Wittich, Walter Arno, and Schuller, Charles Francis. *Audio-Visual Materials: Their Nature and Use.* New York: Harper and Row Publishers, 1967.

Yoakam, Gerald A. *Modern Methods and Techniques of Teaching.* New York: MacMillan Company, 1948.

Chapter XI

DUTIES OF TEACHERS NOT DIRECTLY RELATED TO CLASSROOM INSTRUCTION

The curriculum of any school includes all organized and planned experiences and activities for students at school. The teacher is the principal executor of all these planned experiences, since it is the teacher who determines the *curriculum had.* Because of his central position as chief decision maker about the actual curriculum which students *have,* the teacher must provide leadership in many areas not directly associated with teaching his classes; he sponsors clubs, maintains discipline and control, sponsors student council, sells tickets, coaches plays, goes to faculty meetings and PTA, attends ball games, keeps records, has bus duty, has playground duty, and in many communities is still expected to teach Sunday School and sing in the church choir. In short he is a leader, a model, and an exemplar, if he is a good teacher. Teacher competency is measured by effectiveness of instructional planning and teaching and also by the teacher's effectiveness in handling the many non-instructional tasks with which he is confronted, and justifiably so. Teachers are models for students, whether they wish to be or not.

Classroom Management

Duane Brown asserted that discipline is the sum of those activities not devoted to presenting subject matter.[1] Discipline, he wrote, is all the teacher's efforts to influence student behavior not directly connected with classroom teaching. Both discipline and instruction are designated to help prepare the student to live happily and successfully in his society as an adult. The discipli-

---

1. Duane Brown, *Changing Student Behavior: A New Approach To Discipline* (Dubuque, Iowa: Wm. C. Brown, Company Pub., 1971).

Students develop good citizenship habits by participating in student government.

Photo furnished courtesy of Elmore County Public School, Wetumpka, Alabama.

Social studies teachers usually serve as faculty advisors to the student council.

Photo furnished courtesy of Elmore County Public School, Wetumpka, Alabama.

nary process, of which classroom management is a part, is thus scarcely distinguishable from the instructional process. Both are meant to effect predetermined behavioral changes; both are means of shaping students. Generally the good teacher is also the good classroom manager and disciplinarian, though not necessarily the teacher who maintains the quietest classroom in the building. The teacher's own behavior in class, on the campus, off campus and everywhere is an important part of the disciplinary process. Most undisciplined teachers make poor classroom managers. Teachers who do sloppy work encourage sloppy work in their students. Teachers who are emotionally unstable often have emotionally upset pupils. Teachers who are poor scholars themselves, usually beget poor scholarship in their students, teachers with poor mental health have great difficulty in maintaining enough control to teach.

The authors postulated in chapter one that:

1. Learning of attitudes and human relations is affected by teacher-pupil interaction.

2. Teacher behavior affects what students learn, no matter what the teacher may have planned or hoped.

3. Social studies teachers want their students to grow in mental health, emotional control, self adequacy and self trust, moral commitment, democratic participation, concern for others, and leadership.

4. Effective working groups are prerequisites for developing group goals and providing effective instruction.

5. Leadership in classroom situations is transactional in nature.

6. The United States is a pluralistic society, therefore teachers should value divergent opinion and conduct.

7. The fundamental moral principle of free societies is the worth of each person. Thus we should help each student achieve his potentials.

8. Effective instruction in a free society demands that each student learn how to make his own effective choices, which is the only way he can be free.

9. A main purpose of all education in a free society is to teach pupils how to govern themselves.

10. The purpose of social studies is to teach people how to be better, more effective, more fruitful citizens who are contributing to their own happiness and to that of their neighbors, while maintaining and extending freedom for all.

Taken collectively these assumptions are a cogent argument for effective classroom management as part of teaching students self discipline. As we stated in chapter one, a teacher's personal views of human nature, the nature of learning, and the purpose of schooling influences his every action toward students.

The word discipline sometimes connotes correction and training by punishment. But, whether one uses the term discipline or classroom management, successful instruction is dependent upon its maintenance. Good classroom management does not just happen, it is a function of organization. It is the result of a systematic and regular procedure established to accomplish the goals or purposes of the class. Effective classroom control must always recognize the inherent dignity and rights of every human being.[2]

Misbehavior is learned, and it is caused, just as is productive or socially approved behavior. Any attempt to control or improve the behavior of students in the classroom or elsewhere while at school must, therefore, involve a basic understanding of how people learn and why they behave as they do in given situations. The development of new behavior patterns is generally the result of the student's rearrangement of his phenomenological field, and integration of new behavior patterns into his experiences as appropriate (for him) substitutes for the way he previously behaved. Use of classroom management procedures in effective ways is dependent on careful selection of behavioral objectives, choice of teacher actions, student learning activities, and something different to learn just as effective instruction is dependent on the same steps in careful, thoughtful planning.

The teacher who is effective in improving the behavior (discipline) of his students is the teacher who is successful in transferring control of student actions from the external (fencing in approach) to the internalized (self-actualizing, adequate, self controlled) approach to control of personal actions sublimation of immediate personal needs to other, less immediate, less personal needs. Students have learned to misbehave either because they have had little chance to learn appropriate public behavior, or because maladaptive behavior

2. E. J. Brown and A. T. Phelps, *Managing The Classroom* (New York: The Ronald Press, 1961).

has gotten them desired attention or rewards in their past experiences in similar situations.[3]

Successful teacher attempts to prevent disruption of their classes, or to prevent other undesirable behavior that may interfere with students to learn are dependent on understanding what makes the student behave as he does, understanding how students learn behavior patterns, and unlearn them, and understanding of rewards and punishment systems in student terms. Duane Brown developed a rationale for this in the nine brief principles which follow:[4]

1. Reward and punishment have meaning only in individual terms. One students reward may be another's punishment. Teacher action in giving either must be based on the individual student's reaction to it. This is the analogy of throwing Brer Rabbit into the briar patch!

2. Each teacher has an undetermined ability to influence any given student's behavior either positively or negatively. Any action the teacher takes vis-a-vis particular student will alter the teachers value as a behavior reinforcing agent for each student in his class.

3. Students have taken a long time to learn to behave as they do, thus it takes a long time to alter their behavior much, in a very lasting way. A student may not behave in absolutely predictable ways each time he faces a similar situation.

4. The teacher is only one among many people who influence a student to behave as he does; and the teacher may not even be a significant other for some of his students.

5. If a student is not rewarded and reinforced for adaptive (improved) behavior, maladaptive (misbehavior) may be reinforced and may dominate his conduct.

6. Reward is the most effective device for improving behavior; punishment is basically ineffective as a means of promoting more socially approved behavior. Therefore the classroom teacher should be careful to use punishment only to repress undesirable behavior, not as a way of teaching.

7. Teacher labeling of behavior as good or bad does not make it so for the student. Sometimes teacher labeled bad behavior is socially approved by the peer group.

8. Each student is physically and biologically different, and each student has learned to behave as he does; yet any student responds to the principles set forth here in predictable ways, just as students respond predictably to good teaching.

9. There are a number of relatively simple techniques which most teachers

3. Brown, op. cit.
4. Ibid.

can master and use effectively in controlling the classroom behavior of their students.[5]

The teacher is the most important person in the area of classroom management. It is the teacher who ultimately determines which rules and routines will be established. Excessive rules and routines can be deadly, but a complete lack of rules and routines can be equally devastating. The teacher should establish classroom procedures as early in the school year as possible. This communicates to the class that the teacher knows his job and that he is doing it effectively.

The following list suggests techniques that teachers have found helpful in maintaining successful classroom management.

1. Regulations guiding classroom discussions and activities should be clearly understood by everyone.
2. The environment in which pupils learn should not offend the aesthetic sense. The room is important to learning. It should be neat, orderly, and physically comfortable.
3. All assignments should be specific, achievable, and purposeful.
4. Shouting and threatening as a method of student control should be discouraged. These may work the first time, but are rarely successful for regular usage.
5. An earnest effort should be made to learn the students' names as quickly as possible.
6. Start the class immediately and continue the class until the final bell rings. There has been much research which indicates that most discipline problems begin during the first five minutes of class.

It is important to realize that good discipline does not just happen. There is a great deal of careful planning, sound organization of procedures, and diligent daily application of routines and techniques.

Every teacher has the problems of establishing rules and regulations, as well as school board regulations, and rules made by the administration. Sometimes teachers may think that a rule or regulation is foolish, unenforceable, or actually illegal; however any attempt of the teacher to be selective about which rules to enforce can be, and usually is, deadly to his own efforts to maintain classroom control. Some teachers cause themselves, administrators, and worst of all, students untold problems and misery by their selective application of school dress and conduct regulations. Many administrators view such teacher behavior as undermining the school discipline, and such ambivalent conduct usually does not really endear the teacher to his colleagues or his students. Problems inevitably arise about

5. Ibid.

TABLE 1
Some Specific Goals of Education[6]

Goals Skills, Habits, and Attitudes	How Measured	Means of Attainment
1. For each individual to establish and maintain human relationships	1. Sociometric status 2. Teacher observation	1. Discipline 2. Didactic instruction 3. Counseling
2. Decision-making ability	1. Observation of class responses 2. Appropriateness of educ. and voc. decisions 3. Risk taking in decision-making	1. Instruction 2. Counseling 3. Discipline
3. Completing tasks	1. Observation	1. Instruction 2. Discipline
4. Listening	1. Observation	1. Instruction 2. Discipline
5. Punctuality	1. Observation	1. Instruction 2. Discipline
6. Ability to work cooperatively in groups	1. Observation	1. Instruction 2. Discipline
7. Neatness (personal and in work)	1. Observation	1. Instruction 2. Discipline
8. Acquisition of knowledge that is applicable in work and leisure time activities	1. Teacher made and standardized tests 2. Observation	1. Instruction 2. Discipline

6. Ibid.

how to make rules, how to enforce them, whether they are reasonable or not, and whether a specific rule is socially useful. The two tables which follow indicate some approaches to rule setting that teachers may find helpful. One of the best rules that any teacher can establish for improving the behavior of his students is actually a behavioral rule for teacher conduct, *do not make a rule unless it is absolutely necessary,* and its corrolary is, *do not make a rule you cannot or will not enforce.* A few simple guidelines for administering punishment follow:

1. Punishment should be immediate, and it should fit the infraction.
2. Be fair, do not engage in scapegoating, and above all do not deliver any ultimatums.
3. Withhold judgment until all the facts are obtained.
4. There is no purpose in punishment unless it will improve the behavior of the wrongdoer and prevent recurrence of the infraction.
5. Punishment should always be tempered to the culprit, and should always reflect the needs of the class.
6. Never punish the class for what one person did.

Teach well, have something planned for students to do, arrive on time, begin immediately, and make the lesson interesting and you will have little need for punishment or rules of conduct. Require that all lessons be well done, turned in on time, make certain that all students know what they are to do, how they are to do it, and the purpose of doing it and there will be a more effective learning climate which is what discipline is about anyway. Interesting, well planned, well taught lessons presented by teachers who love their students and their subject is the best disciplinary and classroom management program we have ever seen in operation. The tables reproduced below depict some relations to teaching democratic processes, thus they show the interrelation of instruction and discipline.

Teachers Role in Guidance and Counseling

Guidance is a term that is misused and misunderstood by many people in education. The following five-point definition of guidance by Ira J. Gordon appears to be quite functional for the classroom teacher.

Guidance is the organization of information by the school about the child and his community for the purpose of helping the child learn to make wise decisions concerning his own future. Guidance is the organization of life experiences within the school situation so that the child is provided with

7. Ibid.

TABLE 2
Behavior of Students and Teachers
Two Approaches to Rule Setting[8]

The Process	Teacher Behavior			
	Democratic	Autocratic	Democratic	Autocratic
Extablishing that a problem exists	1. Participates with students 2. Makes suggestions 3. Clarifies 4. Helps state problems	1. Explains problem to students 2. Clarifies 3. States problem	1. Participates in problem definition 2. Makes suggestions 3. Clarifies 4. Helps state problems	1. Passive. He is acted upon
Rule setting	1. Considers alternatives with the group 2. Suggests possibilities 3. Clarifies outcomes or consequences of rules for group 4. Helps to state final rule	1. Considers alternatives alone 2. Sets rule	1. Considers alternative solution 2. Suggests possibilities 4. Helps to state final rule	1. Passive. No behavior required
	1. An active agent in enforcement—may carry out procedures	1. An active agent in Enforcement—may carry out procedures	1. Assists in the enforcement process by exerting peer pressure 2. Self-enforcement as a result of participation	1. Some reaction 2. Some peer pressure to gain teacher's favor

8. Ibid.

TABLE 3
Teacher's Behavior in Enforcement of Rule Outcomes [9]

Behavior	Democratically Developed	Autocratically Imposed
1. Communication of rules	1. Easy to communicate. Students understand readily because of involvement.	1. May be difficult to communicate. Students want to know reasons. Teacher may be unable to explain adequately.
2. Enlisting support for enforcing rules	1. Students are involved by teacher. Peer pressure can be utilized.	1. Students may be resistive to involvement. Some may be openly defiant. Students may cooperate to gain favors.
3. Recognizing rules, infraction	1. Students know that they have broken rule. Other students may support the teacher.	1. Students may not realize that rule was broken or may use this as an alibi. Defiance or rationalization.
4. Punishment	1. Students involved. Teacher may actually have to reduce punishment. 2. Students realize that peer groups do not approve of behavior.	1. Students more likely to resent teacher. 2. Loss of relationship with group.

situations in which he feels completely accepted, in which he is enabled to "take stock" of his potentialities, accept his limitations without threat, and develop a realistic picture of himself and the world around him. Guidance is the provision for satisfactory group experiences in which successful leadership and membership roles are learned and in which the group is able to set goals and solve problems dealing with inter-personal relations. Guidance is the provision of opportunities for the child to understand and value his uniqueness and his relatedness to others. Guidance is the provisions of the above experiences and opportunities for all children.[10]

9. Ibid.
10. Ira J. Gordon, *The Teacher as a Guidance Worker: Human Development Concepts and Their Application in the Classroom* (New York: Harper & Brothers Publishers, 1956), pp. 3-5.

Gordon's definition simply states in writing the responsibilities that good teachers have always accepted. Because of his direct and daily contact with the student, no other person in the school organization has the opportunity to perform the guidance function as readily and effectively as the classroom teacher. It is indeed rare when a student will not identify closely with at least one of his scheduled teachers.

There are definite and recognizable problems of adjustment as the student enters secondary school. He must adjust to more complex organization and curriculum patterns. The student, often for the first time, may be running into real academic competition and pressure. The teacher finds himself in the best position not only to recognize, but also to analyze and help the student to solve these problems.

The teacher is not a therapist and should always be conscious of it. He does have restrictions in counseling situations, but only he can really decide where these restrictions stop and begin. The teacher who is interested in his students as individuals and has their welfare in mind cannot help being a counselor. He will automatically find himself pointing out alternatives to students who come to him with decisions to make. The objective, self-confident teacher will avoid the mistakes of passing judgment and attempting to impose his own value system on the students. The teacher's role in guidance and counseling is active interaction with his students and as a referral agent for more serious problems.

Relationship with Principal and Superintendent

The teacher should clearly recognize his responsibilities to and relationship with his principal and superintendent. These relationships not only affect the teacher's own professional status, but may also affect the learning of the students.

The relationship between the teacher and superintendent should be indirect. The teacher should be in professional communication with the superintendent through the principal. Because the superintendent is responsible to the school board for everything that happens in the school system he will be actively interested in each teacher's success and activities. The superintendent is charged with the responsibility of implementing school policies and it is the teacher's responsibility to know these policies and strive to support them.

The relationship between the teacher and the principal is usually direct. The teacher should recognize that the principal is the official head of the school. He represents the superintendent and the school board in administering the policies of the school. A teacher should always report to the principal first when coming to a new school. Information should be ascertained concerning what the principal expects of the teachers. A few questions a teacher might raise with the principal about personal policies and regulations are:

1. What are the hours a teacher is expected to be in school?

2. How should a teacher report in case he has to be absent?

3. How should a teacher report if he has to leave school during the day because of illness?

4. What is the school policy concerning student misbehavior?

5. What is the school policy concerning extra duty?

There has been an abundance of research to show that the key person in the school situation, as far as the teacher is concerned, is the principal. The principal should be the instructional leader of the school. A quality instructional program then becomes the joint responsibility of the teacher and principal. However, many schools delegate instructional leadership to curriculum directors, department heads, or assistant principals. Many other schools delegate all student behavior problems to an assistant principal or dean.

Larger school systems usually have a number of subject matter or general curriculum supervisors in the central office and teachers are often required to look to these supervisors for instructional leadership. New teachers should find out who is responsible for each area at their school and act accordingly. Also the new teacher should ascertain office procedures, procedures for marking and grading, and for handling student records.

Directing Cocurricular Activities

The curriculum is composed of all the planned learning experiences provided for students at school. That part of the planned experiences which occurs outside the regular courses of study is the cocurriculum.

Cocurricular activities play an important role in the total program of every secondary school. These activities can contribute to the learning opportunities of every student or they can be largely a waste of the time of both students and teachers. Most teachers will be asked to sponsor one or more cocurricular activities. Therefore, teachers must be familiar with the kinds of activities, which a school may provide and the problems of sponsoring these activities.

Not all educators give unqualified support to the cocurriculum. There have been periods in American educational history when most teachers and administrators opposed these out of class, but school sponsored activities. Some observers of secondary education are critical of such activities. However, it is expected that most present day student activities will continue and others will undoubtedly be added. Almost all secondary schools have some form of student government, honor societies, band, athletic contests (both interscholastic and intramural), social clubs, subject clubs, service clubs, hobby or special interest groups, and many other kinds of regularly organized cocurricular programs.

Purposes

Any cocurricular activity should serve an educational purpose. The activity should make a contribution to the growth of individual students, to curriculum improvement through reinforcement of classroom learning, to more effective administration through fostering teamwork and a spirit of group cooperation, to the community through promotion of community interest in school activities.

Some more specific purposes of activities are:

1. Helping students learn profitable uses of leisure time.

2. Promotion of personality growth.

3. Developing student initiative and a sense of responsibility.

4. Learning how to participate in group activities, democratically.

5. Developing student social contacts and skills.

6. Establishing a base of common, shared experience which can lead students of varying backgrounds to understand each other better.

7. Promoting school spirit and enthusiasm.

8. Providing opportunities to develop special interests of an exploratory nature in many subjects, hobbies, and recreations.

9. Supplementing classroom instruction.

10. Developing student creativity.

The sponsor

Activities of a cocurricular nature are part of almost every secondary school, thus most teachers are expected to sponsor or assist with at least one activity or club, even in very large schools. Many times when an administrator has several applicants about equally qualified for a teaching position, he chooses one over the other because of the ability to sponsor a particular cocurricular activity.

Many administrators assign sponsors on the basis of interest in an activity rather than teacher knowledge of it. Teachers should be careful to accept responsibility for only those activities they can reasonably direct in a successful way. Generally students should not be permitted to elect homeroom teachers or club sponsors. Department heads and principals should make the assignments on the basis of teacher interest and competence.

Once appointed the sponsor should:

1. Attend all meetings of the activity, or club.

2. Meet regularly with officers and committees.

3. Determine his legal obligations and discharge them properly.

4. Keep the administration informed of all important matters.

5. Cause adequate and appropriate records to be kept.

6. See that all finances are managed according to school regulations and properly.

7. Encourage student initiative, responsibility, and morality.

8. Make certain the activity contributes something worthwhile to *each* member *and* to *the student body at large.*

9. Provide appropriate safety measures for the students.

10. Keep the activity in proper perspective as it relates to the total school program.

11. Be enthusiastic about what the activity can and does do.

12. Provide for continuity from school year to school year.

There are a number of problems any teacher may encounter in sponsoring any cocurricular activity. The teacher should watch for these potential trouble spots and act to avoid them when possible. Some commonly encountered problems are:

1.   Scheduling the activity and finding a meeting place. The time and place should be open to all potential members.

2.   Organizing the club or activity so that it functions smoothly, but the students run it.

3.   Alumni involvement. Problems with alumni arise most frequently with athletics, band, and social events such as dances, but these troublesome situations can arise with any activity. Even the election to the honor society can be troublesome if good public relations principles are not followed.

4.   Financing can be a problem. Sponsors should not permit students to charge anything to the club or activity without a school purchase order, properly cosigned. All money should be deposited in the *school* bank account. Two signatures should be required on all checks or requisitions, one of them should be the *sponsor's.* Money should not be kept overnight. A proper set of books should be devised and maintained *at all times!*

5.   Elections of officers. Students should not be permitted to hold a major office in more than one activity, exclusive of student council and the honor society. Membership in activities should be arranged so that each student can be a member of two activities plus student council and the honor society and *no more.*

6.   Providing continuity of leadership can be a problem, yet the activity should not become the creature of a teacher.

7.   Keeping records. Adequate minutes must be kept as well as careful financial accounts.

8.   Evaluation of the usefulness of the club in serving school purposes can be an important part of sponsorship.

Cocurricular activities are likely to be more successful when sponsors and administrators are enthusiastic but clear-eyed supporters of the program. Some principles which should govern such a program are listed below.

1. The purpose of all school activities is to educate students.

2. The cocurriculum should help students integrate classroom learning into their total experience in their search for meaning.

3. Membership in a club or activity is a privilege dependent upon responsible discharge of duty.

4. All students should have an opportunity to participate in appropriate cocurricular activities.

5. Student leadership of cocurricular activities should be as wide spread as possible, not in the hands of a few highly popular students.

6. The cocurricular program should be well balanced, with many kinds of activities.

7. The leadership and creativity of the sponsor largely determines the success of an activity.

8. The cocurriculum is supplementary to not a substitute for the regular course of study.

9. A sense of achievement gained in an activity is likely to be transferred to the classroom.

The cocurriculum is meant to supplement not to supplant the regular classroom teaching program of the school. It is a place where students try ideas, learn procedures, develop social and political skills and integrate classroom learnings into their total experiences. Social studies teachers sponsor every conceivable kind of club and activity; but the student council is the activity which is sponsored most often by the social studies teacher, at some time in his career. Therefore, a separate section is devoted to the student council and its contributions to the curriculum.

Sponsoring Student Council or Student Government

The advisor's role

The student council advisor should possess all the personal and professional qualities which make a good teacher. He should be loyal, reliable, honest, objective, knowledgeable, and interested in sponsoring student council. He should genuinely like and trust young people. He will need to have tact, poise and maturity. He will need a good working relationship with colleagues, parents, administrators, students, and he will need to provide forthright, energetic leadership for the council.[11]

The student council advisor helps the students set up goals, he listens to their point of view, he consults with them, but he does not run the council as his little show. He can counsel with students, thereby influencing their character growth, he can advise them thus promoting student growth in self government. His primary task is to work with and through students to carry out a phase of their civic education. Council officers and committee chairmen meet with the advisor frequently and the entire council usually meets with him semi-monthly.[12]

The principal appoints the student council advisor in most schools, however advisors are chosen in many other ways. Sometimes the principal or a counselor acts as advisor, sometimes the advisor is chosen by the students. A fairly common practice in larger schools is for the chairman of the department of social studies to choose the advisor or serve as the advisor himself.[13] However the advisor may be chosen, he should know the students, the community, the school, and he should want to serve. Generally, the more he knows about government and about how people function in small groups, the more effective he will be as advisor to the student council.

The student council can and should be an integral part of the instructional program of a school. It can be an educational experience for the participants, and it can be used to teach the workings of democracy. Participation in student government can help students gain insight into the operation of pressure groups, committees, and how rules are used to structure the process of democratic decision making, this kind of firsthand experience is very instructive.[14]

Through the student council students can become partners in their own education by sharing responsibility.[15] Student government can and should involve all students. Involvement of students in decision making that affects the school program means administrative and faculty relinquishment of control over some of the formal and informal activities and events of the school. Students can participate through council representation in curriculum making and revision, though many administrators and teachers really do not want

11. Gerald M. Van Pool, et al, *The Student Council in The Secondary School.* (Washington, D. C.: NASSP, 1962).

12. William S. Sterner, *The Student Council Advisor* (Washington, D. C.: NASSP, 1963).

13. Ibid.

14. John D. L'Hote, "Detroit Fights Theft and Arson," *American School and University* (July, 1970), pp. 19-21.

15. James E. Howse, "Can The Student Participate in His Own Destiny?", *Educational Leadership.* (February, 1970), pp. 442-45.

bona fide student participation in such activities. Students in today's schools
are increasingly demanding some voice in programs and events which affect
their lives directly, as the curriculum does. [16]

The main purpose of student council is to provide learning experiences for
students. It is intended to provide practice in self government and good citizenship. A properly organized and run student council is a good place to learn
about government. Another function of the council in some schools is to
regulate the club activities of students at school, however the council does not
exist to do chores for the faculty or administration. [17]

Types of Student Councils

There are a great many types of councils, some writers maintain that no
two student council organizations are alike. McKown classified councils on
the basis of: source of membership, responsibilities assigned, and general structure of the organization. [18]

Among those student councils organized according to source of membership McKown listed: representation by special interest (such as class or club
membership); automatic representation (homeroom or class president); by
appointment (by principal or sponsor); appointment by student leaders such
as class president; some schools have alumni representation or other adult
members; election from unspecialized units such as homeroom; representation
at large either by appointment or election; a few schools have political parties
which are represented; and a few schools have geographical representation.

Student governments may be classified according to powers such as: informal council chosen by a principal to do something specific, sometimes this is
an ad hoc student advisory committee; the forum type, it talks but has no
power to act; service council, this is really an overseer of the cocurricular
program; general council at large which represents the entire school, some
teachers think this is one of the better types of councils.

There are several types of councils according to the way they are organized,
some of these are: single house council, a very simple form of organization,
easy to operate and it works well with younger students, but does not teach
students much about American government; multiple house council, usually
house and senate, this is a very popular form of council as it teaches much
about our system of government, but it is slow to act and harder for young

16. Mark A. Chesler, "Shared Power and Student Decision Making," *Educational Leadership.*
(October 1970), pp. 9-14.
17. Van Pool, et al, op. cit.
18. Harry Charles McKown, *The Student Council* (New York: McGraw-Hill, 1944).

children to understand; city council form; city commission form, both of these follow the general lines of typical city governments.

Much can be taught through a genuine student government which has bona fide power to commit the school to appropriate courses of action. Many students do not think very highly of student government because it is run as a popularity contest with only a few students having any real voice in it. The authors have noted that in larger schools many students can not even recognize the photograph of their student association president, quite a few will not know his name. Student councils are held in low esteen by many, if not most, students, especially ethnically different, or lower class students. Many teachers and administrators are afraid to trust students with any real power to decide anything for themselves. Many communities do not think too highly of the things students sometimes do when left to their own devices.

One of the authors was chairman of a department of social studies in a medium sized junior-senior high school for several years, and sponsor of the student council as it was called when he first went there. Several students, some not part of the student power structure, expressed dissatisfaction and disillusionment with the council as it then existed. They thought it did more talking than acting, some felt it was the principal's creature, others felt it was the apparatus of the sponsor. Some called it Mister _____'s railroad! These students were asked what kind of student council they would like if they could have anything they wanted. The response was that they wanted a student government with some power, one that was representative of all kinds of students, and one that held fair elections. The student body was surveyed to discover how much sentiment there was for these reforms, it appeared that most students at least favored some kind of change. Permission to hold a constitutional convention was secured from the principal and the superintendent. The students held a special election to choose the delegates to a constitutional convention, which began to meet near the end of school in the spring, and continued to have committee meetings and meetings of the entire convention throughout the summer, a new constitution was written along the lines of the United States Constitution, and approved for presentation to the student body for ratification in September. All this was done by the old student council system with a lame duck set of officers. The students ratified the new constitution about a month after school started, by a big margin, but not until after a long debate. The new constitution called for use of the state registration system and use of the state type of printed, secret ballot, an election commission, a two party system, party primaries, runoff elections, a bicameral legislature with two senators from each grade at large and presided over by the vice president who could be either a junior or senior. The lower house was based on actual student population count in each actual voting precinct in the county. One precinct had nine representatives, while several others had only one each. The president, vice president, treasurer, and supervisor of elections were all elected at large, with only the president required to be a senior, the supervisor could not succeed himself. The president had several appointive cabinet posts, all subject to senate approval. There were many more details about this unusual and highly effective student government organization, however in the interest of brevity suffice it to say that it was a very effective device for teaching government. Student scores on standardized tests of knowledge of government went up phenomenally. The students liked the government they had created because it had carefully delineated powers, which teachers could not easily take from them, because they were free to run their own show to some degree, and because as some students said governing yourself was fun. The administration seemed comfortable with the experiment; but many of the faculty never accepted it because it was so time consuming, and because they thought it made smart-alecks of youngsters. Some people in the community disliked it; but it survived and flourished until the sponsor took another position, the principal went to the central office, and a new principal came to the school. He killed it before the end of the first semester and returned to a simple one house student council form, which pleased those faculty who always complained that the system patterned after that of the United States was too complex for any young person to understand! Now youngsters about the same age have the right to vote in real United States elections!

Problems of student councils

Most student councils are not democratic, are not representative, and do not teach students much, except that student council is playing at government. In many schools student council is a "rubber stamp" for the administration, the faculty, the sponsor or all three. Students are sensitive to being treated in such cavalier fashion, in these times. Apathy and militancy have their roots in the long history of students' bona fide representatives being either ignored or coerced or manipulated. There are numerous instances in some schools of repeated requests by student councils being rewritten, resubmitted again and again because the people in power did not believe students should have any voice in making even the decisions the student council charter called for.[19] We teach students that democracy is a process in which all people have a voice in making decisions which affect the common welfare, *students make such decisions through regularly established channels and are then either ignored or overruled.*

19. Robert L. Armstrong, "Student Council: Whither Goest Thou?" *Clearing House.* (April 1970).

The student council has been widely criticized because its role has not been defined, its makeup is neither democratic nor representative, and because of the nature of what it does and how it does it. Too many schools hedge councils in with restrictions so that the normal student leadership loses the confidence of the great mass of students, thus a sort of paralysis of no leadership sets in. Out of such situations new and often dangerous student or faculty leadership can arise. Student council can be an important part of any good secondary school curriculum. It can be a great contributor to student growth and learning or it can be a negative and harmful influence in the school. Each school usually makes of its council what it wants.

Other Tasks of Teachers

Teachers are expected to do many non-instructional tasks beside sponsor a club or activity or serve as sponsor of the student council. These tasks and expectations vary from school to school so greatly that it is not possible or practical to attempt discussion of many of them in detail. There is a trend in the professional associations such as the National Education Association's Department of Classroom Teachers and with the membership of the American Federation of Teachers to say that any duty not stated in the contract will not be performed. Many teachers feel that extra work should mean extra pay, and that extra duty should be voluntary. The authors' subscribe to the view that teachers are often called upon to do more out of school work on their own time without compensation than is either necessary or right; but we also believe that a professional person is just that—*professional,* i.e. he does what he must and can for his clients *all the time.*

Many larger secondary schools have elaborate committee systems which teachers will staff. There are such groups as: the textbook selection committee, the committee that screens new applicants for teaching positions, disciplinary committees, committees of class or grade sponsors, groups or individual teachers that direct beauty contests, make floats for parades, plan homecoming activities, make exhibits for the fair, attendance committees, curriculum development councils, faculty welfare or grievance committees, and many more. In smaller schools teachers are more likely to be asked to serve on ad hoc task force type committees, or to serve as an individual in some out of class, after school capacity.

Most teachers have a homeroom which requires extra, non-instructional work, many teachers keep a study hall and most despise it. Strictly speaking, both study hall and homeroom are part of the regular school day and regular load of teachers, but both pose special kinds of drains on the time and energy of the teacher. Most social studies teachers will serve as sponsor of a class, many will be called upon to judge oratorical contests and debates. Every teacher has record keeping chores such as posting grades, keeping up with attendance, issuing library and hall permits, preparing report cards, posting the permanent records, and many more. Some states require that the individual classroom teacher keep the teacher's register. This may even be required by law, in some cases the administration may still provide a clerk to keep the register, but the teacher can not escape the legal requirement to be responsible for its accuracy. It is very important that the register be accurate in states which have a minimum foundation plan since average daily attendance of the students is computed from the register and next years budget is computed from ADA, most states now have some form of minimum foundation. Many teachers look upon record keeping as clerical drudgery and beneath their dignity, however, it is doubted if any professional person is much better than his attention to detail.

Serving on committees, keeping records, having homeroom, serving as senior sponsor, sponsoring a club, and such duties are onerous and burdensome enough to annoy and exhaust many teachers; but at least most of this type of non-instructional work is done at school during regular school hours. There are other things teachers do on their time after school.

Teachers sell tickets to ball games, take tickets, coach plays and musicals, attend PTA, attend faculty meetings, attend student performed functions, participate in back to school night, help with alumni affairs, and in some communities they still are expected to teach a Sunday School class and sing in the choir.

Teachers are exemplars, students copy them and model their behavior after what the teacher is, not what he says in class, alone. Pupils learn through cognition, through their value system, through perception, through study; but they also are shaped by those with whom they come in contact, and they do pattern after those whom they admire, and in some cases after those whom they only know not necessarily admire. Because of these factors, and because of community expectations of teacher behavior, it may be a long time before teachers are able to only teach their classes, if ever. Some doubt that a teacher should want to get rid of out of class chores, since it is in these activities that a teacher gets to know his students best, and is able to exert the most influence on student behavior.

PROBLEMS AND QUESTIONS FOR STUDY OR DISCUSSION

1.   Why should a teacher be concerned about discipline?

2.   Has fear of punishment, or hope of reward any place in a teacher's efforts to maintain good classroom control?

3. Make up a list of rules for student conduct in your class.

4. What are a teacher's responsibilities for controlling student behavior out of class but on other parts of the campus?

5. Examine the postulates reasserted by the authors in this chapter and decide whether you think an adequate case has been made for classroom management as a means of helping students learn self-discipline.

6. What do you think of the rationale of Duane Brown for attempting to prevent disruption of classes because of inadequate discipline?

7. If you don't think Brown has made a good enough case, why not make up a rationale of your own?

8. The assertion is often made that all young prople want to know what is expected of them in terms of behavior. Do you think this is true? If so, why is it true? If not, why do you think it isn't true?

9. What should an inexperienced teacher expect in the way of backing from the principal's office when students are disruptive?

10. Describe the teacher's role in counseling students, and decide how you will do it.

11. Make a set of general rules to guide your relationship with the principal, department head, various levels of supervisors, and colleagues.

12. Decide which club or activity you are best fitted to sponsor, and most interested in, then make a plan for providing leadership for such an activity.

13. Get a copy of the teacher's handbook, the student's handbook, and the teacher's register and study them so that you will know how teachers and students are expected to act.

14. Get a copy of a typical permanent record card and study the information that would ordinarily be on it, so you will have some idea of the kind of records schools keep about students.

15. Study the types of student councils that typically exist and try to determine means of making yours more effective as an outlet for student opinion and as a device to teach students the value of representative government and due process.

16. Do you think that teachers should be required to sponser clubs, sell tickets, go to PTA, go to faculty meetings, coach the play, and obey local norms for dress and behavior? Why? Why not?

REFERENCES

Armstrong, Robert L. "Student Council: Whither Thou Goest?" *Clearing House.* (April, 1970).

Brown, Duane, *Changing Student Behavior: A New Approach to Discipline.* Dubuque, Iowa: Wm. C. Brown Company Publishers, 1971.

Brown, E. S. and Phelps, A. T. *Managing The Classroom.* New York: Ronald Press, 1961.

Burgess, Richard and Judith, Sister M. "Self-Governing School." *Instructor.* (March, 1969).

Chesler, Mark A. "Shared Power and Student Decision Making." *Education Leadership.* (October, 1970).

Emmerling, F. C. "Student Council: A Vehicle for Self-Improvement." *National Elementary Principles.* (May, 1967).

Gordon, Ira J. *The Teacher as a Guidance Worker: Human Development Concepts and Their Application in the Classroom.* New York: Harper and Brothers Publishers, 1956.

L'Hote, John D. "Detroit Fights Theft and Arson." *American School and University.* (July, 1970).

House, James E. "Can the Student Participate in His Own Destiny?" *Education Leadership.* (February, 1970).

McGuire, Thomas C. "Help Your Student Council Justify Its Existence." *Journal of Secondary Education.* Vol. XLV (April, 1970).

McKown, Harry Charles. *The Student Cquncil.* New York: McGraw-Hill Book Company, 1944.

Miklos, Laszlo and Miklos, Mary. "Student Council: Useful or Useless?" *Clearing House.* (December, 1970).

Morganti, M. D. "Total Involvement in Student Government." *Social Education.* (October, 1967).

Pool, Gerald M. Van. "Student Council." *National Association of Secondary Schools Principles Bulletin.* (October, 1964).

Pool, Gerald M. Van., and Others. *The Student Council in the Secondary School.* Washington, D. C.: National Association of Secondary-School Principals, 1962.

Sterner, William S. *The Student Council Advisor.* Washington, D. C.: National Association of Secondary-School Principals, 1963.

Svoboda, W. S. "Student Government: Contradiction in Theory and Practice." *Social Education.* (March 1966).

Vaigo, A. C. "Scandinavia's Lead in Pupil Participation." *Times Education Supplement.* (March, 1969).

Webster, Staten W. *Discipline in the Classroom.* San Francisco: Chandler Publishing Company, 1968.

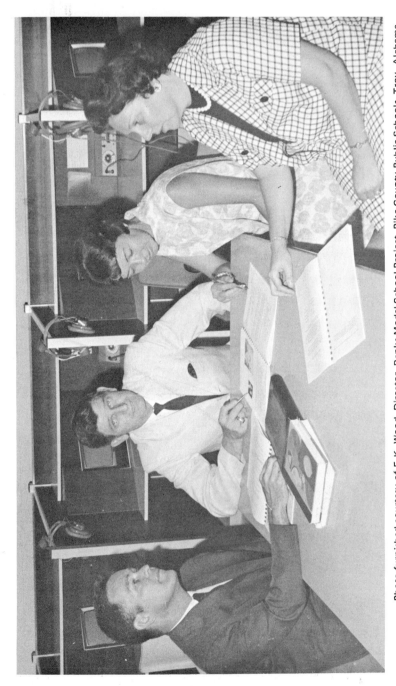

Photo furnished courtesy of E.K. Wood, Director, Banks Model School Project, Pike County Public Schools, Troy, Alabama.

A teaching team not only teaches together but must also plan and evaluate together.

Chapter XII

THE
MAKING
OF
A
PROFESSIONAL

The typical professional education of beginning social studies teachers is at least a baccalaureate degree, as it is for other beginning elementary and secondary teachers in each of the United States. A few states require more than four years of college education for entry into the profession of teaching with a standard certificate, but most require only a baccalaureate for the initial certificate. Requirements for certification as a secondary social studies teacher vary from state to state. However, teachers who have completed an NCATE approved degree program are granted appropriate certificates in most states on a reciprocity basis. Many states require the social studies teacher to earn credit in a course in local history, geography, government, conservation, or some combination of these areas. But those teachers who graduated from NCATE approved programs usually have ample time to schedule such courses in their new state.

Typical Social Studies Degree Program

Typical baccalaureate degree programs for social studies teachers include the following areas in some combination that totals from 124 to 132 semester hours or the equivalent in quarter hours.

General Education	Semester Hours
English, Composition and Literature	12
Speech	3
Physical Science	6
Biological Science	6
Mathematics	3-6
Fine Arts or Humanities	3-6
General Psychology	3-6
Health and Physical Education	3-6
	38-48

Social Sciences	Semester Hours
United States History, including State History	12
World or European History	6-9
History Electives	6-9
Economics	3-6
Sociology	3-6
Political Science	6-9
Geography	3-6
Social Science Electives	6-9
	45-60

Professional Education

General Psychology	3
Human Growth or Adolescent Psychology	3
Educational Psychology and/or Learning Theory	3
Foundations of Education (Social, Historical, or	
Philosophical or a survey of all three)	3
Curriculum	3
General Methods or Principles of High School Teaching	3
Methods of Teaching Social Studies	3
Student Teaching or other full time field experience	6-12
	21-30
Total Hours	126-132

Various colleges require or permit many variations of the course of study listed above. Some colleges permit and encourage prospective teachers to acquire greater concentrations in one or two of the social sciences and most schools have flexibility enough in their preparation programs to permit majors in only one of the social sciences to meet graduation and certification requirements.

Initial Certification

Most states certify teachers in the broad area of social studies grades seven-twelve, some certify them grades five-eight, or even five-twelve. Many subject matter specialists think of this as a very poor practice. Few people know enough to teach in five or six different subject areas at six or more age and grade levels. Most states require teachers to earn six semester hours credit each five years for certificate renewal. One weakness of many preparation programs is that few courses beyond the sophomore, survey level are required. This makes it easy for many college students who are psychologically and academically unsuited to teaching secondary social studies to seek minimum certification in the field. These practices also have contributed to the over supply of persons certified to teach social studies. Furthermore, these practices have contributed greatly to the almost universal dislike of social studies, especially history, expressed by adolescents. Poorly taught courses by poorly prepared teachers, who are not really interested in their subject, have created the attitude of students that social studies is easy, dull, boring, unrelated to life, and in fact, farcical.

Adequate Preparation for Teaching Social Studies

We think that social studies teachers, who wish to be adequate, should have at least a master's degree with a subject matter major of fifteen semester hours in one discipline and a subject matter minor of nine to twelve semester hours in another but related discipline. Furthermore, social studies teachers who want to be excellent should have graduate work in curriculum, instructional practices, uses of the media, and psychology. This means that a social studies program for preparing really good social studies teachers would require about forty five graduate hours above the usual baccalaureate preparation.

Professionalism and the Teacher

A professional person must have formal training before practicing in his field. The members of a profession make up an organization that keeps its members informed, and the profession regulates its own members practice, excluding those that violate the rules of the profession. The profession has a set of standards and code of ethics that its members abide by, and a professional has a body of theory that guides his practice.

Teaching has come a long way since the one teacher little red schoolhouse era of fifty or sixty years ago; yet, in spite of more and better college preparation, teaching is not widely believed to be a profession. Many people believe that teaching should be a profession but that it isn't yet. Why is it not a profession? One reason may be the number of people who teach as a supplement to another income, such as a woman supplementing her husband's income. The large turnover of teachers in the educational system may be another reason. Some women may not be as devoted to their career as men because their main interest in life is homemaking. Many men teachers in the past have used the field of education as a stepping stone to other professions because they could not make enough money or find enough satisfaction in teaching.[1]

Teachers are expected to conduct themselves in an ethical manner at all times. Teachers are looked on as examples for young people and they are

---

1. Howard Vollmer and Donald Mills, *Professionalization* (Englewood Cliffs, N. J.: Prentice-Hall, Inc., 1966), p. 340.

models for many. Communities do not expect to control as much of teachers' private lives as they formerly did; but teachers are still expected to obey community norms, especially in many smaller communities. Those who do not live according to the accepted community norms may lose their position. Those who engage in unethical practices should be removed from the profession.

Most teachers subscribe to the code of ethics of the National Education Association. A condensed version of the code is given below:

1. The teacher should be courteous, just, and professional in all relationships.

2. Desirable ethical standards require cordial relations between teacher and pupil, home and school.

3. The conduct of the teacher should conform to the accepted patterns of behavior of the most wholesome members of the community.

4. The teacher should strive to improve educational practice through study, travel, and experimentation.

5. Unfavorable criticism of associates should be avoided.

6. Testimonials regarding other teachers should be truthful and confidential.

7. Membership and active participation in local, state, and national professional associations is expected.

8. The teacher should avoid endorsement of educational materials for personal gain.

9. Great care should be taken by the teacher to avoid interfering with other teachers and pupils.

10. Fair salary schedules should be sought, and, when established, carefully upheld by all professionals.

11. No teacher should knowingly underbid a rival for a position.

12.   No teacher should accept compensation for helping another teacher to get a position or a promotion.

13.   Professional contracts, when signed, should be respected by both parties and dissolved only by mutual consent.

14.   Official business should be transacted only through properly designated officials.

15.   The responsibility for reporting all matters harmful to the welfare of the school rests upon each teacher.

16.   Professional growth should be stimulated through suitable recognition and promotion within the ranks.

17.   Unethical practices should be reported to local, state, or national commissions on ethics.

Some teachers shrink as a professional person after their first year of experience. Fear of students, fear of administrators, community pressures, discipline problems, inadequacy in subject matter or methodology, and personality disorders cause such teachers to get in a rut. Positive professionalism comes from a real desire to keep up and grow. Growth during the preparatory period and after actual entry into teaching is necessary to help the teacher keep up with changes in subject matter and practice.

The teacher, like the doctor or engineer, has much to learn after leaving college. Among other things, he needs to learn the personal and professional concerns peculiar to his particular community.

The rights of parents and children should be placed above his personal interest. Teachers should do the best they can at their work. They should be careful about what they say about the school and other teachers.

The student teacher, as well as the regular teacher, should respect the confidence of his pupils. When he has a confidential talk with a student he should not discuss it with unauthorized persons. The teacher must remember that he is an example to his students physically, mentally, intellectually, morally, and ethically. The teacher must not try to convert his students to his religious or political beliefs. The teacher should treat each pupil fairly.

The teacher should conduct himself so that he will be respected within his professional field by his associates as well as by his students, community, and administrators. A person should show pride in belonging to the teaching profession. He should try to keep up with academic, professional, and current affairs. He should know the legal aspects of his profession and keep up with changes in them. He should be active in helping his professional organizations solve problems that are found within the educational system. He should use professional methods in obtaining a job and furthermore, he should be honest about his capabilities as a teacher.

Faculty Morale and Welfare

The teacher's professional performance depends upon high morale. The personal satisfaction of the teacher determines to some extent how long he will remain in the teaching profession. It therefore becomes necessary to find the things which contribute to high or low teacher morale and welfare.

There are many factors that contribute to teacher morale. Some of the factors that have been identified are: responsibility, salary, achievement, working conditions, job security, personal life, status, policy and administrative supervision, and the work itself.

Secondary school teachers have many anxieties and discontents in teaching. At the present time no clear cut distinction is made between skilled performance and incompetence of the secondary school teacher. The teacher has been denied, because of the nature of his work, any clear cut profit from his effectiveness. He has no dependable means of tracing the consequences of his efforts to help students to learn. Improvement of teaching is dependent upon the availability to the teacher of reliable information about the effectiveness of his efforts.

Many teachers are burdened with clerical duties and overcrowded classrooms. Most teachers feel that teacher influence on curriculum is too little. They are also concerned about lack of supplies and equipment. Teachers are also concerned about their personal professional careers in areas such as academic freedom, dismissal policies, sick and emergency leave policies, administrative confidence in teachers, and salaries.

One of the most frequent causes of low morale is the teacher's inability to control the student. Many teachers interpret all acts of disobedience as acts of defiance aimed directly at them. Many student malbehaviors that appear to be directed toward teachers are only reactions of students to environmental factors of the school or community and the class and toward the teacher's role as an authority figure, not toward the teacher as a person. The main function of all school discipline is to encourage student self-discipline.

The effectiveness of the teacher's work in the classroom is determined to some extent by the instructional equipment and supplies available to the teacher. The school system should provide audio-visual equipment, projector equipment, screens, blackboards, and film provisions. These are important materials used in the classroom. If the school does not provide these materials, the teacher will be forced to work with what material is available in the most efficient and economic manner. The teacher should be familiar with the school system's policies as they pertain to supplies.

Although it is not ordinarily left to the classroom teacher to select the site for the school in which he teaches, it is wise to check the working conditions of the school system before accepting a job. The building should have been planned and constructed to meet the needs of the students it is to serve. Safety should be given careful consideration. Corridors and stairways should be broad and free from obstructions. A large portion of the teacher's time, at least seven hours a day, is spent in the classroom. Careful measures should be taken to see that the classroom has proper lighting, heating, and ventilation.

The single most important factor determining the morale of the faculty in a school building is the principal. Some decisions are arrived at democratically. Some decisions are made by the principal alone. The faculty should know this and accept it, just as in the teacher's classroom there are decisions which the teacher alone must make. The administrator should settle his own problems and not tie up his teachers with needless and meaningless committee work. A principal who confronts his teachers with a problem that they feel he alone should solve, brings about much irritation and lowers the morale of the faculty members.

The support of the principal in disciplinary problems is an important ingredient in building faculty morale. All teachers appreciate a fair hearing of their side of the story as well as the pupil's side. Until investigation proves otherwise, the principal should back the teacher. If investigation proves that the criticism is unjustified, he owes the pupil a complete explanation of his findings and the teacher's full support.

The salaries of the teachers in secondary schools have a far-reaching influence on welfare and morale. High salaries influence the quality of teaching because salary scales control the quality of the personnel available to teach in the school. Salary determines the number and quality of new teachers a school system will have each fall. Therefore, one cannot disregard the salary factor as a morale booster for teachers.

Tenure laws vary from state to state. The state legislatures control the individual laws regarding teaching tenure. The fact that tenure is not permanent may be disturbing to some teachers. Most schools automatically renew a teacher's contract at the end of the school term. This type contract is of a continuing nature between the teacher and the school district or between the teacher and the state. The teacher should know what kind of contract he has with his school. A recent study of school tenure shows that most secondary-school teachers are of the opinion that tenure legislation reduces the number of resignations, and makes the teachers more willing to express themselves to the administration.

Many citizens believe that tenure protects incompetent and malcontented teachers; and there may be some truth to the belief. Many teachers gain great satisfaction from teaching, others do not gain as much satisfaction. The degree of teacher satisfaction is dependent, at least in part, on working conditions.

Measuring Teacher Competency

A teacher can scarcely glance at any journal in the field of education without seeing something about *accountability.* No matter how you define it, accountability comes out meaning *evaluation of teaching effectiveness,* since it is difficult to evaluate what a person does without also passing a value judgment on the person himself. The literature is full of suggestions on how to evaluate teacher performance without involving personality, but it is doubted if such a thing can ever be accomplished.

For years teachers and teacher associations have insisted that teaching cannot be effectively measured or evaluated. Admittedly such a task is difficult but that does not mean that it should not be attempted. The public is showing its disapproval of education in a growing tide of defeated bond issues, and growing verbal criticism of teacher classroom effectiveness. The United States Office of Education talks of accountability. The professional associations demand autonomy in developing curriculum, controlling teacher preparation programs, having a voice in administering schools, and in policing their own profession. It seems evident that teacher effectiveness is being evaluated by everyone: students, colleges, learned societies, the public, administrators, and private industry. All this evaluation of teacher competency is being done without any well established criteria of what is being evaluated or any generally accepted instrument to measure performance.

It seems that decisions ought to be made about *what* teachers are to be held accountable for, *how* they are to be held accountable, to *whom* they are to be held accountable, and *what* teacher competency is. It seems one way of doing this is to decide that teachers ought to be competent to move students toward the teacher's own behavioral goals. Thus teachers could be measured on the basis of pre-test growth of students toward a teacher's behavioral objectives in terms of student abilities. Teachers ought to be accountable to the administration and the students. Teachers ought also to be accountable to themselves, and to the profession for doing their best in an ethical fashion.

Evaluation may be broadly defined as a systematic attempt to gather evidence regarding changes in student behavior that accompany planned educational experiences. A major purpose of evaluation is to measure adaptation of instruction to the differing capacities and needs of individual pupils. Evaluation of their teaching can make teachers more aware of the nature of children, can aid in curriculum development, and by establishing the degree to which the educational objectives have been achieved, can contribute to curriculum modification.

The purposes for teacher evaluation are:

1. To determine the effectiveness of the instructional program. Though teaching is only a means to an end, it may be possible and necessary to infer the achievement of ends through effective means.

2. To determine the effectiveness of personnel policies and procedures.

3. To provide the basis for supervisory and inservice development programs and activities. Such programs should grow out of the particular needs of teachers and should be based on objective evidence.

4. To provide the basis for administrative decisions. Decisions on personnel and on programs are based on evidence.

5. To facilitate accounting for responsibility. Those who are given authority and responsibility must be able to account for the exercise of the responsibility.

6. To motivate teachers to strive for a higher level of performance.

7. To provide the basis for rewards and sanctions.

8. To assist the teacher in achieving success.

There is only one fully defensible criterion for judging teacher effectiveness: *results.* A major obstacle to developing valid procedures for predicting teacher effectiveness has been inconsistency in the way teachers are evaluated and lack of unanimity about desirable results.

Some of the methods used in evaluating teachers are as follows:

1. Self-ratings: This has long been emphasized and advocated. However, few people are able out of casual introspection to arrive at accurate analysis of their own behavior under any circumstances.

2. Peer Ratings: This involves having teachers evaluate each other. Research studies have found this approach to be of limited value.

Under the usual conditions of teaching, there is little opportunity for one teacher to observe the work of another and most teachers do not like it.

3. Pupil Ratings: This has been the subject of a considerable amount of research. The findings have shown that pupils are able to make more valid and reliable rating of teachers than any other group, including adminstrators, supervisors, and experts; but teachers often resent it.

4. Ratings by supervisors: This is common practice and has been the subject of much of the reported research.

5. Rating by experts: This method, usually done by university personnel, was at one time common in this country.

Most permanent secondary school teachers favor formal evaluation programs as a means of securing organizational approval of their work. Teachers will accept such programs under the following conditions:

1. That they are initiated with the help of teachers.

2. That they are based upon agreed criteria.

3. That they are evaluated at least once a year.

4. That evaluations are explained and discussed with teachers.

5. That follow-up is maintained.

6. That the program is revised as needed.

Under these conditions teachers feel that formal evaluation programs can benefit them and thus provide a better education for the pupils they serve.

The evaluation of the instructional process needs to be separated from evaluation of teacher personal characteristics. Teacher personal characteristics are poor measuring sticks for evaluating instruction. A great deal more research is needed about evaluation of the instructional process.

As far as teacher evaluation is concerned, there needs to be a continued refinement of systematic observation tools. Researchers need to develop less time-consuming methods of observing and recording classroom behavior. Researchers need to establish criteria of satisfactory performance. They need also to determine the nature of the evidence needed to determine whether the criteria are met. Lastly, a method for gathering and interpreting evidence of success must be developed. One of the better devices being used at present is video-taping. There are also many scales available to measure various aspects of teaching.

Professional Growth

Every teacher, regardless of whether he has been teaching a few days or many years, soon realizes that despite good initial training he still has a need to learn more and the social studies teacher is no exception. As he goes into the field of teaching he may find that his knowledge of subject matter or methodology is sketchy and incomplete. There may be gaps in his knowledge of which he was not aware, and some ideas that he felt sure of as a student may now require further study. A good teacher sets out to remedy any deficiencies in his knowledge of subject or pedagogy and does not stop in his efforts to become a master teacher.

Professional growth and development for social studies teachers is largely a matter of continuing self-directed education. Most teachers are aware of the wide variety of resources and means for learning which are available to the educated public. They will find many uses for the reading materials found in libraries and bookstores for professional improvement and for satisfying more personal interests. Fiction, nonfiction, current affairs periodicals, newspapers, books, and magazines of all kinds are potential sources of knowledge. Teachers, like their students, may also learn from observing. Attendance at public lectures and exhibits, political rallies, and meeting of public boards and agencies all offer opportunities for additional learning. So does attention paid to radio and television programs. Travel can be regarded as an educational experience, when the traveler is a curious and observant person.[2]

No matter how much he learns in college, the social studies teacher will need to continue learning after he leaves school. Teachers interested in furthering their professional growth have found the following types of activity helpful:

1. Use of a planned reading program.
2. Community participation.
3. Travel.
4. Graduate study.
5. Attendance at workshops.
6. Participation in local in-service programs.

2. Morris R. Lewenstein, *Teaching Social Studies in Junior and Senior High Schools* (Chicago: Rand McNally and Company, 1963), pp. 540-541.

7. Professional service.
8. Membership in professional organizations.

The teacher of social studies today must be well qualified in a number of subject areas within the field. He must have a broad background and willingness to expand it in order to keep up with the challenges of his profession. Each teacher must have pride in his job to such an extent that he will find that self-motivation answers most of his needs and pushes him forward in his efforts toward professional growth.

There are only two ways to improve the effectiveness of teaching in any school. One is to employ more competent teachers to fill all vacancies left by the death, or retirement, or resignation of teachers in the system. The other way, and it is far more effective, is to provide opportunities for professional growth or in-service education for all teachers, administrators, and other staff persons. Each teacher should want to become more uniquely himself and should direct his efforts at professional growth toward that end. School systems should strive to promote individuality in the professional growth of teachers. Teachers should not be driven toward attainment of some mythical average competency but should strive instead to do those things which they already do well, supremely well.

PROBLEMS AND QUESTIONS FOR STUDY OR DISCUSSION

1. Make a list of the qualities that make a professional person. How many of the professional attributes do you think teaching now has? Do you favor teacher associations controlling their own profession and thus evaluating teachers and policing its own ranks against unethical and incompetent conduct?

2. Read the recommendation made by the authors for initial certification to teach social studies and the assertion that a masters degree and fifteen semester hours of graduate work in a single discipline is probably prerequisite to real competency as a social studies teacher. Do you think the recommendation is too much? Too little? Just ridiculous?

3. What is accountability?

4. Many writers are asserting that the American public is showing a loss of faith in public education. Could greater professionalization of teachers restore their faith?

5. Develop a ten year professional development plan for your self.

6. Study and report to the class on one or two of the better known systems being used to evaluate instruction.

7. State the means you find most satisfactory for having your teaching evaluated.

8. What is the appropriate role for social studies teachers to play in the development of new and better social studies curricula?

9. Discuss ethical conduct of teachers and administrators when negotiations are in progress, when a strike vote is being taken, when a strike is actually in progress?

10. Do you think teachers should strike? Or do you think that teacher strikes should be against public policy? What is the professional viewpoint on such matters?

11. Should teachers have more voice in certification procedures?

12. What is the professional obligation of a teacher for working with student teachers?

13. What are fringe benefits? What is faculty welfare? What things should you learn about working conditions, retirement, sick leave, business leave, sabbaticals, insurance, credit unions, and housing before you accept a position?

14. What professional obligations does a teacher have to his clients, the students, and their parents?

15. Why should a professional teacher keep up with his subject and with changing technology?

16. What does a teacher owe his professional associations? Should a classroom teacher strive to actually become involved in research?

17. What can a teacher get that will help him professionly from examining the work of other classroom teachers?

REFERENCES

Gauerke, Warren E. *Legal and Ethical Responsibilities of School Personnel.* Englewood Cliffs, N. J.: Prentice-Hall, Inc., 1959.

Gayles, Anne Richardson, "In-Service Education: A Key to the Improvement of Instruction in the Social Studies." *The Social Studies,* Vol. LVII, No. 6 (November, 1966).

Kearney, Nolan C. *A Teacher's Professional Guide.* Englewood Cliffs, N.J.: Prentice Hall, Inc., 1958.

Lewenstein, Morris R. *Teaching Social Studies in Junior and Senior High Schools.* Chicago: Rand McNally and Company, 1963.

Liberman, Myron. *Education as a Profession.* Englewood Cliffs, N. J.: Prentice-Hall, Inc., 1956.

Stinnett, T. M. *Professional Problems of Teachers.* New York: Macmillan Company, 1968.

Vollmer, Howard and Mills, Donald. *Professionalization.* Englewood Cliffs, N. J.: Prentice-Hall, Inc., 1966.

Appendices

SAMPLE
COURSES
OF
STUDY
AND
TEACHING
UNITS

Included in Appendix A are examples of courses of study for grades five and six. These courses of study outline the subject matter content that would typically be covered in these grades. Five and six have been included because of the trend toward middle schools. Courses of study are presented for these grades instead of shorter teaching units to give the secondary teacher an opportunity to see what social studies content is taught at this level.

Included in Appendix B are teaching units for each of the grades, seven through twelve, and for some elective subjects which may cross grade lines. These courses of study and units were developed by in-service teachers under the authors' direction and leadership and are being used in middle and secondary schools. The courses of study are brief in the interest of conserving space, but they do show a variety of objectives, methods, content, and measurement. The teaching units are presented in more detail and should serve as models to assist teachers in developing additional teaching units of their own.

The units vary in length, completeness and thoroughness, but all have been used by social studies teachers in actual classroom situations. These units and courses of study have been reproduced with a minimum of editing and revision, in order to retain their practical, field oriented character. The writing is that of the teachers who made them, with few changes or additions.

Several brief problem oriented lessons and a number of project type assignments have been included in this section in an effort to give some examples of how to plan lessons in other ways than unit plan teaching. Sample tests have been included in some teaching units, and some of them have a number of complete daily lesson plans incorporated in them. These lessons, units, and courses of study are representative of short and long range teacher planning. Some are more complete than others; different ones have been included so the reader would have an opportunity to examine various kinds and levels of planning. No explanation of these plans has been included, since we believe the reader will prefer to make his own judgments about the adequacy of various kinds of planning.

The authors have simply reproduced these plans; we make no claim of having verified the correctness of the references cited by the teachers who did the units and courses of study. We believe the citations to be generally accurate, however.

It is hoped that readers will find these units and courses of study useful as references as they make their own long and short range plans for teaching the social studies.

Appendix A

COURSES
OF
STUDY
GRADES
FIVE
AND
SIX

Students in the fifth and sixth grades have a wide variation of maturity both physically and mentally. They are energetic and inquisitive. These traits should be encouraged.

In the fourth grade the children are given an opportunity to contrast the familiar with the unfamiliar by making imaginary visits across our country and to each of the continents and by being introduced to maps and globes. They learn something of land, climate, natural resources, people, and that man must learn to control certain natural features to his advantage.

In the fifth grade earlier concepts are developed, and an in depth study of the United States is made. The students learn of their heritage, the discovery of the western hemisphere, early explorers, colonization of the new world, the Revolution, the beginning of our new country, and the settling of the sections from the Atlantic to the Pacific Oceans, and from the Great Lakes to the Gulf of Mexico (including all fifty states).

The sixth graders widen their horizon by going from their own country into other countries of the western hemisphere, adding many new geographical concepts, learning of the likenesses and differences of regions, peoples, and of their inter-dependence for their economic and national security.

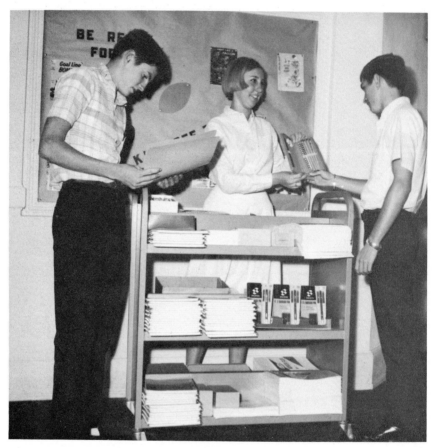

Photo furnished courtesy of Elmore County Public School, Wetumpka, Alabama.

FIFTH GRADE
SOCIAL STUDIES

Statement of Purpose

The fundamental purpose of fifth grade social studies is to develop student growth in social behavior. This social studies program is designed to help students learn how the free society of the United States developed by study of the history and geography of the United States with special emphasis on their own state.

A survey of the discovery, exploration, settlement, and development of the United States from the earliest explorations to the present are the broad areas of emphasis through which the child is provided the knowledge, understanding, appreciations, and values he needs in order to take his place as a worthwhile citizen in society.

Objectives

1. A. Students will acquire respect for the courage, sacrifices, and achievements of the early explorers.
   B. They will be able to write or tell the story of one Spanish, one French, and one English explorer showing the contribution of each to American life.
2. A. Students will develop an appreciation of the contributions of the first Americans to our life today, and a desire to use wisely the rich resources of the Americas.
   B. They will be able to show their appreciation by writing an essay about conservation of resources or by telling the story of several early conservation efforts.
3. A. Pupils will recognize and appreciate the part played by different classes of people in building our country.
   B. They will be able to tell the story of several famous craftsmen and traders.
4. A. Pupils will understand the basic principles of the American way of life.
   B. They will show their understanding of freedom by granting it to other students.

5. A. Children will gain understanding of the American way of life, the Constitution, the Bill of Rights, and basic law.
    B. They will be able to list five freedoms guaranteed to all by the Constitution.
6. A. Pupils will be able to point to each state on a map.
    B. Students should be able to recognize and write most of the fifty states and their capitals.
7. A. Children will be able to tell about the differences in the climate, topography, resources, and people for each region of the country.
8. A. Students will have a conception of the interdependence of people in different sec*:ons of the country.
    B. They will demonstrate this by listing the products consumed at home which come from other states or countries.
9. A. Students should show interest in the way geography and history influence the lives of people.
    B. They will be able to tell the story of the Eskimo and of the plains Indian and how geography made them different.
10. A. Students will be aware of the effect which the many ways of transportation has had upon the development of the United States.
    B. They will be able to write a paragraph about each of four modern means of transportation and its contribution to their life.
11. A. Students will be able to define in writing most of the words and terms introduced in each unit.
12. A. Students will establish the relation of person and place in their mind by matching person, time, event, and place on a test.
13. A. Pupils will use maps in locating places in the United States.
    B. They will be able to locate a state, city, river, or event on an outline map.

Suggested Activities

A. Student activities

1. Depict famous events by painting or drawing.
2. Read and report orally or in writing on the adventures of explorers.
3. Make booklets about historical places, persons, or events.
4. Share daily current news reports, this is a structural activity with each student doing assigned current event topics. None will be read, all will be told.
5. Keep a scrapbook about space travel developments.
6. Keep a scrapbook on the presidency, congress, the Governor, the legislature, Vietnam, foreign policy, or some other topic.

7. Make oral and written reports about people, places, products, or events.
8. Recognize, locate, and learn the states by use of maps and globes.
9. Work with puzzles.
10. Homework, which includes some of the above, reading assignments, and the use of workbooks for some students.
11. Take tests.
12. Make picture maps showing products of the various sections of the United States.
13. Broaden vocabulary.
14. Use library and other resources to find materials on problems.
15. Study maps of the world, the United States, the western hemisphere, and Canada.
16. Trace voyages of early explorers.
17. Prepare exhibits of colonial and pioneer life.

B. Group activities

1. Compare and discuss the ways of life in different sections of America, then and now.
2. Use Weekly Readers in class.
3. Participate on panels.
4. Participate in discussions.
5. Make a time line as a class project.
6. Dramatize historical events.

C. Teacher activities

1. Show films and filmstrips of places of interest in the states.
2. Explain material, help students understand.
3. Help in the selection and use of materials other than the text.
4. Ask questions to motivate and evaluate.

Content

I. American People and Lands
   A. The coming of people to America
   B. Geography, climate, and resources of America
   C. Indians and their contributions
II. Discovering the New World
   A. How the Norsemen found a new continent
   B. How Columbus found America
III. The Northeast

   A.   Mountains, hills, plateaus, plains, rivers
   B.   Settling the Northeast
       1.   Religious groups
           a.   Separatists
           b.   Puritans
           c.   Pilgrims
           d.   Quakers
       2.   Early English Colonies
           a.   Plymouth
           b.   Massachusetts
           c.   Rhode Island
           d.   Connecticut
           e.   New Hampshire
           f.   Maine
           g.   Vermont
           h.   New York
           i.   New Jersey
           j.   Delaware
           k.   Pennsylvania
       3.   Leaders
           a.   Roger Williams
           b.   Thomas Hooker
           c.   Peter Minuit
           d.   Peter Stuyvesant
           e.   William Penn
   C.   Earning a living in New England
       1.   Farming
           a.   Dairy
           b.   Poultry
           c.   Truck gardening
           d.   Fish trade
       2.   Industries
           a.   Textile
           b.   Leather
           c.   Metal
           d.   Electronics
       3.   Fishing and hunting
 IV.   Living and working in the Middle Atlantic States
   A.   New York Region
       1.   New York State Barge Canal
       2.   Trade and industries

B.   The Pittsburgh area
    1.   Ship building
    2.   Mining coal
C.   Manufacturing
    1.   Iron
    2.   Steel
    3.   Textile
    4.   Oil and Gas
D.   The Erie Canal
E.   The early railroad
F.   St. Lawrence Seaway
G.   Farming
    1.   Dairy
    2.   Fruit
    3.   Truck
    4.   Special crops
H.   Fishing

V.   The Southeast
A.   Topography
B.   Settling the Southeast
    1.   Virginia
       a.   Jamestown
       b.   Self-government
       c.   Williamsburg
    2.   Maryland
       a.   Lord Baltimore
       b.   English Catholics
    3.   Carolinas
       a.   Pirates and Indians
       b.   Dividing Carolina
    4.   Georgia
       a.   Debtor's Prison
       b.   Oglethorpe
       c.   Government
    5.   Mississippi
    6.   Florida
    7.   Alabama
C.   Money Crops
    1.   Tobacco
    2.   Rice
    3.   Indigo

        4. Cotton
  D. Settlement of the Southwest
        1. Beyond the Appalachians
        2. Four routes to the West
        3. Pioneer life
VI.   How the United States Became a Nation
  A. How England won most of North America
        1. English and French in the Ohio Valley
        2. The French and Indian War
            a. General Braddock's defeat
            b. The fall of Quebec
        3. France's loss of the New World
  B. How the English Colonies became independent
        1. Events leading to war with England
            a. The Molasses Act
            b. The Stamp Act
            c. The Boston Tea Party
            d. The closing of the port of Boston
        2. Committees of correspondence
        3. Two meetings in Philadelphia
  C. The War For Independence
        1. Early days of the war
        2. Fighting at Lexington and Concord
        3. The Battle of Bunker Hill
        4. Washington's Army
            a. Washington as Commander
            b. Washington crossing the Delaware
            c. Winter at Valley Forge
        5. Battle of Saratoga
        6. Fighting in the Southern Colonies
            a. General Greene's Plan
            b. Trapping of Cornwallis
  D. A free and independent nation
        1. Winning of the Northwest
        2. Declaration of Independence
  E. How the United States Built a strong Government
        1. The Articles of Confederation
        2. A wise plan of government
            a. The Constitutional Convention
            b. Adopting the constitution
        3. Our National Government

a. Putting the constitution to work
b. Inaugrating the first President
c. The Story of George Washington
4. Our Capitol City
a. Building our capitol city
b. Washington, D. C. today
F. How the United States won freedom on the seas
1. Growth of trade
a. Captain Gray's voyage to China
b. United States and the Barbary pirates
2. The War of 1812
3. The Saving of the Northwest
4. Victories by the American Navy
a. The burning of Washington, D. C.
b. Jackson and the battle of New Orleans
c. The results of the war
5. Trade with the Far East
G. How the United States Became a United Nation
1. Quarrels that divided the nation
a. The quarrel over tariff
b. The quarrel over slavery
tariff
b. The quarrel over slavery
c. Three Negro leaders
d. Agreement by compromise
2. Election of a Republican President
a. The Story of Abraham Lincoln
b. Secession of the South
3. The war between the states
a. Blockade of Confederate parts
b. Failure to capture Richmond
c. Robert E. Lee
d. Cutting the Confederacy in two
4. The Emancipation Proclamation
5. After the war
a. Death of Abraham Lincoln
b. Problems of the south
c. Amendments of help the freedom
6. The "Solid South"
7. Our United Nations
VII. Living in the Southeast Today

    A. Farming in the Southeast
        1. Life in the cotton belt
           a. From planting to picking
           b. Preparing cotton for market
           c. Uses of the cotton plant
           d. Pests
           e. Sharecroppers and tenant farmers
        2. Tobacco Land
        3. Mixed farming
           a. Legumes and nuts
           b. Fruits and other special crops
           c. Truck crops
        4. Livestock and Dairying
    B. Fishing
    C. Lumbering
    D. Mining
    E. Chief cities
    F. TVA
VIII. The North Central States
    A. Location, topography, and climate
    B. Northwest territory
        1. History
        2. Government
        3. Settlement
           a. Life in the new settlement
           b. Farming on the prairies
        4. Travel
           a. On foot
           b. By horseback
               (1) Building roads
               (2) Steamboat
               (3) Early railroads
           c. Covered Wagons
           d. By boat
           e. Improvement
    C. Growth of the United States
        1. Missouri Compromise
        2. Louisiana Purchase
        3. New states
           a. Ohio
           b. Illinois

c. Indiana
d. Kansas
e. Nebraska
IX. Living and working in the North Central States
A. Farming
1. Corn
2. Wheat
3. Dairy
B. Lumbering
C. Mining
D. Manufacturing
E. The Great Lakes
1. Transportation
2. Vacation Lands
3. St. Lawrence Seaway
F. Cities of Importance
1. Chicago
2. Detroit
3. Cleveland
4. Toledo
5. St. Louis
6. Kansas City
7. Twin Cities
a. St. Paul
b. Minneapolis
X. The South Central States
A. Location, topography, climate
B. States
1. The story of Louisiana and Arkansas
2. How Texas became a state
a. History
b. Texas Revolution
c. War with Mexico
3. The settling of Oklahoma
a. History
b. Indian reservation
c. Oklahoma land rush
C. Earning a living
1. Farming
a. Cotton
b. Rice

        c.   Sugar

        d.   Wheat, corn, fruit, vegetables

    2.   Lumber, fish, furs

    3.   Mining

        a.   Oil and natural gas

        b.   Sulphur

        c.   Salt quarrying

        d.   Bauxite

        e.   Lead and zinc

        f.   Helium

  D. Houston, America's Space City

XI. The Rocky Mountain States

  A. Features

    1.   Land Surface

    2.   Climate

    3.   The Continental Divide

  B. Early Days

    1.   Spanish

    2.   Mission Settlements

    3.   The Santa Fe trail

  C. Settlement

    1.   The Mormons in Utah

    2.   Nevada and Colorado

        a.   The Comstock Lode

        b.   Pike's Peak or Bust

  D. Making a Living

    1.   Grazing and farm land

    2.   Mining

    3.   Lumbering

  E. Scenic Wonders

    1.   The Rockies

    2.   National and International Parks

XII. The Pacific States

  A. Features

    1.   Climate

    2.   Land Surface

    3.   Location

  B. States

    1.   California

        a.   Settlement

           (1)   Fremont

           (2)   Kit Carson
           (3)   The forty-niners
    b.   Making a living
           (1)   Farming
           (2)   Lumbering
           (3)   Fishing
    c.   Cities
           (1)   Los Angeles
           (2)   San Francisco
  2.   Oregon and Washington
    a.   Lewis and Clark Expedition
    b.   Astoria
    c.   Marcus and Narcissa Whitman
    d.   The Oregon Trail
    e.   Government
    f.   Mining, Fishing, Farming, Lumbering
    g.   Cities
           (1)   Salem
           (2)   Portland
           (3)   Seattle
           (4)   Spokane
  3.   Alaska
    a.   History
    b.   Making a Living
           (1)   Farming
           (2)   Industry
               (a)   Fur
               (b)   Fish
    c.   Scenic Beauty
    d.   Anchorage
  4.   Hawaii
    a.   History
    b.   Settlement
           (1)   Captain Cook
           (2)   Settlers from many lands
    c.   Farming
           (1)   Sugar Cane
           (2)   Pineapples
    d.   Importance of location
    e.   Tourist Land
C. Connecting East and West

       1.   Transcontinental mail service
       2.   Telegraph
       3.   Transcontinental Railroad

XIII.   The United States in the World Today
     A. Our islands in the Atlantic
       1.   Puerto Rico
          a.   As a Commonwealth
          b.   San Juan
          c.   Its Progress
          d.   Crops
             (1)   Sugar
             (2)   Tobacco
             (3)   Fruit
       2.   The Virgin Islands
     B. Our Islands in the Pacific
       1.   Midway
       2.   Wake
       3.   Guam
       4.   Samoa
     C. Panama Canal
       1.   Important Crossroads
       2.   Construction
       3.   Hardships
     D. Peace
       1.   A belief in freedom
       2.   Equal rights for all
       3.   The United States and other Nations
     E. Progress
       1.   At home
       2.   Through inventions
       3.   Lands added

Names of explorers to be learned

Vikings	Cartier
Amerigo Vespucius	Champlain
Columbus	Marquette and Joliet
Balboa	La Salle
DeSoto	Cabot
Ponce de Leon	Squanto
Diaz	Samoset
Magellan	Samuel Slater
Cortez	John Winthrop

Prince Henry   Miles Standish
Coronado   William Bradford
Vasco da Gama

Vocabulary

silt	shellfish	Mayflower Compact
upland	refrigerate	fertilize
glacier	sterling silver	surrender
natural region	quarry	Royal Colony
piedmont	imports	freedom of religion
navigation	industry	textiles
continental shelf	mixed farming	capital
head of ocean navigation	deep-sea fishing	recreation
silo	charter	spinning jenny
capital	assembly	specialized farming
exports	constitution	slag
powerloom	representative	coke
inshore fishing	factory	canal
dory	stockade	smelt
electronics	town meeting	tipple
strip mining	reservoir	lava
pig iron	wood pulp	inlet
ingot	newsprint	sound
bituminous	soil erosion	Tundra
anthracite		sequoia
locomotive		current
drift mining	sod	volcano
clipper ship	toil	interior
shaft mining	gridle	trade winds
blast furnace	prairie	crater
transportation	buckskin	conveyor
merchant marine	flatboat	breakwater
	keelboat	crossroads
	homespun	Forty-niners
gap	territory	spawning place
basin	patchwork	transcontinental
indigo	expedition	suspension bridge
burgess	husking bee	Great Circle Route
smuggle	quilting bee	
overseer	house raising	
plantation	surplus products	atom
money crop	hold	submarine
flood plain	open-pit mining	atomic

debtor's prison   chute   civil rights
tidewater region   hatch   segregated
permanent settlement   taconite   commonwealth
government   processing   cable
frontier
salt lick
cotton gin   levee
cotton belt   delta
indentured servant   mission
                         dry farming
                         reservation
secede   blimp
tariff
freedman
amendment   helium
compromise   drill
                         gusher
                         mohair
emancipate   sulphur
free state   derrick
confederacy   refinery
slave state   raw sugar
abolitionist   flowing well
carpetbagger   hogan
Emancipation   fleece
Proclamation   pueblo
                         geyser
dam   uranium
bauxite   shearing
generate   international
phosphate   Continental Divide

Evaluation

After educational goals and objectives have been established, evaluation is the means by which growth is measured. Evaluation should take place whenever the teacher or the teacher and pupils need to gauge the progress which is being made. It should be a continuing process.

Evaluation in social studies may be set up under three headings: (a) Have the pupils extend their knowledge and basic *understandings?* (b) Have they grown in social-studies *skills?* (c) Have they developed appropriate *attitudes?*

Evaluation not only measures student growth, but it also measures objectives, content, and educational instruction.

Answers must be sought to the following questions:

1. Do the students understand the meaning of the democratic way of life to the extent that they are willing to respect the opinions and rights of others?

2. Is there evidence of increased knowledge and appreciation of early inhabitants of America?

3. Are they becoming more interested in the affairs of their community, state, nation, and world?

4. Have they gained skill in using maps, globes, charts, and graphs?

5. Do they take responsible roles as citizens of their school?

6. Is there a desire on the pupils' part to become responsible citizens of their community, state, and nation?

7. Do the students have an understanding of the American Indians and their contributions?

8. Do the students discuss intelligently the great variety of climate, land surfaces, and natural resources of America?

9. Do students understand how the natural environment and the skills of the people make their life what it is?

10. Do the students understand that good transportation binds the country together and makes possible wide distribution of goods in the United States?

11. Can the students use the vocabulary correctly and with confidence?

12. Do the students show skills in the use and interpretation of maps and charts?

Evaluation can be accomplished by:

Teacher-made Tests

Standardized Achievement Test in the spring

Pre-test from the Standardized Achievement test the year before for placement

Open-book test to teach pupils to read for main ideas and facts

RESOURCE MATERIALS

Textbook: *Living in the United States:* MacMillan Company

Workbook: *Living in the United States:* MacMillan Company

Maps: World, United States, Physical, Geographical Terms, and Political

Art Materials

Brochures

Reference Books

Weekly Readers

Films

Filmstrips:
26E   Citizens in a Democracy
40E   Desert Community Life
14E   Early Explorers and Pioneers
16E   Louisiana Purchase and Florida
11E   Mexican Secession and Gadsden Purchase
33E   Mormon Trail
12E   Original Thirteen Colonies
15E   Pioneers and Settlers of the Oregon Territory
34E   Transportation
31E   Why We Have National Parks
   (Source: Encyclopedia Brittanica, Chicago, Illinois)
5983   The Birthplace of Civilization
   (Source: Life Filmstrips, 9 Rockefeller Plaza, New York 20, New York)
21   The Opening of the West
   (Source: McGraw-Hill Filmkare Products Co., New York City, U.S.A.)
 4E   Middle Atlantic States
 5E   Middle West
 1E   Pacific Coast States
 6E   Southern United States
 7E   Southwestern United States
 2E   Western United States

Tapes: Imperial Productions, Inc.
America Settled
Civil War
Cold War
Depression
Early California and Gold Rush
First President and Democracy Begins
Louisiana Purchase–Lewis and Clark
Mr. Lincoln
Revolutionary War
Seeds of Civil War
Settling West of the Appalachian Mts.
South Builds Again
Texas History
To a New Land
War of 1812
West on the Oregon Trail and Settling the Northwest

World War I
World War II
35th President Killed
49th and 50th States and America in Space

Transparencies: School Material Center

2520 Global Directions and Location Skills
2501 World
2524 Discovery of the New World
2502 North America
2504 The United States
2505 Physical Map of the United States
2512 Growing Season of the United States
2513 Agriculture Regions of the United States
2514 Land Use of the United States
2531 Regions of the United States
2549 United States
2508 Average Annual Rainfall
2525 Revolutionary War-Major Campaigns in the South, West, and North
2529 The Union-The Confederacy
2532 New England States
2533 Middle Atlantic States
2522 How a Bill Becomes a Law
2516 Coal and Iron Ore-Mfg. Areas
2534 Southern States
2535 Midwestern States
2536 Southwestern States
2537 Rocky Mountain States
2539 Alaska
2540 Hawaii

Sample Daily Lesson Plan

Subject: Introduction to the Pacific States

Objectives: The students will locate, identify, and name the Pacific States on a map.

Pupils will list in writing their ideas and opinions of the ways of living in the Pacific states from viewing the pictures in the unit.

Activities: Fill in outlined map of the Pacific States.

Share with the class pictures pertaining to the Pacific States.

Subject: Early Days in The Pacific States

Objectives: The child will develop skill in the use of biographies and stories of adventure, to gain information, ideas, and enjoyment. Pupils will refer to an encyclopedia for further information and to try to evaluate the accuracy of the story or biography they have chosen to read.

Activities: Give oral reports.

Use reference books.

Practice locating and organizing information.

SIXTH GRADE
SOCIAL STUDIES

Statement of Purpose

The sixth grade child begins to see his life as it interacts with other peoples of the hemisphere. He learns about the problems of life in his home, community, state, and country, and compares and contrasts them with those of Canada, Mexico, South America, and the smaller countries of Central America. He begins to recognize, appreciate, and compare the ways climate, terrain, topography, natural resources, and technology affect the livelihood and social life of the peoples of these countries and of the United States.

Students are helped to select and study materials which enable them to use problem solving in their life in this hemisphere.

Objectives

1. A. The students will learn of the simultaneous exploration and development of Canada and the United States.
    B. They will name three explorers of each country and give the region each explored.
2. A. The child will be able to explain to his classmates how Canada's government is patterned after that of the British Commonwealth.
    B. He will orally describe to the group how their history is interwoven.
3. A. The sixth grader will use maps, population, natural resources, temperature, etc. to write the reasons why most people live in the southern part of Canada.
    B. Using the same maps he will show why this area has developed industrially.
    C. The students will make a detailed study of the province of Quebec with a short paper describing their homes, food, clothing, crops, and industry.
4. A. The students will locate six major cities on an outline map of Canada and give the latitude and longitude of each.
5. A. The students will explain the significance of the St. Lawrence Seaway to Canada and the United States.
    B. He will list six benefits derived from the use of the Seaway.

Photo furnished courtesy of AUM Learning Resource Center and Montgomery County Public Schools, Montgomery, Alabama.

6. A. The sixth grader will develop insight into the increasing importance of northern Canada in our national economy and defense.
   B. They will do research and list raw materials found there which are presently being used in industry.
   C. They will show on a map the air miles (across Canada) from unfriendly nations to our own country.
7. A. After class study, the students will participate in discussions to compare the needs, reasons, and benefits of good relations between Canada and their own country.
8. A. The students will gain insight into the interdependence of the different geographical areas of Canada.
   B. He will understand the interdependence of Canada and the United States.
   C. After the above he will list six benefits and three liabilities associated with these.
9. A. The children will present a program showing how the people of Latin America are more like us than different.
10. A. The students will demonstrate (by pantomine) the importance of friendly relations between the countries of Latin America and the United States.
    B. They will draw maps showing political borders and explain how hard they would be to defend from unfriendly countries.
11. A. The sixth graders will describe who our Latin American neighbors are: their race, their culture, their history, and their government.
    B. They will give written reports to small groups on the above.
12. A. The children will make oral comparisons of the diverse ways of living in the natural regions of South America.
13. A. The students will investigate the highly developed Indian civilizations found in Latin America.
    B. They will list their contributions to the early settlers of the western hemisphere.
14. A. The students will report what happened to the South American Indians with the coming of the Spanish.
    B. They will compare this with the treatment of Indian tribes by French and English explorers of North America.
15. A. The students will orally describe the struggle for freedom of the people from different countries of Europe.
16. A. The students will demonstrate their growth and appreciation of the democratic way of life as they use these in class discussions and other school activities.

17. A. The sixth grader will show greater skill in the use and interpretation of maps, globes, charts, graphs, symbols, resource materials, and current events.
    B. Students will use these to present information to small or large groups.
18. A. The children will discriminate in selecting pictures and other content material used in writing reports.
19. A. The students will compare the interests as well as the differences of the peoples of the regions and countries of this hemisphere.
20. A. The students will compare the contributions of different kinds of transportation of the countries and list them according to cost to shipper.
21. A. The child will list some of the many contributions of the different countries in discoveries, inventions, raw materials, manufacturing, science, medicine, art, music, and literature.
    B. They will divide into groups and have a contest to see which side can identify the contributing country.

Suggested Activities (Methods)

Note: Most of these suggestions can be used with either of the countries; others will be designated.

A. Teacher activities:

1. The teacher will introduce, lecture, or lead discussion on each new lesson or assignment.
2. The teacher will use pictures, filmstrips, films, tapes, records, and personal experiences to familiarize students with areas being studied.
3. The teacher will invite resource people to work with students.
4. The teacher will direct individual or group projects (listening for any student suggestions and ideas).
5. The teacher will make arrangements for field trips and other inter-class activities.
6. The teacher will direct students to needed materials for research.
7. The teacher will make, or approve, all assignments.
8. The teacher will provide maps, outline maps, encyclopedias, and supplementary texts for use in class.
9. The teacher will observe students closely, and request conferences to encourage students toward the expected objectives.

10. The teacher will provide and administer tests on the material studied.

B. Student activities

Students will:

1. View a film of the country, or area, to get an overview of physical features, boundaries, climate, and geographical divisions.
2. Collect and read books about countries.
3. Become familiar with the language of each country and why it is spoken. Learn some French, Spanish, and Portuguese words.
4. Use maps to show population of places and other maps to show why. (latitude, winds, rainfall, and temperature).
5. Use maps and globe to show that some mountain ranges continue on either side of both continents.
6. Use pictures of farms, homes, cities, industrial, and rural areas of any country to make displays.
7. Make reports on explorers and early leaders such as: the Vikings, Drake, Balboa, Champlain, Henry Hudson, John Cabot, LaSalle, Joliet, Father Marquette, Simon Bolivar, San Martin, Pizzaro, the Incas and the Aztecs.
8. Keep a current events bulletin board of the country being studied from news and television.
9. Dramatize events that led to the independence of each country.
10. Select one city or country, and make a booklet using pictures to show products, etc.
11. Listen to tapes and records of book reviews, biographical sketches, songs, poems, and plays of some countries.
12. Exchange letters with a pen pal.
13. Make a time line of events in Canada's early history and compare it with that of the United States.
14. Make a product map, or show real products.
15. Study climate and see how it determines rainfall.
16. Compare Indian tribes and their contributions in South America with those in Canada.
17. Choose a tourist attraction, do indepth research of it and share the findings with the class, using pictures, slides, records, folders, books, and encyclopedias.
18. Invite a local traveler to visit with group.
19. Discuss the wars and boundaries of countries.

20. Make a model of dams on the Panama Canal or the Great Lakes, and explain its significance.
21. Keep a list of important people and their contributions (early and present day) to each country. Late in the study of countries play the "Who Am I" game.
22. Dramatize or make a frieze of the fall of Quebec, the landing of Columbus, Pizzaro and the Incas, or Cortez, and Montezuema.
23. Use modeling clay to make relief maps to show natural regions.
24. Use the globe to review latitude, longitude, time zones, equator, and temperature belts.
25. Exhibit things collected from other countries and label and invite visitors to see them.

Content

I. Our Northern Neighbor
   A. Canada
      1. Geographic conditions and how they differ from other countries
         a. Location
         b. Climate
         c. Surface features
         d. Natural resources
         e. Size
      2. People of the region and their early history
         a. Explorers
         b. Early settlements
      3. Canada's relations with other countries
         a. Great Britain
         b. France
         c. United States
         d. Other countries
      4. People of the regions and how they live now
         a. Homes
         b. Food
         c. Clothing
         d. Crops and industries
         e. Customs and culture
         f. Transportation and communication

5. Principal cities
6. Provinces and territories
   a. Population
   b. Contrasts in topography
   c. Products
   d. Natural resources
7. Natural regions
   a. Rocky Mountains
   b. Laurentian Uplands
   c. Appalachian Uplands
   d. Great Lakes
   e. St. Lawrence Seaway
   f. Hudson Bay
   g. Oceans
   h. Other lakes and rivers
8. Contributions to world trade and culture
   a. Minerals
   b. Foods
   c. Government
   d. Manufactured products
9. Map reading
   a. Altitude
   b. Latitude
   c. Latitude
   d. Time zones
   e. Population
   f. Vegetation
   g. Scale
   h. Vegetation and products
   i. Growing seasons
   j. Other map uses

II. Our Southern Neighbors
   A. Mexico
      1. Geographic conditions (differences)
         a. Terrain
         b. Altitude
         c. Latitude
         d. Surface features
      2. People of the regions and their early history
         a. Early Indian civilization
         b. Spanish conquerors

        c.   Mestizos
- 3. People of regions and present day living
  - a. Food
  - b. Clothing
  - c. Homes
  - d. Economic geography and reasons for occupational differences
  - e. Education
- 4. Principal cities
  - a. Mexico City
  - b. Monterrey
  - c. Guadalajara
  - d. Other cities
- 5. Transportation
  - a. Railroads
  - b. Airlines
  - c. Harbors
  - d. Highways
- 6. Natural resources
- 7. Farm products
- 8. Tourist attractions

III. Our Latin American Friends
- A. Central America and West Indies
  - 1. Location
  - 2. Geographical features
  - 3. Size of countries
  - 4. Natural resources
  - 5. Homes, food, and education of people
  - 6. Geographic reasons for occupation
  - 7. Panama Canal
- B. South America
  - 1. Geographic differences
    - a. Latitude
    - b. Altitude
    - c. Rainfall
    - d. Rivers
  - 2. Early and present day history and customs
    - a. Language differences
    - b. Size of countries (reasons for)
      - (1) Major cities
      - (2) Seaports

        c.   Governments
        d.   Schools
        e.   Products
        f.   Natural resources
        g.   Exports and imports

3.   Divisions
        a.   Hot wet lands
        b.   Dry areas
        c.   Cold southern region

4.   Interdependence
        a.   Between countries of South America
        b.   Between South America, U. S., and Canada
        c.   South American countries & Central American countries
        d.   These countries and countries of other continents

5.   Interpreting maps
        a.   Political and Physical
        b.   Rainfall
        c.   Product
        d.   Temperature
        e.   City maps
        f.   Vegetation
        g.   Transportation

6.   Importance of friendly relations between all neighbors of the Western Hemisphere

Social Studies Vocabulary

1.   *Altitude:* The height above sea level.
2.   *Antarctic:* The cold region around the South Pole.
3.   *Arctic:* The cold region around the North Pole.
4.   *Basin:* An area of land largely enclosed by higher land.
5.   *Bay:* Part of a body of water which reaches into land.
6.   *Branch:* A river or creek which flows into a large river.
7.   *Canal:* A man made channel for transportation or irrigation.
8.   *Canyon:* A deep narrow valley with steep sides.
9.   *Cape:* A point of land sticking out into a body of water.
10.   *Channel:* A deep, narrow body of water connecting two larger bodies of water; also the deeper part of a waterway.
11.   *Cliff:* A high steep wall of rock.
12.   *Climate:* The kind of weather a place has through the years.

13. *Continents:* The largest bodies of land on earth; larger than islands.
14. *Current:* The movement of a stream of water.
15. *Delta:* The land deposited at the mouth of a river.
16. *Desert:* A land too dry or too old to grow many plants.
17. *Dike:* A man made wall of earth or stone built to keep out water.
18. *Divide:* A height of land which separates river basins.
19. *Downstream:* The direction toward which a river flows.
20. *Elevation:* The height above sea level.
21. *Equator:* An imaginary line around the earth that is the same distance from the north and south poles.
22. *Fiord:* A narrow inlet of the sea with steep banks; usually formed by a glacier.
23. *Foothills:* Hill at the base of mountains.
24. *Glacier:* A body of slowly moving ice.
25. *Globe:* A map of the earth on a round ball.
26. *Growing Season:* The number of days when the weather is warm enough for plants to grow without being injured by a frost.
27. *Gulf:* Part of a body of water which reaches into the land.
28. *Harbor:* A sheltered place where ships may anchor safely.
29. *Highland:* High or mountainous land.
30. *Hill:* A rise and more or less rounded part of the earth's surface; smaller than a mountain.
31. *Iceberg:* A floating mass of ice which has broken off from a glacier.
32. *Inland:* Way from seashore.
33. *Inlet:* A narrow strip of water extending inland.
34. *Island:* Land entirely surrounded by water, smaller than a continent.

Sample Daily Lesson Plan I

Subject: People of Canada
Objective:
>   The child should be able to write or tell about the homes, food, clothing, and crops in the province of Quebec in Canada.

Activities
1. Assign reading from textbook about their homes, food, clothing and crops.
2. Assign one group of the class to make written reports of homes.
3. Assign one group to make written reports about clothing.
4. Assign one group to give written reports on crops.
5. Assign one group to make questions from these reports, if the class can answer most of them, they have learned something about each.

Sample Daily Lesson Plan II

Subject: Map Reading About Canada
Objective:
    The child should be able to contrast the difference in these two terms *Latitude* and *Longitude.*

Activities
1. Use a map of Canada.
2. Teacher will explain how to find *latitude* and *longitude.*
3. Give cities to locate on map.
4. Assign different pupils to find each city on the map.
5. After pupils know where cities are and can tell what latitude and longitude they are, they understand the difference. If not, drill and give more practice on these terms. If needed, divide class into two groups, have a time race to see which group can first give latitude and longitude of five given cities.

Evaluation

    Evaluation is accomplished by teacher observation, different kinds of tests administered by the teacher to check the growth of students on objectives set forth at the beginning of the course, and by class participation and discussion about material found in textbooks, resource materials, and personal experiences shared by class members. Final evaluation will be made by comparison of present and past achievement tests.

A. Sample Test Items
1. Write a short research paper naming three people, or groups who explored or settled southern Canada, and three groups who explored, or settled the northern part of the United States in the seventeenth century.
2. Explain orally Canada's form of government, and tell how Canada is related to Great Britain.
3. Using maps explain why most of Canada's people live in the southern part of Canada, and why it has developed industrially.
4. Tell how the governments of Canada and the United States cooperated in building the St. Lawrence Seaway, and list six benefits derived from its use.
5. Name, and describe five raw materials found in the northern part of Canada. Tell how each is used in industry. Describe the significance of Canada's friendship to the United States from a military defense standpoint.

6.   Have a debate on needs, reasons, and benefits of good relations between the two major countries of North America.

7.   List how the different geographical areas of Canada are dependent upon each other, and how these countries are also dependent upon each other. List the benefits and liabilities associated with this interdependence.

8.   From research, a program of stories, pictures, dolls, (and tourists) will be presented by the students showing the many ways people of Latin America are like the people of the United States.

9.   Through class discussion and with maps the students will demonstrate the need for friendship, and show how hard it would be to defend the borders of some countries of Latin America from unfriendly nations.

10.   In small groups make written reports on the background of the people in Central and South America giving their race, country of origin, history, and government—each student will choose a country for his research.

11.   From maps and research write a comparison of the differences of living conditions in three natural regions of South America.

12.   List some of the contributions of the Aztec, and Inca Indians to the early settlement of Latin America.

13.   Explain what happened to the leaders of the Indians with the coming of the Spanish.

14.   Enumerate some of the hardships experienced by the South American colonists in their struggle for freedom from their mother country.

15.   The teacher should *gauge* the students' growth in democratic principles by special observation of his class participation on a number of occasions, and indicate his progress in symbols agreed upon by the class.

16.   From maps, each student will present (at a set time) three different kinds of information, using globes, charts, graphs, symbols, pictographs, etc. as needed.

17.   Select pictures, and other suitable pictorial material to illustrate material selected for a research paper, and explain why it was selected.

18.   From the above material compare the differences and likenesses of people in the United States and Argentina, or any two leading countries of the western hemisphere.

19.   Name the kinds of transportation which have helped to develop the different areas, and give the advantages of each.

20.   From a multiple choice test, the students will identify twenty people who have made contributions to the western hemisphere devel-

opment in the fields of discovery, invention, manufacturing, science, medicine, art, music, and literature.

21. Final evaluation will consist of a fifty item true and false test, and an open book test (using out-line maps) to place countries, provinces, mountains, bodies of water, farm products, minerals, natural regions, and some major cities in their proper location, giving the longitude, latitude, and altitude of three.

B. Instruments

1. Class discussion
2. Student reports
3. Student and teacher-made tests
4. Open book tests
5. Map tests
6. Teacher-made tests
7. Weekly Reader Social Studies Tests
8. Metropolitan Achievement Test

RESOURCE MATERIALS

I. **Textbook—** *Canada and Latin America*
Utley, Marguerite, and Whittemore,
Katherine Thomas—Ginn and Company

II. **Textbooks supplementary—** 1. *The United States and Canada*
Whittemore, Katherine Thomas
Ginn and Company
2. *Neighbors on Our Earth*
Whipple, Gertrude, and James, Preston E.
Macmillan and Company
3. *Exploring the New World*
Follett, Dwight W.
Follett Publishing Company
4. *South America* (The Illustrated Book)
Appel, Benjamin
Grossett and Dunlap, Publishers
5. *Travel Atlas of Scenic America*
Hammond, C. S. and Company
6. *World Atlas*
Goode, Paul J.

Rand McNally and Company
7.   *World Atlas* (School and Library)
Foster, Fred W.
School and Library Publishing Co.

III.   Audio visual
A.   Aids (Mechanical)
1.   Overhead Projector
2.   Opaque Projector
3.   Film Strip Projector
4.   Motion Picture Projector
5.   Tape Recorder
6.   Record Player
B.   Aids (Other)
1.   Film Strips
a.   36 E   (1)   Highland Indians
b.   32   (1)   Lowland Indians
c.   33   (1)   The Old and New In South America
d.   34 E   (1)   Transportation
e.   35 E   (1)   Hot Wet Lands-Mexico
f.   21 E   (1)   Amazon Village
g.   Amazon Village East and Southern Lands
h.   39   (1)   Agriculture
i.   27 E   (1)   Friends and Neighbors to the South
j.   5734   (2)   The Pan American Highway—Along the
Andes
k.   5718   (2)   New Coffee Lands in Brazil
l.   5731   (2)   Along the Equator in Equador
m. 5732   (2)   The New Venezuela
n.   5722   (2)   Desert To Forest In Chile
o.   5719   (2)   People of Paraguay
p.   5721   (2)   Farmers of Argentina
q.   5720   (2)   Ranch and City In Uraguay
r.   5730   (2)   Mountain Farmers of Colombia
s.   5729   (2)   Inca Lands In Peru
(2)   *Encyclopedia Brittanica*
Chicago, Illinois
(3)   3M Company
St. Paul, Minnesota
2.   Transparencies
a.   2501 World

      b. 2502 North America—Political
      c. 2503 North America—Physical
      d. 2508 Canada
      e. 2509 Mexico and Central America
      f. 2510 South America
      g. 2517 Landforms
      h. 2518 Standard Time Zones of North America
      i. 2519 The Americas on the Globe
      j. 2520 Global Directions and Location Skills
      k. 2521 River City
      l. 2523 The World of European Discovery
      m. 2524 Discovery of the New World
      n. 3M Map Reading, Latin America Part 1 & 2 Grades 4, 5, 6.
      o. 2542 North America
      p. 2543 South America

3. Films
      a. 135 Arts and Crafts of Mexico
      b. 107 Airplane Changes Our World Map
      c. 2505 Amazon, The
      d. 114 America For Me
      e. 133 Argentina
      f. 167 Brazil
      g. 207 Central America
      h. 210 Children of Chima
      i. 437 Great Lakes, The: How They Were Formed
      j. 180 Great Lakes, The: Their Link with Ocean Shipping
      k. 508 Industrial Provinces of Canada
      l. 582 Land of Mexico
      m. 638 Maritime Provinces of Canada
      n. 2712 Mediterranean Africa
      o. 690 Navajo Children
      p. 691 Navajo Indians
      q. 725 Pacific Canada
      r. 726 Panama: Crossroads of the Western World
      s. 732 People of Mexico
      t. 2753 Peru: People of the Andes (Color)
      u. 737 Peru: People of the Andes (B & W)
      v. 784 Reading Maps
      w. 230 Columbus, Christopher
      x. 580 La Salle, Robert Cavelier Sieur De
      y. 839 Spanish Conquest of the New World

z.   2828 Vikings, The: Life and Conquest
4. Tapes
   a.   Imperial—Famous Moments in History (set of 20)
5. Maps
   a.   World
   b.   North and South America
   c.   Outer space
   d.   Universal Data
   e.   Cosmopolitan World
6. Charts
   a.   Map symbols and geographic terms (set)
   b.   American History
7. Globes
8. Planetarium
9. Encyclopedias
10. Library Books
11. *National Geographic Magazine*

FREE TEACHING MATERIALS——SOCIAL STUDIES

Arabian American Oil Co.
Public Relations Dept.
505 Park Avenue
New York   10022

Pictures of Arabia and
oil production

Belgium Inf. Service
50 Rockefeller Plaza
New York   10020

Posters

Standard Oil Co. of Calif.
Public Relations Dept.
225 Bust Street
San Francisco   94120

Developments in music poster

Freedom's Foundation at Valley Forge
Valley Forge
Penn.   19481

Large packet of materials on
patriotism, democracy, and America

American Trucking Assoc.
Ed. Division
1616 P Street, N. W.
Washington   20036

Land transportation development
chart

New Zealand Embassy
Inf. Service
19 Observatory Circle, N. W.
Washington   20008

Information on New Zealand

Union Pacific RR Co.

Advertising Dept.

1416 Dodge Street
Omaha, Nebraska   68102

Am. Telephone and Telegraph Co.
Booklet Editor
Room 833, 195 Broadway
New York   10007

U. S. Dept. of Ag.
Farmer Cooperative Service
Washington, D. C.

U. S. Dept. of Interior
Bureau of Indian Affairs
1951 Constitution Ave.
Washington   20242

Turkish Tourism and Inf. Office
500 5th Ave.
New York   10036

American Friends of Middle East
Dept. of Dev. and Inf.
1605 N. H. Avenue, N. W.
Washington   20009

Swedish Inf. Service
161 E. 42nd St.
New York   10007

Nestle Co. Inc. (Consumer Service Dept.)
Consumer Service Dept.
100 Bloomingdale Rd.
White Plains, N. Y.   10605

India Tourist Office
685 Market St.
San Francisco   94105

German Inf. Center
410 Park Ave.
New York   10022

Australian Consulate General
636 5th Ave.
New York   10020

Danish Inf. Office
280 Park Ave.
New York   10017

Casa de Portugal
570 5th Ave.
New York   10036

Information on trains, pictures, posters, etc.

Bell telephone developments

Interior, Indians

Booklet on Middle East Countries

Cookies from other lands

Pakistan, Consulate General
Pakistan House
2606 Pacific Ave.
San Francisco   94115

South African Inf. Service
655 Madison Ave., 14th Floor
New York   10021

Swiss National Tourist Office
661 Market St.
San Francisco   94105

Senators
Representatives
Library of Congress–Gutenberg Bible
Metropolitan Life Ins. Co.

Secretaries of States
Chamber of Commerces
Highways Departments
Oil Companies for maps

Alaska Travel Div.
Pouch E
Juneau, Alaska   99801

Denoyer–Geppert Co.
5235 Ravenswood Ave.   Maps, teaching hints, etc.
Chicago, Ill.   60640

National Cotton Council of Am.   Large amount of material on
P. O. Box 12285   growth,
Memphis   38112   Manufacturing and use.

Cram Co. Inc.
P. O. Box 426   Teaching information
Indianapolis, Ind.   46206

Field Enterprise Ed. Corp.
Ed. Services   How a Bill Becomes a Law, police
Merchandise Mart Plaza
Chicago, Ill.   60654

American Bankers Assoc.
Banking Ed. Committee
90 Park Ave.   Economics, Banks
New York   10016

Manufacturer's Hanover Trust Co.
Public Relations Dept.   Banking
350 Park Ave.
New York   10022

United Nations
Public Inquiries Unit
New York   10017

Chinese Inf. Service
100 West 32nd St.
New York   10001

U. S. Nat. Com. for UNESCO
Secretarial   Large group of materials on
Dept. of State   various phases of organization
Washington, D. C.   20520

Federal Bureau of Investigation
Dept. of Justice Bldg.   How it works, job, etc.
Washington, D. C.   20535

Social Security Inf.   What social security is, who
Office of Inf., Room 107   can get it, etc. history
Baltimore   21235

Internal Revenue Service   Taxes, etc.
local

Pop. Reference Bureau Inc.
Inf. Service   Poster on a population of countries
1755 Massachusetts Ave., N. W.
Washington, D. C.   20036

U. S. Dept. of Defense, Office of Civil Defense
Office of Civil Defense, U. S. Army AG Publications Center
Civil Defense Branch
2800 Eastern Blvd.
Baltimore   21220

General Motors Corp.
Public Relations Staff
1-101 Gen. Motors Bldg.   History and study of autos
Detroit   48202

Assoc. of American R. R.
Ed. Relations   Great amount on development and
Transportation Bldg.   use of railroads
Washington   20006

Canadian Gov. Travel Bureau
Ottawa, Ontario, Canada   Large amount on Canada

Canadian Consulate Gen.
Suite 2110 International Trade Mart   Large amount of materials
2 Canal Street
New Orleans   70130

Newfoundland and Labrador Tourist Dev. Office
Confederation Bldg.
St. John's, Newfoundland, Canada

Canadian Embassy
1746 Mass. Ave.
Washington   20036

U. S. Dept. of Interior, Geographical Survey Information Office Washington, D. C. 20242	Amazon
Columbia Inf. Service 140 East 57th St. New York 10022	
Panama Embassy 2601 29th St. N. W. Washington, D. C. 20008	
VFW National Headquarters Americanism Dept. Broadway at 34th street Kansas City, Mo. 64111	Patriotism Flag
Nat. Consumer's Finance Assoc. Mr. Frances A. Kalvacher, Dir. 1000 16th St., N. W. Washington, 20036	Information on economics
Belgium Inf. Service 50 Rockefeller Plaza New York 10020	Information on Belgium, government, people, land
U. S. Dept. of State Bureau of Public Affairs Office of Media Services, Distribution Services (Room 5819A), Washington, D. C. 20520	Relations
People to People P. O. Box 1201 Kansas City, Mo. 64141	Population poster
Instituto Italino di Cultura 686 Park Ave New York 10021	People, land, government Constitution of Italy
Hancock Mutual Life Ins. Co. Community Relations Dept. 200 Berkeley St. Boston 02117	John Hancock, Constitution, other documents, flags
Treasury Dept. Bureau of Customs Inf. Office 2100 K Street Washington 20026	Customs, entering country, etc.
State Mutual Life Ins. Co. Dept. of Public Relations 440 Lincoln St. Worcester, Mass. 01605	Fifty state flags
American Red Cross local Chapter	History, work

TEACHING
UNITS
GRADES
SEVEN
THROUGH
TWELVE

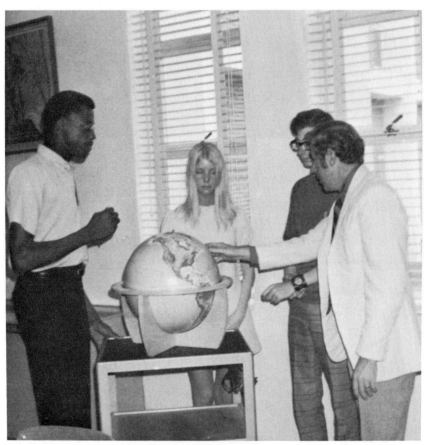

Photo furnished courtesy of AUM Learning Resource Center and Montgomery County Public Schools, Montgomery, Alabama.

SEVENTH GRADE
WORLD GEOGRAPHY:
Australia, New Zealand, and Antarctica

Introduction

One of the fundamental purposes of the secondary social studies is shaping student attitudes toward people of other lands. A knowledge of place, climate, industry, agriculture, terrain, culture, and government of other nations is vital to good citizenship. Geography is a powerful and important contributor to what students come to believe about other countries and the people who live there. The social studies teacher should not try to indoctrinate his students with the teacher's or the textbook writer's point of view; but a good social studies teacher does serve as bridge between the natural provincialism of his students and a more mature and worldly outlook.

This unit is intended to teach the students about the European heritage of Australia and New Zealand. Comparisons between the experiences of these people and the experiences of the people of the United States and Canada will be made. Students should gain some knowledge of what life is like in each of these nations. A knowledge of the terrain, climate, flora, fauna, agriculture, manufacturing, government and life styles of the Anzac peoples will be promoted. The students will also study about the Antarctic region.

This unit is designed to cover the last six-weeks of the seventh grade world geography course. The material is presented in a simple, straight-forward style and the students natural curiosity is utilized as a main means of motivation and teaching.

Behavioral Objectives

Cognitive domain:
1. The students will discuss the comparative sizes of New Zealand, Antarctica, Australia, and the United States.
2. On a map, the students will locate the capitals of New Zealand and Australia, as well as two other large cities in each country.
3. In a brief paragraph the class will compare and contrast the climate and weather conditions of Antarctica, Australia, and New Zealand.

4. The "upside-down" seasons of Australia and New Zealand and the six-month days and nights of Antarctica will be explained by each pupil in one or two short paragraphs.

5. The class will write a one page paper comparing the Australian Outback to the Old West of America.

6. Each student will list three animals found in 1)New Zealand, 2)Antarctica, and 3)Australia, including two characteristics of each animal.

7. The pupils will compare orally the forest lands of New Zealand and Australia as to size and importance to the economy.

8. The students will write a research paper comparing life in an Aborigine, a Maori, and an American Indian village.

9. Each student will differientiate between a marsupial and a monotreme.

10. Each pupil will list six ways that Australia and the United States are similar.

11. The class will explain orally why the Dutch did not back up their discovery of Australia and New Zealand with exploration and settlement.

12. Each pupil will write two reasons explaining why the British became interested in settling Australia and New Zealand.

13. The class will discuss the similarities between the California gold rush of 1849 and the Australian gold rush of 1851.

14. The present day life of a Maori will be compared with that of an Aborigine and an American Indian in a two page paper.

15. In less than a page each class member will discuss the political structures of Australia and New Zealand.

16. The class will discuss orally the role of tourism in the economies of both Australia and New Zealand.

17. Given a list of descriptive phrases, the students will match the phrases with either North Island, South Island, Australia, New Zealand, or Antarctica.

18. The class will construct a time line showing the exploration and development of Australia, New Zealand, and Antarctica.

19. Each student will exhibit his mastery of library skills by making a notebook on these three lands.

20. The class will describe three English customs that are proudly honored by New Zealanders.

21. In a few sentences each student will describe how the prime minister and the cabinet are selected in New Zealand.

22. The class will explain in class discussion why Antarctica is considered a continent while the Artic regions are not.

23. All students will explain in a brief paragraph the importance of the International Geophysical Year to Antarctic exploration.

24. The students will list five of the countries with established bases on Antarctica.
25. Each student will write a one page description of Operation Deep Freeze.
26. The class members will discuss orally Australia's policy of maintaining a "white Australia."
27. On a mimeographed map, each pupil will fill in the names of the seven political territories of Australia as well as the names of the surrounding bodies of water.
28. Each student will color code a rainfall map of New Zealand and Australia.
29. The class will compare the cattle stations of Australia with the sheep stations of New Zealand in a paragraph.
30. Each pupil will explain briefly why grass is the most important crop grown in New Zealand.
31. The students will briefly outline the major explorations in Antarctica.
32. Each student will write a one page analysis of the question on Antarctica.

Affective domain:

33. Each student will value good citizenship by showing respect for others in the class.
34. The students will exhibit a willingness to learn.
35. The pupils will respond to questions in class and will show their interest in the subject by asking questions themselves.
36. Each class member will exhibit scholarship and neatness in all classwork and homework assignments.
37. Students will develop a positive attitude about social studies in general and seventh grade geography in particular.
38. All pupils will show value for opinions of their classmates and will accept others for what they are.
39. Each student will develop a positive attitude about himself.

Skills:

40. Class members will exhibit skills in the use of maps by coding and labeling maps in class.
41. The students will show skill in the use of library facilities by making a notebook on Australia, New Zealand, and Antarctica.
42. Each pupil will exhibit skill in the use of time lines by taking part in the construction of a time line for class use and study.

43. All students will exhibit skill in working individually by turning in outside assignments and classwork.
44. Each child will exhibit skill in working in small groups by actively participating in a small group panel discussion.
45. Every student will exhibit skill in speaking before the class by giving one oral report from a list of several topics.
46. The student will show skill in making things with their hands by constructing one project of their choice.
47. Students will spell correctly and use vocabulary in proper context.

Teaching and Learning Activities

Code: T.C. Teacher centered
                S.C. Student centered
                G.C. Small group or class centered

Introductory activities:

Pretest: A pretest will be given to the class to determine what the students already know and can do. This test will be similar to the one that they will take after completing this unit.

1. **Guest speakers:** If arrangements can be made, Mrs. _____, a native of Australia will speak to the class about life in her homeland. Her general statements about the people and customs of Australia will serve as an introduction to this unit of study and should capture the attention of the students. This will be an excellent opportunity for the class to hear an authentic "Aussie" accent. Mr. _____, an American who has lived in both Australia and New Zealand will speak the same day, giving the class the viewpoint of an American who has spent some time in Australia and New Zealand. (Teacher Centered Obj. # 34, 35)
2. **Filmstrips:** If the guest speakers are unable to come, three filmstrips can be shown—"Australia," "Portrait of Antarctica," and "Introduction to New Zealand." (T.C. Obj. # 34, 35)
3. **Question and Answer:** A question and answer period will follow either the speakers or the filmstrips to see what the class is interested in learning about these three lands. They may bring up interesting points that will be worth covering in the unit. (Group Centered Obj. # 34, 35)

Developmental activities:

1. **Lecture:** Straight lecture will be avoided as much as possible since there are so many other teaching methods available. Brief lectures will be necessary from time to time to explain some of the material. An example

lecture will be entitled, "Three Strange Australians," and will cover the kangaroo, the koala, and the platypus. (T.C. Obj. # 3, 4, 6, 12, 26, 29, 31)

2. **Discussion:** After each lecture period, there will be class discussion so that the students can discuss any part of the lecture that they feel they did not understand. Members of the class will answer all questions if possible, thereby reinforcing what they have learned. (G.C. Obj. # 3, 4, 6, 26, 12, 29, 31)

3. **Panel Discussion:** We will have several panel discussions, enabling every pupil to do outside research with a small group. Using this method the students will find out for themselves the things they should know. The teacher will fill in information that the panel members may have overlooked. Two examples of topics for the discussions are: (1) A Comparison of Life in an Aborigine, a Maori, and an American Indian Village, and (2) A Comparison and Contrast of the Political Structures of Australia and New Zealand. (G.C. Obj. # 8, 12, 16, 25, 31, 44)

4. **Small Group Projects:** The class will be divided into groups of five or six students each to work on a group project chosen from a list of about seven suggested projects. Included on this list will be (1) Make cloth replicas of the flags of Australia and New Zealand. (2) Make a model of an Aborigine village. (3) Make a model of a Maori village. (4) Make a relief map of Australia and New Zealand. (5) Make a relief map of Antarctica with flags showing the location of bases. (6) Construct an appropriate bulletin board about Australia today. (7) Construct an appropriate bulletin board about New Zealand today. (G.C. Obj. # 2, 8, 14, 16, 24, 27, 40, 44, 46)

5. **Written Reports:** Each pupil will be required to write a two to five page report on any acceptable phase of life in these three lands. The purpose of these reports is to encourage individual study outside of class. (S.C. Obj. # 36, 38, 39, 43, 45)

6. **Oral Reports:** The students will share with the rest of the class the information in their written reports. Each pupil will get experience in speaking before a group and the class will benefit from all students' research. (S.C. Obj. # 36, 38, 39, 43, 45)

7. **Projects:** Each student will be required to make a notebook on these three lands, including in it any information that he can find. This will require individual research and use of library skills. Also each pupil will be required to construct one project of his choice during the school year. (S.C. Obj. # 19,36,42,43)

8. **Time Line:** The class will construct a time line showing the exploration and settlement of these three lands. The students will add to the time line as new explorations and developments are covered in class. This will

be the chief method of teaching chronological order to the class. (G.C. Obj. # 18, 31, 41)

9. **Posters:** Students will be encouraged to bring pictures or make posters to illustrate life in these lands. Several posters will be displayed to illustrate (1) animals of New Zealand, (2) animals of Australia, (3) animals of Antarctica, (4) native dress of the Aborigine, (5) native dress of the Maori. (S. C. or T. C. Obj. # 6, 8, 9)

10. **Maps:** Large maps showing rainfall, topography, political divisions, and cities in Australia and New Zealand will be displayed in the room for the students to use. A large map of Antarctica will also be displayed. Mimeographed maps will be given to the class for them to color and fill in. (S. C. Obj. # 2, 24, 27, 28, 40, 43)

11. **Travel Folders and Pamphlets:** Various free materials from travel agencies and from Australia and New Zealand are available to teachers for classroom use. These pamphlets will be left on a table for the students to use in class. Several of the materials already collected from travel agencies have excellent photographs and interesting information about both New Zealand and Australia. The pictures of the unusual tourist attractions are especially good since the available textbooks rarely include this type of information. (S. C. Obj. # 3, 4, 16, 19, 29, 37)

12. **Question and Answer:** Allow time for the students to ask questions after each new section of material is covered. It is important for them to feel free to ask any questions pertaining to the material. The teacher can determine from their questions which parts of the material they do not understand. The rest of the class will be encouraged to answer the questions; their answers can be supplemented whenever necessary. Often another student is able to explain a point to a classmate more effectively than the teacher. Also this method involves more members of the class than if the teacher answers all their questions himself. (G. C. Obj. # 35, 37, 38, 39, 45)

13. **Pass the Question:** This is an especially effective way to involve members of the class who do not often contribute to class discussion. A good way to bolster the self-image of the student who does not frequently contribute is to ask a question that he is capable of answering. The student's anxiety is lessened by allowing him to pass the question on to another student of his choice when unsure of the answer. Neither confirming nor correcting their answers encourages students to think for themselves and arrive at conclusions on their own. After the class catches on to this method of teaching, it is one of the better ways to encourage participation and thinking. (G. C. Obj. # 1, 3, 4, 5, 7, 9, 10, 11, 14, 16, 20, 22, 26, 37, 39)

14. **Field Trips:** A field trip will be made to the local zoo where the animals

of Antarctica, Australia, and New Zealand can be observed. The field
trip will be particularly beneficial for the culturally deprived children
in the class. This will be an enjoyable way for the class to learn about
these animals and should serve to improve the students' attitudes toward
social studies. (G. C. Obj. # 6, 9, 37)

15.   **Films, Filmstrips, and Slides:** There are many good films and slides
available that can add greatly to this unit. There are several filmstrips
available on various aspects of life among the Maoris of New Zealand
making lecture on this phase of the unit unnecessary. There are three
films on Antarctic exploration that should supplement the text well.
There are also sets of slides on Australia and New Zealand available to
teachers. These are particularly good methods of teaching since films do
hold the students' attention when other methods are less successful.
Visual aids of this type make the material come to life for the students
and are usually an enjoyable way to learn. A complete list of free films,
filmstrips and slides on Australia, New Zealand, and Antarctica are
listed in the appendix. (T. C. Obj. # 1, 4, 8, 14, 16, 20, 23, 25, 31, 37)

16.   **Magazine and Newspaper Articles:** Pupils will be encouraged to look for
articles about Australia, New Zealand and Antarctica in newspapers and
in magazines. They will be given the opportunity to discuss their findings
with the rest of the class. Several issues of National Geographic have
excellent information and pictures of these three lands, which will be
available for the class to use. These articles are a very good way to teach
the class about the more recent studies of this part of the world since
their texts and other resources do not include information that is current. (T. C. Obj. # 3, 4, 5, 6, 13, 14, 15, 19, 21, 38)

17.   **Encyclopedias and Reference Books:** Students will be urged to use the
school library facilities when they are making their notebooks and when
they are preparing oral and written reports for class. A list of pertinent
resource material is available at the Municipal Library and other possible sources of information are available nearby. These resources will be
useful as the students are preparing their panel discussions. (T. C. Obj.
8, 15, 19, 36, 42)

18.   **Vocabulary Drill:** There are several vocabulary words connected with
this unit of study with which students need to be familiar. One way of
teaching important words and definitions is by a vocabulary drill which
is similar to a spelling bee. The class is divided into two teams according
to rows so they may remain in their seats. The first person in group one
must ask the first person in group two the spelling and definition of the
vocabulary word of his choice. If he is unable to spell or define this word
correctly the other team gains a point and the next person in line must
try to spell and define the word. Points are gained either by answering

correctly or by stumping the other team. (G. C. Obj. # 44, 46)

19. **Overhead Projector:** Lectures will be accompanied by use of an overhead projector to show the class an outline of the material; a mimeographed study guide will be given each student. This is especially important since seventh graders are not always skilled at note-taking. (T. C. Obj. # 3, 4, 6, 12, 26, 29, 31)

20. **The Textbook:** The text will serve as a framework for this unit of study, supplemented by much additional information provided by the teacher and the members of the class. Few textbooks have adequate coverage of this material so additional research by the students will be necessary. (S. C. Obj. # 1, 2, 3, 7, 10, 11, 17, 20, 23, 24, 29, 30, 31, 36)

21. **Artifacts:** Weapons used by the Maoris and the Aborigines would be both educational and interesting if displayed in the classroom. A borrowed boomerang and a blowgun will be on display in the classroom. Students may have other artifacts they want to display. If real artifacts are not readily available, perhaps the students could construct replicas. (T. C. unless students make these objects themselves. Obj. # 8, 37, 44, 46)

22. **Homework:** Homework will be assigned for the purpose of motivating the class to do research and study outside of class. The assignments will not consist of merely copying down answers from an encyclopedia; but will usually involve finding information not included in the text or they will require the student to think a problem through and arrive at his own conclusions. Two examples of assignments are: (1) Each student will write a one-page paper explaining how the platypus reproduces and cares for its young. (2) Considering what we have discussed in class about life in New Zealand today each pupil will list several ways that life in the United States is similar to life in New Zealand and several ways that it is different. (S. C. Obj. # 5, 6, 8, 12, 15, 20, 21, 22, 26, 29, 32, 36, 43)

23. **Tests:** Pop tests, as such, will not be given, but a brief quiz will be given weekly to evaluate the students' progress toward objectives. These quizzes will consist of ten or less questions that can be answered in a brief paragraph. Such weekly tests will cover the material covered during that week. The tests will be discussed as soon as all the papers are turned in so that the pupils can learn the information they missed. (G. C. Obj. # 1, 3, 4, 5, 7, 9, 10, 11, 12, 13, 15, 16, 17, 21, 23, 25, 26, 29)

24. **Baseball Review Game:** This game is a good method of reviewing the class before the test on this unit. It is a fun way for the class to go back over the material they need to review and it is a painless way to study for the test. The class is divided into two teams. Each student writes five review questions on separate slips of paper and puts them in a box along

with several others prepared in advance. The class is divided into two teams and the desks are moved aside and bases and home plate are marked on the floor in chalk. The team "at bat" lines up and the first player draws a question which is read aloud. If he answers correctly he goes to first base and the next person draws a question. An incorrect answer constitutes an "out." In order to score a run four people must answer correctly before three outs are made. (G. C. Obj. # 33, 35, 39, 49)

Culminating activities:

1. **Summary:** As this unit of study is concluded, the class will discuss the similarities and the differences of these three lands and compare them to the United States. They will discuss the effects this study has had on the students' attitudes about people in other countries and about themselves as members of society. Since this unit is the last one to be studied they will spend time reviewing some of the main points covered during the school year.

2. **Analysis and Evaluation:** Time will be set aside for analysis of some of the beliefs and attitudes developed by the class during the year. This will be the time to tie together the various units studied in the course. We will discuss the fact that the people are much alike all over the world regardless of their differing life styles. The students will be given an opportunity to express their evaluation of the material covered during the year and of the various teaching methods used. We will discuss ways that they feel the study of World Geography will affect their study of later social studies courses. The class may talk about possible influences this course will have on them as citizens and community members.

3. **Measurement of Student Growth:** One way of measuring growth toward the objectives is by comparing the pretest scores with those of the six-weeks tests. This way the teacher can see how far each pupil has progressed from his original starting place. Growth of intangibles such as attitudes and values will be measured largely by observing each student's outward behavior throughout the six-week period.

4. **Marking and Grading Procedures:** No predetermined distribution of marks will be used. Most assignments will carry variable credit. Oral and written reports, homework assignments, and projects will be graded according to content, correctness, effort put forth, and ability of the student. Most test questions will be objective and will be graded by a key. All essay type questions will be graded according to set criteria established before the test is given. Notebooks will be graded largely according to effort put forth by the student, and individual ability. Quality

rather than quantity will be stressed regarding all reports, panel discussions, essay questions, and notebooks.

Outline of Content

I.   Australia, Smallest of the Continents
   A.   Location and Size
      1.   Located in the Southern Hemisphere
      2.   Remains the smallest and the least populous continent
   B.   Physical Description
      1.   Imaginary tour of Australia
         a.   The cities
         b.   The Outback
         c.   The forest lands
         d.   Tasmania
      2.   Upside- down seasons
      3.   Varying climate and weather conditions
   C.   Unique Animal Life
      1.   Kangaroos and Koala Bears
      2.   The Platypus
   D.   People: Past and Present
      1.   The Aborigines
      2.   European discovery and exploration
         a.   Dutch discovery of Tasmania
         b.   Australia claimed for England by Captain James Cook
         c.   First settlement by English prisoners and land-hungry men
         d.   Population increased by the gold rush in 1851
      3.   Similarities between Australians and Americans today
   E.   Political Structure
      1.   The six states of the Commonwealth of Australia
      2.   The Australian Parliament
      3.   The state and federal governments
   F.   Economic Structure
      1.   The role of farming and ranching
      2.   The role of mining and industry
      3.   The role of tourism
II. The Two Islands of New Zealand
   A.   Location and Size
      1.   Located southeast of Australia in the Pacific
      2.   Includes North Island, South Island, and several smaller islands

        3.   Is smaller than Australia
   B.   Physical Description
        1.   Imaginary tour of New Zealand
           a.   The cities
           b.   North Island
           c.   South Island
        2.   Temperate climate and rainy weather
   C.   Unique Animal Life
        1.   Parrakeets and owls
        2.   Kiwi birds and penguins
   D.   People: Past and Present
        1.   The Maoris
        2.   European discovery and exploration
           a.   Dutch discovery of New Zealand
           b.   New Zealand claimed for England by Cook
           c.   Settlement by whalers, traders, and missionaries
           d.   Increased settlement in 1840 when New Zealand became part of British Empire
        3.   English customs in New Zealand today
   E.   Political Structure
        1.   Closely patterned after British government
           a.   The prime minister
           b.   The cabinet
        2.   One of first countries allowing woman suffrage
        3.   One of first to establish a social security system
   F.   Economic Structure
        1.   The role of sheep, cattle, and dairying
        2.   The minor role of mining and industry
        3.   The role of tourism
III.   Antarctica, the White Continent
   A.   Location and Size
        1.   Located on the extreme southern tip of the globe
        2.   Is twice the size of the United States
   B.   Physical Description
        1.   Imaginary tour of Antarctica
        2.   Extreme winds and temperatures
        3.   Ice-covered land mass
   C.   Unique Animal Life
        1.   Gulls, penguins, and snow petrels
        2.   Seals and whales
   D.   Exploration: Past and Present

1. First sighted in 1820
2. Roald Amundsen's search for the South Pole
3. Admiral Byrd's flight across the South Pole
4. The importance of the International Geophysical Year to Antarctic exploration
5. Bases established by many countries
6. Operation Deep Freeze

Evaluation

Of students

1. **Tests:** The students will be given a brief quiz on the material covered each week to determine student progress. These tests will consist of several questions that can be answered sufficiently in one short paragraph. These tests will stress over-all understanding and the grasping of relationships we have discussed in class. The six-weeks test will be mainly objective and will test for the student's understanding of the entire unit of study. An example of a weekly quiz and a copy of the six-weeks test is included at the end of this section.
2. **Observation:** Another method of student evaluation that will be used is observation of the students as they work individually, in small groups, or as a class. This will be one method of determining whether attitude change and the desired learning have taken place. Many things that cannot be measured on a test such as enthusiasm and cooperation are evident in the pupil's classroom behavior. Most of the objectives in the affective domain will be measured chiefly through observing pupil behavior.
3. **Objectives:** The students will be evaluated according to how well they reached the objectives established in advance. If necessary, an objective will be adjusted or discarded if it does not appear to be relevant to the class.
4. **Participation:** The quality of participation in classroom discussions and question and answer sessions will also be another means of evaluating the students' progress. It is the teacher's responsibility to see that each student has ample opportunity and encouragement to participate in class.
5. **Reports and Projects:** Students will also be evaluated on all reports, panel discussions, group projects, and notebooks according to the guidelines mentioned under Culminating Activities.
6. The final grade will be broken down as follows:

Four weekly quizzes..25 Per cent
One unit quiz...25 Per cent
Panel discussion...15 Per cent
Notebook...15 Per cent
Small group project...10 Per cent
Class participation..10 Per cent

Of materials

1. **Student Reaction and Observation:** Evaluation of the various materials used in class—such as the text, reference materials, maps, films and slides, posters, overhead projector transparencies, guest speakers, and travel pamphlets—will be made largely by watching the students' reactions to these teaching aids. If it is evident that a particular material is of little interest or value to the majority of the class, it may be dropped from next year's unit plan. Materials that are of value to the class will be improved upon and included the next time this unit is taught.

2. **Teacher Evaluation:** Evaluation check lists will be given to each student so that he can rate the various materials and methods of teaching used in this class.

Of questions and student learning activities

1. **Student Reaction:** If students react negatively to a planned learning activity then, perhaps, that particular activity does not have worth for this class. Student reactions to the questions asked in class are a good indication of the worth of the questions in stimulating interest.

2. **Observation:** By observing the students as they work together in groups, as they present oral reports and as they ask and answer questions in class, these various learning activities can be evaluated.

Teacher self-evaluation

1. **Unit of Study:** The effectiveness of the unit in causing pupil growth toward objectives is the best measure of the overall worth of the unit.

2. **Method:** Through student reaction, particularly the presence or absence of interest and a willingness to learn more, the teacher will know whether his teaching methods were effective.

3. **Self:** The teacher can evaluate his abilities as a teacher by measuring students' progress in acquiring knowledge of the subject, good personal habits, and worthwhile attitudes about themselves and others.

Sample Weekly Test

Answer any one of the following questions in not over one page.

1. Compare New Zealand, Australia, Antarctica, and the United States as to size.
2. Briefly discuss the climates and the weather conditions in Australia, New Zealand, and Antarctica.
3. Explain the difference between the four seasons here in America and those in Australia and New Zealand.
4. Compare the Australian "OutBack" to the Old West of America.
5. Write a brief description of an Australian marsupial.
6. Write a paragraph describing life in an Aborigine Village.

Unit Quiz

I. **MULTIPLE CHOICE:** Circle the answer that is most correct.

  1. Which of the following is the largest?
      a. Australia
      b. Antarctica
      c. New Zealand
      d. United States

  2. The first Australian settlers were:
      a. Dutch
      b. the Maoris
      c. French colonists
      d. English prisoners

  3. Australia and New Zealand have upside-down seasons because:
      a. They are so close to the South Pole.
      b. They are both in the Southern Hemisphere.
      c. The sun's rays only reach them half of the year.
      d. Their climates vary so greatly from the climate in the United States.

  4. The part of Australia that receives the most rain is:
      a. Near the West Coast
      b. In the interior
      c. Along the Northern Coast
      d. Near the East Coast

  5. Australia is:
      a. The most densely populated small continent
      b. The smallest continent
      c. The most sparsely populated continent
      d. Slightly larger than Antarctica

6. The largest city in southwest Australia is:
   a. Perth
   b. Canberra
   c. Adelaide
   d. Melbourne
   e. Sydney
7. New Zealand differs from Tasmania in having:
   a. Heavy rainfall
   b. An English heritage
   c. Farms and forests
   d. Large cities
8. Tasmania is:
   a. An independent territory
   b. An Australian state
   c. An Australian colony
   d. An island off the southwest coast of Australia
9. Which three of the following would New Zealand be most likely to export?
   a. Wheat
   b. Butter
   c. Meat
   d. Iron ore
   e. Wool
   f. Manufactured goods
10. Which of the following had the most advanced culture?
    a. The Aborigines
    b. The American Indians
    c. The Maoris
11. The British government first became interested in settling in Australia because:
    a. They suspected there was gold there.
    b. They needed a place to send convicts.
    c. They didn't want the Dutch to gain control of Australia.
    d. They needed the raw materials available in Australia.
12. Which of the following is not an English custom kept by New Zealanders?
    a. Drinking afternoon tea
    b. Rule by Parliament
    c. Driving on the left side of the road
    d. Coronation of a king or queen
13. Which of these countries does not have a base on Australia?
    a. Norway

    b. Japan

    c. Chile

    d. Argentina

    e. France

    f. Germany

14. Which of the following political territories of Australia is not a state:

    a. Queensland

    b. New South Wales

    c. Victoria

    d. Northern Territory

    e. South Australia

    f. Western Australia

    g. Tasmania

15. The crop most important to New Zealand's economy is:

    a. Wheat

    b. Sugar cane

    c. Grass

    d. Rice

II. **TRUE-FALSE:** Write out the words *True* or *False* beside the statements.

1. Wellington, New Zealand, is located on North Island.

2. A marsupial is a mammal that lays eggs and nurses her young.

3. The kangaroo is a native of Australia and New Zealand.

4. Penguins are found in abundance in New Zealand and Antarctica.

5. The English were the first Europeans to discover Tasmania.

6. The governments of Australia and New Zealand are both patterned after the British form of government.

7. There are nearly twenty times as many sheep in New Zealand as there are people.

8. Mining and industry play an important role in the Australian economy.

9. Antarctica is nearly twice as large as the United States.

10. The first settlers in New Zealand were whalers, traders, and missionaries.

III. **MATCHING:** Fill in the blank on the left with a letter of a country on the right.

1. Wheat producer   A. Antarctica

2. "One of the world's great   **B.** North Island
dairy farms"   **C.** South Island
3. Geysers and mineral springs   **D.** Australia
4. Large numbers of whales   **E.** New Zealand
caught here
5. Has more sheep than any
other country

IV. Write a short description of one of the following:(not over one page)
1. The animal and bird life of Antarctica.
2. Describe a cattle station.
3. Describe a sheep station.

BIBLIOGRAPHY

Teacher's sources:

Borchert, James R. and McGuigan, Jane. *Geography of the Old World.* New York: Rand McNally and Company.

Cooper, Kenneth S., and Sorensen, Clarence W. *The Changing Old World.* Atlanta: Silver Burdett Company.

Meyer, J.G., and Hamer, O. Stuart. *The Old World and Its Gifts.* Chicago: Follett Publishing Company.

Pounds, Norman J. G., and Cooper, Edward L. *World Geography.* Cincinnati: South-Western Publishing Company.

Silver, James F. *Old World Lands.* Chicago: Silver Burdett Company.

Uttley, Marguerite, and Aitchison, Alison E. *Lands and Peoples of the World.* Chicago: Ginn and Company.

Suggested sources for students:

Alexander, Fredrick. *Australia and the United States.* Boston: World Peace Foundation.

Belshaw, Horace. *New Zealand.* Berkeley: University of California Press.

Bursey, Jack. *Antarctic Night.* New York: Rand McNally.

Byrd, Richard E. *Alone.* New York: G.P. Putnam's Sons.

Byrd, Richard E. *Discovery.* New York: G.P. Putnam's Sons.

Caldwell, John Cope. *Our Neighbors in Australia and New Zealand.* New York: John Day Company.

Christie, Eric. *The Antarctic Problem.* London: Allen and Univin.

Clark, Charles. *A History of Australia.* New York: Cambridge University Press.

Clemens, Samuel Langhorne. *Following the Equator.* New York: Harper and Brothers.

Dalton, Brian J. *War and Politics in New Zealand.* Sydney: Sydney University Press.

Davies, Alan F. *Australian Society.* New York: Atherton Press.

Day, Arthur G. *The Story of Australia.* New York: Random House.

Debenham, Frank. *Antarctica: The Story of a Continent.* New York: Cambridge University Press.

Department of Internal Affairs. *Introduction to New Zealand.* Wellington: Whitcombe and Tombs, Ltd.

Dufek, George J. *Operation Deep Freeze.* New York: Harcourt, Brace, Inc.

Frazier, Paul Wilson. *Antarctic Assault.* New York: Dodd, Mead, Inc.

Gould, Laurence M. *Antarctica in World Affairs.* New York: Foreign Policy Association.

Grattan, Clinton H. *Australia.* Berkeley: University of California Press.

Grattan, Clinton H. *Introducing Australia.* New York: The John Day Company.

Henry, Thomas R. *The White Continent.* New York: The Sloane Company.

Hunt, Erling M. *American Precedents in Australian Federation.* New York: Columbia University Press.

MacInnes, Colin. *Australia and New Zealand.* New York: Time, Inc.

McLintock, A. H., ed. *An Encyclopedia of New Zealand.* Wellington: R. E. Owen, government printer.

The Modern Encyclopedia of Australia and New Zealand. Sydney: Horwitz-Grahame.

Mountevans, Edward R., and Russell Evans, Garth. *Man Against the Desolate Antarctic.* New York: W. Funk.

Mulvaney, Derek J. *The Prehistory of Australia.* New York: Praeger.

Nash, Walter. *New Zealand: A Working Democracy.* New York: Duel, Sloan, and Pearce.

News and Information Bureau. *Australian Panorama.* Canberra, Australia.

Pike, Douglas. *Australia: The Quiet Continent.* Cambridge: Cambridge University Press.

Ress, Henry. *Australasia: Australia, New Zealand, and the Pacific Islands.* London: Macdonald and Evans.

Resse, Trevor R. *Australia, New Zealand, and the United States.* London: Oxford Press.

Roberts, Stephen H. *History of Australian Land Settlement.* New York: Johnson Reprint Corporation.

Robson, Lloyd L. *The Convict Settlers of Australia.* New York: Cambridge University Press.

Schulthess, Emil. *Antarctica, A Photographic Survey.* New York: Simon and Schuster.

Sinclair, Keith. *The Origins of the Maori Wars.* Wellington: New Zealand University Press.

Soljak, Philip L. *New Zealand, Pacific Pioneer.* New York: The MacMillan Company.

Spate, O.H.K. *Australia.* New York: Praeger.

Sperry, Armstrong. *All About the Artic and Antarctic.* New York: Random House.

Sullivan, Walter. *Quest for a Continent.* New York: McGraw-Hill Book Company.

Taylor, Paul W. *Antarctic Adventure and Research.* New York: D. Appleton and Company.

Wright, Harrison M. *New Zealand: 1769-1840.* Cambridge: Harvard University Press.

Ziegler, Oswald L. *Australia From the Dawn of Time to the Present.* Sydney: O. Ziegler Publications.

Zubrzycki, Jerzy. *Immigrants in Australia.* Parkville: Melbourne University Press.

Other suggested sources of information:

National Geographic Magazine
Reader's Guide to Periodical Literature
Goodes World Atlas
Webster's Geographical Dictionary
Other Lands and Other Peoples, A country by country fact book published by NEA.
World Almanac

SOURCES OF FILMSTRIPS

1. *Educators Guide to Free Films.* Educators Progressive Service, Inc. Randolph, Wisconsin, 30th annual edition. (Films available from this source are listed below.)

    (1) *Australia,* 16mm, sound, 12 mins.
    This film covers the social, political, and industrial structure of Australia. (Dept. of the Air Force)

    (2) *Plein Sud,* 16mm, sound, 55 mins.
    This film, in full color, presents a Belgian expedition to Antarctica in 1957 and 1958. Narration is English. (Belgian Embassy)

    (3) *Portait of Antarctica,* 16mm, sound, 28 mins.
    Describes the work of the Navy in Antarctica during the International Geophysical Year and the work being continued on that continent. (Dept. of the Navy)

    (4) *Power for Continent Seven,* 16mm, 30 mins.
    Shows scientific efforts in the Antarctic, the installation of the nuclear power unit, and the Navy's work in support of the national Antarctic research effort. (Dept. of the Navy)

    (5) *First Impressions,* 16mm, sound, 11 mins.
    Air trip to Australia and other lands with a stewardess as guide. (Associated Films, Inc.)

2. *Educators Guide to Free Filmstrips.* Educators Progressive Service, Inc. Randolph, Wisconsin, 22nd annual ed. (Available filmstrips are listed below.)

   (1) *Antarctica,* Silent, 30 frames

   New Zealand's research in the Antarctic; shows some scientists conducting their summer studies of penguin and seal life, geology, and meterology. (New Zealand Embassy)

   (2) *Australian Way of Life*

   Shows hunting, fishing, gathering equipment, ornaments.

   (4) *Gold in New Zealand.* Silent

   Sketches and old photography of how gold was obtained by dredging and panning in New Zealand in 1852. (New Zealand Embassy)

   (5) *Introduction to New Zealand,* Silent, 72 frames

   Gives general view of New Zealand including scenery and the life of the people. Views of the better known tourist attractions as well as the beautiful mountains and lakes. (New Zealand Embassy)

   (6) *The Maoris,* Slides with script, 30 slides

   Shows the way the Maoris lived before the European settlers came to New Zealand and how New Zealanders live today. (New Zealand Embassy)

   (7) *Making a Maori Basket*

   (8) *Maori Cloak*   (New Zealand Embassy)

   (9) *Maori Food*

   (10) *Maori Village*

   (11) *New Zealand Flax,* Silent, 25 frames

   Shows that the Maoris had no wool or cotton and relied on the flax plant for their daily needs.

   (12) *New Zealand Paths of Progress,* Silent, 48 frames

   Shows that New Zealand's economic development rests largely on the growth of her natural and agricultural resources. Dairy products form the basis of primary industry and meat is processed for exportation.

   (13) *Traditional Maori Life,* Silent, 50 frames

   Ways of life of the Maoris in pre-European times. Includes their customs, crafts, clothing and cooking methods, their weapons, their games, and their dances.

   (14) *Young New Zealand,* Silent, 54 frames

   Shows that New Zealand is a young country and much importance is laid upon the education and welfare of its young people. The benefits of health care are shown, the schools and encouragement of the open air life and sports.

   (15) *How We Carry Things in New Zealand,* Silent, 30 frames

Shows that transportation by rail, road, air and sea are important factors in developing New Zealand's industry and economy.

(16) *North Island Scenery,* Slides with script, 40 frames

Depicts views of Tongariro National Park in the North Island. New Zealanders and visitors can ski in wintertime on slopes of active volcanoes. They can admire in the distance the extinct volcano around which is some of the country's richest farm land. There are also beautiful lakes and excellent harbors.

(17) *South Island Scenery,* Slides with script, 40 frames

Presents some of the scenery of the South Island of New Zealand, which is famous for its Alps which run the length of the west coast and have mountains over ten thousand feet. It includes the incredible glaciers, beautiful clear lakes, and rolling countryside.

(18) *Starshine Under the Earth,* Silent, 35 frames

Shows New Zealand's Waitomo Caves which have fascinating stalactite and stalagmite formations, as well as a glow-worm grotto. A boat glides gently down the river, which winds through the cavern enabling the visitor to admire the canopy of tiny winking "stars"—the lights of the glow-worms.

(19) *New Zealand Birds,* Slides with script, 40 slides

Shows some of the birds of New Zealand. New Zealand has no native animals, but does have a great variety of native birds.

(20) *New Zealand Birds of Sea and Shore,* Silent, 24 frames

Shows variety of sea and shore birds such as albatros and the penguin in their native habitats.

3. Addresses to write for further information concerning this unit.

    1. Australian News and Information Bureau
       636 Fifth Avenue
       New York, New York 10020

       (Ask for list of available publications or single copies of pamphlets that are usually given free to educators—also filmstrip list.)

    2. Beckley-Cardy Company
       1900 North Narragansett Avenue
       Chicago, Illinois
       (Request Geography Poster Maps Series on Australia.)

       Buffalo Museum of Science
       Humboldt Park
       Buffalo, New York
       (Catalog of sales items.)

4. Columbia University Press
    Internation Documents Service
    2960 Broadway
    New York, New York

    (A selected checklist of UN and UNESCO books, pamphlets and periodicals.)

5. The Visual Instruction Bureau
    University of Texas
    Austin, Texas

    (Bridge to Ideas Series: "Better Bulletin Board Displays," 62 pages.)

6. National Geographic Society
    School Service Division
    16th and M Streets, N. W.
    Washington, D. C.

    (List of publications, including back issues of *National Geographics Magazine* currently available. Also separate color sheets from the *National Geographics Magazine* and the ten color wall maps.)

7. Owen Publishing Company, F. A.
    Dansville, New York

    (Catalog of teaching aids.)

8. Information Classroom Picture Publishers
    31 Ottawa Avenue, N. W.
    Grand Rapids, Michigan

    (Leaflets describing units of teaching pictures and filmstrips on Australia and the Polar Regions.)

9. Free catalogs of maps, globes, charts and models from the various commercial publishers or their distributors.

Problem Solving Lesson

On the first day of this unit the class will be given a problem that they consider important to them as a class. Since this is a seventh grade class, the problem must be suited to the maturity level and the abilities of the students. Also, materials suitable for researching the problem must be available for the class to use.

A sample problem for this class to solve would be devising a plan to improve the living conditions of the Australian Aborigines, who live on reservations much like our American Indians. This would be an appropriate problem since they will already be familiar with the Aborigines' present living conditons.

The case study method of problem solving can be used with this problem, since the class will be given basic information on the problem. From this they could have class discussion which would lead them to their own conclusions.

Another example of problem solving is giving the class the problem of setting up their own rules and regulations for student behavior in the school in general and in this classroom in particular. Students will work out for themselves the basics of classroom order and discipline—from rules governing when a student may sharpen his pencil all the way to establishing punishments for misbehavior. It is believed that students are less likely to break rules that they had a hand in making.

In order to solve either the problem of the Aborigines or that of classroom discipline, the same steps of problem solving must be applied.

The first day the *problem will be defined* and the class will be broken down into smaller groups to further *analyze the situation and set up tentative hypotheses.* Each group will be assigned a particular aspect of the problem to *study outside of class.*

The second day will be spent *organizing the data* that the groups have collected. Each group will choose a leader to present his group's findings to the rest of the class. After all this information has been shared with the class, the remainder of the class period will be spent *evaluating and interpreting the data.*

The third day's class period will be spent *forming conclusions* about the possible solutions to the problem. The practicality of each suggested solution will be discussed by the class until a final conclusion is reached by the majority of the pupils. Sometimes in problem solving the group never reaches a satisfactory conclusion. The real value of problem solving is that it forces the students to think and seek conclusions of their own.

Project Method of Teaching

The project method of teaching is an activity centered approach to learning. As the student strives to reach the objectives defined by his project he is experiencing growth through his own efforts. This method of teaching allows the individual pupil to be as creative as he wants since he uses his own initiative to construct his project. This method is often misused when projects are assigned that have no real value as a part of the unit of study. Ideally, the project method of teaching is a type of organized, student centered activity, that is directed toward the reaching of a particular objective.

In order to promote individual study the class will be required to complete a notebook on Australia, New Zealand, and Antarctica which may include any information of interest to the individual pupil. Reports and summaries of articles concerning any aspect of life in these three lands should be included in the notebooks. Photographs and drawings may also be used to make the notebooks more interesting.

Each student will also be required to work on a small group project (mentioned previously under Developmental Activities) which will involve the construction of one of the following:

1. A relief map of Australia and New Zealand.
2. A relief map of Antarctica.
3. A bulletin board of Australia.
4. A bulletin board on Australia.
5. Replicas of the flags of Australia and New Zealand.
6. A model of a Maori village.
7. A model of an Aborigine village.

Each student will also do one special project of his own choosing during the school year. Every person in the class will become an expert on this one thing and will know more about this subject than anyone else in the class, including the teacher. The main purpose of this project is to increase the pupil's feeling of self-worth and importance. The students will each be given time to present their special projects to the rest of the class.

TIME LINE

EXPLORATION & SETTLEMENT

	1606	1642	1769	1770	1787	1820	1840	1851 1911	1929
Australia	Sighted by Dutch Ships	Tasman Discovers Tasmania		Capt. Cook Reaches Australia	First English Settelment			Australian Gold Rush	
New Zealand		Tasman Discovers New Zealand	Capt. Cook Reaches New Zealand				New Zealand Made Part of British Empire		
Antarctica						Antarctica Mainland Discovered		Amundsen Reaches South Pole	Byrd's Flight Over the Pole

(To be constructed and filled in by the students as the material is covered.)

321

Daily Lesson Plan

Class and Grade __7th grade Geography__ _____ Unit Title __Australia, New Zealand, and Antarctica__

Teaching Method: Discussion __X__ Illustration ____ Demonstration ____
Conference ____ Lecture __X__ Project ____

Type of Objective:
1. Behavioral Objective —

A. Psychomotor _____	B. Affective _____	C. Cognitive _____
1. Skills _____	1. Perceiving _____	1. Memorize facts _____
2. Combination of	2. Responding __X__	2. Association _____
skills & mental	3. Valuing __X__	3. Application _____
set _____	4. Organizing _____	4. Inquiring _____
3. Habit _____	5. Attitude _____	5. Discovery __X__
		6. Thinking _____

2. Educational Objective — Knowledge __X__   Understanding _____
Appreciations __X__   Values _____

Lesson Objective: __The students will show their interest in the unit we are beginning by listening to the speakers__ and by asking questions during the class discussion.

Student Assignment: __Read Chapter 32 in the text as background for the material to be covered in class tomorrow.__

Concepts to be Taught	Teaching Method or Activity	Time	Materials for Students
1. Introduction of the speakers, Mrs._____, and Mr._____.	Students will move chairs into a circle so all can hear the speakers.	5 minutes	
2. Mrs._____will give background information about her homeland.	Lecture.	10 minutes	Photographs, art objects, and weapons from Australia.
3. Mr._____ gives his views as an American who has visited Australia and New Zealand.	Lecture.	10 minutes	Photographs and Australian currency.
4. Question and answer session where pupils ask specific questions of the speakers.	Question and answer	15 minutes	
5. Preview of what the unit will cover.	Discussion of the printed outline that will be given to each student.	10 minutes	Mimeographed handout.

Relation to Previous and Future Lessons: This lesson is the introduction to a new unit which will be the final topic of study in this school year.

Evaluation: The students' interest in the unit that we are going to be studying will be measured by observing their reactions to the speakers and by the quality of the questions that each student asks about this topic.

Daily Lesson Plan

Class and Grade 7th grade Geography _____ Unit Title Australia, New Zealand, and Antarctica

Teaching Method: Discussion X Illustration X Demonstration _____
Conference ____ Lecture X Project _____

Type of Objective:
1. Behavioral Objective —

A. Psychomotor	_____	B. Affective	_____	C. Cognitive	_____
1. Skills	X	1. Perceiving	_____	1. Memorize facts	X
2. Combination of		2. Responding	X	2. Association	X
skills & mental		3. Valuing	_____	3. Application	_____
set	_____	4. Organizing	_____	4. Inquiring	_____
3. Habit	_____	5. Attitude	_____	5. Discovery	_____
				6. Thinking	_____

2. Educational Objective — Knowledge X   Understanding X

Appreciations _____   Values _____

Lesson Objective: The students will show their understanding of the comparative sizes and locations of Antarctica, New Zealand, and Australia by using maps in their texts and by demonstrating skill in using the larger classroom maps.

Student Assignment: For tomorrow the class will color a rainfall map and a vegetation map of Australia. On a separate sheet of paper they will discuss the effects that the rainfall has had on the economy of Australia.

Concepts to be Taught	Teaching Method or Activity	Time	Materials for Students
1. Australia is the smallest continent; Antarctica is twice the size of the U. S.	Demonstration on large map in the classroom.	10 minutes	Map in test and large wall map.
2. Australia and New Zealand have upside-down seasons because they are in the Southern Hemisphere.	Pass the question.	10 minutes	
3. Australia's weather varies from the rainy eastern coast to the arid interior desert lands.	One of the students will point out the rainfall and vegetation areas of Australia on the large rainfall map.	10 minutes	Mimeographed rainfall and vegetation maps for the class to color.
4. This lack of rain in the interior of Australia accounts for the sparce population in this area.	Lecture and class discussion of similarities between the Outback and the Old West here in America.	10 minutes	
5. The large cities are along the coasts of Australia.	Brief lecture and use of the material in the text.	10 minutes	Material in the text.

Relation to Previous and Future Lessons: This lesson deals with the physical description of Australia. It is important to know the contitions of the land before studying the inhabitants since the geography often affects the people living in the country.

Evaluation: The students will be evaluated according to their ability to use maps effectively.

1⁵

Daily Lesson Plan

Class and Grade 7th grade Geography   Unit Title Australia, New Zealand, and Antarctica

Teaching Method: Discussion _X_ Illustration _X_ Demonstration _____
                    Conference ____ Lecture _X_ Project _____

Type of Objective:
1. Behavioral Objective —

A. Psychomotor _____	B. Affective _____	C. Cognitive _____
1. Skills _____	1. Perceiving _____	1. Memorize facts _____
2. Combination of	2. Responding _X_	2. Association _X_
skills & mental	3. Valuing _____	3. Application _____
set _____	4. Organizing _____	4. Inquiring _X_
3. Habit _____	5. Attitude _X_	5. Discovery _____
		6. Thinking _____

2. Educational Objective — Knowledge _X_   Understanding _X_

                    Appreciations _____   Values _____

Lesson Objective: The pupils will demonstrate their understanding that life in Australia is much like life here in
the United States by comparing American and Australian cities in class discussion.

Student Assignment: Each pupil will meet with members of his small group to begin work on the assigned
group projects.

Concepts to be Taught	Teaching Method or Activity	Time	Materials for Students
1. Australia's European heritage can be seen in her large cities.	—Class discussion of the material in the text; pointing out features in the photographs of Australian cities that are European.	10 minutes	The text and some additional photographs in pamphlets.
2. Sydney is the location of the largest wool market in the world.	—Pass the question—we will cover the entire section in the text about sheep in Australia.	10 minutes	
3. Australia is a land of agriculture— wheat, sheep, cattle—and of large cities.	—Filmstrip, "Australian Way of Life", followed by discussion.	15 minutes	Film strip.
4. Class discussion of the important points in the film.	—Pupils will be free to ask questions about the film or anything else we have covered in class.	10 minutes	
5. The class will be divided into small groups and assigned one of several projects.	—The groups will be decided by me but each group may choose from the list of projects.	5 minutes	

Relation to Previous and Future Lessons: This lesson deals with the cities and the agriculture of Australia
and is a continuation of yesterday's discussion of the physical description of Australia.

Evaluation: The students will be evaluated by the quality of their responses during the pass-the-question session. They
also will be evaluated according to their contributions to the discussion comparing Australian and American cities.

324

Daily Lesson Plan

Class and Grade 7th grade Geography   Unit Title Australia, New Zealand, and Antarctica

Teaching Method: Discussion _X_ Illustration _X_ Demonstration _____
                    Conference _____ Lecture _X_ Project _____

Type of Objective:
1. Behavioral Objective —

A. Psychomotor _____	B. Affective _____	C. Cognitive _____
1. Skills _____	1. Perceiving _____	1. Memorize facts _X_
2. Combination of	2. Responding _X_	2. Association _____
skills & mental	3. Valuing _____	3. Application _____
set _____	4. Organizing _____	4. Inquiring _X_
3. Habit _____	5. Attitude _____	5. Discovery _X_
		6. Thinking _____

2. Educational Objective — Knowledge _X_   Understanding _____
                             Appreciations _____   Values _____

Lesson Objective: The pupils will list three of the unique animals of Australia and will give three characteristics of each.

Student Assignment: For tomorrow each student will write a one page paper telling how the platypus bears its young and how they care for the young.

Concepts to be Taught	Teaching Method or Activity	Time	Materials for Students
1. Australia is noted for its unusual animal life.	—Lecture	5 minutes	Posters of animal life.
2. The kangaroo is a marsupial and has many unusual characteristics.	—*National Geographics* with excellent pictures will be passed around as I lecture.	10 minutes	Photographs.
3. The koala bear is a marsupial that can only live in Australia.	—Lecture.	10 minutes	Photographs and a stuffed koala that will be passed around.
4. Comparison of these two animals to other mammals.	—Class discussion	10 minutes	
5. The platypus is a monotreme.	—I will begin the lecture on the platypus but will assign a paper for the pupils to write so that they will find out much of this information for themselves.	5 minutes	
6. Explanation of the assignment and report from project groups.		10 minutes	

Relation to Previous and Future Lessons: This lesson introduces three of Australia's unusual animals. Since the section on the platypus was not completed today the first part of the period tomorrow will be spent in class discussion of their findings on the subject.

Evaluation: My evaluation of how well the class met this lesson's objectives will be done when I grade the weekly quiz which will have a question on this material.

Daily Lesson Plan

Class and Grade __7th grade Geography_____ Unit Title _Australia, New Zealand, and Antractica_

Teaching Method: Discussion _X_ Illustration ___ Demonstration ____
Conference ____ Lecture _X_ Project _____

Type of Objective:
1. Behavioral Objective —

A. Psychomotor _____	B. Affective _____	C. Cognitive _____
1. Skills ___X___	1. Perceiving _____	1. Memorize facts __X___
2. Combination of	2. Responding __X___	2. Association _____
skills & mental	3. Valuing _____	3. Application _____
set _____	4. Organizing _____	4. Inquiring _____
3. Habit _____	5. Attitude _____	5. Discovery __X___
		6. Thinking _____

2. Educational Objective — Knowledge __X___ Understanding __X___
Appreciations _____ Values _____

Lesson Objective: __The pupils will discuss the early discovery and exploration of Australia when they take the__
test Monday._____

Student Assignment: _Review the material covered in class this week. There will be a quiz Monday on this_
information._____

Concepts to be Taught	Teaching Method or Activity	Time	Materials for Students
1. First part of period will cover the material on the platypus that the students researched.	—Class discussion	10 minutes	Photographs.
2. Life in an early Aborigine village.	—This information will be given to the class in the form of an imaginary tour of an Aborigine village.	15 minutes	
3. European discovery of Australia. a. The Dutch b. Captain Cook c. Early settlers	—Lecture	15 minutes	
4. Divide class into groups for panel discussions of a. Political structure b. Early settlement c. The Aborigines		10 minutes	

Relation to Previous and Future Lessons: This lesson concludes the study of Australian animal life and leads the class into the section on the exploration and settlement of Europeans in Australia.

Evaluation: How well the class reached the lesson objective will be determined by the quiz to be given on Monday.

Daily Lesson Plan

Class and Grade <u>7th grade Geography</u> Unit Title <u>Australia, New Zealand, and Antarctica</u>

Teaching Method: Discussion <u>X</u> Illustration ___ Demonstration ___
Conference ___ Lecture ___ Project ___

Type of Objective:
1. Behavioral Objective —

A. Psychomotor ————	B. Affective ————	C. Cognitive ————
1. Skills <u>X</u>	1. Perceiving <u>X</u>	1. Memorize facts ————
2. Combination of	2. Responding <u>X</u>	2. Association ————
skills & mental	3. Valuing ————	3. Application ————
set ————	4. Organizing <u>X</u>	4. Inquiring <u>X</u>
3. Habit ————	5. Attitude ————	5. Discovery ————
		6. Thinking ————

2. Educational Objective — Knowledge <u>X</u> Understanding ____

Appreciations ____ Values ____

Lesson Objective: <u>The students will demonstrate skill in working with a group and in speaking before the class</u>
<u>by participating in a panel discussion.</u>

Student Assignment: <u>The two panels not heard today will give their presentations tomorrow.</u>

Concepts to be Taught	Teaching Method or Activity	Time	Materials for Students
1. The first part of the class will be the weekly quiz.	—Students will answer the six questions of the test.	25 minutes	
2. Panel discussion on the Aborigines.	—Panel discussion.	15 minutes	
3. Discussion of main points brought out and my comments.	—Question and answer.	10 minutes	

Relation to Previous and Future Lessons: The test given at the beginning of the period serves to tie up the information studied during the previous week. The panel discussions will be continued on the following day.

Evaluation: The pupils will be evaluated on their research and the quality of their contributions on their panel.

Daily Lesson Plan

Class and Grade __7th grade Geography_____ Unit Title __Australia, New Zealand, and Antarctica__

Teaching Method: Discussion __X__ Illustration ____ Demonstration ____
                    Conference ____ Lecture ____ Project ____

Type of Objective:
1. Behavioral Objective —

A. Psychomotor _____	B. Affective _____	C. Cognitive _____
1. Skills __X__	1. Perceiving __X__	1. Memorize facts _____
2. Combination of	2. Responding __X__	2. Association _____
skills & mental	3. Valuing _____	3. Application _____
set _____	4. Organizing __X__	4. Inquiring __X__
3. Habit _____	5. Attitude _____	5. Discovery _____
		6. Thinking _____

2. Educational Objective — Knowledge __X__   Understanding _____

Appreciations _____   Values _____

Lesson Objective: __The students will exhibit skill in working with a group and in speaking before the class by__
__participating in a panel discussion.__

Student Assignment: __Reread the section in the text concerning the economic structure of Australia and be__
__prepared for class discussion.__

Concepts to be Taught	Teaching Method or Activity	Time	Materials for Students
1. Panel discussion on the early exploration and settlement of Australia.	—Panel discussion followed by question and answer.	15 minutes	
2. Panel discussion on the political structure of Australia.	—Panel discussion followed by question and answer.	15 minutes	
3. Return the graded test papers and explain the answers.	—Class discussion or question and answer.	20 minutes	Corrected test papers to keep for future study.

Relation to Previous and Future Lessons: During this period we will finish the panel discussions and go over the test papers before beginning a new topic of study—the economic structure.

Evaluation: The pupils will be graded according to the amount of study that went into their panel presentations and the quality of their contributions to the discussion.

Daily Lesson Plan

Class and Grade 7th grade Geography _____ Unit Title Australia, New Zealand, and Antarctica

Teaching Method: Discussion _X_ Illustration ____ Demonstration _____
Conference ____ Lecture _X_ Project _____

Type of Objective:
1. Behavioral Objective —

A. Psychomotor	_____	B. Affective	_____	C. Cognitive	_____
1. Skills	_____	1. Perceiving	_X_	1. Memorize facts	_X_
2. Combination of		2. Responding	_X_	2. Association	_X_
skills & mental		3. Valuing	_____	3. Application	_____
set	_____	4. Organizing	_____	4. Inquiring	_____
3. Habit	_____	5. Attitude	_____	5. Discovery	_____
				6. Thinking	_____

2. Educational Objective — Knowledge _X_   Understanding _____

Appreciations _____   Values _____

Lesson Objective: The students will show their understanding of the various economic factors discussed in class
by the quality of the contributions they make in class.

Student Assignment: Read the information in the text on New Zealand and be prepared to discuss similarities
between New Zealand and Australia.

Concepts to be Taught	Teaching Method or Activity	Time	Materials for Students
1. The role of farming and ranching in the Australian economy a. Wheat and other crops b. Sheep stations c. Cattle stations	—Lecture. —Student questions and comments.	20 minutes	—Pamphlets on Australian agriculture to be handed out.
2. The role of mining and industry.	—Lecture.	15 minutes	
3. The role of tourism.	—Lecture and class discussion.	15 minutes	—Various travel pamphlets put out by the Australian government.

Relation to Previous and Future Lessons: This lesson ends the discussion of Australia and leads into the
study of New Zealand.

Evaluation: The students will be tested for the information covered in this lesson on the next weekly quiz.

Daily Lesson Plan

Class and Grade _7th grade Geography_ _____ Unit Title _Australia, New Zealand, and Antarctica_

Teaching Method: Discussion _X_ Illustration _X_ Demonstration _____
Conference _____ Lecture _X_ Project _____

Type of Objective:
1. Behavioral Objective —

A. Psychomotor _____	B. Affective _____	C. Cognitive _____
1. Skills _X_	1. Perceiving _____	1. Memorize facts _X_
2. Combination of	2. Responding _X_	2. Association _X_
skills & mental	3. Valuing _____	3. Application _____
set _____	4. Organizing _____	4. Inquiring _____
3. Habit _____	5. Attitude _____	5. Discovery _X_
		6. Thinking _____

2. Educational Objective — Knowledge _X_ Understanding _____
Appreciations _____ Values _____

Lesson Objective: _The students will locate New Zealand on a map and will point out the large cities on North Island and South Island._

Student Assignment: _Be prepared to discuss the Maori Indians in class tomorrow._

Concepts to be Taught	Teaching Method or Activity	Time	Materials for Students
1. Location and size of New Zealand.	–Use of the large maps.	10 minutes	Maps in the text.

2. Imaginary tour of New Zealand
  a. The cities
  b. North Island
  c. South Island
	–Rather than using lecture this information will be given in the form of a narrative tour along with two short filmstrips.	20 minutes	

3. Class discussion of the filmstrips.	–Discussion.	10 minutes	
4. Temperature and climate.	–Pass the question. –Coloring rainfall maps.	10 minutes	Rainfall maps to put in their notebooks.

Relation to Previous and Future Lessons: This lesson begins the study of New Zealand and is really only an introductory lesson.

Evaluation: The students' understanding of this lesson will be evaluated partly by their use of maps and partly by their contributions to the class discussion.

EIGHTH GRADE
UNITED STATES
HISTORY:
"The United States Becomes
A World Power"

Introduction

In teaching eighth grade United States History, the teacher is committed to developing in students an understanding of and appreciation for our country's heritage, an understanding of the responsibilities of a good citizen, a respect for group differences, a realization of the necessity of world cooperation, inquiring minds and critical thinking, more efficient study habits, and self-acceptance. These committments are closely related to the broader purpose of the school and the students' needs.

The specific purposes of the unit "The United States Becomes a World Power" were developed with the needs of the students in mind. The students need to understand the industrialization of the United States in terms of invention, business, production and higher living standards, to see why the United States became interested in lands beyond its borders, to understand the relationship between the United States and other American republics, to develop an understanding of the changing United States foreign policy, and to understand the causes of the world wars and of what importance these wars are to us today.

The unit "The United States Becomes a World Power" will cover the period of 1850 to 1930. The unit begins with the industrial growth of the country and the social changes that resulted from this industrial growth. Next, the ways in which the United States acquired military bases and additional territory and the building of the Panama Canal are to be studied. Students will learn about their country's relations with Canada and Latin American countries and then the First World War and other events, including the Roaring Twenties and the beginning of the Great Depression, that led up to 1930.

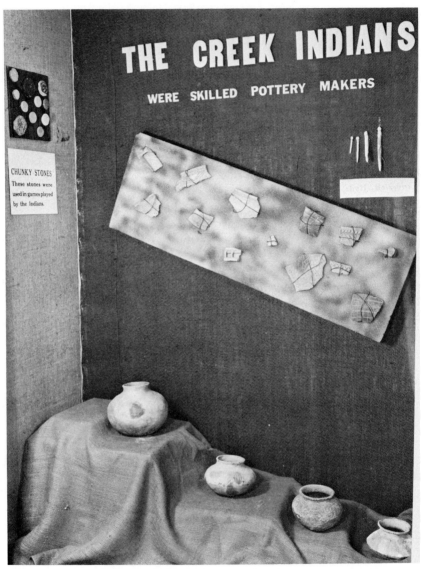

Photo furnished courtesy of AUM Learning Resource Center and Montgomery County Public Schools, Montgomery, Alabama.

Objectives

Cognitive:

1. The students will discuss in class how industrial growth led to the growth of wealth in the United States.
2. The students will identify in writing all major characteristics of the Gilded Age.
3. The students will discuss in class new sports and activities brought from Europe by the wealthy.
4. The students will discuss in writing inventions and discoveries which made home life easier and more pleasant by 1900.
5. The students will discuss in writing journalism of the late 1800's.
6. The students will identify in writing the United States' greatest contribution to the world of architecture.
7. The students will recite in class for what the dates on the timeline stand.
8. The students will discuss in writing the United States' becoming a world power from a cause and effect viewpoint.
9. The students will discuss in writing how Alaska and Hawaii became United States territories and later states.
10. The students will discuss in writing the Spanish-American War as to cause, main events, and results.
11. The students will discuss in writing the need for and the problems confronted in building the Panama Canal.
12. The students will briefly contrast in writing conditions in China just prior to 1900 and today.
13. The students will list six of the islands the United States has under her protection and in what sea or ocean each is.
14. The students will compare Canada and the United States as to topography, area, climate, and living conditions.
15. The students will locate on a map orally and in writing the Canadian provinces, the countries of Central and South America, and the Caribbean republics.
16. The students will briefly identify pertinent dates and acts in Canada's history.
17. The students will identify in writing certain Mexican and South American heroes.
18. The students will contrast in writing the colonization of South America and the founding of the English colonies.
19. The students will contrast in writing past relations between Latin America and the United States with those at present.

20. The students will list the reasons Central America is important to the United States today.
21. The students will give oral reports on the origin, meaning, and composers of some of the music heard in the United States which originated in Latin America.
22. The students will discuss in writing causes of and the United States' role in World War I.
23. The students will list four of the seven main provisions of the Treaty of Versailles ending World War I.
24. The students will contrast in writing the Roaring Twenties and the Great Depression.
25. The students will discuss in writing the factors studied in class that led to United States involvement in World War II.

Skills:
26. The students will gain skill in understanding cause and effect relationships as shown in class and on tests.
27. The students will strive to recognize the difference between fact, opinion and rumor and demonstrate this in class.
28. The students will gain skill in listening, interpreting and communicating as shown in class and in writing.
29. The students will demonstrate skill in working independently and cooperatively in groups.
30. The students will develop the use of skills of time and chronology as shown in class discussion, in writing and in constructing a timeline.
31. The students will show skill in note-taking and keeping a notebook.
32. The students will show skill in talking before the class, in giving oral reports, etc.
33. The students will use the library to find information.
34. The students will develop at least one of their special abilities by optional activities.

Affective:
35. The students will develop an interest in keeping informed about current affairs through all types of communication media and will exhibit this interest in class.
36. The students will demonstrate respect for their peers and their teacher by not disagreeing disagreeably.
37. The students will demonstrate increased self-confidence and self-acceptance in word and work.
38. The students will demonstrate enthusiasm for learning by participation and efficiency in meeting assignments.

39. The students will show in their work and in class motivation to be a patriotic, participating citizen.
40. The students will demonstrate self-discipline in all classwork.

Goals:

1. The students will enjoy the class.
2. The students will learn, not memorize.
3. The teacher will present knowledge in the truest and most realistic way about the community, state, nation, and world.

Teaching and Learning Activities

Code: T—Teacher centered
            L—Learner centered
            C—Class centered
            G—Small group centered
            (Numbers in parentheses after activities
            refer to the specific objectives.)

Introductory:

1. Administer a pretest to determine previous knowledge and acquisition of unit objectives. (T)
2. Show relationship to previous units studied by lecture and visual aids. (T)
3. Pass out to each student the requirements of the unit. (T)

Developmental:

Teacher centered

1. Lecture. (T) (16—Example of type of objective for which this will be used, 28, 31)
2. Question and answer. (T, L) (2—Example of type of objective for which this will be used, 32)
3. Films. (T) (1, 9, 22, 24—See appendix for listing.)
4. Filmstrips. (T) (10, 14, 20—See appendix for listing.)
5. Making posters. (T) (4—Posters on home furnishings in the late 1800's, 8—Characteristics of a world power, 16—Chart on powers of government of Canada and the United States.)
6. Class session in which Latin American music, including the calypso, the rumba, and the tango, is played. (T) (21)
7. Bringing in speakers. (T) (21—Someone who has visited or worked in Canada or a Latin American country will come and tell the class

about such things as the homes, foods, recreation, and daily life of the people, 22—Veteran from World War I to speak on his war experience, 24—Speaker regarding conditions during the depression.)

8. Bulletin board displays. (T) (24—Common elements of a business cycle-period of prosperity, "boom" period, recession period, depression period, recovery period: Example of type of objective for which this will be used.)

Learner centered

1. Written reports from book list handed out in class. (L) (28)
2. Locating places on a map. (L) (13, 15)
3. Using magazines, newspapers, radio and television. (L) (12, 19, 27, 33)
4. Homework assignments. (L) (2—Example of type of objective for which this will be used.)
5. Service activity, such as preparing scrapbook to be used in hospital children's ward. (L) (39)
6. Note-taking and keeping a notebook. (L) (28, 31)

Class centered

1. Problem-solving. (C) (8—Example of type of objective for which this will be used, 27, 28, 29, 33)
2. Discussion. (C) (4, 26—Examples of type of objectives for which this will be used, 28, 30, 32)
3. Bulletin board display. (C) (6—United States skyscrapers, especially the Empire State Building)
4. Making a time line. (C) (7, 30)
5. Taking a test. (C)
6. Playing teaching games connected with Social Studies. (C)

Optional activities

1. Oral reports on books and selected research topics. (L) (2—*The Gilded Age* by Mark Twain and Charles Dudley Warner, 11—Stories pertaining to the building of the Panama Canal, 21—Origin, meaning and composers of some Latin American music heard in the United States, 22—New Weapons in World War I, 25—World War Two, 32, 33)
2. Making posters. (L) (3—Cartoons of people enjoying recreation while machines do the work, 19—Cartoons of Uncle Sam telling European countries to keep "hands off" the Americas, 22—War posters to resemble those used to stimulate Americans to enlist, buy war bonds, etc., 34)

3. Panel discussion. (G) (12—"China: Past and Present," 29, 32, 33)
4. Debate. (G) (23—Resolved: That the United States Should Enter the League of Nations, 32, 33)
5. Making a mural. (G) (24—Contrast between life in the 1920's and life in the 1930's, 34)
6. Constructing a model. (G) (11—Panama Canal, 34)
7. Impersonations. (L) (4—Inventors, with each inventor trying to prove the importance of his invention, 32, 33, 34)
8. Teaching class. (L) (5—Students interested in journalism will do extra research on journalism in the late 1800's and teach it to the class: Example of type of objective this will be used for.)
9. Map construction. (G) (15—Western hemisphere, filling in country boundaries as they are taken up, 34)

Ways to encourage students to develop Their own methods of learning:

1. Relate the teaching to what the students already know.
2. Relate roles played in school to the roles students play out of school.
3. Make methods of teaching as real and lifelike as possible.
4. Try to relate facts and skills to each other meaningfully.
5. Provide for student activity and participation in learning.
6. Provide for firsthand experience.
7. Spend some time preparing learners to learn.
8. Provide for initial successes on which the student may build.
9. Avoid creating emotional tension in the students.
10. Try to sustain student interest.
11. Before trying to teach a student a task, be sure he has the prerequisites.
12. Recognize and strive to meet individual differences.

Culminating:

Summary

1. Review vocabulary, identification of people and historical information. (T, L)
2. Display notebooks and scrapbooks. (L) (31)
3. Display mural, model, map, posters and other work by students. (G) (34)
4. Complete time line. (C) (30)
5. Panel discussions on:
   a. My responsibilities in the United States.

    b.   How I Can Be a Good Citizen.

    c.   People Who Have Improved My Standards of Living. (C) (29, 32, 33, 39)

Articulation

Provisions to aid the students in relating the unit to materials covered earlier and to those to follow and provisions to aid the students in getting the over-all picture of the course will be used throughout the six weeks. These provisions will include time lines, the bringing in of old material in discussion, the mention of new material to be taken up after the present unit, and discussions of cause and effect relationships in class and in writing. A brief review of the year will be given at the end of the last six weeks.

Marking and grading practices

The teacher will follow grading practices that adhere to the grading established by the school. The grades will be based on assignments, class participation, test scores. The teacher will use a version of the supplementary contract method. The students will all be expected to master the basic minimum requirements for a "C". They may contract supplementary assignments and activities early in the six weeks to make a "B" or an "A".

Outline of Content

I.   Life in the United States since 1850
    A. The growth of wealth
        1.   Philanthropists
    B. The Gilded Age—1865 to 1890
        1.   Major characteristics
        2.   Leisure activities
        3.   Inventions
    C. Progress in the arts
        1.   Journalism
        2.   Architecture

II.   Expansion beyond the seas
    A. A new world power
        1.   Requirements
    B. Alaska and Hawaii
    C. Island possessions
        1.   Midway and Wake
        2.   Virgin Islands and others
    D. Spanish-American War

        1.   Causes
        2.   Main events
        3.   Results
            a.   Puerto Rico, Guam and the Philippines
   E. Panama Canal
        1.   Acquisition
        2.   Importance
        3.   Problems
   F. China
        1.   Prior to 1900
        2.   Today

III.   Good neighbors
   A. Canada
        1.   Topography, area, climate and living conditions
        2.   History
            a.   Early Canada
            b.   Steps leading to Dominion government
            c.   Canada's present status
   B. Latin America
        1.   Mexico
        2.   Central America
            a.   Importance to the United States
        3.   Caribbean republics
        4.   South America
            a.   Struggle for independence
            b.   Revolutionary leaders
            c.   Brazil
        5.   Music
   C. Relations between Latin America and the United States
        1.   "Colossus of the North"
        2.   Monroe Doctrine
        3.   Good Neighbor Policy
        4.   Organization of American States

IV.   World War I and the Twenties
   A. Causes of the war
   B. Position of the United States
        1.   Neutral
        2.   Trade with Allies
        3.   U-boat menace
        4.   War is declared
        5.   Part in war

    C. Peace and the League of Nations
    D. Life in the Twenties
    E. The Great Depression
        1. Common elements of a business cycle
    F. Factors leading to United States involvement in World War I

Evaluation

Of students

1. Tests. At least one test a week will be given to encourage students to keep up with assignments and so that their over-all grade on tests for the six weeks will not be heavily influenced by any one test grade. The tests will be short, taking about fifteen minutes to administer.
2. Reconsideration of objectives. This will be done if the need is indicated by the pretest on the unit objectives. It will also be done throughout the six weeks as it is felt to be needed.
3. Observation. This will be the primary method of evaluating a number of objectives, especially under the affective domain and under skills. Evaluation will be made of class participation, leadership qualities, attitude and cooperation, enthusiasm shown, contributions made in the class, and skills.
4. Teacher-pupil conferences will be used to evaluate some assignments.
5. Conduct a questionnaire concerning the students' opinions on United States foreign policy.
6. Evaluation of supplementary individual and group assignments.
7. Pupil self-evaluation.

Sample Objective test

(Numbers of test questions are the same as the specific objectives they are testing.)

1. By 1900 the wealthiest Americans were: (1) Merchants; *(2)* Factory owners; (3) Landholders; (4) Teachers.
2. Which of the following is *not* a characteristic of the Gilded Age? (1) Lasted from 1865-1890; (2) Mansions sprang up; *(3)*Well-to-do began to enjoy the activities of the middle class in their leisure time; (4) The wealthy were unaware of the life of the working people; (5) Most Americans felt they could improve their own situation.
3. The most favored sport of all by 1890 was: *(1)* Bicycling; (2) Tennis; (3) Golf; (4) Football; (5) Basketball.

4. Which of these had *not* been invented by 1900? (1) Telegraph; *(2)* Radio; (3) Telephone; (4) Incandescent lamp; (5) Gas stoves.

5. The paper which fought yellow journalism was: (1) the *Sun;* (2) *Journal;* (3) *World;* *(4) Christian Science Monitor.*

6. The United States' greatest contribution to architecture was: (1) Southern Colonial; (2) American Classical; *(3)* Skyscraper; (4) Modern.

7. The Panama Canal was opened in: (1) 1907; (2) 1848; (3) 1917; *(4)* 1914; (5) 1898.

8. By the middle 1800's the United States had met all the requirements for being a world power but which one? *(1)* Having territory beyond its home shores; (2) Large enough size; (3) Industrialization; (4) Wealth.

9. How much did the United States pay for Hawaii? (1) 2 ¢ an acre; (2) $72,000,000; *(3)* Nothing; (4) $2,700,000.

10. The battleship which is connected with the Spanish-American War is: (1) *The Lusitania;* (2) *The Serapis;* (3) *Clermont;* (4) *Old Ironsides; (5) The Maine.*

11. The right to build the Panama Canal was received from: (1) France; (2) Colombia; *(3)* Panama; (4) Venezuela; (5) Mexico.

12. The main changes in China since the late 1800's have been in: *(1)* Government; (2) Agriculture; (3) Manufacturing; (4) Transportation; (5) Recreation.

13. The island that is a United States possession and is matched with the correct body of water is: (1) Formosa—Pacific Ocean; (2) Philippines—Atlantic; (3) Puerto Rico—Pacific; (4) Wake—So. Atlantic; *(5)* Virgin Islands—Caribbean Sea.

14. Canada and the United States: (1) Are exactly equal in area; *(2)* Canada is slightly larger; (3) The United States is slightly larger; (4) The United States is much larger.

15. British Columbia is: (1) A country in South America; (2) A country in Central America; (3) There's no such country or province; (4) A Caribbean republic; *(5)* A Canadian province.

16. The queen of Canada: (1) Does not exist; (2) Is a Canadian; *(3)* Is the queen of England; (4) Is the real head of the government in Canada; (5) Is elected by the people.

17. Which man do South Americans call "the Liberator"? *(1)* Bolivar; (2) San Martin; (3) O'Higgins; (4) Hidalgo; (5) Morelos.

18. The main difference in the founding of the English colonies and the colonization of South America is: (1) The Spanish conquered the largest country in South America; (2) In North America conquest came first,

followed by colonization; (3) In South America colonization came first, followed by conquest; *(4)* In South America, conquest came first, followed by colonization.

19. Latin Americans: (1) have always trusted the United States; (2) Trusted the United States beginning with the establishment of the Monroe Doctrine; (3) Called the United States the "Comrade of the North; *(4)* Distrusted the United States and the Monroe Doctrine.

20. Central America is important to the United States because: (1) Of its popular tourist cities; (2) British Honduras is an United States colony; *(3)* It supplies our country with certain crops and products; (4) It was also settled largely by the English.

21. The rumba originated in: (1) Argentina; (2) Brazil; (3) Germany; *(4)* Cuba.

22. The main reason the United States entered World War I was: (1) The Allies were blocking the ports of the Central Powers; *(2)* German submarine warfare; (3) The killing of an Austrian archduke; (4) Alliances; (5) Japanese attack on Pearl Harbor.

23. Which was *not* a provision of the Treaty of Versailles? (1) Germany had to pay reparations; (2) Austria, Hungary, Poland, Czechoslovakia and Yugoslavia were established as independent nations; *(3)* All countries that participated in the war must join the League of Nations; (4) Germany's army and navy were limited.

24. One of the main causes of the crash of the stock market in 1929 was: (1) No one was buying stock; *(2)* Overspeculation; (3) An order of the president; (4) The reduction of the national debt.

25. Which was *not* a *cause* of World War II? (1) The depression; (2) Dictatorships; *(3)* Attack on Pearl Harbor; (4) Nazis.

Of materials

1. Students will list individually at the end of the six weeks activities they enjoyed most and activities in which they learned the most.

2. Observation will be made throughout of student enthusiasm and of student progress.

Of questions and student learning activities

1. Student learning activities will be evaluated by observation of their effectiveness in promoting learning.

2. Student reactions to learning activities will be considered in planning future learning activities.

3. Questions asked in class will be evaluated to see if the students were challenged or threatened.
4. Student performance on test questions will be evaluated. Those which everyone missed or got correct will be evaluated as to why.

Teacher self-evaluation

1. Objectives and content will be revised if deemed necessary for further use. Some objectives may no longer seem important.
2. The teacher will evaluate methods of teaching as to their effectiveness with this particular class in meeting the objectives.
3. The teacher will evaluate herself as to how well disciplined the class was, how much they seemed to have learned, and if they did indeed meet the objectives of the unit.

FILMS AND FILMSTRIPS

Films planned for use in unit:

(Numbers in parentheses relate to the specific objectives.)
Andrew Carnegie—EBF (1)

Great Land-Alaska—Modern (9)

Hawaii: U. S. A.—Bailey (9)

Headlines of the Century (Reels 1, 2, 3, 4, 5)—TFC
Part 1:	1897-1905
Part 2:	1905-1910
Part 3:	1910-1923
Part 4:	1923-1928
Part 5:	1928-1932

'29 Boom and '30's Depression—McGraw (24)

World War I—EBF (22)

Filmstrips planned for use in unit:

(Numbers in parentheses relate to the specific objectives.)
Canada—Life (14)

Introducing Central America—McGraw (20)

Introducing South America—McGraw (15)

The Spanish-American War—Eye (10)

Other films related to unit:

Admiral Dewey's Victory at Manila—YA

Alaska: Reservoir of Resources—EBF

Alaska Wonderland—World

Buenos Aires—Academy

Canada: Geog. of the Americas—Coronet

Canadian Boom—McGraw

Central America—EBF

Chicago Fire—McGraw

Cities: How They Grow—EBF

Cities: Why They Grow—Coronet

Fifty Year Barter (Purchase of Virgin Islands)—Almanac

Golden Twenties—McGraw

Hawaiian Native Life—EBF

Immigration—EBF

Immigration in America's History—Coronet

Immigration Quotas: Are They Fair?—McGraw

Inventions in America's Growth: 1850-1910—Coronet

Mexican Village Life—Hoefler

Mexico: Geog. of the Americas—Coronet

People of Mexico—EBF

Peru-Land of the Incas—Hoefler

Report on Puerto Rico—YA

The Lost Battalion—YA

The Philippines—Coronet; EBF

The Sinking of the Titanic—YA

United States Expansion: Overseas—Coronet

Untroubled Border—McGraw

Uranium, New American Frontier—Modern

Virgin Island Visit—YA

World War I: Background—Coronet

World War I: Building the Peace—Coronet

World War I: The War Years—Coronet

Other filmstrips related to unit:

Alaska—EBF; Life

Alaska, the Land & Its People—Rand

America, World Power before 1918—Rand

Art, Literature, Sports, 1865-1900—Eye

Central America—EBF

Changes in American Life—Rand

Foreign Policy (1918-1941)—Rand

Growth in National Power: The Pan American Union—Eye

Land & Peoples of Central America—Rand

Living in the Hawaiian Islands—SVE

Mexico—Life

Nations Need Each Other—Filmstrip

Our Fellow Citizens, Hawaiians—McGraw

Panama and the Canal—EBF

Period of Prosperity (1923-1929)—Eye

Prosperity & Depression—Rand; SVE

Puerto Rico—Eye

Results of the War: The League—Eye

Rise of America as a World Power—Yale

The First World War—Eye

The Great Depression—Eye

The Panama Canal—Eye; Enrich

The United States in World War I—Rand

Producers of films and filmstrips:

ACADEMY
Academy Films
Box 3088, Hollywood, Calif.

ALMANAC
Almanac Films, Inc.
516 Fifth Avenue, New York 36, N. Y.

BAILEY
Bailey Films, Inc.
6509 DeLongpre Ave., Hollywood 28, Calif.

CORONET
Coronet Films
65 E. So. Water St., Chicago 1, Ill.

EBF
Encyclopedia Britannica Films, Inc.
1150 Wilmette Ave., Wilmette, Ill.

ENRICH
Enrichment Teaching Materials, Inc.
246 Fifth Ave., New York 1, N. Y.

EYE
Eye Gate House, Inc.
146-01 Archer Ave., Jamaica 35, N. Y.

FILMSTRIP
Filmstrip House
347 Madison Ave., New York 17, N. Y.

HOEFLER
Paul Hoefler Productions
7934 Santa Monica Blvd., Los Angeles 46, Calif.

LIFE
Life Magazine Filmstrip Division
9 Rockefeller Plaza, New York 20, N. Y.

McGRAW
McGraw-Hill Book Co., Textfilm Dept.
330 West 42 St., New York 36, N. Y.

MODERN
Modern Talking Picture Service, Inc.
3 D. 54th St., New York 22, N. Y.

RAND
Rand McNally and Co.
8255 N. Central Park, Skokie, Ill.

SVE
Society for Visual Education, Inc.
1345 Diversey Parkway, Chicago 14, Ill.

TFC
Teaching Films Custodians, Inc.
25 West 43rd St.
New York 36, N. Y.

YA
Young America Films, Inc.
18 E. 41st St., New York 17, N. Y.

YALE
Yale Univ. Press Film Service
386 4th Ave., New York 16, N. Y.

BIBLIOGRAPHY

Eibling, Harold H., King, Frederick M., and Harlow, James. *Our United States.* Illinois: Laidlaw Brothers.

Dade County Public Schools. *United States History Curriculum Guide—Grade 8 & 11.* Bulletin 9B.

Daily Lesson Plan

Class and Grade __8th grade U. S. History_____ Unit Title __World Power"__

"The United States Becomes a

Teaching Method: Discussion _X_ Illustration _X_ Demonstration _____
Conference _____ Lecture _X_ Project _X_

Type of Objective:
1. Behavioral Objective —

A. Psychomotor	_____	B. Affective	_____	C. Cognitive	_____	
1. Skills	_____	1. Perceiving	_X_	1. Memorize facts	_____	
2. Combination of		2. Responding	_X_	2. Association	_X_	
skills & mental		3. Valuing	_X_	3. Application	_X_	
set	_X_	4. Organizing	_X_	4. Inquiring	_X_	
3. Habit	_____	5. Attitude	_X_	5. Discovery	_____	
				6. Thinking	_X_	

2. Educational Objective — Knowledge _X_ Understanding _X_
Appreciations _X_ Values _____

Lesson Objective: __The students will answer orally questions from their assignment about Canada, will gain skill__
__in listening, interpreting and taking notes, and will draw in and label the Canadian provinces on a map.__

Student Assignment: __Study Latin American countries on a map and today's notes.__

Concepts to be Taught	Teaching Method or Activity	Time	Materials for Students
Characteristics of Canada.	Question and answer period on the assignment on Canada: likenesses to the U. S., length of U. S.– Canada border, etc.	10 minutes	
Powers of government of U. S. and Canada.	Teacher explanation.	5 minutes	Poster.
Canada's history.	Lecture.	15 minutes	
Names and locations of the Canadian provinces.	Students will draw in boundaries of Canadian provinces on a previously made outline of the Western hemisphere and label them. 1 per student.	15 minutes	Map.
	Discussion of the next day's assignment.	5 minutes	

Relation to Previous and Future Lessons: Beginning of a new topic on neighboring countries. Will have
just completed a study of China. Next lesson is on Canada and Mexico.

Evaluation: Students will be evaluated by observation of class participation, performance, and contribution to
the class.

Daily Lesson Plan

"The United States Becomes

Class and Grade <u>8th grade U. S. History</u> Unit Title <u>a World Power"</u>

Teaching Method: Discussion <u>X</u> Illustration <u>X</u> Demonstration ____
                   Conference ____ Lecture <u>X</u> Project ____

Type of Objective:
1. Behavioral Objective –

A. Psychomotor _____	B. Affective _____	C. Cognitive _____
1. Skills _____	1. Perceiving _____	1. Memorize facts <u>X</u>
2. Combination of	2. Responding <u>X</u>	2. Association <u>X</u>
skills & mental	3. Valuing _____	3. Application _____
set <u>X</u>	4. Organizing <u>X</u>	4. Inquiring <u>X</u>
3. Habit _____	5. Attitude _____	5. Discovery _____
		6. Thinking <u>X</u>

2. Educational Objective – Knowledge <u>X</u>   Understanding <u>X</u>
                           Appreciations <u>X</u>   Values <u>X</u>

Lesson Objective: <u>One student will give an oral report on Hidalgo. The students will discuss orally a film on</u>
<u>Canada and will gain skill in listening, interpreting and notetaking.</u>

Student Assignment: <u>Read about Central and South America and Caribbean republics (5 pages). Bring to class</u>
<u>the day after tomorrow a written summary of a magazine or newspaper article on any Latin American country.</u>

Concepts to be Taught	Teaching Method or Activity	Time	Materials for Students
Characteristics of Canada	Filmstrip: Canada (Life)	15 minutes	
	Discussion of film.	10 minutes	
Mexican indepencence and Mexico today.	Lecture.	10 minutes	
Mexican heroes.	Student oral report on Miquel Hidalgo.	10 minutes	
	Discuss assignment.	5 minutes	

Relation to Previous and Future Lessons: Tomorrow will discuss Central America.

Evaluation: Student oral report and class discussion will be evaluated by observation.

348

Daily Lesson Plan

Class and Grade __8th grade U. S. History__ Unit Title __"The United States Becomes a World Power"__

Teaching Method: Discussion __X__ Illustration _____ Demonstration _____
Conference _____ Lecture __X__ Project __X__

Type of Objective:
1. Behavioral Objective —

A. Psychomotor	_____	B. Affective	_____	C. Cognitive	_____
1. Skills	_____	1. Perceiving	__X__	1. Memorize facts	__X__
2. Combination of		2. Responding	__X__	2. Association	_____
skills & mental		3. Valuing	_____	3. Application	__X__
set	__X__	4. Organizing	__X__	4. Inquiring	__X__
3. Habit	_____	5. Attitude	_____	5. Discovery	_____
				6. Thinking	__X__

2. Educational Objective — Knowledge __X__ Understanding __X__
Appreciations __X__ Values _____

Lesson Objective: __The students will discuss orally a film on Central America, will gain skill in listening, interpreting and taking notes, will fill in and label country boundaries of Central America, and will answer questions about the importance of Central America to the U. S.__

Student Assignment: __Bring article to class tomorrow and study your notes.__

Concepts to be Taught	Teaching Method or Activity	Time	Materials for Students
Characteristics of Central America.	Filmstrip: Introducing Central America (McGraw).	15 minutes	
	Discuss film.	5 minutes	
Names and locations of Central American countries.	Students will draw in boundaries of and label the countries on the large map previously made by the students.	10 minutes	Map.
History of Central America.	Lecture.	10 minutes	
Importance of Central America to the U. S.	Discussion	10 minutes	
	Give assignment.		

Relation to Previous and Future Lessons: Tomorrow will discuss South America.

Evaluation: Students will be evaluated on their participation, performance, and contribution to the class.

Class and Grade 8th grade U. S. History _____ Unit Title "The United States Becomes a World Power"

Teaching Method: Discussion _X_ Illustration _X_ Demonstration ____
Conference ____ Lecture ____ Project _X_

Type of Objective:
1. Behavioral Objective —

A. Psychomotor _____	B. Affective _____	C. Cognitive _____
1. Skills _____	1. Perceiving _X_	1. Memorize facts _____
2. Combination of	2. Responding _X_	2. Association _X_
skills & mental	3. Valuing _X_	3. Application _X_
set _X_	4. Organizing ____	4. Inquiring _X_
3. Habit _____	5. Attitude ____	5. Discovery _X_
		6. Thinking _X_

2. Educational Objective — Knowledge ____   Understanding _X_
Appreciations _X_   Values ____

Lesson Objective: The students will discuss orally a film on South America, will fill in and locate country boundaries of South America, and will discuss orally the difference in the colonization of South and North America.

Student Assignment: None for whole class; some students are to give oral reports tomorrow.

Concepts to be Taught	Teaching Method or Activity	Time	Materials for Students
Characteristics of South America.	Filmstrip: Introducing South America (McGraw).	15 minutes	
	Discuss film.	5 minutes	
Names and locations of countries of South America.	Students will fill in the boundaries of and label the countries on the map.	15 minutes	Map.
Contrast the colonizations of North and South America.	Discussion period.	10 minutes	
	Take up article summaries for today's homework.	5 minutes	Make a bulletin board of some of the articles for tomorrow.

Relation to Previous and Future Lessons: Tomorrow will study heroes of South America and Brazil.

Evaluation: Students will be evaluated by observation of participation, performance, and contribution to the class.

Daily Lesson Plan

Class and Grade <u>8th grade U. S. History</u> Unit Title <u>"The United States Becomes a World Power"</u>

Teaching Method: Discussion <u>X</u> Illustration ____ Demonstration ____
Conference ____ Lecture <u>X</u> Project ____

Type of Objective:
1. Behavioral Objective –

A. Psychomotor ____	B. Affective ____	C. Cognitive ____
1. Skills ____	1. Perceiving ____	1. Memorize facts <u>X</u>
2. Combination of	2. Responding <u>X</u>	2. Association ____
skills & mental	3. Valuing ____	3. Application ____
set <u>X</u>	4. Organizing ____	4. Inquiring ____
3. Habit <u>X</u>	5. Attitude <u>X</u>	5. Discovery ____
		6. Thinking <u>X</u>

2. Educational Objective – Knowledge <u>X</u>   Understanding <u>X</u>
Appreciations <u>X</u>   Values ____

Lesson Objective: <u>Several students will give oral reports. The students will gain skill in listening, interpreting and taking notes and will answer questions orally on South America revolutionary heroes and on Brazil.</u>

Student Assignment: <u>Those students who have records on Latin American music see me after class and bring them day after tomorrow if you can. The day after that we will have a map test and the next day we will have a test over all the material on Canada and Latin America.</u>

Concepts to be Taught	Teaching Method or Activity	Time	Materials for Students
South American revolutionary heroes	Student oral reports	25 minutes	
Brazil	Question and answer on reports and Brazil	15 minutes	
	Discussion of the activities for the next two days and tests to be given.	10 minutes	

Relation to Previous and Future Lessons: Tomorrow will have a speaker who has visited a Latin American country.

Evaluation: Students will be evaluated by observation of their oral reports, participation, attentiveness, and contribution made to the class.

351

Daily Lesson Plan

Class and Grade <u>8th grade U. S. History</u> Unit Title <u>"The United States Becomes a World Power"</u>

Teaching Method: Discussion <u>X</u> Illustration <u>X</u> Demonstration ____
Conference ____ Lecture <u>X</u> Project ____

Type of Objective:
1. Behavioral Objective —

A. Psychomotor ____	B. Affective ____	C. Cognitive ____		
1. Skills ____	1. Perceiving <u>X</u>	1. Memorize facts ____		
2. Combination of skills & mental set ____	2. Responding <u>X</u>	2. Association <u>X</u>		
	3. Valuing ____	3. Application <u>X</u>		
	4. Organizing ____	4. Inquiring <u>X</u>		
3. Habit <u>X</u>	5. Attitude <u>X</u>	5. Discovery ____		
		6. Thinking <u>X</u>		

2. Educational Objective — Knowledge ____ Understanding <u>X</u>
Appreciations <u>X</u> Values ____

Lesson Objective: <u>The students will gain skill in listening and interpreting and in distinguishing fact from opinion.</u>

Student Assignment: <u>None except be studying for tests.</u>

Concepts to be Taught	Teaching Method or Activity	Time	Materials for Students
Contrast certain aspects of life in a Latin American country with life in the students' own state.	Speaker who has visited or worked in a Latin American country will come and tell the class about such things as the homes, foods, recreation and daily life of the people.	40 minutes	Samples brought by the speaker for the students to see.
	Question and answer period.	10 minutes	

Relation to Previous and Future Lessons: Tomorrow will have a class session on different types of Latin American music.

Evaluation: The Students will be evaluated on the basis of their attention, respect and intelligence in questioning in class.

Daily Lesson Plan

Class and Grade __8th grade U. S. History_____ Unit Title __"The United States Becomes a World Power"__

Teaching Method: Discussion ____ Illustration ____ Demonstration __X__
                   Conference ____ Lecture __X__ Project ____

Type of Objective:
1. Behavioral Objective –

A. Psychomotor _____	B. Affective _____	C. Cognitive _____
1. Skills _____	1. Perceiving _____	1. Memorize facts __X__
2. Combination of	2. Responding _____	2. Association __X__
skills & mental	3. Valuing __X__	3. Application _____
set __X__	4. Organizing __X__	4. Inquiring _____
3. Habit _____	5. Attitude __X__	5. Discovery _____
		6. Thinking __X__

2. Educational Objective – Knowledge __X__   Understanding _____
                           Appreciations __X__   Values _____

Lesson Objective: __Some students may bring, in addition to the teacher, records of Latin American music to class,__
__and some will give oral reports on the origin, meaning, and composers of some Latin American music heard in the U. S.__
__The students will gain skill in listening, interpreting and note taking and in distinguishing certain types of music.__

Student Assignment: __Continue studying for tests; the map test is tomorrow.__

Concepts to be Taught	Teaching Method or Activity	Time	Materials for Students
Several different types of Latin American music heard in the U. S., including the calypso, the rumba, and the tango.	Playing records.	30 minutes	Records.
Origin, meaning, and composers of the music played.	Student oral reports.	20 minutes	

Relation to Previous and Future Lessons: Tomorrow will discuss relations between the U. S. and Latin America.

Evaluation: Student oral reports will be evaluated by observation.

Daily Lesson Plan

Class and Grade <u>8th grade U. S. History</u> Unit Title <u>"The United States Becomes a World Power"</u>

Teaching Method: Discussion <u>X</u> Illustration ___ Demonstration ___
Conference ___ Lecture <u>X</u> Project <u>X</u>

Type of Objective:

1. Behavioral Objective —

A. Psychomotor		B. Affective		C. Cognitive	
1. Skills	<u>X</u>	1. Perceiving	<u>X</u>	1. Memorize facts	<u>X</u>
2. Combination of skills & mental set	___	2. Responding	<u>X</u>	2. Association	<u>X</u>
		3. Valuing	<u>X</u>	3. Application	<u>X</u>
		4. Organizing	___	4. Inquiring	<u>X</u>
3. Habit	___	5. Attitude	<u>X</u>	5. Discovery	<u>X</u>
				6. Thinking	<u>X</u>

2. Educational Objective — Knowledge <u>X</u>   Understanding <u>X</u>

Appreciations <u>X</u>   Values ___

Lesson Objective: The students will identify in writing the names and locations of the provinces of Canada and the countries of Latin America. They will discuss in class past relations of the U. S. and Latin America, will work on the timeline, and will gain skill in listening, interpreting and notetaking.

Student Assignment: <u>Study for tomorrow's test.</u>

Concepts to be Taught	Teaching Method or Activity	Time	Materials for Students
	Map test.	15 minutes	
Past relations of the U. S. and Latin America.	Class discussion.	15 minutes	
1889—the year the Pan American Union was organized.	Students will draw a picture of the Pan American Union and the date it was organized on the timeline.	10 minutes	Timeline.
Improvements in U. S.–Latin American relations over the years.	Lecture.	10 minutes	

Relation to Previous and Future Lessons: Tomorrow will begin a study of World War I.

Evaluation: Students will be evaluated by observation of class participation, preparation, and contribution to the class.

Class and Grade __8th grade U. S. History_____ Unit Title __"The United States Becomes a World Power"__

Teaching Method: Discussion _____ Illustration _X_ Demonstration _____
Conference _____ Lecture _X_ Project _____

Type of Objective:
1. Behavioral Objective —

A. Psychomotor	_____	B. Affective	_____	C. Cognitive	_____
1. Skills	_X_	1. Perceiving	_X_	1. Memorize facts	_X_
2. Combination of		2. Responding	_X_	2. Association	_X_
skills & mental		3. Valuing	_____	3. Application	_X_
set	_X_	4. Organizing	_X_	4. Inquiring	_____
3. Habit	_____	5. Attitude	_____	5. Discovery	_____
				6. Thinking	_X_

2. Educational Objective — Knowledge _X_   Understanding _X_

Appreciations _____   Values _____

Lesson Objective: __The students will identify and discuss in writing information covered on Canada and Latin America. They will gain skill in listening; interpreting and notetaking.__

Student Assignment: __Be reading on WWI for tomorrow, especially reasons behind the war and American involvement.__

Concepts to be Taught	Teaching Method or Activity	Time	Materials for Students
	Test over material covered on Canada and Latin America.	20 minutes	
World War I	Film: World War I (EBF)	15 minutes	
Immediate cause of World War I.	Lecture.	10 minutes	
	Assignment.	5 minutes	

Relation to Previous and Future Lessons: Tomorrow will discuss new weapons in WWI, reasons behind the war and the position Americans took.

Evaluation: Students' completion of certain objectives will be evaluated on the basis of test performance.

Daily Lesson Plan

Class and Grade <u>8th grade U. S. History</u>   Unit Title <u>"The United States Becomes a World Power"</u>

Teaching Method: Discussion <u>X</u> Illustration <u>X</u> Demonstration ____
                         Conference ____ Lecture <u>X</u> Project ____

Type of Objective:
1. Behavioral Objective —

A. Psychomotor	____	B. Affective	____	C. Cognitive	____
1. Skills	X	1. Perceiving	X	1. Memorize facts	X
2. Combination of		2. Responding	X	2. Association	X
skills & mental		3. Valuing	____	3. Application	____
set	____	4. Organizing	____	4. Inquiring	X
3. Habit	____	5. Attitude	____	5. Discovery	X
				6. Thinking	X

2. Educational Objective — Knowledge <u>X</u>   Understanding <u>X</u>

   Appreciations <u>X</u>   Values ____

Lesson Objective: <u>Some students will give oral reports on new weapons in WWI. The students will answer</u>
<u>questions orally on the day's assignment.</u>

Student Assignment: <u>Certain students are to prepare posters similar to those used to encourage Americans to</u>
<u>buy war bonds, enlist, etc. in WWI. Read about the homefront and our part in fighting and the end of the war.</u>

Concepts to be Taught	Teaching Method or Activity	Time	Materials for Students
	Return tests and discuss.	10 minutes	
New weapons in WWI.	Student oral reports.	15 minutes	
Reasons behind the war and the position the U. S. took.	Question and answer.	20 minutes	Poster on the headlines in the *New York Times* on the sinking of the *Lusitania.*
	Assignment.	5 minutes	

Relation to Previous and Future Lessons: Tomorrow will discuss the homefront, our part in fighting, and the end of the war.

Evaluation: Students will be evaluated by observation of oral reports and answers in class.

356

NINTH GRADE
CIVICS:
State and Local Government

Introduction

The fundamental purpose of the social studies, especially Civics, is to help each student become a good citizen. Therefore Civics should be taught so that students can become thoroughly familiar with the way our government works and with the problems we face as citizens. Opportunities must be given for students to practice the basic principles of problem solving and of democracy in class, in school, and in the community. People generally become what they do.

Almost everything people do is influenced by the laws of their state, and the ordinances of their municipality. It is the state that determines the law of contracts, that charters corporations, that grants driver permits, issues fishing and hunting licences, decides who can teach school, who can practice law or medicine, and gives the city or county the power to grant marriage licenses. These are but a few examples of the many ways that local government influences and controls our lives. Yet, the functions of the state and local governmental agencies are taught less in the schools and are understood less by the typical citizen than those of the national government. Solutions to present problems and the hope of the future is that the citizenry can and will be informed and will make their influence felt on every level of government and public life.

A unit on state and local government is presented in the ninth grade in the hope that an understanding of the state legislature, the executive branch, the state courts, county government, city government, and the way special districts operate will help tomorrow's citizen make wise decisions.

Objectives

Skills:
1. Students will exhibit skill in using the filmstrip projector and the overhead projector.
2. Students will become familiar with the library by doing research and reports.

3. Students will develop good study habits.
4. Students will develop skill in following directions.

Cognitive:

1. The students will list the necessary qualifications for members of the state legislature and their term of office.
2. The students will compare bicameralism and unicameralism.
3. The students will discuss the duties of the speaker of the House.
4. The students will list the seven major steps in making a bill into a law.
5. The students will name and define the two types of direct legislation.
6. The students will discuss the qualifications for becoming governor.
7. The students will discuss the executive powers of the governor.
8. The students will discuss the legislative powers of the governor.
9. The students will list the major executive officers of the state.
10. The students will state the basic functions of the state courts.
11. Beginning with the highest court in the state, the students will name in order the courts that make up our state judicial system.
12. The students will give one type case to be heard in each of the above courts.
13. The students will list the three ways by which a person may become a judge.
14. The students will define and compare the grand and petit juries.
15. The students will name and define the two forms of law.
16. The students will define statutory law.
17. The students will distinguish a civil case from a criminal case.
18. The students will name and define the two classes of crimes under criminal procedure.
19. By using the chart method the students will show the steps in the prosecution of felonies.
20. The students will discuss the criticisms of our state judicial systems.
21. The students will state the main function of county government.
22. The students will name and discuss the duties of the office holders of the county.
23. The students will discuss the county manager plan, showing why it works for some and why not for others.
24. The students will list the officers of a town.
25. The students will define special districts.

26. The students will outline the officers of community or town government and give their duties.

27. The students will compare and contrast the various charters for city governments.

28. The students will discuss the mayor-council form of city government.

29. The students will discuss the commission form of government.

30. The students will discuss the council-manager form of city government.

Teaching and Learning Activities

Key: T—Teacher centered
             S—Student centered
             G—Group centered

I. Introductory activities

A. Invite a judge or lawyer to speak to the class on the topic, the Administration of Justice. (T)

B. Have the mayor speak to the class on his job and the city's government, its functions and problems. (T)

C. Have representatives to Girl's State and Boy's State give reports on their weeks' activities. (S)

D. Have an interview with the school principal or superintendent. Find out how much it costs to operate a school for a year and where the money comes from. Find out how much both the state and community affect the system. (S)

E. Students will be responsible for bulletin boards each week. (S)

F. Use of filmstrips, "Government in Action," to initiate each chapter. (T)

II. Developmental activities

A. Stage a debate on the subject: Resolved: That the state legislature should be reorganized on a unicameral basis. (G)

B. Prepare a chart indicating the course of a bill through the state legislature. (S)

C. Divide the class into two groups and let them form their own legislature, using the state legislature for a pattern. Have them pass bills. (G)

D. Prepare a biography of the governor of our state. (S)

E. Have the class construct a chart of the courts in the state's judicial system. (G)

F.   Have a mock court session, re-enacting the actual steps of a real trial. (G)

G.   Write a report on a prominent court case being reported in the newspapers. (S)

H.   Debate. Resolved: That the state should provide the necessary funds to any person accused of a felony to insure that person's obtaining adequate defense. (G)

I.   Construct a chart of the organization of our county's government. (S)

J.   Debate. Resolved: That this county should adopt the county manager system. (G)

K.   Obtain a copy of our city's charter and discover the exact nature of the organization of its government. Recommend changes to be made. (S)

L.   Obtain a list of the constitutional officials of the state and their duties from the official records. Using additional information, prepare thumbnail biographies of each. (S)

M.   Have a round table discussion on the duties of each official of the county. (G)

N.   Using a transparency, make a diagram showing how municipal, county, and state governments overlap. (S)

O.   Attend a session of court and write a report on what took place. (S)

P.   Read the *Mayflower Compact.* Report on its contents to the class. (S)

III.   Optional activities

A.   Do research on what is being done by your county in the following ways: (a) road building; (b) care of unfortunates; (c) health programs; (d) library service. (S)

B.   Students will make a booklet throughout the unit on each chapter using current events related to chapters. (G)

C.   Discuss: Three particular matters which need urgent attention in your county. (G)

D.   Discuss: Do you think every city should be permitted to frame and adopt its own charter? (G)

E.   Make a study of a metropolitan area. Draw a map of it. List all of the units of local government included in the area. What is the area doing to solve some of its problems? (G)

F.   Have a "What's My Line?" type of show in which class members try to guess the state office a student pretends to hold. (G)

G.   Lecture Objective 1   (T)

H.   Discussion Objective 3   (G)

I.   Drama Objective 4   (G)
J.   Pass the Question Objective 14   (G)

Contract Assignment and Grading

The contract method of giving project type assignments and of grading will be followed in an effort to allow each student to determine his own grade and level of work. A copy of the contract to be used follows.

"A" contract

1.   A report on selected research topics (both oral and written).
2.   Read all basic materials and two articles from the Suggested Reading List after each chapter.
3.   Work on two committees or debates, chairman of one.
4.   Average of 92 on tests.
5.   Exhibit superior citizenship qualities.

"B" contract

1.   A report on selected research topics (given orally).
2.   Read all basic materials and one article from the Suggested Reading List after each chapter.
3.   Serve on two committees or debates and really work on one of them.
4.   Average 84 on tests.
5.   Exhibit good citizenship qualities.

"C" contract

1.   One report either written or oral.
2.   Read all basic material.
3.   Serve on one panel or debate and work at it.
4.   Average 74 on tests.
5.   Show adequate citizenship qualities.

Other Student Assignments

1.   Students will be responsible for the bulletin board each week, correlating it with the week's assignment.
2.   Debate. Resolved: That the state legislature should be reorganized on a unicameral basis.
3.   Prepare a chart indicating the course of a bill through the state legislature.
4.   Prepare a biography of the governor of the state.

5. Write a report on a prominent court case being reported in the newspaper.
6. Debate. Resolved: That the state should provide the necessary funds to any person accused of a felony to insure that person's obtaining adequate defense.
7. Construct a chart of the organization of our county's government.
8. Debate. Resolved: That this county should adopt the county manager plan.
9. Obtain a list of state officials. Prepare thumbnail reports of each.
10. Using a transparency, make a diagram showing how municipal, county, and state governments overlap.
11. Do research on what is being done by your county in the following areas: (a) road building; (b) care of unfortunates; (c) health programs; (d) library service.
12. Students will make a booklet throughout the unit on each chapter using related current events.
13. Make a study of a metropolitan area. Draw a map of the units of local government included in the area. What is the area doing to solve some of its problems

Outline of Content

I. State legislatures
   A. Bicameralism versus unicameralism
   B. Size and apportionment
   C. Qualifications, pay, election and terms
   D. Legislative sessions
   E. Powers of the legislature
      1. Legislative powers
      2. Nonlegislative powers
   F. Organization of the legislature
   G. The legislative process
      1. Source of bills
      2. Voting
   H. A bill becomes law
   I. Improving state legislatures
   J. Direct legislation
      1. Initiative
      2. Referendum
II. The Governorship and state administration
   A. The office

B. The governor at work
1. Executive powers
2. Legislative powers
3. Judicial powers
4. Miscellaneous duties
C. Other executive officers
1. Major officers
2. Lesser officers and agencies
3. Administrative reorganization
4. Interstate agencies

III. State Court systems
A. Organization
B. Selection of judges
C. Advisory opinions
D. Declaratory judgments
E. The jury system

IV. State courts in action
A. Kinds of law
B. Rules of procedure
C. Improving judicial procedures

V. Rural local government
A. Counties
1. Legal status
2. Functions
3. Organization
4. Powers
5. Officers
B. Reform of county government
1. County manager plan
2. County consolidation
3. County-city consolidation
C. The township system
D. County-township system
E. Special districts

VI. Municipal governments
A. Urban growth
B. Village government
C. City government
D. Forms of city government
1. Mayor-council

2.   Commission
3.   Council-manager

Evaluation

1.   Were the students interested in the materials which were presented?
2.   Did all students participate in the activities which were planned?
3.   Did the students understand the material presented to them?
4.   Did the tests meet the needs of all students?
5.   Did the students develop skill in using the library?
6.   Did the students show interest by asking and answering questions?
7.   Were the activities and materials well correlated?
8.   Did the activities and materials meet the needs of the slow learner as well as the gifted?

Sample Unit Test

State and Local Government

Place the letter of the statement which BEST answers the question in the space provided on the answer sheet.

1.   The necessary qualifications for members of the state legislature do *not* include:
     (a)   U.S. citizen
     (b)   residents of their state
     (c)   35 years of age
     (d)   residents of districts they represent   (1) [1]
2.   An argument for bicameralism is:
     (a)   It is easier for public to know what the legislatures are doing.
     (b)   The legislature can easily control lobbying.
     (c)   It is possible to fix responsibility for action or inaction.
     (d)   One house may act as a check on the other to prevent enactment of unwise legislation.   (2)
3.   The presiding officer of the House of Representatives is the:
     (a)   speaker
     (b)   president pro tempore
     (c)   president of the House   (3)
4.   Not listed among the powers of the Speaker is:
     (a)   power of recognition
     (b)   power of veto

1. Refers to the objective being tested.

    (c)   interpretation and application of rules

    (d)   the reference of bills   (3)

5.   Initiative and referendum are types of:

    (a)   direct legislation

    (b)   indirect legislation

    (c)   statutes

    (d)   legislative councils   (5)

6.   List in order the steps in making a bill into a law:

    _____ Debate on the Floor

    _____ Reference

    _____ The Committee stage

    _____ Introduction and first reading

    _____ Action in Second House

    _____ Executive Action

    _____ Engrossment and Passage   (4)

7.   Qualifications for a governor of our state are:

    (a)   live in a populous area

    (b)   may not be an atheist

    (c)   an acceptable record of accomplishment

    (d)   none of these

    (e)   all of these   (6)

8.   Which is *not* one of the executive powers of the governor:

    (a)   law enforcement

    (b)   supervision of administration

    (c)   veto power

    (d)   military powers   (7)

9.   Legislative powers of the governor include:

    (a)   message power

    (b)   special sessions

    (c)   veto power

    (d)   items a and b

    (e)   all of the above   (8)

10.   Which of the following is not considered one of the executive offices of the state?

    (a)   State Board of Health

    (b)   Treasurer

    (c)   Secretary of State

    (d)   Superintendent of Public Instruction   (9)

11.   The basic function of state courts is:

    (a)   to settle disputes

    (b)   to protect the rights of individuals

    (c)   to check the executive and legislative branches of government

      (d)   a and c

      (e)   all of the above   (10)

12.   Rank in descending order beginning with the highest court:

      _____ Municipal courts

      _____ Intermediate Appellate courts

      _____ Justice of the Peace

      _____ General Trial Courts

      _____ State Supreme Courts

      _____ Police Courts   (11)

13.   Match the facts with the courts above:

      _____ review decisions of lower courts

      _____ lowest court in urban area

      _____ deals with minor legal matters

      _____ reviews decisions made by lower courts

      _____ divisions—civil criminal juvenile

      _____ traffic and small claims—circuit, district, county or superior

      _____ courts   (12)

14.   Which method is not used for selecting a judge:

      (a)   city councils

      (b)   popular election

      (c)   appointment by the legislature

      (d)   none of the above   (13)

15.   MATCH:

      (a)   Grand Jury   investigate all indictable offenses

      (b)   Petit Jury   is used in civil and criminal cases   (14)

16.   A body of unwritten, judge-made laws is:

      (a)   statutory law

      (b)   constitutional law

      (c)   equity

      (d)   common law   (15)

17.   The form of law dealing with the legislative acts of Congress, the state legislature, city councils, and county boards is known as:

      (a)   administrative law

      (b)   statutory law

      (c)   constitutional law

      (d)   equity law   (16)

18.   A civil suit differs from a criminal suit in that in a criminal suit:

      (a)   there is a dispute between private parties

      (b)   the State is always a party

      (c)   there are two types of procedure, law and equity suits

      (d)   governmental units are usually involved   (17)

19.   The major and most serious type of crimes is:

(a)   felony

(b)   misdemeanor

(c)   murder, robbery, and perjury

(d)   A and C

(e)   B and C

20.   List in order of occurrence for prosecution of felonies:

_____ Police Department

_____ Grand Jury

_____ Police Court

_____ Felony Committee

_____ Prison

_____ Trial Court   (19)

21.   Some criticisms of our state judicial systems are:

(a)   the delay and cost of obtaining justice

(b)   lack of plans of organizational unity

(c)   the systems are overzealous

(d)   all of the above

(e)   none of the above   (20)

22.   The functions of county government are:

(a)   responsible for collecting federal tax

(b)   set qualifications for county offices

(c)   responsible for administering state laws and county laws

(d)   setting the rate for own percentage for sales tax   (21)

23.   The job of collecting taxes is given to the:

(a)   sheriff

(b)   county clerk

(c)   county treasurer

(d)   county assessor   (22)

24.   The success of the county manager plan depends on:

(a)   local party organization

(b)   the "courthouse gang" who fear their jobs

(c)   the caliber of the manager himself

(d)   the rural residents   (23)

25.   The principle officers of a town are:

(a)   selectmen

(b)   moderators

(c)   sheriff

(d)   clerks   (24)

26.   A local unit created to perform related functions is known as:

(a)   board of supervisors

(b)   board of commissioners

    (c)   special district

    (d)   selectmen   (25)

27. In town government, the council has the power to:

    (a)   determine the tax rate

    (b)   appropriate money

    (c)   levy special assessments

    (d)   all of the above   (26)

28. The principle executive officer in the village is:

    (a)   the clerk

    (b)   the tax collector

    (c)   mayor

    (d)   police officer   (26)

29. The charter under which all cities within the State are grouped according to population and a uniform charter is granted to all cities within the same class is known as the:

    (a)   classified charter

    (b)   special charter

    (c)   optional charter

    (d)   city charter   (27)

30. The oldest and most widely used form of city government is the:

    (a)   mayor-council

    (b)   commission

    (c)   council-manager

    (d)   neither   (28)

31. An advantage of the commission form of city government is:

    (a)   It makes possible the separation of politics and administration.

    (b)   It promotes efficiency.

    (c)   It locates responsibility.

    (d)   The number of commissioners to elect is small and they can act promptly.   (29)

32. Students of government have found that the best of the three major forms of city government is the:

    (a)   mayor-council

    (b)   commission

    (c)   council-manager

Answer Sheet

1.＿＿＿＿＿   21.＿＿＿＿＿
2.＿＿＿＿＿   ＿＿＿＿＿   22.＿＿＿＿＿
3.＿＿＿＿＿   13.＿＿＿＿＿   23.＿＿＿＿＿
4.＿＿＿＿＿   ＿＿＿＿＿   24.＿＿＿＿＿
5.＿＿＿＿＿   ＿＿＿＿＿   25.＿＿＿＿＿
6.＿＿＿＿＿   ＿＿＿＿＿   26.＿＿＿＿＿
      ＿＿＿＿＿   ＿＿＿＿＿   27.＿＿＿＿＿
      ＿＿＿＿＿   ＿＿＿＿＿   28.＿＿＿＿＿
      ＿＿＿＿＿   14.＿＿＿＿＿   29.＿＿＿＿＿
      ＿＿＿＿＿   15.＿＿＿＿＿   30.＿＿＿＿＿
      ＿＿＿＿＿   ＿＿＿＿＿   31.＿＿＿＿＿
      ＿＿＿＿＿   16.＿＿＿＿＿   32.＿＿＿＿＿
7.＿＿＿＿＿   17.＿＿＿＿＿
8.＿＿＿＿＿   18.＿＿＿＿＿
9.＿＿＿＿＿   19.＿＿＿＿＿
10.＿＿＿＿＿   20.＿＿＿＿＿
11.＿＿＿＿＿   ＿＿＿＿＿
12.＿＿＿＿＿   ＿＿＿＿＿
      ＿＿＿＿＿   ＿＿＿＿＿
      ＿＿＿＿＿   ＿＿＿＿＿
      ＿＿＿＿＿   ＿＿＿＿＿

Teacher Evaluation

1. Did I understand fully all materials which were presented to my students?
2. Did I present material in such a way as to motivate my students?
3. Were my objectives purposeful?
4. Did the test effectively measure student growth toward purposes and objectives of this unit?
5. Were my activities student-centered?
6. Did I make allowances for the slow, average, and gifted students?
7. Did I use an adequate number of visual aids and were they effective?
8. Was I fair to each student in my grading practices?
9. Did I plan each lesson so as to reach the objectives?
10. Did the students find the material interesting and worthwhile?
11. Is my classroom arranged and maintained for the best work results?
12. Am I involved in community and extra-class activities?
13. Are the assignments purposeful and clear?
14. Are the students given responsibility in the classroom?
15. Do I encourage the students to be creative in assigned activities?
16. Have I helped create a friendly, courteous atmosphere?

BIBLIOGRAPHY

Dimond, Stanley, and Pflieger Elmer. *Civics For Citizens.* New York: J. B. Lippincott Company.

McClenaghan, William. *American Government.* Boston: Allyn and Bacon, Inc.

Snider, Clyde. *American State and Local Government.* New York: Appleton-Century-Crofts, Inc.

Zimmerman, Joseph. *State and Local Government.* New York: Barnes and Noble, Inc.

SUGGESTED READINGS

Chapter 36—state legislatures

Baker, Gordon. *The Reapportionment Revolution.* New York: Random House.

Dirksen, Senator Everett M. "Rewrite the Constitution?" *U. S. News.*

Reeves, Richard. "Travia: The Other Half of the State Government." *New York Times Magazine.*

Stern, Sol. "The Call of the Black Panthers." *New York Times Magazine.*

Tydings, Senator Joseph D.. "The Last Chance for the States." *Harper's.*

Chapter 37—the governorship and state administration

Baird, Joseph H. "Lester Maddox: Puritan in the Statehouse." *The Reporter.*

Evans, Rowland. "Now That Regan Is Governor." *Saturday Evening Post.*

Frady, Marshall. "Governor and Mrs. Wallace." *The Atlantic.*

Hearnes, Governor Warren E. "What Worries Governors." *U.S. News.*

"It's Time to Change the Guard." *Time.*

Chapter 38—state court systems

Friggens, Paul. "Is That Judge Fit To Sit?" *Reader's Digest.*

Knebel, Fletcher. "How Good Are Our Juries?" *Look.*

"Reforming Juvenile Justice." *Time.*

Ross, Irwin. "The Victims of Crime Deserve a Break." *Reader's Digest.*

Samuels, Gertrude. "A Judge With A Disciplined Indignation." *New York Times Magazine.*

Chapter 39—state courts in action

Bazelon, David T. "Clients Against Lawyers." *Harper's.*

Brooks, Thomas R. "The Finest Could Be Finer." *New York Times Magazine.*

Coughlin, George. "What Every Trial Juror Should Know." *Reader's Digest.*

"Rising Crime and the Courts–State Justices Take A Stand." *U.S. News.*

Wilson, Orlando. "A Police Chief Looks At Crime." *U.S. News.*

Chapter 41—rural local government

Deutsch, Patricia and Ron. "San Mateo Shows the Way to Treat Mental Illness." *Reader's Digest.*

Miller James. "Can Local Government Be Saved?" *Reader's Digest.*

Ornstein, Franklin. "Local Government Is A Farce." *Saturday Evening Post.*

Chapter 42—municipal governments

Arnold, Martin. "City Councilman–Man in a Wind Tunnel." *New York Times Magazine.*

Bollens, John. *The Metropolis: Its People, Politics, and Economic Life.* New York, Harper and Row.

Miller, James. "A City Pulls Itself Together." *Reader's Digest.*

National Municipal League. *Forms of City Government: How Have They Worked?* (New York).

Three Day Problem-Centered Lesson Plan

The problem-centered lesson plan is an excellent method for studying government in the high school. The student gets to select the problem, find his own solutions and test them for effectiveness. The objectives of this lesson are: (1) Students will discuss the advantages of a unicameral and a bicameral government. (2) Students will gain skill in planning. (3) Students will gain skill in forming conclusions.

The teacher will let the class select the problem to be studied. The problem in this plan being: Should we have a unicameral or bicameral government? Why?

The class will be divided into two groups—one taking the side supporting unicameralism and the other bicameralism. These two groups will be divided as deemed necessary by the students in each group.

The group will begin to analyze the problem and collect data. The teacher should have relevant materials available for students to use in the classroom and at home. The second day will be devoted to collecting, organizing and evaluating the data. The third day will be the period alloted for group leaders to give their conclusions.

Project Plan Teaching

The project plan is an excellent method for teaching content by letting the student identify his own objectives. In order for this method to be successful the teacher should know the class and the interests and skills of the students.

The teacher will guide the student so that his activities do not vary from the objectives. The resourceful teacher may suggest activities but should not force them upon the students. The teacher must remember that the project should have value as subject matter and that it is the students who must accept the responsibility for the project. The student then determines his own grade by the work he accomplishes.

The class could compile a history of the city or town and make a replica of it. The school without a paper would be an ideal learning situation for setting up a school paper. The teacher must be prepared in any project which they decide to do!

The creative teacher can make social studies come to life by using this method of teaching.

Daily Lesson Plan

Class and Grade <u>9th grade Civics</u> Unit Title <u>State and Local Government</u>

Teaching Method: Discussion ____ Illustration ____ Demonstration ____
Conference ____ Lecture _X_ Project ____

Type of Objective:
1. Behavioral Objective —

A. Psychomotor ____	B. Affective ____	C. Cognitive ____
1. Skills ____	1. Perceiving _X_	1. Memorize facts ____
2. Combination of	2. Responding _X_	2. Association _X_
skills & mental	3. Valuing ____	3. Application ____
set ____	4. Organizing _X_	4. Inquiring ____
3. Habit ____	5. Attitude ____	5. Discovery ____
		6. Thinking _X_

2. Educational Objective — Knowledge _X_ Understanding ____

Appreciations ____ Values ____

Lesson Objective: <u>The student will list the necessary qualifications for members of the state legislature and their</u>
<u>term of office.</u>

Student Assignment: <u>Read Chapter 36 in textbook.</u>

Concepts to be Taught	Teaching Method or Activity	Time	Materials for Students
Qualifications for members of state legislatures, their terms of office.	Pass the question to begin the lesson, then lecture.	45 minutes	

Relation to Previous and Future Lessons: Relate state government to national government and local
government.

Evaluation: Observation—did the students answer the question or pass it?

374

Daily Lesson Plan

Class and Grade 9th grade Civics _____ Unit Title State and Local Government _____

Teaching Method: Discussion __X__ Illustration ____ Demonstration ____
                     Conference ____ Lecture ____ Project ____

Type of Objective:
1. Behavioral Objective —

A. Psychomotor	_____	B. Affective	_____	C. Cognitive		_____
1. Skills	_____	1. Perceiving	__X__	1. Memorize facts		_____
2. Combination of		2. Responding	__X__	2. Association		__X__
skills & mental		3. Valuing	_____	3. Application		_____
set	_____	4. Organizing	_____	4. Inquiring		__X__
3. Habit	_____	5. Attitude	__X__	5. Discovery		_____
				6. Thinking		__X__

2. Educational Objective — Knowledge __X__   Understanding _____

Appreciations _____   Values _____

Lesson Objective: Students will discuss the duties of the Speaker. Students will discuss qualifications for members
of the state legislature and their duties. _____

_____

Student Assignment: Read pp. 615-627 in textbook. _____

_____

Concepts to be Taught	Teaching Method or Activity	Time	Materials for Students
Duties of the Speaker.	Questions from students.	5 minutes	Paper and pencil.
Qualifications of members of legislatures.	Questions from teacher to lead into general class discussion on the state legislatures.	30 minutes	
	Test.	10 minutes.	

Relation to Previous and Future Lessons: Students will study the unicameral and bicameral legislatures to
decide which is better.

Evaluation: Test.

Daily Lesson Plan

Class and Grade _9th grade Civics_ _____ Unit Title _State and Local Government_ _____

Teaching Method: Discussion _X_ Illustration ___ Demonstration _____
Conference ___ Lecture ___ Project _____

Type of Objective:
1. Behavioral Objective —

	A. Psychomotor		B. Affective		C. Cognitive	
	1. Skills	_____	1. Perceiving	_X_	1. Memorize facts	_X_
	2. Combination of		2. Responding	_X_	2. Association	_X_
	skills & mental		3. Valuing	_X_	3. Application	_____
	set	_____	4. Organizing	_X_	4. Inquiring	_X_
	3. Habit	_____	5. Attitude	_____	5. Discovery	_____
					6. Thinking	_X_

2. Educational Objective — Knowledge _X_ Understanding _X_

Appreciations _____ Values _____

Lesson Objective: _The student will compare bicameralism and unicameralism._ _____

_____

_____

Student Assignment: _Do research on having debates._ _____

_____

Concepts to be Taught	Teaching Method or Activity	Time	Materials for Students
Bicameralism	Students will have a debate on bicameralism versus unicameralism.	45 minutes	Notes taken on the subject.
Unicameralism			Rules for debating.
Debate procedures			

Relation to Previous and Future Lessons: Unicameral government – good or bad?

Evaluation:
Observation: How well did the students know their material? Was it well presented?

Daily Lesson Plan

Class and Grade _9th grade Civics_ Unit Title _State and Local Government_

Teaching Method: Discussion ____ Illustration ____ Demonstration ____
Conference ____ Lecture _X_ Project ____

Type of Objective:
1. Behavioral Objective —

A. Psychomotor	____	B. Affective	____	C. Cognitive	____
1. Skills	____	1. Perceiving	_X_	1. Memorize facts	_X_
2. Combination of		2. Responding	____	2. Association	_X_
skills & mental		3. Valuing	____	3. Application	____
set	____	4. Organizing	____	4. Inquiring	____
3. Habit	____	5. Attitude	_X_	5. Discovery	____
				6. Thinking	_X_

2. Educational Objective — Knowledge _X_ Understanding ____

Appreciations ____ Values ____

Lesson Objective: _The student will list the seven major steps in making a bill into a law._

Student Assignment: _Students will reread the section in the textbook on how a bill becomes a law and be pre-_
pared to follow the steps in class.

Concepts to be Taught	Teaching Method or Activity	Time	Materials for Students
The seven major steps for a bill to become a law.	Lecture. Class discussion and questions.	45 minutes	Chalkboard, charts and paper and pencil.

Relation to Previous and Future Lessons: Tomorrow the students will set up a mock Senate and make a
bill into a law.

Evaluation: Observation of interest and class participation.

Daily Lesson Plan

Class and Grade <u>9th grade Civics</u> Unit Title <u>State and Local Government</u>

Teaching Method: Discussion ____ Illustration ____ Demonstration __X__
Conference ____ Lecture ____ Project ____

Type of Objective:
1. Behavioral Objective —

A. Psychomotor _____	B. Affective _____	C. Cognitive _____
1. Skills _____	1. Perceiving __X__	1. Memorize facts_____
2. Combination of	2. Responding __X__	2. Association __X__
skills & mental	3. Valuing _____	3. Application __X__
set __X__	4. Organizing __X__	4. Inquiring _____
3. Habit _____	5. Attitude _____	5. Discovery _____
		6. Thinking __X__

2. Educational Objective — Knowledge __X__   Understanding __X__

                              Appreciations _____   Values _____

Lesson Objective: <u>Students will demonstrate knowledge of how a bill becomes a law by posing as a body of the</u>
<u>state legislature and passing a bill.</u>

Student Assignment: <u>Read pp. 630-635 in textbook. Have reports on how we can improve our state</u>
<u>legislatures.</u>

Concepts to be Taught	Teaching Method or Activity	Time	Materials for Students
Tests on how a bill becomes a law.		10 minutes	
Steps for a bill to become a law.	Drama moot session.	35 minutes	

Relation to Previous and Future Lessons: Students will study the types of legislation and the part of the people in the process.

Evaluation: Test. Participation in passing the bill.

Daily Lesson Plan

Class and Grade _9th grade Civics_ _____ Unit Title _State and Local Government_ _____

Teaching Method: Discussion _X_ Illustration ____ Demonstration ____
                      Conference ____ Lecture ____ Project _____

Type of Objective:
1. Behavioral Objective —

A. Psychomotor	_____	B. Affective	_____	C. Cognitive	_____
1. Skills	_X_	1. Perceiving	_X_	1. Memorize facts	_____
2. Combination of		2. Responding	_X_	2. Association	_X_
skills & mental		3. Valuing	_X_	3. Application	_____
set	_____	4. Organizing	_____	4. Inquiring	_____
3. Habit	_____	5. Attitude	_____	5. Discovery	_____
				6. Thinking	_X_

2. Educational Objective — Knowledge _X_   Understanding _____
                         Appreciations _X_   Values _____

Lesson Objective: _The student will discuss the problems and give possible solutions of state legislatures._ _____

Student Assignment: _Students will read Chapter 37, giving emphasis to pp. 637-647._ _____

Concepts to be Taught	Teaching Method or Activity	Time	Materials for Students
Problems of state legislatures.	Reports given by students.	25 minutes	Reports researched before class.
Solutions to problems.	Discussion.	10 minutes	Filmstrip.
	Filmstrip.	10 minutes	

Relation to Previous and Future Lessons: Students will begin a study of the governor and other branches of power in state government.

Evaluation: Evaluate the reports, class participation and the filmstrip.

Photo furnished courtesy of AUM Learning Resource Center and Montgomery County Public Schools, Montgomery, Alabama.

TENTH GRADE
WORLD HISTORY:
The Middle Ages

Introduction and Purpose

The purpose of this unit is for the students to gain an understanding of the importance of the Middle Ages. They should have an understanding of past events, especially those which have an effect on the formation of current events. For this reason, a knowledge of the events of the Middle Ages is necessary for an insight into today's world affairs. This unit is planned to present factual and interesting material on life during that time so that the purpose will be fulfilled.

Overview

The following is a unit in tenth grade world history. This unit covers the period of time from the early 400's to the late 1400's which is referred to as the Middle Ages. The Middle Ages is an essential part of world history: many events happened during this time. The feudal system, the beginning of towns and cities, the Crusades, and various inventions are all part of the events. The life was hard and dangerous, as well as progressive. This unit tells of the happenings and the way of life during this era.

Specific Objectives

Skills:

1. Students will develop their ability to relate certain dates with important events in history.
2. Students will improve in reading ability.
3. Students will follow directions in taking tests.
4. Students' abilities to listen and to take notes will improve.

5. Students will develop self-confidence when speaking before a group or audience.
6. Students will use the library and other sources to find supplementary material.

Knowledge:

1. The students will explain three of the following items concerning the development of monasteries:
    a) The importance of monasteries
    b) Spread of Christianity by monks
    c) Contributions of monasteries
    d) Teachers of Christianity
2. The students will list four characteristics of the Gothic style of architecture.
3. The students will list three contributions of the Mohammedan culture.
4. The students will describe three characteristics of the invading Germans.
5. The students will identify the term feudalism.
6. The students will contrast the relations of nobles to that of the serfs.
7. The students will discuss the reasons for growth of towns during the Middle Ages.
8. The students will identify the health hazards of the Middle Ages.
9. The students will list two important literary works of the Middle Ages.
10. The students will identify five inventions of the Middle Ages.
11. The students will identify the following: Pope Urban's appeal, the Magna Charter, Joan of Arc, the Hundred Years' War.
12. The students will differentiate between the Middle Ages and The Renaissance.
13. The students will write a few sentences describing the purpose of the Crusades.
14. The students will identify Charlemagne.
15. The students will describe castle life.
16. The students will list three geographic discoveries during the Middle Ages.

Appreciations:

1. The students will show their understanding of the importance of the Middle Ages and its influences in our lives today.

Methods of Activities

Introductory activities:

1. A week or so before the unit is taught the teacher will assign a topic to each row in the room for reports and research. One row will take the

feudal system, another the manorial system, etc. Then when the unit is started, students will report their findings. (Class centered)

2. As each topic is discussed, the teacher will illustrate with maps, charts, and various drawings that have been prepared to further the interest of the lecture. (Teacher centered)

3. As another introductory activity the teacher will have volunteers to do special reports and posters. (Student centered)

Developmental activities:

1. Readings from the textbook will be assigned to give students a better understanding of class activities. (Class centered)

2. Class discussions will be conducted to maintain interest, to insure understanding and to develop the students' abilities. They will also be able to express their opinions and views. (Class and teacher centered)

3. A bulletin board will be prepared weekly by the students. (The responsibility will be rotated from student to student.) The bulletin boards will be pertinent to the subject. (Student centered)

4. Each student will be required to give an oral book report. (Student centered)

5. The chalkboard and overhead projector will be used to clarify pronunciations and to emphasize the important names, terms, and places. (Teacher centered)

6. Maps will be a regular part of class in teaching specific areas and locations. (Teacher centered)

7. Students will be given a list of references to write to get information to share with the class. (Student centered)

8. A guest speaker will be asked to speak about some phase of the period being studied. This will add interest and knowledge to the course. (Teacher centered)

Culminating activities:

1. The students will participate in a thorough review of the unit. (Teacher centered)

2. Questions will be asked by the students concerning areas of interest to the students. (Student centered)

3. The students will be tested to evaluate their knowledge and understanding of the materials covered. (Class centered)

Outline of Content

AN INTERESTING PERIOD
OF TIME——THE MIDDLE AGES

I. Religion in the Middle Ages
   A. The church and the people
      1. A universal church
         a. Catholic Church
         b. Rome the center
      2. The church and daily life
         a. Was a community center
         b. Sinners——pilgrimage
      3. The church and recreation
         a. Most important source of recreation
         b. Had Biblical skits
   B. The development of monasteries
      1. The importance of monasteries
         a. Devoted lives to service of God
         b. Thousands retired to monasteries
      2. Spread of Christianity by monks
      3. Contributions of monasteries
         a. Helped educate children
         b. Preserved skills
         c. Wrote in Latin
      4. Others teachers of Christianity
   C. The building of cathedrals
      1. Church architecture
      2. Beauty of the Gothic architecture
         a. Pointed arch
         b. Great stained glass
         c. "Bibles carved in stone"
   D. Power of the church
      1. Church organization and authority
         a. Received income various ways
         b. Had trials for people who disobeyed rules
      2. Conflict between church and government
   E. Spread of Mohammedanism
      1. A new religion
         a. In Arabia——Mohammedanism
         b. Prophet Mohammed born in Mecca 570
         c. Mecca religious center for Arabian people

          d.   The Koran

          e.   Hegira

    2.   The spread of Islam

          a.   Carried on by caliphs

          b.   Spread to various countries

    3.   Mohammedan culture

          a.   Far in advance of that of Europe

          b.   Had great respect for learning and science

          c.   Made important contributions

          d.   Bagdad——capital of Moslem world

    4.   Importance of Moslem Empire

  F.   The crusades

    1.   Conflict in the Holy Land

          a.   Mohammedan rule of Holy Land displeasing to the Christians

          b.   Christian often went to the Holy City of Jerusalem

          c.   Nomads from Asia conquered the Holy Land

          d.   Council of French and German bishops met

    2.   Pope Urban's appeal

          a.   Appeal to march against Turks and to reclaim Jerusalem

          b.   Beginning of many new crusaders

    3.   Peter and the Peasants' crusade

    4.   The first crusade

    5.   Later crusades

          a.   Second one——defeat for Christians

          b.   *The Talesman*

          c.   Christians regained city of Acre

    6.   Effects of crusades

          a.   Vast trade

          b.   Zoos

          c.   First book on plant and animal life

    7.   Another religion in the time of the crusades

    8.   The spread of religions

          a.   Christianity

          b.   Mohammedanism

II.   A.   Germans claim Western Europe

    1.   The invading Germans

          a.   Vigorous people

          b.   Dressed in hides, furs, linen, and wool

          c.   Knew how to make earthware

          d.   Hunting means of securing food

    2.   A new way of government
       a.   Christianity accepted by conquering Germans
       b.   Christians—taught Germans more civilized ways of living
    3.   Civilization turns eastward
       a.   Constantinople known as Byzantine Empire
       b.   Emperor Justinian of Byzantine Empire

B. Charlemagne's Empire
    1.   An empire in northern Europe
       a.   Empire found by Frankish king
       b.   Mohammedans defeated in the Battle of Tours
       c.   Charles Martel followed by son Pepin as leader of Franks
       d.   Next Pepin's son Charlemagne or Charles the Great
    2.   Charlemagne
       a.   Wanted to unite all Europe
       b.   Made German tribes between Rhine and Vistula rivers accept Christianity
       c.   Was crowned emperor by Pope Leo III
       d.   Believed heartily in religion
    3.   Charlemagne's successors
       a.   Louis known as "the Pious"
       b.   Charles, Lothaire, and Louis

C. The Norse invasions
    1.   Fighting favorite pastime
    2.   Valhalla
    3.   Discovered easy way to make living——to plunder people of wealth
    4.   Turned to sea for livelihood
    5.   Went westward
    6.   Did considerable damage in France
    7.   Change in tactics
       a.   Became friendly
       b.   Became Christians

D. Feudalism
    1.   What feudalism was
       a.   The political, social, and economic structure of medieval Europe
       b.   Determined a person's place in society
       c.   Had force of law during the Middle Ages
    2.   Theory and practice of feudalism
       a.   Based on holding of land

   b. King owned land of his kingdom
  3. Feudal courts
   a. "Fief and justice" are one
   b. People accused of crimes——might be tested by ordeal
   c. Trial by combat
   d. Compurgation
   e. Lateran Council
  4. The castle as seat of government
  5. A trade and social center
   a. Shops and stores
   b. Wells dug
  6. Castle life
   a. Lord and lady most important persons
   b. Life attractive for nobility
  7. The celebration of knighthood
 E. The manorial system
  1. The relations of nobles to serfs
   a. Serfs lowest level of feudal society
   b. Owned no property——serfs
  2. Wealth based on farming
   a. Agriculture basis for wealth
   b. Income of lords——depended on work of serfs
  3. The passing of feudalism

III. Development of European nations
 A. The rise of England
  1. British Isles most important
  2. Early invasions
   a. Romans
   b. Germans
  3. The coming of Christianity
   a. St. Patrick to Celtics of Ireland
   b. St. Augustine in England
  4. Unification of England
  5. The Norman conquest
   a. William, Duke of Normandy
   b. Harold of Wessex
  6. Reforms in government under Henry II
   a. Jury had its beginning
   b. Judges
  7. Additional freedoms under the Plantagenets
  8. The Magna Charta or Great Charter

           a.   Most important political document in history

           b.   Things a king might not do

      9.   The development of Parliament

    10. Our debt to Medieval England

           a.   Jury system

           b.   Our courts

           c.   Our system of representative government

           d.   Some of our favorite stories

B.   The rise of France

     1.   Roman influence

     2.   France a feudal state

     3.   The Hundred Years' War

           a.   England successful in first part

           b.   Second part, England lost

           c.   Third part, English again

     4.   The increasing power of French kings

           a.   Powerful nobles

           b.   Rise of middle class

C.   The Rise of Spain

     1.   The peoples of Spain

     2.   Triumph of Christianity

D.   The rise of the German states

     1.   An independent people

           a.   Kept their own customs

           b.   Many small states

     2.   The Holy Roman Empire

           a.   Otto king of Italy

           b.   A loose connection or union of German and Italian states

           c.   Emperors elected

E.   Development of other nations

     1.   Origin of several small nations

           a.   Portugal

           b.   Norway and Denmark

           c.   Switzerland

     2.   The origins of Russia

           a.   Laid in Middle Ages (the foundations)

           b.   Established trading posts

           c.   Adopted Greek form of Christianity

           d.   Empire built on military strength

           e.   Mongol Empire

           f.   Golden Horde

       g.   Moscow established as capital city of Russia

  3. The Ottoman Empire

      a.   Founded by a Turkish warrior

      b.   Established in southeastern Europe

      c.   Moscow made Christian capital of eastern Europe

IV.   European culture in the Middle Ages

  A. The growth of towns

      1. Why towns developed

         a.   Need for protection

         b.   Attracted traveling merchants

      2. International trade

         a.   Grew with the development of local industries

         b.   Spices, incense, jewelry

         c.   Merchant leagues set up

      3. The growth of guilds (organization of skilled workers)

         a.   Coppersmiths, furriers, tailors, shoemakers, belt makers

         b.   Set prices

         c.   Determined work day

      4. Duties of citizens

         a.   Maintain street in front of home

         b.   Night watchman

      5. Medieval towns

         a.   Public square in center, usually as a market place

         b.   Maintained courts of justice

      6. Health hazards

         a.   Wells often polluted

         b.   Tossed garbage out of windows to street

         c.   Disease and epidemic common

  B. Medieval education

      1. A superstitious people

      2. Medieval learning

         a.   Schools were the church

         b.   Most learning strictly religious

         c.   St. Augustine——*City of God and Confessions*

         d.   St. Jerome

      3. Development of universities

  C. Literature, art and music

      1. Literature in Middle Ages

         a.   *Song of Roland*

         b.   "Beowulf"

        c.   *Canterbury Tales*
        d.   *Divine Comedy* (by Dante)
        e.   Boccaccio's *Decameron*
    2. Art in the Middle Ages
        a.   Generally religious
        b.   Golds, blues, and reds used
    3. Music in Middle Ages
  D. Invention and discovery
    1. Inventions in Middle Ages
        a.   Progress slow
        b.   Water mills and windmills used
        c.   Drills and lathes common
        d.   Printing press
    2. Discoveries in Middle Ages
        a.   Geographic
        b.   Establishment of universities

Evaluation

What should be measured:

1. The students' skills
2. Major concepts
3. Ability to do critical thinking
4. Values
5. Students' knowledge of the subject matter
6. Ability to communicate
7. Extent of class participation
8. Questions asked by students
9. Work or study habits of students
10. Students' comprehension of subject matter

Methods or techniques of evaluation:

1. Observation by the teacher of individuals, small groups, and classes in many situations
2. Conferences or interviews with students
3. Teacher-pupil planning
4. Self-evaluation by the students
5. Teacher-made tests
6. Standard tests
7. Talks with the parents
8. Essays
9. Participation in skit

Test Questions

1. Explain three of the following items concerning the development of monasteries:
   a) The importance of monasteries
   b) Spread of Christianity by monks
   c) Contributions to monasteries
   d) Teachers of Christianity

2. List four characteristics of the Gothic style of architecture.

3. List three contributions of the Mohammedan culture.

4. Describe three characteristics of the invading Germans.

5. Contrast the relations of nobles to that of the serfs.

6. Discuss the reasons for growth of towns during the Middle Ages.

7. List two important literary works of the Middle Ages.

8. List five inventions of the Middle Ages.

9. Write a few sentences describing the purpose of the crusades.

10. Describe castle life during the Middle Ages.

11. List three geographic discoveries of the Middle Ages.

12. Identify four health hazards of the era.

13. Identify the term feudalism

14. Identify the following: Pope Urban's appeal, the Magna charter, Joan of Arc, and the Hundred Years' War.

15. Identify Charlemagne.

16. Match the following by placing the correct number in the correct space.

a. Victor Hugo	1. Battle of Tours
b. Hegira	2. Parliament
c. Charles Martel	3. Yr. 1 in Mohammedan calendar
d. Great Council	4. "Bibles carved in stone"
e. St. Augustine	5. *City of God & Confessions*
f. Constantinople	6. Byzantine Empire

17. Place T before the statements that are true and F before the statements that are false.

    _____ 1. Lateran Council involved condemning trial by ordeal.
    _____ 2. England was the religious center during the Middle Ages.
    _____ 3. The music during the Middle Ages was extremely pretty.
    _____ 4. The Roman style of architecture involves pointed arches.

BIBLIOGRAPHY

Appel, John C. and Magenis, Alice. *A History of the World.* New York: The American Book Company.

Bettersworth, John K., and others. *Your Old World Past.* Texas: Steck-Vaugh Company.

Drummond, Muriel Jean, and Platt, Nathaniel. *Our World Through the Ages.* New Jersey: Prentice-Hall, Inc.

Habberton, William, and Roth, Lawrence V. *Man's Achievements Through the Ages.* New York: Laidlaw Brothers, Inc.

Slosson, Preston W., and others. *The History of Our World.* Boston: Houghton Mifflin Company.

Wallbank, T. Walter. *Man's Story.* New Jersey: Scott, Foresman and Company.

Welty, Payl Thomas. *Man's Cultural Heritage.* New York: J. B. Lippincott Company.

ELEVENTH GRADE
AMERICAN HISTORY:
The United States, 1919-1945

Introduction

Today's student is tomorrow's citizen. A good citizen must be informed of and understand the happenings around him. To understand much of today's complex society it is necessary to look backward—to the origin. This unit is a study of the United States from 1919 to 1945. The main events covered are: The Roaring Twenties, The Great Depression, The New Deal, and, World War II.

This unit of study is designed to increase the student's knowledge of the period; but, equally as important, the unit is designed to stimulate the student to think. Facts are included, but questions asking "why" and "how" dominate.

This unit is usually taught the fifth six-weeks period of the eleventh year of school.

Behavioral Objectives

Cognitive

1. The student will summarize in a one page essay the Election of 1920, including in this essay the candidates, their party, the main planks of the platforms, the results of the election, and one unusual thing about this election.

2. The student will explain in one sentence the meaning of the term "isolation," as related to Republican diplomatic policy in the 1920's.

3. The student will describe in his own words (written report not over one page) how and when the United States changed from a debtor to a creditor nation.

4. The student will explain in one paragraph why the Pact of Paris (also called the Kellogg-Briand Pact) failed.

5. In Harding's administration the domestic policy was one of "laissez faire." The student will give a specific example of this type of policy which indicates that he understands the term "laissez-faire."

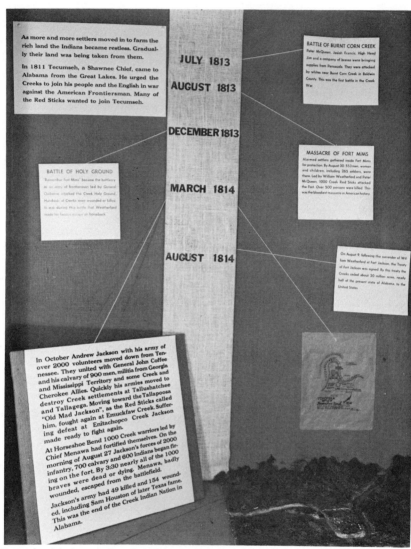

Photo furnished courtesy of AUM Learning Resource Center and Montgomery County Public Schools, Montgomery, Alabama.

6. The student will list three reasons the United States passed laws restricting immigration.

7. The student will evaluate the administration of Calvin Coolidge (who he appointed as Cabinet members, how he handled authority, and how well he knew what he was doing) and make a value judgment as to whether or not he was a good president.

8. The student will write a two page essay entitled "How The Automobile Changed the United States."

9. The student will write a paragraph on "Does a farm bloc exist today?"

10. The student will summarize the tone of the 1920's; indicating the reason for the change in national attitude.

11. The student will discuss, in class, Herbert Hoover's philosophy of the relationship between the people and the government.

12. The student will list four conditions which helped to cause the Depression of 1928.

13. The student will give an example of one public figure today who is similar to Herbert Hoover in his views on public relief and list these similarities.

14. The student will explain, in his own words, why there was starvation in 1930 when there were immense surpluses of food.

15. When prices of farm products are high, farmers tend to cultivate more land and to produce more in order to make more money. When prices of farm products fall, farmers tend to cultivate more land and to produce more in an attempt to maintain their income; but the more the farmers produce, the lower prices go. The student will describe possible solutions to this problem.

16. The student will draw a conclusion from the following statistics: "In 1932, 36,000 immigrants entered the country; 103,000 emigrants left." The student will explain why this situation existed.

17. The student will describe the days of "Normalcy" in a general narrative report not to exceed two pages.

18. The student will list the three general objectives of the New Deal.

19. The student will describe the benefits of the FDIC.

20. In 1932 farmers were desperately in trouble financially. The student will summarize, in one page, steps taken in 1933 to alleviate this situation.

21. The student will describe briefly how Franklin D. Roosevelt dealt with the disillusionment and fear prevalent in the country when he entered office.

22. The student will discriminate between the Civilian Conservation Corps

and the Public Works Administration, listing each program's objectives and if they achieved their objectives.

23. The student will summarize the Tennesseee Valley Authority program, including in this summary the objectives of the project and criticisms directed at it.

24. The student will inform himself on the merits of redistribution of wealth as a means of raising the general standard of living. He will do this by using additional sources found in the library as well as reading the textbook. He will prove this is (or is not) an effective means of raising the standard of living.

25. The student will describe the objectives of the Work Progress Administration, evaluate the program, and decide if it was a successful program.

26. The student will state the principle the Social Security Act of 1935 established.

27. The student will characterize Franklin Delano Roosevelt in one paragraph.

28. The student will compare the American Federation of Labor and the Committee for Industrial Organization as they existed in 1930.

29. The student will write a one page summary of Franklin Roosevelt's "packing the Supreme Court," concluding with his personal feelings toward this event.

30. One assumption underlying sit down strikes is that the job is property belonging to the worker. The student will judge the validity of this statement and participate in a debate entitled: RESOLVED: Sit down strikes are ethical.

31. The student will summarize, in a two page report, the New Deal; including its objectives, accomplishments and shortcomings.

32. The student will list six technological advances occuring in the period between 1920 and 1930 and briefly cite after each some of the changes these advances brought.

33. Many Latin Americans resent the way the United States has monopolized the word "American." The student will suggest ways in which people living in the United States might help break this national habit.

34. In 1933, the United States recognized the USSR. Will Rogers remarked, "The United States would probably recognize the Devil if it could sell him pitchforks." The student will explain the significance of this remark and agree or disagree with the remark.

35. The student will describe the principal features of Fascism (including its doctrine, leader, and place of origin) in a brief report.

36. The student will outline the basic doctrine of Nazism.

37. The student will describe, in a brief paragraph, the treatment Jews received in Germany from 1934-1945.

38. The student will justify America's attitude (in 1935) of non-intervention in World War II.

39. The student will list one result of Britain and France's policy of appeasement and the U.S. policy of isolation on the advance of Hitler.

40. The student will explain in a short report how Hitler removed the threat of Germany fighting a two front war.

41. On an outline map of Europe the student will place the name of each country involved in World War II, indicating which are Allied Powers and which are Axis Powers. He will also locate the Rhineland, Sudentenland, and the Polish Corridor.

42. The student will state the date and reason of the first peacetime draft for the United States.

43. The student will list three major differences between Fascism and Communism.

44. The student will explain (in a short paragraph) Roosevelt's attitude toward intervention in the European War in 1940.

45. The student will describe the provisions of the Lend-Lease Act.

46. In the message to Congress that recommended the Lend-Lease Act, President Roosevelt set forth the famous Four Freedoms. The student will list these Four Freedoms.

47. The student will recall the one event which united Americans and produced American involvement in World War II.

48. The student will outline America's part in World War II.

49. The location of the First World War differed from that of the Second World War. The student will detect these differences, and analyze the disadvantages of the location of World War II to the United States.

50. The student will list the two cities bombed by the United States with the first atomic bomb ever used.

51. The student will describe the effects of World War I on productivity in the United States. (one page essay)

52. The student will investigate any and all sources in an effort to find if he has relatives who served in the Armed Forces in World War II. He will give an oral report in class on his findings.

53. On the home front the war produced many changes. The students will list two groups of Americans which were helped by the war and describe how they were helped.

54. The student will describe the growing tension between Japan and the United States from 1931 (Stimson Doctrine) to 1941 (Pearl Harbor).

55. The student will identify 90 percent of the following men:
    1. Stalin
    2. Benito Mussolini
    3. Winston Churchill
    4. Douglas MacArthur
    5. Dwight D. Eisenhower
    6. Chaing Kai-shek
    7. Adolf Hitler
    8. Frank Lloyd Wright
    9. Fiorello La Guardia
    10. Huey Long

56. The student will select a book from the booklist and write a one page review of the book, using the book review guide given in class.

57. The student will select a topic from a list of topics handed to them and write a five page term paper on the chosen topic using correct grammar, punctuation, and annotation.

58. The student will compare Adolf Hitler and Napolean Bonaparte in a two page report. (Include personalities, efforts to gain power, tactics used to control people and the fate of each man.)

59. The student will become proficient in interpreting maps, globes, charts, graphs and graphic presentations.

60. The student will construct time lines.

61. The student will use the library effectively.

62. The student will evaluate information; determining the reliability of the sources of information and distinguishing fact from opinion.

63. The student will develop skill in finding information, condensing information, and making valid generalizations.

64. The student will write a scholarly term paper, using correct grammar, punctuation, annotation, and recording of bibliographical information.

65. The student will develop skill in public speaking.

66. The student will develop skill in working in small groups— panels, forums, debates, symposiums, buzz groups, etc.

67. The student will develop skill in reading and listening for meaning.

68. The student will create effective posters, graphs, charts, and other audio visuals to use in oral reports as an aid in communication.

Affective domain

69. The student will think for himself, make a decision, and support it.
70. The student will show an awareness of the changing role of the United States in world affairs and the problems she has faced as a world power.
71. The student will accept responsibility for his work and see that it is done neatly and on time.
72. The student will learn the responsibilities of being a good citizen and realize how important it is for him to live up to this responsibility.
73. The student will learn to participate in class discussions in a manner beneficial to him and to his peers.
74. The student will show respect for the rights of others; thus proving that he respects the dignity of the individual.
75. The student will demonstrate a growing appreciation of his heritage, faith in the democratic process, and pride in being an American.
76. The student will demonstrate that he can do something that no other person in the class can do as well.

Teaching and Learning Activities

Code to teaching and learning activities
TC—Teacher centered activity
SC—Student centered learning activity
GC—Small group centered learning activity
or class centered

Introductory activities

A. **Pre-test:** (TC) The purpose of the pre-test is to determine the level on which the majority of the students are functioning at the beginning of the unit. It sets a starting point for growth toward objectives. It is necessary if evaluation of actual progress is to be measured accurately. It is given before the unit is begun. The pre-test is similar to the final test given to measure growth, but is more general.

Self Evaluation Scale: (SC) A self evaluation scale is included for the same reason as the pre-test. It allows the teacher to set a starting point to measure growth toward objectives in the affective domain. Sample questions in this scale are:

1. How well can you make decisions and support these decisions?
   (1) very poorly (2) poorly (3) fair (4) well (5) very well
2. How well do you accept responsibility?
   (1) very poorly (2) poorly (3) fair (4) well (5) very well

3. How effectively do you communicate with others?
    (1) very poorly (2) poorly (3) fair (4) well (5) very well
4. How well do you work with others?
    (1) very poorly (2) poorly (3) fair (4) well (5) very well
5. Do you consider yourself a good citizen?
    (1) Yes (2) No
6. Do you think a democracy is the best form of government?
    (1) Yes (2) No

B. **Lecture:** (with guide sheet) (TC) This is a twenty minute lecture on the objectives of teaching this unit. What is expected of each student will be outlined. An introduction to the 1920's will relate this unit to the previous period studied. Some of the significant persons, events and problems of the period will be presented. Matted pictures with captions (taken from *Life* magazine) will be shown to illustrate the general tone of the Twenties.

C. **Pass The Question Game:** (GC) This game is used to stimulate interest and get attention. Rules of game:
    1. If you know the answer to the question, answer the question in a complete sentence and in a voice loud enough for everyone in the room to hear.
    2. If you do not know the answer, choose a consultant (anyone in the room except the teacher) and ask him to help you.
    3. Do NOT say "I don't know."
    4. Do NOT volunteer an answer.

    Example Questions:
    1. What were three changes which occurred between 1920 and 1930?
    2. Why and how did the national attitude change?
    3. How did the automobile change the United States?
    4. Who was responsible for putting the automobile within reach of the "common man"? How did he do this?
    5. Who were two artists to achieve fame in the "jazz world" during the 1920's?
    7. What was the "national game" in the field of sports in the Twenties?
    8. What is Prohibition?

Developmental activities

A. **Role Playing:** (GC) (Obj. 1, 65, 66, 73)

    The Election of 1920

    Time: July 4, 1920
    Event: Political Rally
    Place: Your Home Town

Characters:
> Narrator—(played by student) This character sets the time, event, place and introduces the characters.
> Warren G. Harding (Republican)—(Played by student)
> Governor James M. Cox (Democrat)—(Played by student)

These two men give a ten minute speech describing their platform. The audience then asks questions they are interested in about the problems of the day. The narrator is moderator and delivers the questions to the participants. After the question and answer period the rally is concluded by the narrator.

B. **Individual Reports:** (SC) (Obj. 61, 62, 63, 65, 67) The student will present an oral report to the class—preferably on his research paper. He will practice good public speaking. The report will not exceed ten minutes and will contain an introduction, several clearly defined concepts, and a summary. This report is due as the class studies events related to the student's individual topics. (Topics for reports are in the appendix.)

C. **Lectures:** Lectures are used to introduce a topic, to give the student information considered valuable which he might not find otherwise, to organize and relate concepts studied, and to summarize. Each lecture will not exceed thirty minutes at any time. A visual aid (poster, transparency, map, etc.) will accompany lectures.

Example:
> The Depression (30 minutes)
> a. causes
> b. stockmarket crash
> c. effects of depression on "common man"
> d. effects on government
> e. lasting results
> Film: "The Great Depression" (15 minutes)
> Question-Answer Period (5 minutes)
> Assignment for following day: Write a paragraph summarizing how the Depression affected your parents, grandparents, or anyone who lived through the Depression.

D. **Buzz Groups:** (GC) (Obj. 62, 65, 66, 67, 69, 73, 74) A list of questions will be placed on the chalkboard. The teacher will divide the class into four groups. Each group will be responsible for answering the question assigned to it. At the end of fifteen to twenty-five minutes the group will choose a leader to give a summary of what the group concluded. (Contradicting ideas may be included in this summary.)

Examples of the questions:

1. What was Herbert Hoover's philosophy of the relationship between the people and the government? Do you agree with his viewpoint?
2. Who is one public figure today who is similar to Herbert Hoover in his views on public relief? What are these similarities?
3. When prices of farm products are high, farmers tend to cultivate more land and to produce more in order to make more money. When prices of farm products fall, farmers tend to cultivate more land and to produce more in an attempt to maintain their income; but the more the farmers produce, the lower prices go. Describe possible solutions to this problem.
4. Why was there starving in 1930 when there were immense surpluses of food in the United States?

E. **Resource People:** (TC) (Obj. 67, 20, 48, 53) Resource people will be used extensively to encourage the realization that historic events being studied actually happened, that common people were affected by them, and that we are making history today. Persons familiar to the students, as well as unfamiliar persons will be invited. Persons highly respected, and "common, everyday" people will be guest speakers.

Examples of guest speakers:
The town historian—Mr. _____ (past superintendent of schools),—will speak on "Grenada in the Second World War."

A town businesswoman—Mrs. _____—will speak on "How the Depression Affected Grenada Businesses."

A farmer — Mr. _____— will tell about "Farmers and the New Deal."

A woman from the community—Mrs. Ann Thornton—will tell of "My Experiences At Home During World War II."

F. **Workshops:** (GC) (Obj. 59, 61, 62, 63, 65, 66, 68, 73, 74) Workshops will be provided where some of the students may go to the library and work up reports. Other students will stay in the classroom and construct posters, bulletin boards, maps, and other audio visuals to supplement the reports being done. Workshops will be preceded by detailed planning of work. The student will write a proposal of what he wishes to do and who he wants to cooperate with, how long his work will take (approximately), what the finished product will be, and how it will be constructed.

Example of a workshop:
The New Deal
Ten students will write reports on the following topics (detailed, not over six pages).

Objectives of the New Deal

FDR—The Man
Abandonment of the Gold Standard
Relief Measures
Tennessee Valley Authority
Criticism of the New Deal
Similarities Between the New Deal and Current War on Poverty
Report on actual work done by CCC and PWA
The FDIC

Their partners will make posters, graphs, charts, maps, etc. to illustrate these reports.

The students will, in teams, give their reports to the class, including use and explanation of audiovisuals.

G. **Debates:** (GC) (Obj. 62, 65, 66, 67, 69, 71, 73, 74) Debates are included in this unit to encourage the individual to develop his ability to involve himself in critical thinking. The student will, at some time, participate in a debate, choosing either side—negative or affirmative. The topic of the debate will be introduced by a student who will guide the debate and see that the debate goes according to rules in a text supplied him by the teacher. Each student will have informed himself on the procedure of debate. Five minutes will be the limit to present a speech. There will be four students on the affirmative side, four on the negative side. Prior organization will have eliminated repetition; each student will bring out new ideas. There will be a two minute rebuttal and the class will have a chance to vote on the issue.

Topics to be debated are:
RESOLVED: The New Deal encouraged socialism in America.
RESOLVED: Sit down strikes are ethical.
RESOLVED: That the federal government should establish a national program of public work for the unemployed.

H. **Brainstorming:** (GC) (Obj. 69, 73) Brainstorming will be used, to a degree, to encourage creative thinking in students. A topic will be introduced and each student will be encouraged to suggest possible solutions or to add personal opinions.

Example of brainstorming question:
The atomic bomb has just been dropped on Pearl Harbor. You are there. What do you do?

I. **Class Discussion:** (GC) (Obj. 65, 66, 67, 69, 73, 74) Class discussion will be entered into extensively. Questions pertaining to the subject being studied will be entertained. Students will be given questions to start discussions. They will be encouraged to talk with each other as well as with the teacher. All students will talk loudly and clearly. Opinions will be heard, but the student must have some authority to back his statements. Off-subject statements will result in a penalty to the asker.

J.   **Films:** (TC) (Obj. 67, 75) Films will be shown to give the student a picture of how events they are studying really were. They will stimulate interest and develop questions in students. Films will be followed by a question-answer period.

Examples of films to be used:

The Three Faces of Evil (28 minutes). This film shows the build-up of Fascism, Nazism, and Japanese Militarism.

Tale of Two Cities (14 minutes). This film tells the story of the atomic bombing of Hiroshima and Nagasaki which brought the war to an end. (See instructions in the appendix for obtaining films.)

K.   **Filmstrips:** (TC) (Obj. 59, 67) Filmstrips will be used to illustrate lectures, to give a vivid interpretation, and to depict the general "tone" of the times. They will be used as aids to lectures since they can be adjusted to the rate of the lecturer.

Example of filmstrips used:

Story of TVA. This filmstrip, in full color, presents a factual account of the operations of the TVA. It is accompanied by a script. (To obtain, see instructions in the appendix.)

L.   **Time Lines:** (GC) (Obj. 59, 60, 68) A time line will be constructed, initially, by a committee of students who volunteer. They will be responsible for obtaining the materials and constructing the time line. They may do this in any way they wish but must satisfy the following conditions:

1.   The time line must be large enough for everyone to see.
2.   It must have separate lines for (1) presidents, (2) wars, (3) the arts, (4) technoligical developments, (5) governmental programs, (5) important legislation, (6) home events, (7) European events.
3.   Each line must be in a different (and vivid) color.
4.   The time line must be placed above the chalk board or some other obvious place.

Students (all students) will be responsible for keeping the time line up to date. Each student will be assigned one of the topics for a week. During that week he will be responsible for that topic being up to date. (An example of time line is in the appendix.)

M.   **Agree-Disagree Sessions:** (GC) (Obj. 62, 65, 66, 67, 69, 73) Several controversial topics will be written on the chalkboard. The student will prepare for the next day a report supporting either viewpoint he wishes. As each topic comes up, students will give their decision and support it.

After hearing all arguments on each topic, the students will take a vote on the issue.

Example of a topic discussed in the session:

(1) The New Deal encouraged (did not encourage) socialism in America.

(2) In 1933 the United States recognized the USSR. Will Rogers remarked, "The United States would recognize the Devil if it could sell him pitchforks." Do you agree with this statement?

N. **Committee Reports:** (GC) (obj. 62, 63, 65, 66, 67, 69, 73, 74) The students will divide into committees of four or five individuals. A chairman will be elected. The committee will be handed a problem or job to do. The chairman will appoint members to be responsible for different segments of the project. Each student will do his part and the results will be reported to the chairman. The chairman will organize the findings and summarize them; reporting them to the class.

Example:

Is redistribution of wealth an effective means of raising the general standard of living?

O. **Book Reports:** (SC) (Obj. 56, 61, 62, 65, 67, 69, 71) Book reports will be given orally in class. They will not exceed two minutes in length. The student will introduce the book and give his evaluation of it. In reviewing the book he will use the following outline:

1. State title, author, and position of author (what he does for a living).
2. State why you think the author is qualified to write the book (or why he isn't qualified).
3. Give what you feel to be the author's purpose.
4. Write a BRIEF summary of the content.
5. Did author achieve his purpose?
6. Your opinion of the book.
7. Do you recommend this book to your classmates?

Book reports will be summarized on one page and handed to the instructor.

P. **Bulletin Boards:** (SC) (Obj. 66, 68, 71) (Optional activity) The construction of bulletin boards will be assigned to volunteers. Volunteers may work in teams. They will be given free reign in their presentation. It *must,* however, pertain somehow, to what is being studied. (Extra credit will be given for volunteer work.)

A smaller bulletin board will be placed in the classroom for miscellaneous items to be placed on it. Articles of interest, coming TV programs (concerning the subject), good books to read (again on the subject), pictures, cartoons, post cards and announcements of school related events may be placed on this board. Current events which the students feel will "make history" may be placed here. Consent of the instructor must be obtained before posting.

Q. **Maps:** (SC) (Obj. 59) Maps will be used frequently and locations of places studied will be emphasized. A world map will be placed in the classroom and places studied will be outlined and shaded as they are studied. Individual map construction will be encouraged. Transparencies of countries, their location and principal cities will be shown on the overhead projector.

R. **Case examples:** (SC) (Obj. 63, 67, 71, 73, 74) The students will find examples of how the events being studied affected people in the local area.

Example of a case study:
Interview the president of the local power company to find out if TVA affected his company.

S. **Interviews:** (SC) (Obj. 63, 66, 74) The student will, during the six weeks, interview one person who lived through the period we are studying. He will set up the interview at least one week in advance. He will, before the interview, prepare a list of questions to ask. He will dress carefully for the occassion and take a classmate along with him. He will report to the class on his findings in a two minute report.

T. **Audio-visual material:** (TC) (Obj. 59)
Pictures shall be used to supplement lectures, show details, and give a visual interpretation to a happening. The picture shall be presented on a mat with a caption attached.
Slides will be included when there is only one such item available to the class.
Overhead projectors will be used to portray something graphically which is difficult to portray otherwise. Cartoons, maps, graphs, and lists will be shown in this manner when possible.

U. **Study guides:** (TC) (Obj. 63, 67) Guides to structure notes taken during lecture will frequently be provided. This is to help the student learn to organize his notes. (An example of a study guide is found in the appendix.)

V. **Homework:** (SC) Homework assignments will be given in an effort to get students to increase their knowledge. This cannot be done completely inside the classroom. Homework assignments will be a stimulant to further study and a method of encouraging the student to develop his own method of studying. Homework assignments will be fairly short.

W. **Personal Conferences:** (TC) (SC) Personal conferences will be used to come to the root of any problem which develops in the classroom. Lack of interest or poor class attendance might be the reason for the conference. The purpose of the conference is to individualize instruction as much as possible.

Culminating activities

A. **Lecture:** The lecture will be used to summarize and conclude; show relationships; and relate study to other areas of student life.

B. **Question-Answer:** Question and answer periods will be held to answer any questions or provide help in relating events. Question-Answer periods will be used to evaluate student growth toward objectives.

C. **Time Lines:** The time line will be viewed in an attempt to teach the relationship of one event to another, to teach chronology and time sequence, and to review major points.

Optional activities (Bonus will be given.)

A. Bulletin Boards

B. Construction of audiovisual materials for use in lectures and oral reports

Marking and Grading Procedure

Methods used to evaluate student growth toward objectives:

Formal tests

Anecdotal Records

Participation in class activities

Outcome of project

        a. interest shown in doing project

        b. work actually done in project

        c. final results

Evaluation of book reports

Evaluation of oral reports

Term paper

Personal Conferences

Cooperation in Group Work

Homework Done

Optional Activities undertaken

Grading procedure:

Formal Tests

    a.   Three weeks test .... 25 percent

    b.   Six weeks test.. 25 percent

Oral and Written Book Report.. 10 percent

Term paper.. 10 percent

Project... 20 percent

Class Participation .... 10 percent

(Bonus for optional activites undertaken)

Outline of Content

I.   Normal
- A. The Election of 1920
- B. Foreign Affairs
  1. European Affairs
  2. The World Court
  3. The League of Nations
  4. The Washington Conference, 1921-1922
  5. Kellogg-Briand Treaty (Pact of Paris)
  6. Latin American Policies
- C. Domestic Affairs
  1. Federal Finances
  2. Immigration Restrictions
  3. Death of President Harding
  4. Calvin Coolidge
  5. Election of 1924
- D. The Golden Twenties
  1. Technological Advances
  2. The Automobile
  3. Radio and Motion Pictures
  4. The Plight of Agriculture
  5. Cultural Achievements
  6. Women and Their Changing Status

II.   The Depression of 1928
- A. Election of 1928
- B. Herbert Hoover in Office
- C. Causes of the Depression
- D. Attempts to Stem the Depression
- E. The Collapse of the Stockmarket

     F. Immediate Effects of the Depression

     G. Election of 1932

III.   The New Deal: Recovery and Relief

     A. Franklin Delano Roosevelt

     B. Banking Securities and Currency

     C. Aid to Agriculture

     D. Industry and Labor

     E. Relief Measures

     F. Attacks on the New Deal

IV.   Second Phase of the New Deal: Reform

     A. Work Relief

     B. Social Security Act

     C. Advance of Labor

     D. Election of 1936

     E. Supreme Court Fight

     F. Recession 1937-1938

     G. Estimate of the New Deal

V.   The Good Neighbor and the Axis Threat

     A. The Good Neighbor Policy in Latin America

     B. Relations with Europe

         1. Reciprocal Trade Agreements Act, 1934

         2. Recognition of the USSR, 1933

     C. Fascism

     D. Nazism

     E. Attitude of Isolation and Appeasement

     F. Europe at War

         1. Conquest of Poland: "Blitzkrieg"

         2. Lifting the Arms Embargo

         3. Russian Attack on Finland

         4. Germany pushes through Denmark, Norway, Netherlands, and Belgium

         5. Fall of France

     G. Debate over Foreign Policy

VI.   The Second World War

     A. The Battle of Britain

     B. The Election of 1940

     C. Battle of the Atlantic

     D. Japanese Aggression in the Far East

         1. Attack on Pearl Harbor

         2. Alliance with Germany and Italy–1940

     E. Axis Victories

    F.   Difficult Military Problems
    G. The Russian Front
    H. Attack From the West
    I.   Dwight D. Eisenhower
    J.   Conquest of the Pacific Islands
    K. The Atom Bomb
    L.   Japanese Surrender
    M. On the Home Front
        1.   Battle of Production
        2.   Attempts to Control Inflation
        3.   Civil Liberties
    N. The Election of 1944
    O. Wartime Diplomacy
    P.   Wartime Conferences
    Q. Death of Franklin Roosevelt
    R. Birth of the United Nations
    S.   San Francisco Conference, 1945

Sample Test Items

Multiple Choice

Objective No.

_____ 1   The main issue in the Election of 1920 was:
    a.   isolation versus involvement in world affairs
    b.   lowering of tariffs
    c.   unemployment
    d.   poverty
    e.   immigration restriction

_____ 3   When did the United States change from a debtor to a creditor nation?
    a.   between World War I and World War II
    b.   during the Korean War
    c.   after the Revolutionary War
    d.   after the Civil War
    e.   1969

_____ 5   Under a policy of "laissez faire" a government would most likely:
    a.   enforce anti-trust laws against business combinations
    b.   *not* enforce antitrust laws against business combinations
    c.   make regulatory agencies, such as the Interstate Commerce Commission as powerful as possible
    d.   consider private enterprise a threat to government

_____ 6   The United States passed laws restricting immigration mainly
            because of the:
            a. closing of the frontier
            b. development of labor saving devices
            c. growth in power of organized labor
            d. nationalistic sentiment
            e. fear of radicalism

_____ 7   Calvin Coolidge's philosophy of government was:
            a. economy and laissez faire
            b. intensive governmental regulation of business
            c. extensive aid to the unemployed
            d. liberal welfare programs

_____ 10   The national attitude of the 1920's was one of:
            a. faith and high hope
            b. despair and discouragement
            c. "devil may care"
            d. none of these

_____ 12   Which of the following was _NOT_ a cause of the Depression?
            a. World War I
            b. Depressed condition of agriculture
            c. Overproduction
            d. Stock market speculation
            e. tight money

_____ 16   In 1932 103,000 emigrants left the country. Which of the follow-
            ing is _NOT_ a reason they left?
            a. Depression
            b. shortage of jobs
            e. starvation
            d. tuberculosis epidemic

_____ 18   The three specific objectives of the New Deal were:
            a. removal of fear; a gain in the gross national product, and
                eradication of poverty
            b. change in national attitude, rise in level of living, and crime
                prevention
            c. radicalism, reform, and relief
            d. socialism, communism, and commercialism
            e. recovery, relief, and reform

_____ 20   Which of the following programs were undertaken to aid the
            farmer (1935):
            a. AAA
            b. PWA

        c.   WPA

        d.   CCC

        e.   NLRA

___ 32   Which of the following technological advances did *NOT* take place between 1920 and 1930?

        a.   automobile

        b.   radio

        c.   moving pictures

        d.   use of the atomic bomb

___ 38   America's attitude toward the Axis threat which arose in 1935 was one of:

        a.   anger

        b.   indifference

        c.   welcome

        d.   ignorance

        e.   avoidance (isolation)

___ 39   Which of the following choices best describe the results of Britain's and France's policy of appeasement?

        a.   The policy aided Hitler's advances

        b.   The policy hindered Hitler's advances

        c.   The policy had no effect on Hitler's plans

___ 42   In whose presidency did the first peacetime draft in the United States occur?

        a.   Herbert Hoover

        b.   Theodore Roosevelt

        c.   Calvin Coolidge

        d.   Franklin Roosevelt

        e.   John F. Kennedy

___ 50   The cities bombed by the United States with the first atomic bomb ever used were: (Choose two)

        a.   Hiroshima

        b.   Manchuria

        c.   Pearl Harbor

        d.   Nagasaki

        e.   Berlin

___ 53   Two groups in the United States were helped by World War II. Who were they? (Choose two)

        a.   American Negroes

        b.   Jews

        c.   Italian Americans

        d.   Irish Americans

        e.   Women

___ 47   The incident which united Americans and produced American involvement in World War II was:

        a.   "blitzkrieg" (conquest of Poland)

        b.   Battle of the Atlantic

        c.   Fall of France

        d.   bombing of Pearl Harbor

        e.   Fall of Denmark

True-False

Directions: Place true or false by each question. Write out the words *true* and *false*.

Objective No.

19 _____   Every bank in the United States is a member of the FDIC.

21 _____   "Fireside chats" with Franklin D. Roosevelt were an attempt to overcome the fear and disillusionment prevading the country in 1932.

26 _____   The Social Security Act of 1935 established the principle that an industrial society has a responsibility toward those it casts out of work and those too old to work.

44 _____   Franklin D. Roosevelt, in 1940, felt the United States would have to enter the war in the near future.

51 _____   World War II caused productivity at home in the U.S. to drop.

Matching

Match the following terms with the phrase which best describes it. There is only one correct answer for each term.

Objective No.

22 _____ Civilian Conservation Corp

22 _____ Public Works Administration

23 _____ TVA

25 _____ Works Progress Administration

28 _____ CIO (in 1925)

28 _____ AFL (in 1925)

45 _____ Lend-Lease Act

        a.   relief measure which employed men to build dams, sewer systems, waterworks, etc.

        b.   federal agency designed to restore a specific area by building

dams, reforesting areas, and
establishing power plants

c.   relief agency set up to provide
jobs for white collar workers

d.   relief measure employing young
men between ages of 18 and 25
to work toward conservation and
restoration of our country

e.   craft union

f.   industrial union

g.   act enabling the president to send
supplies and weapons to a foreign
country to protect the U.S.

h.   act lifting the arms embargo

i.   relief measure designed to aid farmers

Match the following men with the phrase at the bottom of this page which best describes them (with what they are most identified). There is only one correct answer.

Objective No.

55 _____ Huey Long

55 _____ Fiorella LaGuardia

55 _____ Stalin

55 _____ Benito Mussolini

55 _____ Winston Churchill

55 _____ Adolf Hitler

55 _____ Frank Lloyd Wright

55 _____ Chiang Kai-shek

55 _____ Douglas MacArthur

55 _____ Lenin

     a.   leader of Bolshevik Party after 1924

     b.   Italian dictator–fascist

     c.   Nationalist governor of China

     d.   famous American architect

     e.   author of the "New Deal"

     f.   Fascist leader of Germany

     g.   leader in Bolshevik Revolution

     h.   mayor of New York City 1933-1945,

known for bringing honesty to
that city's government

i.   senator from Louisiana who
believed in "sharing the wealth"

j.   England's war minister during
World War II

k.   America's ambassador to Britain

l.   U.S. general in World War II

Short Answer

Answer the following questions in one or two sentences.

Objective No.

2   Explain the meaning of "isolationism" as related to Republican diplomatic policy of the 1920's.

4   Why did the Kellogg-Briand Pact (Pact of Paris) fail?

8   Explain some of the changes brought by the automobile.

9   Does a farm bloc exist today?

11, 13   What was Herbert Hoover's philosophy of the relationship between the government and people? Who is a public figure today who shares his views on public relief?

14   In one paragraph explain why there was starvation in the 1930's when there were immense surpluses of food?

15   When prices of farm products are high, farmers tend to cultivate more land and to produce more in order to make more money. When prices of farm products fall, farmers tend to cultivate more land and to produce more in an attempt to maintain their income; but, the more the farmers produce, the lower prices go. Describe a solution to this problem.

27   Briefly characterize Franklin D. Roosevelt as a person.

31   What were the main objectives of the New Deal? Did the program achieve its objectives? Support your answer.

33   What are some other words people in the United States might use besides "American" to refer to themselves?

35, 36   Compare Nazism and Fascism in regard to doctrine, leaders, and place of origin.

37   Describe briefly treatment Jews received in Germany during 1934 to 1945.

38   List three major differences between Communism and Fascism.

Essay

48   Summarize (in outline form if you like) America's part in World
            War II.

49   The location of World War I differed from the location of World
            War II. What were these differences and what were the disadvan-
            tages to the United States of the location of World War II.

54   Trace the growing tension between Japan and the United States
            from 1931 (Stimson Doctrine) to 1941 (Pearl Harbor).

Map Exercise

41   On the following outline map of Europe locate these areas:
            Germany
            France
            Britain
            Austria
            Hungary
            Czechoslovakia
            Poland
            Yugoslavia
            Denmark
            Netherlands
            Italy
            The Polish Corridor
            Sudentenland
            Rhineland

Time Line

            Explain the following time line, showing relationships, causes,
            and results. In explaining the time line, take three events and
            discuss them in some detail, using the remaining as transition
            points. (Time line in the appendix)

Evaluation

Evaluation of material

A.   Student reaction to the material will be used as a criterion for
      evaluating material. Did the students consider it (a) too hard; (b) too easy
      (c) boring (d) out of date?

B.   The reaction of other educators to the material will be taken into consid-
      eration. After they studied it, what was their opinion?

C.   Where did I get the material and who prepared it? Was the material
      prepared by professional educators or authorities in that field?

TIME LINE

Presidents	Woodrow Wilson 1913-1921	Warren G. Harding 1921-1923 (died in office)	Calvin Coolidge 1923-1929	Herbert Hoover 1929-1933	Franklin Roosevelt 1933-1945
"Name of the Times"	The Roaring Twenties 1920-1930			The Great Depression 1929-	The New Deal 1933
European Affairs			Rise of Dictators	Policy of Appeasement	Neutrality Legislation	World War II in Europe 1939	U. S. Enters World War II 1941-1945
Technological Advances	Automobile, Radio, Moving Pictures, Electricity 1920-1930				Atomic Bomb

417

Evaluation of questions and student learning activities

A. **Questions:** To evaluate test questions an item analysis will be made. Questions which 50 percent or less of the students got right will be thrown out of the test and restructured if used in the future. Evaluation of the objective behind that question will be done.

   If more than 80 percent of the students get a question correct, the question will be thrown out on the basis the question is too easy. The objective the question is measuring will be studied.

B. **Lecture:** Lectures will be evaluated by audience reaction. Were the members of the audience bored; did they yawn, talk to each other, fiddle and squirm, etc.?

C. **Pass The Question Game:** This learning activity will be evaluated mainly by student participation. Did it stimulate interest?

D. **Role Playing:** Questions to ask: Do the students really learn about people they are characterizing? What is the student's attitude toward this activity?

E. **Buzz Groups:** Buzz groups will be evaluated by determining if this is the most effective manner in which the students work. Do the students seem to enjoy this and do more students participate in this manner?

F. **Resource People:** Resource people will be evaluated by questions students ask after the speech or presentation. Each will be considered separately.

G. **Workshops:** Workshops will be evaluated by the teacher as to how much actual work is done, what the students learn in cooperation, and how well they participate in the work.

H. **Debates:** Debates will be evaluated by student participation and facts brought out in speeches. Learning to debate will be considered important.

I. **Films and Filmstrips:** These learning activities will be evaluated in class discussions after each presentation.

J. **Time Line:** The time line will be considered successful if the students develop some sense of chronology.

K. **Class discussion:** Class discussion will be judged by the participation of the students, if dialogue is free and plentiful, and how well these dialogues stimulate thinking.

L. **Individual Reports:** Oral reports will be evaluated on the basis of their aid to the student in learning to communicate to others.

Evaluation of self

A form to evaluate the instructor will be passed to the students. They will be encouraged to be objective, honest, and fair and will be assured that they will remain anonymous. The evaluation will be administered by a student.

Evaluation of unit of study

To evaluate the unit of study growth toward the objectives outlined will be the main criterion. Did the students learn and do what was intended?

SOURCES CONSULTED

Textbook:

Bragdon, Henry W., and McCutchen, Samuel P. *History of a Free People.* New York: The Macmillan Company.

Other sources:

Allen, Frederick Lewis. *Only Yesterday.* New York: Harper and Brothers, Publishers.

Capp, Glenn R., and Capp, Thelma R. *Principles of Argumentation and Debate.* New Jersey: Prentice Hall.

Leuchtenburg, William Edward. *The Perils of Prosperity, 1914-1932.* Chicago: University of Chicago Press.

Mowry, George E., Hick, John D., and Burke, Robert E. *Problems of American Democracy.* Boston: Houghton Mifflin Company.

Weiss, John. *The Fascist Tradition.* New York: Harper and Row.

Films and filmstrips:

Educators Guide to Free Films. 30th ed. Randolph, Wisconsin: Educator's Progress Service.

Educators Guide to Free Filmstrips. 22nd ed. Randolph, Wisconsin: Educator's Progress Service.

Educators Guide to Free Social Studies Material. Randolph, Wisconsin: Educator's Progress Service.

Films:

Flames on the Horizon. TV636, 16mm, Sound, (28 minutes)
    This film presents a prelude to the action of World War II. It depicts how the Nazis and the Fascists overran both Europe and North Africa, and then follows the darkest day–Pearl Harbor.

Spreading Holocaust. TV 637, 16 mm, Sound, (28 minutes)
    This film shows the United States girding to meet the challenge, the mightiest crusade for freedom the world has ever known.

Army in Action. TV 639, 16 mm, Sound, (28 minutes)
    This film shows the army in action during World War II, with special emphasis

on the progress of the war on all fronts, including the gigantic pre D-Day buildup for the amphibious invasion of Europe.

Command Decision: The Invasion of Southern France. TV 572 (1962), 16 mm, Sound, (28 minutes)
This film presents Operation "Dragon" which features Roosevelt, Stalin, Chiang Kai-Shek, and Churchill.
>   (The above films may be obtained from:
>   3rd U. S. Army
>   Attention: Audio-Visual Support Center
>   Fort McPhereson, Georgia 30330)

Fight for the Sky. SFP 1563 (1965), 16 mm, Sound, (28 minutes)
This film documents the heroism of American fighter pilots who flew escort missions over Germany during World War II. Footage of fierce battles includes some captured German film.
>   (The above film may be obtained from:
>   USAF Central Audio-Visual Library
>   AF Audio-Visual Center
>   Norton AFB, California 92409)

Filmstrips used:

Hall of American Costume Flapper Period 1920-1930. Dress of Georgette Crepe, about 1925. Satin Dress, about 1927. Etc. # 68 1128.

Accessories of the Flapper Period. # 68 1136.

Other Materials:

Pictures from *Life Magazine* "The Roaring Twenties"

1929 issue of *Life Magazine*

World Map, Rand McNally Atlas Company.

ADDITIONAL SOURCES
(For Student Reference)

General works:

Beard, Charles Austin. *America in Midpassage.* New York: The Macmillan Company.

Longsam, Walter Consuelo. *The World Since 1914* New York: The Macmillan Company.

Shannon, David A., *Twentieth Century America: The United States Since the 1890's.* Chicago: Rand McNally and Company.

Secondary sources:

Allen, Frederick Lewis. *Only Yesterday.* New York: Harper and Brothers, Publishers.

Allen, Frederick Lewis. *Since Yesterday.* New York: Harper and Brothers, Publishers.

Allen, Frederick Lewis. *The Big Change.* New York: Harper and Brothers, Publishers.

Bliven, Bruce. *Twentieth Century Unlimited.* (This book is about the arts of the Twentieth Century.)

Colvin, David Leigh. *Prohibition in the United States.*

Faulkner, Harold. *From Versailles to the New Deal.* New Haven: Yale University Press, (A Chronicle of The Harding–Coolidge–Hoover Era.)

Greene, Laurence. *Era of Wonderful Nonsense.* New York: Bobbs Merrill Company,

Leuchtenburg, William Edward. *The Perils of Prosperity, 1914-1932.* Chicago: University of Chicago Press.

Lippman, Walter. *Men of Destiny.* New York: The Macmillan Company.

Merz, Charles. *Great American Bandwagon.* New York: The Literary Guild of America.

Morris, Lloyed R. *Not So Long Ago.* New York: Random House.

Murray, Robert A. *Red Scare.* Minneapolis: University of Minnesota Press. (A Study in National Hysteria, 1919-1920.)

Schlesinger, Arthur M. Jr. *The Age of Roosevelt: The Crisis of the Old Order.* Boston: Houghton Mifflin Company.

Taylor, A. J. P. *The Origins of the Second World War* (paperback). Connecticut: Fawcett Publications, Inc.

VonLaue, Theodore H. *Why Lenin? Why Stalin?* New York: J. B. Lippincott Company,

Weiss, John. *The Fascist Tradition.* New York: Harper and Row, Publishers.

Wilbur, Ray Lyman, and Hyde, Arthur M. *The Hoover Policies.* New York: Charles Scribner's Sons.

Hoffman Frederick J. *The Twenties.* New York: Collier Books. (American Writing in the Post War Decade.)

Hofstadter, Richard. *The Age of Reform* New York: Vintage Books. (From Bryan to F.D.R.)

Leuchtenburg, William Edward. *F.D.R. and the New Deal, 1932-1940.* New York: Harper and Brothers, Publishers.

Individual Projects

The individual is required to do a project of his own during the six-week period. This project has only one requirement. It must be done by the student to the very *best* of his ability. It can be any undertaking that he desires. It does not have to relate to history or any subject being studied in the classroom. You must get the instructor's approval before beginning, however. It must be done by the student *only.*

The purpose of this project is to increase the student's confidence in himself. Without a sense of confidence and some pride a person does not strive for his best. Thus, he never fulfills his potential. The project will be presented to the instructor and viewed by the class.

Topics for Projects

Fashions of the Twenties
Changing Youth after World War I
Henry Ford
Corruption in Politics in the Twenties
Prohibition
Music of the 1920's
Suffrage and the Changes in the Status of Women
Literature of the Twenties
Sports During the Twenties
Life on a Farm during the Twenties
Life in an Apartment House during the Depression
Causes of the Depression
Buying on Margin
Songs of World War II
Moving pictures (early)
Changes in education between 1920 and 1930
Ernest Hemingway
Changes in values and morals in the Twenties
F. Scott Fitzgerald
Famous Immigrants
Frank Lloyd Wright
Rodgers and Hammerstein
Charles Lindbergh
Radio
The New Deal
Life in these United States during World War II
The Red Scare
General Douglas MacArthur
Crime in the Twenties
Prohibition
Events leading to World War II
Winston Churchill
Franklin Delano Roosevelt
Immigration Restriction
"black" Thursday
Will Rogers
Fiorello La Guardia
Battles of World War II
Technological Advances during the Twenties
Negroes in the War

Pearl Harbor
The Bombing of Nagasaki and Hiroshima
Japanese Militarism before World War II

EXAMPLE OF STUDY GUIDE
The New Deal

Relief Measures	Recovery Measures		Reform (Social Planning)
	Industry, Banking	Agriculture	
WPA			TVA
	NRA	AAA	
			Social Security
PWA	FDIC		
		Advance of Labor	
CCC	SEC	Norris LaGuardia Act	Housing
	Gold Standard	Section 7-a	
	CIO		
		NLRA	

Daily Lesson Plan

Class and Grade <u>11th grade U. S. History</u> Unit Title <u>U. S. History 1919-1945</u>

Teaching Method: Discussion _____ Illustration _X_ Demonstration _____
Conference _____ Lecture _X_ Project _____

Type of Objective:
1. Behavioral Objective —

A. Psychomotor _____	B. Affective _____	C. Cognitive _____	
1. Skills _____	1. Perceiving _X_	1. Memorize facts _____	
2. Combination of	2. Responding _____	2. Association _____	
skills & mental	3. Valuing _____	3. Application _____	
set _____	4. Organizing _____	4. Inquiring _____	
3. Habit _____	5. Attitude _____	5. Discovery _____	
		6. Thinking _X_	

2. Educational Objective — Knowledge _____ Understanding _X_

Appreciations _____ Values _____

Lesson Objective: <u>The student will summarize the "tone" of the 1920's.</u>

Student Assignment: <u>Read pp. 581-590 of textbook. Answer questions 8, 9, and 10 on p. 591. (Tomorrow:</u>
<u>Assignment of roles and rules for preparing roles.)</u>

Concepts to be Taught	Teaching Method or Activity	Time	Materials for Students
Changes taking place between 1920 and 1930.	Pass the Question Game.	20 minutes	Mimeographed list of objectives for course.
	Lecture.	10 minutes	
The 'mood' of the 20's.	Pictures on The Roaring Twenties (on mats with captions).	10 minutes	Pictures of 1920's.
Why the national attitude changed.		10 minutes	Filmstrips of 1920's (Fashions).
Cultural achievements during the 20's.			

Relation to Previous and Future Lessons: Introduction to the 1920's.

Evaluation: This lesson will be evaluated by student participation in Pass the Question Game; attentiveness during lecture; and questions asked about pictures.

Daily Lesson Plan

Class and Grade <u>11th grade U. S. History</u> Unit Title <u>U. S. History 1919-1945</u>

Teaching Method: Discussion ____ Illustration ____ Demonstration <u>X</u>
Conference ____ Lecture <u>X</u> Project ____

Type of Objective:
1. Behavioral Objective —

A. Psychomotor		B. Affective		C. Cognitive	
1. Skills	____	1. Perceiving	<u>X</u>	1. Memorize facts	____
2. Combination of		2. Responding	____	2. Association	<u>X</u>
skills & mental		3. Valuing	____	3. Application	<u>X</u>
set	____	4. Organizing	____	4. Inquiring	____
3. Habit	____	5. Attitude	____	5. Discovery	____
				6. Thinking	<u>X</u>

2. Educational Objective — Knowledge <u>X</u> Understanding ____

Appreciations ____ Values ____

Lesson Objective: <u>The student will summarize the Election of 1920 and identify the change in foreign policy of</u>
<u>the U. S. in 1920's.</u>

Student Assignment: <u>Read pp. 572-581 of textbook. Answer question 1 on p. 591.</u>

Concepts to be Taught	Teaching Method or Activity	Time	Materials for Students
Election of 1920 a. Candidates b. Main issue c. Platform of each d. Results	Role playing.	20 minutes	
Foreign policy a. Kellogg-Briand Treaty b. Washington Conference	Lecture.	20 minutes	Study guide.
Domestic Policy a. Immigration restriction b. Federal spending			
Death of Harding	Question-Answer Session.	10 minutes	

Relation to Previous and Future Lessons: In studying the 1920's the election is vital to understanding the times; the foreign and domestic policy is determined by the winner of the election; the death of Harding determines future events.

Evaluation: The success of the roleplaying would be evaluated by student participation and interest. Attitude of audience would evaluate the lecture. Type of questions asked in Question-Answer Session will determine success of it.

Daily Lesson Plan

Class and Grade 11th grade U. S. History   Unit Title U. S. History 1919-1945

Teaching Method: Discussion _X_ Illustration ____ Demonstration ____
Conference ____ Lecture _X_ Project ____

Type of Objective:
1. Behavioral Objective —

A. Psychomotor ____	B. Affective ____	C. Cognitive ____
1. Skills ____	1. Perceiving _X_	1. Memorize facts ____
2. Combination of	2. Responding ____	2. Association _X_
skills & mental	3. Valuing ____	3. Application ____
set ____	4. Organizing ____	4. Inquiring _X_
3. Habit ____	5. Attitude ____	5. Discovery ____
		6. Thinking _X_

2. Educational Objective — Knowledge _X_   Understanding _X_

Appreciations ____   Values ____

Lesson Objective: The student will list the causes of the Depression and analyze the condition of the United States during the Depression.

Student Assignment: Read pp. 592-602 of textbook. Answer questions 2, 3, and 5 on p. 611. Ask parents or grandparents what they remember about the Depression.

Concepts to be Taught	Teaching Method or Activity	Time	Materials for Students
Causes of the Depression. Effect of Depression on the Common Man	Resource person ("Effects of Depression on Local Businesses" Mrs. ____ ____ Local Business-woman).	30 minutes	
Stock Market Crash.	Class discussion	20 minutes	

Relation to Previous and Future Lessons: The Depression was a result of many things—most of which occurred during 1920-30. It left a lasting impression on future generations.

Evaluation: Evaluation of this lesson will be consideration of pupil interest; what the resource person added to knowledge content and student interest; and quality of class discussion.

Daily Lesson Plan

Class and Grade __11th grade U. S. History_____ Unit Title __U. S. History 1919-1945_____

Teaching Method: Discussion ____ Illustration ____ Demonstration ____
Conference ____ Lecture ____ Project ____

Type of Objective:
1. Behavioral Objective —

A. Psychomotor _____	B. Affective _____	C. Cognitive _____
1. Skills _____	1. Perceiving _____	1. Memorize facts_____
2. Combination of	2. Responding_____	2. Association __X__
skills & mental	3. Valuing _____	3. Application _____
set _____	4. Organizing _____	4. Inquiring _____
3. Habit _____	5. Attitude __X__	5. Discovery _____
		6. Thinking _____

2. Educational Objective — Knowledge __X__ Understanding __X__

Appreciations _____ Values _____

Lesson Objective: __The student will describe Herbert Hoover and the New Deal._____

Student Assignment: __Read about Herbert Hoover in any source you can find. Consult the source file on him (in__
the appendix of this unit)._____

Concepts to be Taught	Teaching Method or Activity	Time	Materials for Students
Herbert Hoover—the man.	Individual reports. Herbert Hoover. Life on a Farm During the Depression.	10 minutes	List of possible references.
Hoover's philosophy of the government.			
Farmer's plight during the depression.	Buzz groups. (plus reporting of find-ings of groups).	40 minutes	

Relation to Previous and Future Lessons: Herbert Hoover is the man held responsible for the Depression. He must be understood to fully understand the government. Farm problems were also a large part of the reason for the Depression.

Evaluation: Findings of buzz groups and cooperation in working together will be a test for the effectiveness of this day's work.

Daily Lesson Plan

Class and Grade __11th grade U. S. History_____ Unit Title __U. S. History 1919-1945_____

Teaching Method: Discussion __X__ Illustration ____ Demonstration ____
                       Conference ____ Lecture __X__ Project ____

Type of Objective:
1. Behavioral Objective —

A. Psychomotor		B. Affective		C. Cognitive	
1. Skills	X	1. Perceiving		1. Memorize facts	
2. Combination of		2. Responding	X	2. Association	
skills & mental		3. Valuing		3. Application	
set		4. Organizing		4. Inquiring	
3. Habit		5. Attitude	X	5. Discovery	X
				6. Thinking	X

2. Educational Objective — Knowledge __X__   Understanding ____

                       Appreciations ____   Values ____

Lesson Objective: __The student will recognize the author of the New Deal and list the objectives of this author in__
creating this program.

Student Assignment: __Read pp. 617-632 in textbook. Answer question 1 on p. 632.__

Concepts to be Taught	Teaching Method or Activity	Time	Materials for Students
Franklin D. Roosevelt's concept of "try something"	Lecture.	20 minutes	
Objectives of New Deal.	Problem solving.	30 minutes	Definition of Problem Rules for problem solving.

Relation to Previous and Future Lessons: The New Deal was unique. It was a type of experiment. The student should see in the New Deal how daring it was to undertake such an experiment. It could fail.

Evaluation: Student participation in problem solving; creative thinking exhibited; and attention paid to lecture will be used to evaluate this daily lesson.

Class and Grade <u>11 grade U. S. History</u> Unit Title <u>U. S. History 1919-1945</u>

Teaching Method: Discussion ____ Illustration ____ Demonstration __X__
                  Conference ____ Lecture ____ Project __X__

Type of Objective:
1. Behavioral Objective —

   A. Psychomotor _____ B. Affective _____ C. Cognitive _____
      1. Skills __X__   1. Perceiving _____   1. Memorize facts _____
      2. Combination of   2. Responding _____   2. Association _____
         skills & mental   3. Valuing _____   3. Application _____
         set _____   4. Organizing __X__   4. Inquiring __X__
      3. Habit _____   5. Attitude _____   5. Discovery _____
                                                       6. Thinking __X__

2. Educational Objective — Knowledge __X__   Understanding __X__

                           Appreciations _____   Values _____

Lesson Objective: <u>The student will write a report on one of the following topics which demonstrates he under-</u>
<u>stands the concept fully.</u>

Student Assignment: <u>Workshop Activity: Ten students will go to library, research a subject (chosen from the</u>
<u>list) and organize it into a 10 minute report. He will have his partner stay in the class and construct some type visual aid.</u>

Concepts to be Taught	Teaching Method or Activity	Time	Materials for Students
Objectives of the New Deal.	Workshop.	50 minutes	Access to Library.
FDR—The Man		(to be finished at home.)	Access to Art Supplies and other materials to construct posters, graphs, charts, flannel boards, etc. to illustrate report.
Abandonment of the Gold Standard.			
Relief Measures.			
TVA			
Criticisms of New Deal.			
Similarities between New Deal and Current War on Poverty.			
Report on actual work done by CCC and PWA.			
FDIC			

Relation to Previous and Future Lessons: The New Deal was the solution to the depression. It paved the way for much of our present type of legislation today.

Evaluation: Cooperation between students will be the main type of evaluation for this workshop.

(Note: THIS WORKSHOP COULD TAKE TWO DAYS)

430

Daily Lesson Plan

Class and Grade <u>11th grade U. S. History</u> Unit Title <u>U. S. History 1919-1945</u>

Teaching Method: Discussion _____ Illustration _X_ Demonstration _____
Conference _X_ Lecture _____ Project _X_

Type of Objective:
1. Behavioral Objective —

A. Psychomotor		B. Affective		C. Cognitive	
1. Skills	_X_	1. Perceiving	_____	1. Memorize facts	_____
2. Combination of		2. Responding	_____	2. Association	_____
skills & mental		3. Valuing	_____	3. Application	_X_
set	_____	4. Organizing	_X_	4. Inquiring	_____
3. Habit	_____	5. Attitude	_X_	5. Discovery	_____
				6. Thinking	_____

2. Educational Objective — Knowledge _X_ Understanding _X_

Appreciations _____ Values _____

Lesson Objective: <u>The student will demonstrate skill in giving public speeches and communicating with his peers.</u>

Student Assignment: <u>The student, with his partner, will give a five-minute report done in workshop yesterday.</u>
<u>His partner will demonstrate his visual aid.</u>

Concepts to be Taught	Teaching Method or Activity	Time	Materials for Students
Objectives of New Deal.	Student reports.	10 minutes each	Any visual aid which might have been constructed.
FDR – The Man.	Explanation of visual aids.	50 minutes in all	
Abandonment of Gold Standard.			
Relief Measure.			
Tennessee Valley Authority.			
Criticism of New Deal.			
Similarities between New Deal and Current War on Poverty.			
Report on actual work done by CCC and PWA.			
FDIC			

Relation to Previous and Future Lessons: The New Deal was the solution to the Depression. It paved the way for much of our legislation of today.

Evaluation: The quality of reports, manner presented, and attention gained from audience will be evaluators of this type lesson. Also visual aids constructed will be evaluated by quality of construction and neatness.

Daily Lesson Plan

Class and Grade 11th grade U. S. History _____ Unit Title U. S. History 1919-1945 _____

Teaching Method: Discussion X Illustration ____ Demonstration ____
                   Conference ____ Lecture ____ Project _____

Type of Objective:
1. Behavioral Objective —

A. Psychomotor	_____	B. Affective	_____	C. Cognitive	_____
1. Skills	X	1. Perceiving	_____	1. Memorize facts	_____
2. Combination of		2. Responding	_____	2. Association	_____
skills & mental		3. Valuing	_____	3. Application	X
set	_____	4. Organizing	X	4. Inquiring	X
3. Habit	_____	5. Attitude	X	5. Discovery	_____
				6. Thinking	X

2. Educational Objective — Knowledge X   Understanding _____

Appreciations _____   Values _____

Lesson Objective: The student will make a critical judgment on whether the New Deal encouraged socialism in America.

Student Assignment: The students will participate in a debate entitled "RESOLVED: The New Deal encouraged socialism in America." Come prepared to be a debator.

Concepts to be Taught	Teaching Method or Activity	Time	Materials for Students
Definition of socialism. How the New Deal might have encouraged socialism.	Debate (student).	50 minutes	Instructions for debating will be given to the students a week before the debate; also sources to obtain information.

Relation to Previous and Future Lessons: This is an evaluation for the student to make (on his own) of the New Deal. It encourages him to consider all aspects of the New Deal.

Evaluation: Student participation and interest in the debate will be criteria for evaluation of this lesson.

Daily Lesson Plan

Class and Grade __11th grade U. S. History__ Unit Title __U. S. History 1919-1945__

Teaching Method: Discussion ____ Illustration ____ Demonstration ____
Conference ____ Lecture __X__ Project ____

Type of Objective:
1. Behavioral Objective –

A. Psychomotor _____	B. Affective _____	C. Cognitive _____
1. Skills _____	1. Perceiving ____	1. Memorize facts _____
2. Combination of	2. Responding ____	2. Association __X__
skills & mental	3. Valuing ____	3. Application ____
set _____	4. Organizing __X__	4. Inquiring ____
3. Habit _____	5. Attitude ____	5. Discovery ____
		6. Thinking ____

2. Educational Objective – Knowledge __X__ Understanding ____
Appreciations ____ Values ____

Lesson Objective: __The student will list the major recovery, reform , and relief measures under the New Deal__
__and relate it to its purpose.__

Student Assignment: __Study Chapter 26 and 27 in text familiarizing yourself with the numerous measures of__
__relief originated by the New Deal.__

Concepts to be Taught	Teaching Method or Activity	Time	Materials for Students
Relief measures WPA PWA CCC	Lecture.	30 minutes	Guide for taking notes (example in appendix).
Recovery measures NRA FDIC SEC AAA Noris-LaGuardia Act CIO NLRA	Agree-disagree session.	20 minutes	
Reform measures TVA Social Security			

Relation to Previous and Future Lessons: These acts were the catalysts which enabled the New Deal
to enact its objectives. They must be understood before the New Dial can be understood.

Evaluation: Reaction of audience to lecture.

Photo furnished courtesy of AUM Learning Resource Center and Montgomery County Public Schools, Montgomery, Alabama.

ELEVENTH OR TWELFTH GRADE SOCIAL STUDIES: The Soviet Union, 1917-1971

Introduction

Several states require that a six-weeks unit on Americanism versus Communism be taught. Many other states strongly urge the teaching of something about communism or the Soviet Union or both. Sistrunk found in his 1968 nationwide survey of chief state school officers that something about Americanism versus communism is taught in over ninety percent of the nation's schools.[2] Many of the laws and executive decrees requiring the unit were explicit about the content of the unit which was to be taught, when the requirement first became commonplace about 1963-64. Usually these laws specified that the fallacies of communism, the evils of communism, the failures of communism, the means used by communist states to subvert our government, the lack of freedom in communist countries, and the way in which the international communist apparatus is organized and the way it functions were the points to be emphasized. It appears from several recent surveys of what teachers are setting up as objectives for the unit that some of the emphasis on the negative side of communism and the Soviet Union has subsided. It also appears that many teachers feel little pressure while teaching the unit now, while they felt great pressure several years ago. Many teachers are now approaching communism and the Soviet Union from the viewpoint of history or of comparative government and economics.

The unit on Americanism versus Communism chosen for inclusion in this book is a unit on the Soviet Union since the revolution of 1917. It is not typical of the units used by teachers five or six years ago, but it does seem to be representative of the approach now becoming more common. This unit uses a historical approach to studying the Soviet Union and communism, rather than a comparative one. It is a unit that could be included in several senior high school social studies courses.

The unit begins with the events of March 1917, and goes through the rule of Lenin, Stalin, World War II, Khruschev, the cold war, the several five year

2. Walter E. Sistrunk, *The Teaching of Americanism Versus Communism in Secondary Schools,* Bureau of Educational Research, Mississippi State University, State College, 1968.

plans, the geography of the Soviet Union, and the ideas of Marx and Engels as presently interpreted. The primary purpose of the teacher who devised the unit, was understanding of the culture, government and life of the people of the Soviet Union. Emphasis is not on the ways communism differs or is similar to our system, though this is treated in the unit in a number of places.

Educational Objectives

1. Each student will interpret simple maps and charts.
2. Each student will cooperate with his classmates.
3. Each pupil will demonstrate by his attitude in class that he respects the right of other people to have ideas different from his own.
4. All will work effectively with other students.
5. By turning projects in on time and having homework prepared on time, all will show that they assume responsibility.

Each student will do the following:

6. Define and show the significance of two of the basic theories of Karl Marx.
7. Write a short paragraph on two characteristics of a communistic society (according to Marx or Lenin).
8. Write a short comparison of the two revolutions of March, 1917 and November, 1917 as to the leadership, ease with which changes were accomplished, and permanence of each.
9. Write a one-page discussion dealing with social and military difficulties in Russia in late 1916 and early 1917.
10. List two conditions which existed during the Russian civil war concerning the relationship of government to the people.
11. List three reasons why Trotsky's Red Army was victorious in the civil war.
12. Briefly write an explanation of the economic conditions prompting Lenin to formulate his New Economic Policy.
13. List one of the main issues during the struggle for power between Stalin and Trotsky.
14. List three goals of Stalin's Five-Year Plans.
15. Write one reason for the purges of the party by Stalin.
16. List two great weaknesses of the Soviet Union during the Khrushchev administration.
17. List five civil liberties of both the Soviet and American people. Briefly write how three of these differ in actual practice.

18.   Write a short paragraph showing the similarities between the U.S. Congress and the Supreme Soviet.

19.   List two ways by which dictatorship is preserved in the Soviet Union.

20.   Write the significance of the term "agitation" applying it to events prior to and during elections.

21.   List two social conditions (for example, age, duties, social status) of Communist party members today.

22.   List three advantages of belonging to the Communist party if you lived in the Soviet Union.

23.   Write an explanation of why the church was de-emphasized by Stalin.

24.   Write an explanation of the present relationship between the party and the church.

25.   List three purposes of Soviet education.

26.   Compare the importance of women in the United States and Soviet Union.

27.   Write a page on the failure of the USSR to produce a classless state (as forseen by Marx) including mainly evidence of social classes present in the Soviet Union.

28.   List one example of a Soviet writer, musician, or dancer who was purged by Soviet authorities.

29.   Briefly explain the manner in which the Soviet Union generally obtained satellite countries.

30.   List three reactions to prevent the spread of communism.

31.   State one purpose in collectivizing farms.

32.   Write a short criticism of Marx's theory of history using at least two reasons why he was wrong.

33.   State three unique features of Soviet geography.

34.   List a reason for the change in the Soviet Union's power structure.

35.   Write the main reason why the Germans allowed Lenin to return to Russia in April, 1917.

36.   Define four of the following terms giving the significance of each:
Red Terror
Comintern of 1919
Russo-German Pact
Gosplan
"Peaceful co-existence"
Bolshevik

37.   Write a short comparison of the growth rate of Soviet industry as compared with that of the United States.

38. Write a paper of at least 2-3 pages evaluating the success of the Soviet system in improving the life of the average Soviet citizen. Each student will express his ideas logically, using good form and grammar.

39. When given a world map, each student will mark the following areas:

1. The areas where communism is predominant
2. The areas that are predominately anti-communist
3. Neutral areas

40. Each student will read *one* of the following books and write a 1-2 page report on things he learned from the book:

Communism in Latin America by Robert J. Alexander
The Soviet Image of the United States by F.C. Barghoorn
The Room on the Route by Godfrey Blunden
Communism in Our World by John C. Caldwell
Khruschev's Russia by Edward Crankshaw
The God that Failed by R.H. Crossman
All Things New by Sonia Daugherty
Communism in Western Europe by M. Einaudi
Why They Behave Like Russians by John Fischer
Inside Russia Today by John Gunther
Russia, A History by Sidney S. Harcave
I Chose Freedom by Victor A. Kravchenko
Siberia by Emil Lengyel
Cradle of Conquerors by Erwin C. Lessner
Communism in Action by Library of Congress
Russia: Past and Present by Anatole G. Mazouur
The Land of the Russian People by Alexander Nazaroff
Russia and America by Henry L. Roberts
The Dynamics of Soviet Society by W. W. Rostow
American in Russia by Harrison E. Salisbury
Three Men Who Made a Revolution by Bertram D. Wolfe

Another book selected by the student may be substituted for one of these books if the teacher approves.

41. Each student will write a paper of about five pages on a topic chosen by himself. Possible topic titles could be "Contributions of Soviets in Science," "Expansion in Siberia" or "The Kremlin." The papers must be logically and gramatically correct, and at least five different sources must be used.

42. Each student will be a member of a group which will participate in each of these activities for a period of one week:

      (1)   Making a time line
      (2)   Publishing a newspaper
      (3)   Making a bulletin board to illustrate current class lessons
      (4)   Presentation of informal book reports
      (5)   Preparation of special charts and graphs and other learning aids to be shown in class
      (6)   Preparation and presentation of panel discussion or informal debate

Activities

Teaching methods

Introductory Activities:
1. Guest speaker who has been to the Soviet Union. He will show slides of his visit and students will ask him questions. (Group)
2. Film introducing the country and its geographical features (Group)

Developmental activities:
1. Lecture (T) (14, 34)
2. Make assignments (T) (6, 9, 17, 37-42)
3. Both teacher and students will ask and answer questions (T and S) (11, 17, 33)
4. Pass-the question game (G) (27, 35)
5. Use overhead transparancies showing the birth of communism, Marx's theory on destruction of communism, growth of party, the planned economy, basic educational reforms, Soviet agriculture, and Soviet advantages in possessing Eastern Europe (T) (9, 14, 25, 31)
6. Reading Assignments—These assignments will be chosen so that they coincide with topics discussed in class. (S) (6, 9, 17)
7. Written Research Reports—The topic may be from those suggested by the teacher but will be chosen by the student. At least five different sources must be used, and the paper should be approximately five pages in length. An oral report will be required of some students. From doing this research, they will acquire skill in finding information and organizing it into a well written report. (S) (41)
8. Committee work—The class will be divided into six equal groups. Each group will be responsible for a different project each week. The next week a different project will be assigned to them. Each student will serve as chairman of a committee for at least one week. The following projects will be included in the plan:

1. A time line will be made by the students, each one working on it for one week. The time line will be drawn in different colors, and it will extend across the front of the room. So that all may see it, it will be above the black board.
2. Each group will be responsible for bulletin board decorations for one week. The display should pertain to the subject currently being studied. (G) (42)
3. Each group will give a short summary of their book report before the class. (S) (42)
4. Special charts and graphs will be made available to students to help clarify lectures. This group will work closely with the teacher. (For example, a chart or graph may be made to illustrate the rate of growth of the Soviet economy in contrast with that of the U.S.) (G) (42)
5. Each group will be responsible for one panel discussion or debate on the subject currently being discussed in class (for example, collective farms or labor unions). (G) (42)
6. A "newspaper" will be published each week. One student will be editor while others are reporters and typists. They will pretend that they are living in the USSR during Stalin's purges. For example, they will write as though they were an eyewitness to the extermination of the Kulaks. These "newspapers" will be mimeographed and distributed to all members of the class. (G) (42)
7. Take tests—There will be one large unit test and several less important announced daily tests. (G) (42)
8. Some students will report to the class on the results of their independent study. Whether or not a student reports will depend on his topic. (S) (42)

Culminating activities:

1. A day will be devoted to summarizing what we have studied during the unit. Students will ask questions and answer questions. They will discuss the value of various aspects of Soviet life, and they will evaluate the Soviet system. (G)
2. One of the culminating activities to be done by all class members is to write a page or more stating how the Soviet form of government has affected the life of the average Soviet citizen. This is to be based on class discussion and facts learned through individual study. (S)
3. A unit test will be given. The next day the test and its results will be discussed in detail with the students.

Outline of Content

I. Introduction
  A. Geographic Setting
    1. Size
    2. Climate
    3. Types of land
    4. Natural resources
    5. Implications of geography
  B. Diversity of people
  C. Industrial growth
II. Marx and his theories
  A. His background
  B. Theory of history
  C. Theory of labor value
  D. Why Communism is inevitable
  E. Nature of communism
    1. Lenin: "From each according to his ability; to each according to his need."
    2. Classless society
    3. State will wither away
    4. Concept of morality
  F. Weaknesses of theories
    1. Class struggle was not the only cause of all history
    2. If communism is inevitable, why do they recruit?
    3. Not acceptable to major religions
    4. Workers don't usually see themselves as exploited
III. Life before the revolution
  A. Nicholas II and World War I
    1. Influence of Rasputin
    2. Discontent in cities and country
    3. Conditions of Russian army
      a. Almost 4,000,000 killed in first year of war
    4. Bolshevik vs. Menshevik
  B. Strikes and bread-riots in Petrograd
IV. First revolution (March, 1917)
  A. Establishment of Provisional Government
  B. Formation of Soviets
  C. Kerensky replaced Prince Lvov
  D. Lenin and his return
V. Second Revolution (November, 1917)

A. Led by Bolsheviks
B. Provisional Government is run out
C. Lenin becomes leader by force
D. Treaty of Brest-Litovsk
E. Summary of the two revolutions

VI. Civil War—Period of War Communism
A. Conditions
1. Private property abolished
2. Banks, railroads, etc. nationalized
3. Severe famine—Kulaks, as a protest, kill animals
4. Naval mutiny
B. Allies invaded Russia to help fight Bolsheviks
C. The Red Army organized by Trotsky
D. Reasons for Communist victory
1. Withdrawal of Allies allowed Bolsheviks to concentrate their efforts.
2. Central position of Bolsheviks
3. Lenin's fanatical spirit
4. Resentment of foreign involvement
5. White Russians did not promise land or social reforms. They included many groups who could not agree.

VII. The Union of Soviet Socialist Republics established
A. Lenin's New Economic Policy
1. Reason: When government took land from the peasants, they revolted. They refused to plant crops; and famine and unrest were the results in the cities.
2. A revert to capitalistic policies in some businesses
3. Graduated wage scales
4. United States aid was accepted to help bolster the faltering economy.
B. The Struggle for Power after Lenin's death
1. Trotsky
a. Wanted world communism immediately
b. Leader of Red Army in Civil War
2. Stalin
a. Had studied for priesthood but was rejected for his Marxist ideas
b. Felt communism should be built up at home first
C. Policies of Stalin
1. Five Year Plans
a. Goals

           1.   Rapid industrialization

           2.   Improvement of agricultural production

           3.   Elimination of private production

           4.   Strengthening USSR's defense against outside world

      b.   Success because of much sacrifice

   2.   Purges

D.   Khrushchev

   1.   Bitter attack of Stalin

   2.   Advocate of "peaceful co-existence."

   3.   Space conquests

   4.   Economic growth rate high

   5.   Missile bases in Cuba

   6.   Weaknesses

      a.   Agriculture—In 1963-4, the Soviet Union had to buy meat from West

      b.   Way of passing power from one leader to another

      c.   Increasing inability to dominate Communist countries

E.   Replaced by Leonid Brezhnev and Alexei Kosygin

VIII.   The Soviet Union today

A.   Government

   1.   Constitution of 1936

      a.   Democratic

      b.   Federal republics

      c.   Civil liberties

          1.   Guarantee of job

          2.   Free education

          3.   Free medical care

          4.   Old-age care

          5.   Minimum voting age is 18

   2.   Supreme Soviet

      a.   Bicameral

      b.   Basis of representation

   3.   Dictatorship rests upon

      a.   Communist party

      b.   Censorship

          1.   Government papers

             a.   Izvestia

             b.   Pravda

          2.   Purpose: to prevent publication of anti-communistic ideas

        c.   Police
    4.   Election Procedure
        a.   How to get name on ballot
            1.   Nominated by approved organization
            2.   Legally qualified
            3.   Willingness to run
        b.   Role of agitator
            1.   Before election he tells of good deeds of party
        c.   On election day
            1.   Over 99 percent of eligible voters participate
            2.   Agitators make sure everyone votes

B. The Communist Party
    1.   Only party allowed
    2.   Size
    3.   Duties of members
    4.   Youth organizations
    5.   Types of people who are members

C. Religion
    1.   Controlled by Party
    2.   Churches were nationalized and turned into offices or museums
    3.   In World War II, to gain support, churches were allowed to exist
    4.   Number of members now
    5.   Why was religion denounced?
        a.   It kept the people content with bad conditions
        b.   Priests were example of upper class
        c.   Communism is itself a religion

D. Education
    1.   Purposes
        a.   Literate, intelligent population
        b.   Economic specialists
        c.   Political indoctrinations
        d.   Mass training for industrial workers
    2.   Extent of education
        a.   Very little illiteracy exists
        b.   Kindergartens allow women to be in labor force

E. Society and Culture
    1.   Changes
        a.   Importance of Women
        b.   Increase in industrial laborers
        c.   Increase in urban population

      2.   Social classes
          a.   Party members, scientists, economic planners, etc.
          b.   Urban working class
          c.   Peasants
          d.   Criminals, political prisoners
      3.   Writers
          a.   Boris Pasternak
      4.   Musicians
          a.   Prokofiev
          b.   Stravinsky
      5.   Ballet
      6.   Concept of Art
      7.   Importance of Science
   F. Foreign Policy
      1.   The Soviet Union did not come to be accepted until the 1930's
          a.   Reason:
              1.   Comintern of 1919
      2.   World War II
          a.   Russo-German Pact
              1.   USSR—would get half of Poland
              2.   USSR—would have a free hand in Finland, Estonia, and Latvia
              3.   USSR would remain neutral but would furnish supplies to Germany
          b.   Germany invaded Soviet Union
              1.   Cities fell to Germans
              2.   As they almost lost Moscow, the Soviets determined to halt the Germans who were not used to the severe Soviet winters.
          c.   Hitler tried to take oil fields in USSR
          d.   Soviets recaptured much of their lost land
              1.   7,000,000 Soviet citizens dead
              2.   Because of much needed repair, technicians were taken to Soviet Union from Eastern Europe
          e.   Poland and much of Eastern Europe were overun by Soviet troops
          f.   Soviet Union emerged as a major world power
          g.   Permanent member of United Nations' Security Council
      3.   Postwar Soviet Policy
          a.   Communist parties were set up in these countries

            1.   Poland
            2.   Czechoslovakia
            3.   East Germany
            4.   Bulgaria
            5.   Romania
            6.   Hungary (Rebellion of 1956)
            7.   Yugoslavia
            8.   Albania (allied to Red China)

      b.   Korean War
            1.   Soviets overran area north of 38° parallel
            2.   U.S. overran area south of 38° parallel
            3.   Soviet Union set up Communist dictatorship in North Korea
            4.   Land was given to peasants
            5.   Industry nationalized
            6.   Soviets withdrew but supplied weapons

      c.   Communism in Asia
            1.   China
            2.   North Korea
            3.   North Vietnam
            4.   Much of Laos
            5.   Parts of South Vietnam

      d.   Large and influential Communist parties set up in many other countries

    4.   Western Reactions against Communism
      a.   Marshall Plan
      b.   NATO
      c.   CENTO
      d.   SEATO

G. Agriculture
    1.   State Farms
      a.   Workers are civil servants
      b.   Models of agriculture
    2.   Collective farms
      a.   Combination of small individual farms
      b.   All share in work and profits
      c.   Small private plots are allowed in order to make agriculture more efficient and allow more people to go to city factories to work

H. Industry
    1.   Each factory has an allotment of raw materials, labor and money

        2.   Each has a quota to produce

        3.   Goods are sold to government

        4.   Labor force

           a.   There is a union responsible to government

           b.   There are no strikes

  I.   Gosplan

        1.   Local units funnel up to national level requests for resources

        2.   Allotments and quotas are funnelled down

        3.   Controlled by party and government

        4.   Emphasis is on heavy industry, not consumer goods

IX.   Summary

 X.   Analysis of Soviet Success

      A.   Does not give people a choice.

      B.   Is Marxism-Leninism relevant to our times?

      C.   For its purposes, it has been most successful.

Evaluation

Grading will be on the point system in order to make it easier for the teacher to assign each activity a different value. The following table will show the maximum number of points that can be assigned to each activity.

Unit test	300 points
Daily tests	50 points
Written book report	50 points
Research paper	100 points
Committee work	500 points
Bulletin Board	50 points
Time Line	75 points
Oral book report	25 points
Newspaper	150 points
Special charts, graphs, etc.	75 points
Panel discussion or debate	125 points
TOTAL	1000 points

The total number of points received by each student will be added and this number will be divided by 10. The result will be the six weeks average of the student.

On any essay question on the tests, a list of facts which should be included will be made in advance. Since points will be deducted from the value of the question for any information that is missing, students should organize their thoughts in a logical manner. Writing should be legible and proper grammar

should be used. All daily tests will be pre-announced.
On the following rating scales, this system will be used:

5—Excellent
4—Good
3—Average
2—Fair
1—Poor

For the Written Book Report, this rating scale will be used:

____ Appropriateness of book
____ Report written appropriately (according to directions)
____ Book contributes to student's knowledge
____ Report logically organized
____ Report gramatically correct
____ Report reflects a considerable amount of thought
____ Unbiasly written
____ Appropriate writing style

RATING SCALE FOR RESEARCH PAPER

____ Thoroughly prepared
____ Covers subject
____ Benefit to student
____ Logically written
____ Appropriate writing style
____ Gramatically correct

RATING SCALE FOR BULLETIN BOARD

____ Works well with group
____ Makes useful contributions to group
____ Creativity
____ Appropriateness of display
____ Attractiveness of display

The Bulletin Board will be graded by the members of the class.

Unit Test

Place the letter of the BEST answer in the blank to the left of the question.

____ The Soviet Union: (obj. 33)
    a.   Covers 1/6 of the total land surface of the globe
    b.   Is covered with deserts called steeps
    c.   Is more densely populated than the United States
    d.   Has an abundance of good ports

____ Which of the following does *not* apply to conditions in Russia just before the March, 1917 revolution? (9)

a.   Nicholas II was a powerful czar, and he was able to protect his country from the enemy.

b.   The military was discouraged because of numerous defeats.

c.   There was severe famine.

d.   Many Russians had died in the cities.

____ The Germans allowed Lenin to return to Russia in April, 1917 because (35)

a.   His prison sentence was completed.

b.   He was being transferred to a Soviet prison.

c.   He would take Russia out of the First World War.

d.   He promised to obtain supplies for the Nazis.

____ Which were conditions existing during the Russian Civil War? There may be more than one answer. (10)

a.   Widespread famine

b.   Railroads were nationalized

c.   Lenin met little opposition

d.   Property was equally divided up and given to all citizens.

____ According to the theories of Marx and Lenin, which of the following would characterize a communistic society? There may be more than one answer. (7)

a.   Classless society

b.   Bureaucracy

c.   No Secret Police

d.   All people will receive equally

____ Lenin devised his New Economic Policy: (12)

a.   To pacify the unhappy people who, in protest because their land had been taken away, refused to plant crops and caused widespread famine

b.   To promote the manufacture of consumer goods

c.   To equalize wealth

d.   To raise the standard of living among peasants

____ Stalin and Trotsky disagreed over: (13)

a.   The area of the world that should be made communistic immediately

b.   The importance to be played by the Secret Police

c.   How one should become a party member

d.   The tactics used by the Red Army during the Civil War

____ Which was *Not* a goal of Stalin's Five Year Plans? (14)

a.   Rapid industrialization

b.   Hastening world communism

c.   Improvement of agricultural production

    d.   Elimination of private production

_____ A purpose of the purges of Stalin was: (15)

    a.   To lower the population in the cities

    b.   To eliminate those who were anti-communistic

    c.   To punish the kulaks

    d.   To consolidate his position as supreme dictator

_____ Which of the following were two of the great weaknesses of Khruschev's time? (16)

    a.   Agriculture

    b.   Failure to maintain dominance over all communist world

    c.   Industry

    d.   Educational level of its citizens

_____ Which of the following is *not* an advantage given to party members? (22)

    a.   Higher social status in general

    b.   Better vacation areas

    c.   Easier jobs

    d.   Better chance of education for his children

_____ The main purpose of collectivizing farms was: (31)

    a.   To bring the people closer together so that government officials could supervise more easily

    b.   To eliminate competition among farmers

    c.   To show the rest of the world that a communal society was best

    d.   To make agriculture more efficient and thus to allow more people to go to the city factories to work

_____ A Soviet writer who was severely criticized by Soviet authorities was: (28)

    a.   Sergei Prokofiev

    b.   Boris Pasternak

    c.   Rudolf Nureyev

    d.   Leo Tolstoy

_____ The growth rate of Soviet industry is: (37)

    a.   Two to three times that of U.S.

    b.   Less than the growth rate of U.S. industry

    c.   Much higher than that of U.S. for consumer goods

    d.   Is approximately equal to that of the U.S.

_____ The status of the Soviet woman: (26)

    a.   Has risen from its level under the czars so that women are more important to the labor force in USSR than in U.S.

    b.   Is equal to that of the American woman

    c.   Is shown to be high by the fact that several women have been members of the Presidium

    d.   Has risen because family life was not emphasized

____ The church exists in the Soviet Union because: (24)
   a.   There are many who want to go to church
   b.   Those who attend are usually the very old
   c.   The church has consented to being controlled by the Communist Party
   d.   Its existence gives the Western world a more positive attitude of the Soviet Union
____ Which of the following is *not* a purpose of Soviet education: (25)
   a.   to develop individualism
   b.   to produce economic specialists
   c.   to have a more literate population
   d.   training for industrial work
____ Those who explain and justify the actions of government officials are called: (20)
   a.   Propagandists
   b.   Agitators
   c.   The Establishment
   d.   Apparatus
____ Which of the following is *NOT* a characteristic of the U.S. and Soviet legislatures? (18)
   a.   Lower house represents population
   b.   Upper house represents regions
   c.   Membership is elected by the people
   d.   Administrative branch of the government is appointed by it.
____ Which of the following was *NOT* a reaction to prevent the spread of communism: (30)
   a.   NATO
   b.   SEATO
   c.   Marshall Plan
   d.   ABC Alliance
____ Since World War II, the Soviet Union's power: (34)
   a.   Has seriously been challenged by Communist China
   b.   Has greatly expanded through her complete domination of satellite countries
   c.   Has been shown through her position as a permanent member of the UN's Security Council
   d.   Was able to suppress uprisings in East Germany

Write *True* or *False* in the blank preceding each of the following sentences:

____ A main reason for the de-emphasis of religion in the Soviet Union is that religion tries to make the oppressed content with their life here on earth. (23)

___ Most of the members of the Communist party are relatively old. (21)

___ Thirty percent of the Soviet population are members of the Communist party. (21)

___ One method the USSR uses to obtain satellite countries is to set up strong communist parties which gain control of the police in the area. (29)

The following are characteristics of the Russian Revolutions of March and November, 1917. Put 1 in the blank if it is a characteristic of the first revolution and 2 if it is a characteristic of the second revolution. Some may be characteristics of both revolutions. If so, put both numbers in the blank. (8)

___ Led by Bolsheviks

___ Was followed by Prince Lvov's Provisional government

___ Relatively little bloodshed

___ Lenin had a major role

___ Began with bread-riots in Petrograd

Define four of the following terms and give the significance of each: (36)

Red Terror
Comintern of 1919
Russo-German Pact
Gosplan
"Peaceful Co-existence"
Bolshevik

Define and show the significance of two of the following of Marx's theories: (6)

Theory of history
Theory of surplus value
Theory of labor value

List two valid reasons why Marx's theory of history was inaccurate. (32)

Name two Soviet institutions whose prime duty is to preserve the dictatorship. (19)

The USSR has failed to produce the type of classless society predicted by Marx. List two evidences of this fact basing your answer on the social class system of the Soviet Union. (27)

List three reasons that the Red Army defeated the White Army in the Russian civil war. (11)

List five civil liberties shared by Soviet and United States citizens. For three of these tell how they differ in actual practice. (17)

BIBLIOGRAPHY AND LIST OF MATERIALS

Textbook: *Story of Nations*
Workbook: *Story of Nations*

Magazines

Encyclopedias

The Soviet Image of the United States by F. C. Barghoorn

The Room on the Route by Godfrey Blunden

Communism in Our World by John C. Caldwell

Khrushchev's Russia by Edward Crankshaw

The God that Failed by R. Crossman

All Things New by Sonia Daugherty

Communism in Western Europe by M. Einaudi

Why They Behave Like Russians by John Fischer

Inside Russia Today by John Gunther

Russia, A History by Sidney S. Harcave

I Chose Freedom by Victor A. Kravchenko

Siberia by Emil Lengye

Cradle of Conquerors by Erwin C. Lessner

Communism in Action by Library of Congress

Russia: Past and Present by Anatole G. Mazour

Russia and America by Henry L. Roberts

The Dynamics of Soviet Society by W. W. Rostow

American in Russia by Harrison E. Salisbury

Three Men Who Made a Revolution by Bertram D. Wolfe

Man's Cultural Heritage A World History

Civilization Past and Present Vol. 2

Man and Civilization

History of Western Civilization

The Government of the Soviet Union

A Short History of Western Civilization

A History of Civilization

Maps

Globe

Overhead Transparencies on:
1. Birth of Communism
2. Marx's Theory on Destruction of Communism
3. Growth of Party
4. Planned Economy
5. Basic Educational Reforms
6. Soviet Agriculture
7. Soviet Advantages in Possessing Eastern Europe

Films

Pretest

Slides

Pictures

Charts, Graphs, and other learning aids

Resource Person

Three Week Teaching Unit

ELEVENTH AND
TWELFTH GRADE ECONOMICS:
The Economic Activities of Government

Introduction

The purpose of this unit is to help students discover the ways in which governments influence economic activities in a free society. Abraham Lincoln justified these activities when he said:

> The legitimate objective of government is to do for a community of people whatever they need to have done but cannot do at all, or cannot so well do, for themselves.

This unit is a survey of the economic activities of government. It will consider the conflicting opinions of the role that government should play in a free society with a private enterprise economy. It will also consider the conflicting views of the rising cost of government.

Consideration will be given to the economic activities of the state, and local, as well as the Federal government.

Objectives

Cognitive:

1. The student will list the five major economic activities of government.
2. The student will describe in writing the major services provided by local and state governments.
3. The student will describe in writing why the enforcement of contracts is vital to business.
4. The student will list the main arguments for and against public power projects.
5. The student will describe in writing the activities of government in the following fields:
   establish minimum standards
   enforcing competition
   regulating public utilities
   regulating the economic system during war

Photo furnished courtesy of AUM Learning Resource Center and Montgomery County Public Schools, Montgomery, Alabama.

        providing unemployment insurance and social security
        promoting housing and slum clearance
        aiding small business and farmers
        promoting prosperity and full employment

6.   The student will discuss both orally and in writing the pros and cons of governmental expenditure.

7.   The student will identify the following terms by writing not more than one sentence about each:

public power	unemployment insurance
private power	social security
creeping socialism	national security
public assistance	

8.   Each student will participate in a classroom debate of a controversial economic issue.

9.   Each student will participate in preparing a chart showing various governmental agencies that regulate industries.

10.   Each student will give a speech from five to eight minutes on a major economic issue.

11.   The student will solve both orally and in writing economic problems when they are presented with them by the teacher.

Affective:

12.   The student will show an increased appreciation of how tax money is spent by writing an essay showing which governmental service they would be willing to delete in their local community.

13.   The student will indicate their value of government services by describing in writing what they would have to do to provide one of the following services for themselves:

        aid for needy and handicapped
        free public education
        coining of money

Skills:

14.   Each student will show a knowledge and understanding of economic charts by using and making various charts.

15.   Each student will show an increased knowledge of the library by using it to prepare papers, speeches, and debates.

16.   Each student will learn to write and give speeches.

17.   Each student will learn the basics of debating by participating in a debate.

Teaching Activities

Legend: TC—Teacher centered
SC—Student centered
GC—Group centered

Introductory methods:
1. Filmstrip (TC)
2. Speaker (TC)
3. Discussion (GC)
4. Reading assignment (SC)

Developmental methods:
1. Student assignment (SC)
2. Speeches (SC)
3. Discussion following speeches (GC)
4. Problem-solving (GC)
5. Debates (GC)
6. Class Discussions (GC)
7. Lecture, Question and Answer (to be used only when necessary) (TC, GC)
8. Charts (GC)
9. Tests (GC)

Culminating methods:
1. Summary (GC) (Through discussion)
2. Tie in of past material and relate its significance to future material to be covered. (TC)
3. Test to find out whether or not objectives have been achieved. (GC)
4. If objectives were not met, evaluate to determine why not. (TC)

The Economic Activities of Government

I. Economic Activities of Government
   A. Protection of Life, Liberty, and Property.
      1. Perserving of public order is the most fundamental economic function of government.
      2. An essential function of government is the enforcement of business contracts.
      3. Included in the protection that government provides is that of defense against possible enemy attack.

    B.   The Government Provides Necessary Services.
        1.   Free public education.
        2.   Aid to needy and handicapped.
        3.   Provide parks and playgrounds.
        4.   Build bridges, highways, pave, clean, repair, and light streets.
        5.   Collects and distributes the mail.
        6.   The government prints and coins money.
    C.   Government Regulates Private Economic Activities.
        1.   Establishes minimum standards.
        2.   Enforcing competition.
        3.   Regulating public utilities.
        4.   Regulation in time of war.
    D.   Government Provides Economic Aid and Insurance in the following areas:
        1.   Unemployment insurance.
        2.   Social security.
        3.   Promoting housing and slumclearance.
        4.   Public housing.
        5.   Urban renewal.
        6.   Mortage Insurance
        7.   Aid to small business.
        8.   Aid to farmers.
        9.   Support of International Trade.
    E.   Government Promotes Economic Stability and Growth by:
        1.   Helping large groups of people to maintain a minimum level of living.
        2.   Maintaining the purchasing power of consumers.
II.   Views About The Cost Of Government.
    A.   The View That Government Costs Are Too High.
        1.   Some people believe that the rising costs are a positive danger to our economy.
        2.   Every dollar the government spends it takes from the people in the form of taxes.
        3.   People cannot continue to bear the heavy burden of taxes.
        4.   As a result of rising taxes, business enterprise slows down, economic activity stagnates, production drops and the standard of living declines.
        5.   The remedy is for people to serve themselves.
    B.   The View that Government Costs Are Not Too High.
        1.   Advocates of this position say that no price is too high for national security.

2.   Prices have gone up a good deal, and government must pay more for the goods and services they buy.
3.   Increased population means increased service.
4.   Services have been expanded on all governmental levels.
C.   Comparing Government Costs As Percentages Of Total Production.
1.   What percentages of the total national production does government use?
2.   There has been little increase in the *relative size* of government expenditure over the years.
D.   Government Costs May Go Higher.

Grading Criteria

The teacher-made tests will be graded on a representative scale. Approximately sixty to seventy percent of the test will be objective. Discussion or essay type questions will count for twenty to thirty percent. Short answer or short discussion will usually count ten percent.

The criteria for the grading of speeches are:

10% Body (posture, facial expression, eye contact, gestures).
10% Voice (volume, enunciation, rate of speaking, inflection).
10% Language (choice of words, pronunciation).
40% The Speech Itself (beginning, organization, practice, interest aroused, ending).
20% Information Presented, Research.
10% Conclusions drawn.

The debate will be graded on much the same criteria as the speech.

Reports written by students will be based on the following criteria:

15% Correct word usage, grammar, spelling, and writing style.
10% Footnoting and Bibliography form.
35% Content.
35% Conclusions drawn.
5% Presentation, attitude, opinion of teacher (general over-all quality and appearance).

Written assignments (homework, essays) will be graded the same as the above.

Problem-solving questions will be graded on the above basis with primary emphasis on correctness of solution reached.

BIBLIOGRAPHY

Fairchild, Fred R. *Understanding Our Free Economy.* Princeton: Van Nostrand.

Goals of Economic Policy, Report of the Committee on Economic Policy. Economic Research Department, Chamber of Commerce of the U.S.

Hailstones, Thomas J., Martin, Bernard L. and Wing, George A. *Contemporary Economic Problems and Issues.* Chicago: South-Western Publishing Co.

Heilbroner, Robert L. *The Making of Economic Society.* Englewood Cliffs, N.J.: Prentice-Hall, Inc.

Hughes, R.O. *Fundamentals of Economics.* Boston: Allyn and Bacon.

Samuelson, Paul A. *Economics: An Introductory Analysis.* New York: McGraw-Hill.

Smith, Augustus H. *Economics for Our Times.* New York: McGraw-Hill.

FILMS

"Everybody Knows." (Chamber of Commerce of U.S., Washington, D.C.), 15 minutes.

"Productivity—Key to Plenty." (EBF), 22 minutes.

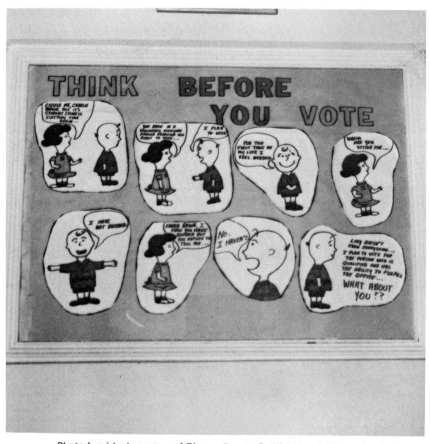

Photo furnished courtesy of Elmore County Public School, Wetumpka, Alabama.

TWELFTH GRADE
AMERICAN GOVERNMENT:
The Federal Courts, and Their Relation to State and Local Governments

Introduction

This six weeks unit of American Government deals with the actions of the court systems of the United States, the operation of the state government and how the governments of the cities and counties function. The unit is intended to stress the learning of information which can better enable the student to function properly when dealing with political situations.

Overview

This unit of government goes into three different subject areas. The first section deals with civil rights and the different types of courts in the country. The relationships of the laws, civil rights and the court systems are all pointed out to the students. The government of the state and its operation is the second topic area that will be studied. This section deals with the problems of running a state and how these problems are overcome. The last subject area concerns itself with the local governments, both city and county. The local officials and their duties, the functions of the different county and city departments and the organization of the local governments are discussed so that the student can gain a better grasp of the political structure of the area in which he lives.

Objectives

1. The student will list four types of Federal Courts.
2. The student will describe, in a sentence or two, the major jobs of four Federal Courts.
3. The student will, in one or two sentences each, describe the major jobs of three officials of the Federal Judiciary system.
4. The student will, in a few sentences, describe the Ex Post Facto law.
5. The student will, in a few sentences, describe a Bill of Attainer.

6. The student will answer true-false questions about the Ex Post Facto Law.

7. The student will answer true-false questions about a Bill of Attainer.

8. The student will answer true-false questions about the Bill of Rights.

9. The student will list four civil rights given by the Constitution of the United States.

10. The student will list three occasions when the state can regulate freedom of the press and freedom of speech.

11. The student will, in several sentences, discuss the idea of Habeas Corpus, telling what it is and what the laws say about it.

12. The student will list four parts of a state constitution and tell the purpose of each part listed.

13. The student will discuss in a paragraph the Committee System of the state legislature, how they are made up and what their functions are.

14. The student will, in a brief paragraph, tell what lobbyists are and what they do.

15. The student will discuss, in a paragraph or two, (not over one half page) the *basic* principles of passing a bill in the state legislature.

16. The student will list three powers of the governor and in a sentence or two describe those powers.

17. The student will list three major officials of the state (excluding the governor) and tell briefly what their jobs are.

18. The student will list three state courts and briefly tell the jurisdiction of each.

19. The student will, in a paragraph, discuss the Grand Jury, what it is and what it does.

20. The student will, in a paragraph, tell how a jury is selected.

21. The student will, in a paragraph, tell the difference between a Grand Jury and a Petit Jury.

22. The student will, in a paragraph, tell the difference between a Law Suit and an Equity Suit.

23. The student will briefly tell what a felony is and give four examples of crimes considered felonies.

24. The student will briefly tell what a misdemeanor is and give two examples.

25. The student will briefly describe a Bill of Indictment and tell who brings it about.

26. The student will list four tax restrictions placed on the state.

27. The student will describe the differences in real property and personal property.
28. The student will list three types of state taxes and tell by whom they are paid and what things are taxed.
29. The student will list four elected county officials and in a sentence or two each describe their major duties.
30. The student will, in a paragraph not over a half a page, discuss the operation of the town meeting.
31. The student will list three types of city government and describe, in several sentences each, the operation of each type.

Teaching and Learning Activities

1. Introductory activities:
    A.   Films
    B.   Guest Speakers
    C.   Prelecture Discussion
    D.   Demonstration
2. Teacher Activities:
    A.   Films
    B.   Lecture
    C.   Question and Answer
3. Student Activities:
    A.   Creation of hypothetical problems
    B.   Outside Reading
    C.   Demonstrations
    D.   Mock-ups (Simulated situations such as town meetings, criminal trials, etc.)
4. Joint Activities:
    A.   Discussions
    B.   Tests
    C.   Field Trips
5. Optional Activities:
    A.   Reports on subjects related to the study topics
    B.   Projects and demonstrations other than those required for class
    C.   Panel discussions on governmental problems
    D.   Class project such as researching and helping solve a school or governmental problem
    E.   Suggestions will be considered from any member of the class.

6. Encouragement of study will come through the class activities. The mock-ups will require the student to research some area of the situations being simulated. A wide variety of optional and required work is hoped to encourage the student to branch out and develop his interests and study methods.

Teaching Areas and Methods Used

The Judiciary:
    Methods: (1)C, (2)B, (3)A and (4)B
    Objectives: 1, 2 and 3
Civil Rights:
    Methods: (1)A, (1)B, (2)B and (3)A
    Objectives: 5, 6, 7, 8, 9, 10, 11 and 4
State Courts:
    Methods: (1)A, (2)B, (2)C, (3)D-Jury selection and indictment pro-
        ceedings, (3)A, (4)B, and (4)C-to watch a court trial
    Objectives: 17, 18, 19, 20 and 21
Criminal and Civil Procedure:
    Methods: (1)A, (1)B-Lawyer, (2)B, (3)D-Court trial, (4)A and (4)B
    Objectives: 22, 23, 24 and 25
State Constitution:
    Methods: (1)C, (2)B, (2)C, (4)B and (3)D
    Objectives: 12
State Legislature:
    Methods: (1)C, (2)B, (3)D-Passing of bill in legislature, and (4)B
    Objectives: 13, 14 and 15
State Governors:
    Methods: (1)A, (2)B, (2)C and (4)B
    Objectives: 16 and 17
State Finance:
    Methods: (1)A, (2)B, (2)C, (4)A and (4)B
    Objectives: 26, 27 and 28
Township and County Government
    Methods: (1)A, (2)B, (3)D-Town meeting and election of county
        officials
    Objectives: 29 and 30
City and Town Government

Methods: (1)A, (1)D, (2)B, (3)C-Three forms of city government, (4)A and (2)C
Objectives: 31

Culminating Activities

The unit will be ended by the students viewing a film on corruption in the government and how to spot it. There will also be a review of the material by means of questions and answers. In addition, the most important facts covered will be enumerated to aid the student in studying. The relationships of one subject area to another will be a process that will continue throughout the teaching unit. The unit has been prepared so that each subject area is the basis for the next section of study. The relations of one subject to another can better be pointed out if the material is closely associated and not disjointed.

Tests and participation in class are two methods to be used in determining the growth and learning of the students. Homework assigned to be handed in will be another factor in considering student growth. The students will also be graded on the basis of how well they research their parts in the mock-ups. The objectives of the course are to be used as a basis for deciding how much the students have improved and how much they have learned during the six weeks. Question and answer periods can help give some idea of how the students are progressing toward the objectives.

Tests will consist of multiple choice, true-false and discussion questions. The true-false and multiple choice questions will be graded with the aid of a stencil. The discussion questions will be graded on the basis of how many factors are included when compared to the teacher's list of needed information. The students will have had these factors pointed out to them during lectures and reviews. Tests will be given at the end of each week and will last only part of the period. A pretest will be given to the students at the beginning of the six weeks and the same test will be given at the end of the term in order to understand how much the students retained.

Outline of Content

The Judiciary

I. District Courts
   A. Lowest regular court

        B.   At least one district and one judge per state
        C.   Has no power when
             1. state is a party
             2. suits involve representatives of other countries
             3. it is a customs case
             4. there are claims against the U.S.

II.   Court of Appeals
        A.   Each judicial district has a court of appeals.
        B.   They relieve the Supreme court of some cases.
        C.   They have no original jurisdiction.

III.   Supreme Court
        A.   One chief and eight associate justices
        B.   Gives final interpretation of Constitution
        C.   Has original jurisdiction in cases
             1. between states
             2. against ambassadors and public ministers
             3. against consuls
        D.   Appelate jurisdiction from lower courts

IV.   Court of Claims
        A.   Five judges
        B.   Hears cases against U.S.
        C.   Congress appropriates money to pay claims

V.   Customs Court
        A.   Hears claims about goods and the duties collected on them
        B.   Nine judges at major ports

VI.   Court of Customs and Patent Appeals
        A.   Five judges in Washington and New York
        B.   Hears appeals from court of customs and handles cases of patent disputes

VII. Tax Court
        A.   Branch of executive division
        B.   Sixteen judges
        C.   Jurisdiction in Internal Revenue cases only

VIII. Court Officials
        A.   Judges
        B.   D.A.
        C.   U.S. Marshals
        D.   District Court Commissioner

Civil Liberties

I.   Restrictions of Constitution

      A. No slavery
      B. No punishment under Bill of Attainer
      C. No punishment by Ex Post Facto Law
      D. No deprivation of life, liberty or property

II.   Bill of Rights
      A. Restricts Congress only
         1. State can in certain cases restrict these rights
      B. Three restrictions on states
         1. No laws to impair contract obligation
         2. No state can use anything besides what the national government designates as legal tender
         3. No denial of equal protection of the law
      C. Guaranteed Civil Rights
         1. Religion
         2. Freedom of Speech and the Press
         3. The Right to Petition
         4. The Right of Habeas Corpus
         5. Protection against Unreasonable Searches and Seizures
         6. The Right to a Jury Trial

State Courts

I.   Organization
      A. Justice Courts
         1. Jurisdiction in misdemeanors
         2. Small Money claims
         3. Property ownership
         4. Wrongs or damage to property
      B. County Courts
         1. Minor felonies
         2. Major misdemeanors
         3. Civil cases above a certain amount of money
      C. Superior, Circuit or District Courts
         1. Major felonies
         2. Civil cases
      D. Supreme Court
         1. Handles appeals from lower courts
      E. Probate Courts
         1. Problems of wills and estates
      F. Court of Small Claims
         1. Handles small cases usually without lawyers

II.   Juries
      A. Grand Jury

      1. Hears evidence and determines if person should be brought to trial

      2. Bring True Bill of Indictment

      3. Bring a presentation or accusation

  B. Petit Jury

      1. Decide disputed facts of a case

      2. Usually made up of twelve people

  C. Jury selection

      1. Selected by board or commission

      2. Selected from tax or poll books

      3. Criminals, illiterates or people under twenty one or over a certain age are not eligible

Criminal and Civil Procedures

I. Civil Cases

  A. Law Suits

      1. Sues for damages

      2. Usually a jury trials

  B. Equity Suit

      1. Sues for stoppage of wrong doing

      2. Deposition

      3. Judge trial

  C. Criminal Trial

      1. Felonies

      2. Misdemeanors

  D. Criminal Procedure

      1. Warrant issued

         a.   states crime

         b.   arrest by police, sheriff or peace officer

      2. Misdemeanor arrest

         a.   no warrant if crime is committed in the presence of law officer

         b.   warrant needed if crime was not committed in presence of law officer

      3. Indictment

         a.   Prosecuting attorney looks into case

         b.   Brings Bill of Indictment

         c.   Grand Jury decides if there is enough evidence to try the person

State Constitution

I. Constitutions parts

A. Preamble

    B. Bill of Rights
    C. Provisions for organizing branches of state government
    D. Miscellaneous articles
    E. Provisions for change
    F. Schedule

II.   Constitutional convention
    A. Delegates chosen by voters
    B. Legislative proposal
    C. Popular Initiative
    D. All but one state requires ratification by the public

III.   Authority of Constitution
    A. Supreme law of state
    B. Legislation cannot interfere with the constitution
    C. State constitutional laws cannot conflict with the United States Constitution

State Legislature

I.   Type Legislature
    A. Unicameral or Bicameral
        1. Senators
        2. Representatives
            a. gerrymandering
    B. Rights of members
        1. No arrest during session
            a. doesn't amount to much today
    C. Power
        1. Any power not delegated to the United States or prohibited by the state

II.   Organization of the Legislature
    A. House
        1. Lt. governor or elected official heads Senate
        2. Selects own rules for procedure and qualification
        3. Officers and duties similar to Congress
    B. Committee System
        1. Work horse of legislature
        2. Studies bills of certain types
        3. Pigeon holing
    C. Senate
        1. State usually divided into Senatorial Districts
        2. Each district has about equal population

III.   Passage of Laws

      A. Bill introduced in either House or Senate
      B. Referred to proper committee
      C. Passage in house in which it originated
      D. Introduced in other house
      E. Goes to committee and readings
      F. Passed and certified
      G. Goes to original house where it is enrolled and signed
      H. Goes to second house where it is enrolled and signed
      I. Approved and signed by governor
      J. Goes to Secretary of State and filed

IV.   Lobbyists
      A. Pressure groups
      B. Regulations for these groups

State Governors

I.   Powers of Governor
      A. Executive
          1. Appoints officers
          2. Sees that laws are enforced
      B. Legislative
          1. Veto bills
          2. Call extra sessions of the legislature
          3. Send messages to Legislature
      C. Judicial
          1. Pardoning persons for crimes
      D. Assisted in powers by state police, sheriff, etc.

II.   Executive Officers of State
      A. Lt. Governor (not all states have one)
          1. Serves when governor can't
          2. President of Senate in some states
          3. Succeeds governor if he dies or is impeached
      B. Secretary of State
          1. Chief clerk and recorder of official acts of governor and legislature
          2. Has charge of state papers
      C. Auditor
          1. Audits accounts of state officers who collect or distribute state money
      D. Treasurer
          1. Distributes money on orders of auditor
      E. Superintendent of Public Education
          1. Heads public schools and school boards

        2. Issues regulations for schools and sees that they are enforced

        3. Distributes school funds

        4. Collects school statistics

  F. Boards

      1. Board of State Institutions

        a.   regulates educational, charitable and correction institutions

      2. Board of State Functions

        a.   Board of Health, Agricultural Board, or Highway Commission

      3. Examining Boards

        a.   Board of Medical Examiners, Civil Service Commission, etc.

State Finance

I.   Tax Restrictions

  A. Must be used for public purposes only

  B. Must apply uniformly to those taxed

  C. Persons or property must come under government levying the tax

  D. Certain guarantees prevent injustices

  E. No taxing of Federal property

  F. No taxation of imports or exports without Congressional consent

  G. No taxation of interstate commerce

  H. States can't tax vehicles or vessels on basis of capacity

  I. Churches, schools and certain properties are taxed exempted

II.   Property Tax

  A. Real property

      1. Land, buildings, etc.

  B. Personal Property

      1. Tangible

        a. visible wealth-cars, boats, etc

      2. Intangible

        a. rarely seen wealth-bonds, stocks, etc.

  C. Sales Tax

      1. Tax on amount of sales

  D. Income Tax

      1. Progressive

      2. Taxes total income minus deductions

      3. Some people pay state, city and Federal income tax

  E. Business Tax

1. Tax on corporations, electric companies, private businesses, etc.

Township and County Government

I.   County Officials
- A. County Board
  1. Acts to administer state laws in county
  2. Set tax rates
  3. Determine how certain money should be used
  4. Has charge of county buildings
  5. Has charge of county road building and maintenance projects
- B. County or District Judge
- C. Probate Judge
- D. District Attorney
  1. Brings criminals to trial
- E. Sheriff
  1. Prevents breech of peace
  2. Arrests offenders of law
  3. Carries out orders of courts and clerk
- F. Coroner
  1. Holds investigations on bodies where foul play is suspected
- G. County Clerk
  1. Prepares ballots
  2. Issues licenses
  3. Records deeds, wills, etc.
- H. Auditor
  1. Goes over county accounts
  2. Issues warrants for use of money
- I. Treasurer
  1. Guards and takes in county money
  2. Job performed by Tax Collector in some states
- J. Superintendent of Schools
  1. Collects information on schools
  2. Examines teachers
  3. Helps with selection of teachers
  4. Observes schools operation
  5. Helps with finance problems

II.   Townships
- A. Powers over
  1. Roads
  2. Schools
  3. Libraries

4. Taxation
5. Public works
B. Town Meetings
   1. Selectmen elected by the people
   2. Meetings usually held once a year
   3. Public warrants state business to be discussed
   4. Officers elected
   5. Past finances and future business discussed
   6. Allows people to be closer to what is going on in the government of the township

Village and City Government

I. Village
  A. Small Towns
  B. Powers of Village
    1. Provide sidewalks
    2. Provide sewers
    3. Provide police protection
    4. Provide lights
    5. Provide fire protection
  C. Village ruled by Council
    1. Elected by people
    2. Set tax rates
    3. Issues funds for certain purposes
  D. Mayor
    1. Presides over Council meetings
    2. May enforce village ordinances

II. City
  A. Mayor Council Type Government
    1. Council makes laws
      a. enacts city ordinances
      b. sets tax rates
      c. approves revenue
    2. Mayor enforces laws
      a. head of city
      b. presides over council meetings
      c. vetoes ordinances of council
  B. Commission Type
    1. Has legislative and executive power
    2. Each commissioner has charge of one department
      a. public affairs
      b. finance

        c.   safety

        d.   parks

        e.   street improvement

C. City Manager

    1. Council

    2. Manager selected by council

Evaluation

Evaluation of students:

A.   Tests

B.   Performance in mock-ups

C.   Hand-in homework

D.   Participation in class

E.   Reports

F.   Observations of changing attitudes and actions in class

Examples of test questions:

1.   List four types of Federal Courts.

2.   In a sentence or two each, describe the major jobs of the above listed courts.

3.   List three officials of the Federal Judiciary and in one or two sentences each describe their duties.

4.   In a paragraph describe the *Ex Post Facto Law* and tell how it relates to your civil rights.

5.   In a paragraph discuss a *Bill of Attainder* telling what it is and how it applies to your civil liberties.

6.   The Ex Post Facto Law deals with *civil law* only. (False)

7.   Under a *Bill of Attainder* a man can be sent to prison without a trial. (False)

8.   A *state legislature* has the right to pass a law saying that it is legal to use something besides gold and silver as legal tender. (False)

9.   List four civil rights given by the Constitution of the United States.

10.   List three occasions when the state can regulate the freedom of speech and the freedom of the press.

11.   List four parts of the state constitution and tell the purpose of each part.

12.   Discuss in a paragraph what the idea of *Habeas Corpus* is and what the law says about it.

13. Discuss in a paragraph the Committee System of the state legislature, how the committees are made up and what their functions are.

14. Discuss in a paragraph what lobbyists are and what they do.

15. Discuss in a paragraph or two (not over one page) the *basic* principles of passing a bill in the state legislature.

16. List three powers of the governor and in a sentence or two each describe those powers.

17. List three officials (major officials) of the state (excluding the governor) and briefly describe their jobs.

18. List three state courts and briefly state the jurisdiction of each.

19. Discuss in a paragraph the *Grand Jury,* what it is and what it does.

20. Discuss in a paragraph how a jury is selected.

21. In a paragraph, point out the differences in a *Grand Jury* and a *Petit Jury.*

22. Discuss in a paragraph the differences between a *Suit at Law* and an *Equity Suit.*

23. Tell briefly what a *Felony* is and give four examples of crimes considered felonies.

24. Briefly tell what a *Misdemeanor* is and give two examples of misdemeanors.

25. Describe briefly what a *Bill of Indictment* is and tell how it is brought about.

26. List four tax restrictions placed on the state.

27. In a paragraph, tell the differences between *Real Property* and *Personal Property.*

28. List three types of state taxes and tell by whom they are paid and what things are taxed.

29. List four elected county officials and in a sentence or two each describe their major duties.

30. Describe the operation of a town meeting (not over a half page).

31. List three types of city government and in several sentences each describe the operation of each type.

Material evaluation

Evaluation of the course material will be based chiefly on student reactions. Direct questioning of the students will yield a good deal of information on how the students feel about the material. Having the students fill out a rating sheet can also give much insight into the feelings of the students about the material. Class participation and test scores will also be used as an indicator of the difficulty and worth of the material used. Ratings and suggestions about the materials from respected teachers will also be considered.

Question and learning activities evaluation

Student reactions will again be a major factor in this area of evaluation. If the students have a hard time understanding certain questions, then those questions will be considered inadequate and altered. Also considered will be suggestions from students and respected teachers about how to make the questions more readily understood. Class reactions to films, slides, mock-ups and other activities will be used as an indicator of how good those methods are. Tests and question answer periods will be used to measure how much information is gained in the classroom and how well the students are progressing under the methods being used.

Teacher self-evaluation

Evaluation of the teacher's methods and materials will be based on how interested the class is in what is being presented and how well the students retain the information. If the students are bored and make poor grades on tests, then the teacher can assume the methods are inappropriate. Another method of evaluation that will be used is the rating sheet. Students, other teachers who have observed the teaching and the teacher himself will all fill out a rating sheet in order for the classroom teacher to gain a better understanding of himself and his methods.

BIBLIOGRAPHY

The text:

McClenaghan, William A. *Magruder's American Government,* rev. Boston: Allyn and Bacon Inc.

Additional material:

Beth, Loren P., *Politics, The Constitution and The Supreme Court.* Evanston, Ill.: Row, Peterson and Co.

Bloch, Charles J., *States Rights, The Law of the Land.* Atlanta: The Harrison Company.

Hand, Learned. *The Bill of Rights.* Cambridge: Harvard University Press.

Harris, Joseph P., *Elements of American Government.* New York: McGraw Hill.

Films:

Our Civil Rights

Basic Court Procedure

Justice Under Law

State Capital

Property Taxation

County Government

Community Government

You the People

Problem Solving Lesson

The students will participate in a three day problem solving lesson dealing with jury selection, indictment proceedings and a courtroom trial. The day before the simulation begins there will be a discussion of what is to take place. Any problems the students have will be discussed before the mock-up starts.

Objectives

The student will in a paragraph discuss the Grand Jury, what it is and what it does.

The student will in a paragraph tell how a jury is selected.

The student will in a paragraph discuss the difference between a Grand Jury and a Petit Jury.

The student will briefly describe a Bill of Indictment and tell how it is brought about.

Methods

The students will begin preparing several days before the mock-up is scheduled to start. An election of the major people needed in the simulation (Judges, Lawyers, District Attorney, etc.) will be held before the trial. Each of these elected people will be required to research his role so that he will be able to perform well during the mock-up. To insure a good knowledge of the role, each elected person will hand in a written paper on the duties of the official he is to play.

Every member of the class will be involved in the mock-up in some *useful* way. Nobody will be made to feel that they are left out. The number of jurors may have to be increased, but it is very important that everyone is involved with the trial.

The first step of the simulation will be to select a grand jury and a petit jury. Then the grand jury will be required to find the accused eligible or ineligible for trial. The actual trial will take place after the indictment proceedings. The defendant will have before the trial and indictment proceedings, set up the crime and what evidence was to be found.

All members of the class will be required to hand in a brief statement of the guilt or innocence of the accused. The statement will also include why the student felt the way he did.

The trial will be as realistic as is practically possible. There may, however, have to be some deviation from actual courtroom procedure. For example, it may be difficult to find a person with the proper qualifications who can act as court stenographer. The idea behind the mock trial is to give the students a *basic* understanding of courtroom procedure. Details should and will be included in the simulation, but not to the point where they cloud the basic working factors of the court.

Culminating activities

The problem solving lesson will be concluded by a question and answer period. The important factors of the trial will be written on the blackboard or on an overhead projector. The day after the question and answer period there will be a test to determine what the students have learned.

Audio-visual aids

Each student will be required to wear an easily readable sign stating his role in the proceedings. The use of signs is a good way to help the students to learn to relate the roles with the role players.

Time Line For American Government

It is a difficult task to create a really good time line for a course in American Government. The difficulty arises from the fact that government is not studied on a chronological basis. An example of a time line for government would be the arrangement of the amendments to the Constitution in order of their passage date. On the chart would be a long line with the basic ideas of the amendments and when they were passed. Another line on the chart could list the different departments of the government and when they were organized. Using this type time line can point out the relationship of dates, but it fails to point out more important relationships of *ideas*. For this reason, the time line will be modified for this unit in government. The basic principles will be the same, but there will be a de-emphasis of dates and time.

The basic objective of the modified time line will be to point out sequential relationships and relationships of one subject to another. The students will still write and draw on a long piece of butcher's paper and it will be displayed in the front of the class. An example of the modified time line is given on this page. The line visually points out the steps taken in the arrest and trial of a person. The detail of the information can easily be increased or decreased to suit the needs of the students. For example, the steps of the indictment proceedings could be listed under that heading. A problem with clarity arises when too much detail is used. Simplicity will aid the student in relating one fact to another.

The time line makes a very good visual aid, since it is left up in front of the classroom every day. The relationships, similarities and differences of the time order and the subject material can be visually pointed out on the chart, thus allowing the students to see the material and not just hear it.

The Process of Arrest and Trial

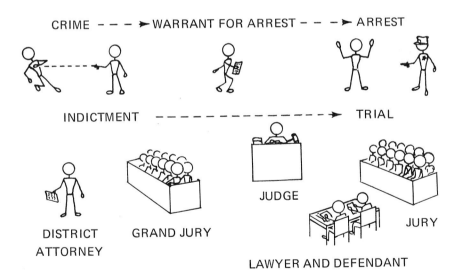

INDEX

Abington High School, 152
Accountability, 246
Advanced Placement, 155
American Association of School Administrators, 3
American Library Association, 181
Anthropology, 65
Assumptions:
  about knowledge and learning, 27
  basic, 11
Audio-Visual Guide, 191
Augustine, St., 50
A.V. Materials, 186
  selection of, 188

Bachman, John W, 181
Beard, Charles A, 52
Behavioral Objectives, 103, 107-113
  purpose of, 107
Bernard, Harold W, 2
Brevard County Board of Public Instructors, 79
Brown, Duane, 213, 217
Brown, James W, 181

Carr, Edwin R, 36, 76
Charts, Basic Types of, 195
Chronology, Teaching, 197
Civic Education Project (1965), 9
Citizenship Education, Goals of, 9
Cochran, Lee W, 181
Cocurricular Activities, 224
  problems, 227
  purposes, 225
  sponsor, 226

Code of Ethics, NEA, 242
Competency, Teacher, 246
Computer Assistant Instruction:
  advantages, 203-204
  critics, 204
  limitations, 204
Comte, Auguste, 59
"Cone of Experience," 76, 77, 80, 83
Contracts, Examples of, 90-91
Controversial Issues, Techniques, 169
Course Outlines, 101
Courses of Study, 103
  format for, 104-105
  procedure for developing, 105
Current Events, 167
  selection of topics, 168
  teaching techniques, 168
Curriculum:
  emerging patterns in social studies, 38
  future social studies, 43
  junior high social studies, 39
  senior high social studies, 40
  "Space Curriculum Guidelines," 79
  typical social studies patterns, 39
  what should be taught, 37
Curriculum Had, 5, 213
Curriculum Planned, 5

Dale, Edgar, 76, 181
Danforth Foundation, 9
Das Kapital, 64
De Bernardis, Amos, 184
Degree Program, Typical, 239
deKieffer, Robert E, 181

Democratic Participation, 10
Dewey, John, 84
Directory of 16mm Film Libraries,
    192
Disciplines, Structure of, 47
Discovery Learning, 47-49

Economics, 63
Educational Film Guide to Free Films,
    192
Educational Media Index, 191, 192
Educational Screen and A.V. Guide,
    191
Educationally Disadvantaged:
    problems, 160
    teaching, 159
Educator's Guide to Free Filmstrips,
    191
Evaluation, Purposes of, 123
Evaluation of Teachers:
    methods, 247
    purposes, 247

Filmstrips, 191
Franklin, Benjamin, 178
Fraser, Dorothy McClure & Edith
    West, 5
Frey, Sherman, 22

Galbraith, John K, 65
Geography, 62
Globes, 193
Gordon, Ira J, 220, 223
Graphs, 194-195
    area, 195
    bar, 195
    circle, 194-195
    pictorial, 195
    pie, 194
Guidance, Teacher's Role, 220
Guide to Content in the Social Stud-
    ies, A, 6

Hanna, Lavone A, 8
Harcleroad, Fred F, 181
Hass, Kenneth B, 181
Haugen, Earl, 22
Hegelian Dialectic, 52
Herbart, Johann, 104
Herodotus, 50

Heyl, Elsie P, 192
History, 50
    schools of, 52
    sources of, 51
Humboldt, 63

Imperatives in Education, 3
Independent Study, 151
Individual Study, 150
Ingraham, Leonard W, 205
Inquiry Method, 47, 65

Jefferson, Thomas, 64
Josephus, 50

Kenworthy, Leonard, 74
Keynes, John M, 65

Laboratory, Community as a, 172
Large Group Instruction, 151
Learning Experiences, Student, 74
Learning, Principles of, 22
Lesson Plans, Daily, 105 samples,
    113-118
Lewis, Richard B, 181
Library Books, 181

Management, Classroom, 213
Maps, 193
Marking, Purposes of, 133
Marx, Karl, 64
Malthus, 64
Maxson, Robert C, 170
McCreary, Eugene, 9
Media:
    sources, 206
    types, 178
Melbourne High School, 42
Method, Contract, 88
Methods:
    criteria for selecting, 76
    discussion, 81
    expository, 80
    individualizing instruction, 85
    lecture, 80
    non-expository, 81
    problem solving, 84
    project, 82
    socialized recitation, 81
    Socratic dialogue, 81

teaching, 73
teaching games, 91
The Art of Questioning, 86
Mill, John Stuart, 64
Misbehavior, 216
Moffatt, Maurice, 8
Morale, Faculty, 244
Morrison, Henry, 104
Munice Community Schools, 7

National Association of Secondary School Principals, 2
National Council for Social Studies, 9
National Council of Social Studies, 202
NCATE, 239
NEA, 169, 182
Nongraded Schools, 42

Opaque Projector, 190
Overhead Projector, 190

Packer, Harry Q, 181
Personal Policies, 224
Pimlico Jr. High School, 152
Planning:
    for teaching, 101
    long range, 103
Plutarch, 50
Political Science, 53
    as a discipline, 54
    fields of study, 55
Prince George's County Public Schools, 5
Professional Growth, 249
Professionalism, 241
Programmed Instruction, 199
Psychology, Principles of, 27
Pupil Progress, Marking and Reporting, 132

Quillen, James I, 8

Reading Problems, Causes of, 159
Remedial Reading, 157
Report Cards, 135
Ricardo, 64
Ritter, 63
Roselle, Daniel, 9

Salaries, 245
Seminar, Historical, 50
Seminars, 153
Shores, Louis, 181
SIMPLE, 44
Skills to be Learned, 76
Slide Projector, 192
Slow Learner:
    evaluation of teaching methods, 157
    teaching methods, 156
Small Group Instruction, 150
Smith, Adam, 64
SOCC, 44
Social Darwinism, 52
Social Studies:
    goals of, 5-10, 14
    in the middle schools, 43
    philosophical positions of teachers, 19
    progress in change in, 36
    purposes of, 14
    specific purposes of teaching, 10
    trends in curriculum, 38
Sociology, 58
Spencer, Herbert, 48
Spengler, Oswald, 52
Sputnik, 35
Student Attitudes:
    changing, 170
    hypotheses, 170-171
Student Council, 228
    advisor, 228-230
    problems, 232
    types, 230

Teaching Games, Examples of, 95-96
Teaching Units, 101, 103
    origins, 104
    steps in writing, 104
Team Teaching, 147
    advantages, 150
Technological Change, 35
Ten Imperative Needs of Youth, The, 2
Tenure Laws, 245
Tests:
    commercial, 136

    teacher-made, 126   Ugly Americans, 35
    scoring, 130   Urbanization, 35
Testing: U.S. Office of Education, 246
    effects on students, 132
    purposes of, 126   Van Ranke, Leopold, 50
Textbooks, 178
    evaluating, 180   Welfare, Faculty, 244
    methods, as, 183   Wiles, Kimball, 177
Thucydides, 50   Workbooks, 186
Time Lines, 196
Toynbee, Arnold, 52